Taisan may be high;
        yet it is under the sky.
If you climb and climb again,
        there is no reason why
        you should fail.
People do not try and only say
        that the mountain is too high.

                        Yang Sa-un
                        (1517–1584)

SEOUL CALGARY 1988

THE OFFICIAL PUBLICATION OF THE U.S. OLYMPIC COMMITTEE

PUBLISHER Mikko "Mike" Laitinen, President
Commemorative Publications
Salt Lake City, Utah USA

MARKETING COORDINATOR Judd Parr

MANAGING EDITOR Lisa H. Albertson

ASSOCIATE EDITOR John Robinson, *Deseret News*

USOC ADMINISTRATION EDITING The U.S. Olympic Committee Public Information and Media Relations Division: Mike Moran, Director; Gayle Plant, Barbara Gresham, Bob Condron, Jeff Cravens

CAPTIONS Lee Warnick

PRINTING A.B. Hirschfeld Press, Inc., Denver

BINDING Hiller Bindery, Salt Lake City

PAPER Metsä-Serla, Äänekoski Paper Mill, Finland / supplied by: The Madden Corporation, Rockefeller Plaza, New York

INK Spectrum Ink Company Division of Midland Color

COLOR SEPARATIONS Ernest D. Miller Guaranteed Colour, Salt Lake City

TYPESETTING Type Center, Salt Lake City

STATISTICS Special thanks to Amateur Athletic Foundation of Los Angeles, Joanna Payne, Barbara Gresham, Jeff Cravens, David Heim, Bob Hughes, Jed Williamson

SPECIAL THANKS Baaron B. Pittenger, Executive Director, U.S. Olympic Committee; John Krimsky, Jr., Deputy Secretary General, USOC; James A. Schaeffler, Esq., William B. Campbell, Gregory L. Harney, C. Robert Paul, Jr. (USOC); The U.S. National Governing Bodies of Sport; Richard L. Smith, Tarja Laitinen, Len Corbosiero, Mikko Tuomarila, Dale Reiman, A.W. "Buz" Smith, Ridgely H. Gilmour

Published under license from the U.S. Olympic Committee by Commemorative Publications P.O. Box 1988, Sandy, Utah 84091

ISBN 0-918883-02-4

PHOTO-GRAPHERS

Long Photography, Inc. (LPI) Los Angeles
   George Long
   Bob Long
   Tim Long
Robert Hagedohm (LPI) / Los Angeles
Michael Yada (LPI) / Los Angeles
pressfoto team / Helsinki
Hannu Vierula (pressfoto) / Helsinki
Esa Pyysalo (pressfoto) / Helsinki
Lauri Kautia (pressfoto) / Helsinki
Leonora V. Goldberg / New York City
Lori Adamski-Peek / Park City, UT
David Black / Colorado Springs
Norbert Schmidt / Munich
Roger Lean-Vercoe / Devon
David Finch / London
Tish Quirk / Carlsbad, CA
GES / Karlsruhe, FRG
Nancie Battaglia / Lake Placid
Scott Rupp / Herndon, VA
Ned Bonzi / Denver
Lehtikuva Oy / Helsinki
Chris Wilkins (Lehtikuva Oy) / Helsinki
COLOS (Lehtikuva Oy) / Helsinki

PHOTOGRAPHY COORDINATOR Brian C. Peterson

ABOVE / *Fast and steady shooters: A well-bundled, armed photographer records images of biathletes at Canmore.* (LPI)

OPPOSITE / *Not far from where the world's athletes are performing their Olympian feats, this Korean weightlifter hefts his daily burden with far less fanfare.* (George Long/LPI)

PAGE 1 / *In a dizzying swirl of color, Korea exhibits her culture — here a Flower Crown dance — at the Opening Ceremonies.* (Bob Long/LPI)

PAGE 2 / *Another of Korea's deep-rooted (and deep-hued) traditions, the Dragon Drum procession.* (Bob Long/LPI)

PAGE 3 / *These Canadians stand perfectly still to form, in heroic scale, the five interlocked Olympic rings during the Opening Ceremonies.* (LPI)

SUCCEEDING PAGES / *The ice inside Calgary's Saddledome is seemingly set aflame by a precision group of skaters during the Closing Ceremonies extravaganza.* (R.L. Hagedohm/LPI)

CONTENTS

A TOAST TO THE HOSTS:

They were the biggest, longest, best-attended, most expensive, most competitive, and most peaceful in history, the XVth Olympic Winter Games and the Games of the XXIVth Olympiad, and they were perfect examples of Citius, Altius, Fortius—and then some.

From the chinooks and rugged grandeur of the Canadian Rockies to the Land of the Morning (and evening) Calm below the 38th Parallel, the Games covered two hemispheres, encompassed a record 160 nations between the two celebrations, another record 11,169 athletes and ran the athletic gamut—from East German swimmer Kristin Otto's six gold medals in Seoul on one end of the spectrum, to British ski jumper Eddie Edwards' death-defying, yet futile, leaps in Calgary on the other.

When the fireworks from the Closing Ceremonies in Seoul cleared in early October, other than the usual ranting and raving over judgment calls, no one had staged a protest of any consequence.

When Juan Antonio Samaranch, president of the International Olympic Committee, called on the youth of the world to assemble again in four years, in Albertville, France, and Barcelona, Spain, for the XVIth Olympic Winter Games and the Games of the XXVth Olympiad, no one could think of any good reasons not to.

So the Olympic movement not only survived the Games of '88, it set for itself a new standard. In the Winter Games, Calgary's sparkling new facilities, built at a cost of $223 million, included a state-of-the-art hockey rink, an indoor speedskating oval and a new ski resort with high-speed quadruple chairlifts. At Seoul, for the Summer Games, the Koreans spent a total budget of approximately $3.1 billion that included the building of two stunning sports parks with no less than 11 brand new specialty arenas, and still had enough left over to line the city's boulevards with flowers.

Calgary's Games—extended to 16 days, the longest in Winter Olympics history—had more sports (seven, with 47 events) and more nations (57) than ever before,

ABOVE / *Olympic Plaza was where the action was in Calgary. Thousands gathered nightly for a spirited, and sometimes spontaneous, mix of entertainment, medal ceremonies and live Olympic events projected onto a huge screen.* (R.L. Hagedohm/LPI)

PRECEDING PAGES / *A mask of glittering new sports facilities conceals a city whose soul drips with history, like the branches that frame tranquil Hyangwonjŏng Pavilion, which is a mere 150 Olympics old . . .* (George Long/LPI)

(INSETS - TOP TO BOTTOM) / *. . . Korea honors and reveres its past, and one of its aged pays homage to the ages with a stroll on the grounds of historic Kyŏngbokkung Palace . . . as do the not-so-aged during a school field trip to nearby Ch'angdŏkkung Palace. .. Perhaps such cultivation has helped to create this Land of the Morning Calm, with a culture as serene as a lotus blossom on a still pond.* (insets - R.L. Hagedohm/LPI)

SEOUL AND CALGARY

ABOVE / *Smiles, smiles, everywhere in Seoul were smiles, as the Koreans charmed their guests with extra mile hospitality.* (R.L. Hagedohm/LPI)

while Seoul's Games, also 16 days in length, not only featured, with 23, the most summer sports in history but, with 160 entered nations, more participants than ever in Olympic history.

Of the world's 167 recognized National Olympic Committees, only North Korea, Cuba, Nicaragua, Ethiopia, Albania, the Seychelles and Madagascar failed to participate athletically in Seoul. North Korea and Cuba boycotted the Summer Games because North Korea was not permitted to co-host the Games, while Nicaragua had other domestic problems.

In the face of the stiffest competition in the world, the United States—if you were keeping score—stayed more than competitive even though the inflated medal counts from 1984 declined. The United States went from eight Winter Games medals in '84 to six medals (two golds, one silver, three bronzes) in '88 and from 174 Summer Games medals in the Eastern Bloc-boycotted Olympics of '84 to 94 medals (36 golds, 31 silvers, 27 bronzes) in Seoul. The United States' performance in Seoul, however, was cause for enthusiasm.

The Soviet Union and the German Democratic Republic re-established themselves as the sporting world's one-two punch. The Soviets led the count in Calgary with 29, followed by the GDR with 25; in Seoul, the Soviets collected 132 medals (55 golds, 31 silvers, 46 bronzes), while the East Germans edged the United States for runner-up honors with 102 medals (37 golds, 35 silvers, 30 bronzes).

At the Winter Games, once they'd given the chinooks—strong warm westerly winds that act not unlike a huge blow dryer—a chance to run their course, the Swiss were the real showoffs, winning 11 of the 30 available medals in alpine skiing, the crown jewel of the Winter Games. The Finns did their usual high-flying act at the jumping hill, where the newest Flying Finn—Matti Nykänen—won three gold medals, a $40,000 bonus, and living legend status in his countryland. Nykänen's total dominance of the 70-meter and 90-meter jumping events drew almost as much applause and attention as Edwards, the first and only British ski jumper to ever compete in the Olympics. Eddie the Eagle, as he came to be affectionately known, finished last but, nonetheless, was successful at achieving his goal: He lived to tell about it.

America's lowest Winter Games medal output in 52 years went hand in hand with the highest incidence of injuries in the U.S. Ski Team history and tragedy on the men's speedskating team, where the top skater, Dan Jansen, competed the morning his sister died, and fell on the ice for the first time in three years.

The most magical American moments came in women's speedskating, where 23-year-old Bonnie Blair, financed by the police department in her hometown of Champaign, Ill., won at 500 meters and flashed a smile that even had the homicide detectives teary-eyed, and in men's figure skating, where, in the battle of the Brians, Brian Boitano of the United States edged Brian Orser of Canada.

In Seoul, it was 17-year-old American swimmer Janet Evans, on leave from her senior year of high school in California, and diver Greg Louganis, granting the world a final encore, who replaced the enthusiasm and artistry of Blair and Boitano. Evans, oblivious to the machine-like East German women, who were winning everything she wasn't, swam to three golds with equally as much "what-me-worry?" nonchalance as when Blair beat Christa Rothenburger, the East German world champion. And Louganis, needing a nearly perfect last dive on the platform to edge China's Ni Xiong and make it two golds, not to mention a career-for-the-ages, came through with, as ordered, a near-perfect dive.

The most decorated American, and overall Olympian in Seoul was Matt Biondi, who swam with dolphins before the Games to pick up a few moves and then won five gold medals, one silver and one bronze.

The U.S. swimming and boxing teams distinguished themselves well, and often. But it was on the track where the United States' medals came the fastest. Carl Lewis and Florence Griffith Joyner were king and queen of speed, and Joe DeLoach sneaked in for a piece of the crown by nipping Lewis at 200 meters. There was a changing of the guard in the 400-meter hurdles, where Edwin Moses lost to Andre Phillips. Jackie Joyner-Kersee became the undisputed first lady of track and field, winning gold medals in both the long jump and the heptathlon, where she broke her own world record.

The United States defeated the Soviets in men's volleyball, but lost to them in basketball in a game that left the nation that invented hoops stunned and wondering. The Soviets defeated coach John Thompson's U.S. team, 82-76, only the second loss in Olympic history for the U.S. men's team, which may include professionals by 1992.

America's loss to the Soviets was a mere tremor in Seoul compared to the shock waves sent out when it was announced that Ben Johnson had tested positive for use of a banned substance.

Johnson had set a world record at 100 meters in the Olympic final with a 9.79 clocking that left Carl Lewis' American record of 9.92 back with the rest, choking in the dust.

But Johnson's urine sample revealed traces of an anabolic steroid. He was stripped of his gold medal—it was later awarded to Lewis—and disqualified from international track competition for two years. He was one of 10 positive drug tests in Seoul—one less than in the Games of L.A.—but by far the most infamous.

The Games of Seoul didn't stop in the wake of the Johnson drug bust, or even slow down. Before long, there was talk of the positive side of the scandal—that Johnson's example would deter others tempted to use drugs in the future—and the Games

ABOVE (TOP) / *Only Mother Nature could have messed up Calgary's meticulous Olympic plans, so every so often she sent a stiff wind to show the world who was still boss.* (R.L. Hagedohm/LPI)

ABOVE / *In Korea, the chief concern centered around a more human-based issue — security.* (Bob Long/LPI)

OPPOSITE (TOP) / *The world marveled at the continuing athletic exploits of two who flew through the air with the greatest of grace and ease: Matti Nykänen of Finland in ski jumping . . .* (Leif Rosas)

(BOTTOM) / *. . . and Greg Louganis of the United States in diving.* (Michael Yada/LPI)

TOP RIGHT / *The bottom line: This quadrennial festival of sport is a lonely, and lovely, beacon to the world -- displayed both in Seoul and here in Calgary's Closing Ceremonies -- of brotherhood and peace.* (R.L. Hagedohm/LPI)

continued. Soon after, the hottest topic of the Games became the host Koreans' irritation with the way NBC-TV was broadcasting the Olympics and with the behavior of Americans, in general—who, to put it politely, they thought were impolite.

Now that was more like it.

What's an Olympic Games, anyway, without some good old-fashioned, basically harmless nationalism?

That's as serious as it got in Seoul, where 120,000 policemen had nothing more to do but lean on their rifles—and where the world, as it turned out, got together to get it together.

The message from Korea, and from Canada too, is perfectly clear in hindsight: When it comes to the Olympics, the more the better. And if the movement was on shaky ground before 1988, it couldn't be more solid after East met West. ☐

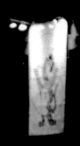

Imagine the look on their faces if the ancient Greeks, never ones to shy away from a little opulence and grandeur themselves, had been introduced to the Olympic stage of Seoul, Korea, in 1988 A.D.

"Now this," they'd have no doubt said, "is what we had in mind."

Never, in all the history of the Olympiads, have the Olympians had it so good—or safe, either, as it turned out. A sport for every arena and an arena for every sport—and a metal detector for every body.

There wasn't a bad seat in the city.

When those in the Seoul delegation made their pitch to the IOC in 1981, bidding for the Games of '88, they were much like the tailor standing in front of his "Savile Row Tailor Shop" in It'aewon, saying, "Come on in. I make you special good deal."

The IOC just had to trust them.

There was no Olympic Park, where six of the finest arenas several zillion won could buy would be constructed. There was no Olympic Stadium with an adjoining Sports Complex complete with its own subway stop and 14-lane highway out front. As a matter of fact, the Seoul suburb of Chamshil, where the stadium and Sports Complex were to be con-

structed—barely existed at all. And, the beautiful Han River, which flanks Chamsil and was the sight of the regetta venues, was still a polluted, unattractive waterway.

In the span of seven short years, the people of Seoul turned their city into a veritable sporting mecca. Their effort was Olympian. The city that had rebuilt itself from the ground up after the devastating effects of the civil war 35 years ago—indeed, this is a city where the sign "In business for 35 years" qualifies for patriarch status—took its Olympic host city assignment with equal seriousness.

The two main Olympic centers, the Sports Complex and Olympic Park, were located less than five miles apart in southeast Seoul and, between them, they housed no less than 11 arenas that offered separate, state-of-the-art facilities for track and field, baseball, water polo, boxing, basketball, fencing, weightlifting, tennis, cycling, gymnastics and swimming.

Seoul's dedication to a memorable Olympics didn't stop with the flower-lined boulevards, major cleanups or construction. The city went the extra mile—adopting an odd-even system to lessen traffic congestion.

If your car's license plate ended in an odd number then you could drive on odd-numbered days, and vice versa.

ABOVE / *Surrounded by a bucketful of tears worth of onions, these women at Seoul's bustling Karak Market can sort and package a bagful of the pungent vegetables faster than Florence Griffith Joyner can run the 100.* (R.L. Hagedohm/LPI)

PRECEDING PAGES / *The recently cleaned up Han River, whose banks hosted a diverse festival of arts, entertainment and food throughout the Olympics, sparkled as never before . . .*

(INSET) / *. . . and, on the eve of the Opening Ceremonies, exploded in flashing flames of fireworks.* (both photos - R.L. Hagedohm/LPI)

ABOVE / *It seemed in the city of Seoul, where taxis were plentiful but plenty full, that the deluge of foreigners weren't the only ones exploring new territory. Many of the taxi drivers were "imported" to lend a hand in Seoul.* (Michael Yada/LPI)

RIGHT / *This woman in the Karak Market is a veteran of many corn harvests — and Olympic years.* (R.L. Hagedohm/LPI)

SUCCEEDING PAGES / *Its head almost in the clouds, the Daehan Life Insurance Building, at 63 floors, wins a gold medal as Asia's tallest edifice . . .*

(INSETS TOP TO BOTTOM) / *. . . while far below things are a great deal more crowded, both during busy morning hours at the Karak Market . . . and on Seoul's congested streets, where a rich diversity of vehicles (cars, trucks, buses, motorcycles, bicycles and handcarts) makes for interesting, and adventurous, driving . . . action-packed I'taewon, a shopper's paradise, proves that all that glitters is just not gold.* (all photos - R.L. Hagedohm/LPI)

Only taxis, buses, and government cars were exempt. The result was, oh, only about 300,000 less cars on the streets of downtown Seoul on any given Olympic day.

For that reason alone, a lot of natives—enjoying less smog and more highway—hoped the Games would last forever.

Recognizing that there would be cultural differences when West met East, the people of Seoul tried to anticipate these, and counter them if they could—which is why they banned the serving of dog meat in restaurants during the course of the Olympics.

Seoul's biggest and most concerted effort came in the area of security. Since there were threats of terrorist violence both from outside and within—such are the problems of hosting an Olympics when you've got an unresolved civil war on your hands—extreme steps had to be, and were, taken. No less than 120,000 troops were on call or on duty around the clock. Armed guards patrolled the athletes' village and press village and all the Olympic venues.

Metal detectors were in place in front of every arena. Mirrors were regularly rolled underneath cars and buses, the better to spot bombs or contraband with. All removable covers to sewer lines, air conditioning vents and other ducts were marked with tape, easily identified if tampered with.

If Houdini had been a terrorist, he might have been able to get out of South Korea. But he'd have never gotten in.

But Seoul's style wasn't protection through intimidation. The police force adopted a non-macho posture. Their attitude was cordial like the signs at the innumerable security checks: "Your cooperation with the security would be most appreciated."

The Games rolled on unfettered.

They began in a morning calm at the Chamshil Stadium, where the Opening Ceremonies stamped Seoul's unique signature on the 16 days that would follow.

While the new facilities and construction represented—at a total budget of $3.1 billion—the modern Korea, the Opening Ceremonies, fraught with symbolism, represented the enduring traditional philosophies of the ages-old "Harmony and Progress"—the motto of the Seoul Games.

Most poignant was when Yoon Tae-oong, a first grader at Chamwon Elementary School, entered the stadium floor alone, rolling a hoop. In silence he walked across the grass. Yoon was born on Sept. 30, 1981, the day the Games were awarded to Seoul in Baden-Baden, the Federal Republic of Germany (FRG). As explained in the official program, he was "symbolic of the bright future of mankind by showing to the world that a new life had grown old enough to play with a hoop while Korea had prepared to host the world for the Olympics."

The Koreans had a certain homecourt mentality after all their hard work, and did not take at all kindly to criticism, or to what they perceived as disrespect. Hence, a kind of smoldering media feud developed with the United States, initially because the members of the U.S. team behaved rather boisterously when entering the stadium for the Opening Ceremonies, and after that because of NBC's television coverage—which was broadcast throughout South Korea on the U.S. Armed Forces Network—of an incident at the boxing venue, where the Koreans violently protested a loss, and a New Zealand official was attacked in the ring.

Such East-West collisions were no doubt inevitable. But in the end, neither deterred greatly from Seoul's overall Olympic effort, or kept the charms of Seoul from coming through loud and clear.

It'aewon was open for business as usual.

The world's largest, and most popular, factory-direct marketplace did a bustling Olympic trade, offering its usual fare—silk, eel skin, tailor-made suits and coats, leather, T-shirts, Reeboks, sweatsuits, you-brand-name-it—at its usual rock bottom, special deal prices. And then throwing in a new set of luggage to get it all home.

And how about a Rolex for $30?

The markets at Tongdaemun and Namdaemun and Myŏng-dong and Insa-dong and elsewhere were Olympic hot-spots as well, as were the traditional Korean restaurants—where dog steaks weren't available but kimchi (spicy cabbage, to be brief and kind) was, in abundance. The not-so-traditional Korean restaurants also did an Olympian trade: Wendy's, Kentucky Fried Chicken, Burger King, McDonald's, and Dunkin' Donuts.

For culture lovers, the Seoul Olympic Arts Festival went the distance of the Games, offering everything from sculpture to painting to dances to a performance by the La Scala Opera Company. In the arts, East met West without a whimper.

At the Closing Ceremonies, the Seoul Games ended with more symbolism, as the lights in Olympic Stadium were shut off and lanterns were lit, both on the stadium floor and in the stands, allowing old Korea to traditionally light the way for guests leaving.

They had successfully pulled off the most elaborate Olympics in history. And as they hang up the "In business since 1988" signs on their arenas, the people of Seoul must know that, as a result of their considerable efforts, neither their city, nor the Olympic movement, will ever be the same again. □

ABOVE / *A pageantry of the arts: 13,000 colorful participants gather 'round.*
(Michael Yada/LPI)

ABOVE / *Korean heritage: Strength rising from gentleness.*
(Leonora V. Goldberg)

OPENING

RIGHT / *A triumphant trio:
A teacher, graduate student
and high school student do
the honors.* (Bob Long/LPI)

LEFT / *Waiting in the wings: One of the 88 participants who was born on the auspicious day of September 30, 1981.* (Leonora V. Goldberg)

BELOW / *Faces of the world: Masked confusion tells a story of human emotions and conflict.* (Bob Long/LPI)

CEREMONIES

RIGHT / *Konori: A folk game representing yin and yang where confrontation dissolves into harmony.* (Bob Long/LPI)

BACKGROUND / *Thousand-fold precision: Practitioners of taekwondo demonstrate harmony.* (Michael Yada/LPI)

HEART 'N

How many friends have I? Count them:
Water and stone, pine and bamboo —
The rising moon on the east mountain,
Welcome, it too is my friend.
What need is there, I say,
To have more friends than five?

Yun Sŏn·do (1587 1671)
Songs of Five Friends

PHOTOS / Leonora V. Goldberg

ARCHERY

The object of concentration is a gold circle, 11.4 cm in diameter. At 90 meters, the farthest distance in this competition, a shooter's pin sight completely obscures it; spectators must use binoculars to follow the action. The event proceeds languidly for five days. At its conclusion, winners and losers alike retire to relative obscurity. The event is archery.

Two-time U.S. individual gold medal winner (' 76 and ' 84) Darrell Pace calls archery "an athlete's sport, a doing sport." "It is," he says, "a very difficult spectator sport."

Those who did it best in Seoul were the host Koreans and American Jay Barrs.

In the women's competition the Koreans swept all of the medals, as Kim Soonyung took the gold, Wang Hee-kyung the silver and Yun Young-sook the bronze. That didn't come as a surprise as the Koreans were expected to do very well before the Games.

In the tense atmosphere of the men's competition, Barrs of Mesa, Ariz., mentally withdrew from the shining green field, the popping arrows, the methodical precision of the white-clad archers, into a deep well of concentration. The strategy worked for Barrs, who came from behind on the last day to edge Korea's Park Sung-soo for the gold. The Soviet Union's Vladimir Echeev took the bronze.

The first two days every athlete shoots 144 arrows—men at 90, 70, 50 and 30 meters, women at 70, 60, 50 and 30 meters—for the right to advance to the third day. Only the top 24 make the cut. Finally, by noon of the fourth day, only eight advance to the shooting line.

The fifth day featured an entirely new Olympic program, archery team competition. Again, Americans and Koreans dueled for gold in the men's competition, but this time, the Americans finished second with Great Britain third.

The individual medals eluded the American women, but the Olympic experience did not. "It was worth every minute of it. I worked so hard for it," said Melanie Skillman, who placed 10th in the competition. At 33, the oldest of the American women, Skillman practiced her sport in an automotive garage between rows of junked cars in her hometown of Laureldale, Pa.

While the Koreans dominated the women's competition individually, there was considerable drama in the team competition.

Archery competitions are a lot like golf tournaments. They take all day to play, and often come down to the final arrow. The women's team final was like that.

Twelve teams had qualified for the medal-round competition that began the morning of Oct. 1 at the Hwarang Archery Field, but the real battle for the medals centered among four teams—Korea, the United States, the Soviet Union and Indonesia.

Indonesia started fast and snagged first place from the favored Koreans after the 30-meter shoot, only to have the Koreans overtake them in the 50-meter round.

Meanwhile, the Soviet Union slipped into fourth after a bad 50-meter round. Twenty points behind the United States, the Soviets, it seemed, were too far back to seriously challenge the Americans, now in third place.

But, with just nine arrows left the Soviets rallied and moved to within two points of the United States—871 to 873. Indonesia was in second with 879 and Korea, with 901, held a comfortable lead that it never relinquished.

It was then to be a battle for the silver and bronze. And, fortunately for the U.S. team, that's when the youngest American Olympian, 14-year-old Denise Parker, came through. She scored a bull's-eye (10) and a pair of nines for 28 points. Her score, combined with 51 points by Skillman and Debra Ochs, enabled the United States to finish one point ahead of the Soviet Union and to tie Indonesia for second.

ABOVE / *Denise Parker, at 14 the youngest U.S. Olympian, placed 21st, but was still able to take a medal home to show classmates at her Utah middle school when she helped the U.S. women's team to a third place finish.* (George Long/LPI)

A shoot-off, where all three team members step to the line to shoot three arrows in a 2-1/2-minute period, determined the silver and bronze medalists. Skillman's first arrow missed the target and that bizarre mishap put the Americans in too deep of a hole to overcome Indonesia. Still, the U.S. trio, relative newcomers to team competition, went home with the bronze. □

ABOVE / *Jay Barrs of Mesa, Ariz., outshot the competitors including hometown favorite, Park Sung-soo (silver), and world champion Vladimir Esheev of the USSR (bronze) to win the individual gold.* (George Long/LPI)

ATHLETICS

The nine dramatic days of the 1988 Olympic track and field competition came and went, leaving behind a collage of stark and vivid images that, even by Olympic standards, may long be remembered. Drug scandals. Flo-Jo. Hooded uniforms. Upsets. Kenyan distance runners. American sprinters. Photo finishes. Record times and distances . . .

They were all of the things that Olympic track and field competitions have come to mean—and some that weren't.

There was Ben Johnson, running at speeds no human being had ever approached; there was Johnson again, fleeing Seoul sans his gold medal and his glory, an exclamation point on the growing drug problems of sport. There was Florence Griffith Joyner, the fashion plate with the designer nails and Flo-ing hair, taking women's sprinting into the men's territory and leaving a trail of records for another generation to challenge. There was Flo-Jo's sister-in-law, Jackie Joyner-Kersee, the modern-day Babe Didrikson, running, jumping, hurdling and throwing like no woman before her. There was Carl Lewis, racing to replace the medal he had buried with his father and to duplicate his quadruple gold performance of L.A., but coming up short, a victim of circumstances and rising young teammates . . .

And there were those American kids . . . including 19-year-old Steve Lewis, just barely old enough to vote, stealing the 400-meter dash, and 21-year-old Joe DeLoach, taking the gold from his friend and training partner, the other Lewis, in the 200. Must be time for a changing of the guard. There were the passing of eras right before our eyes, as Edwin Moses, Mary Slaney and Daley Thompson were all run down by time and younger legs.

Curiously, when all was said and done, the track and field competition seemed to reveal something about our nationalities, if not our lifestyles. "Spheres of excellence endure," wrote *Sports Illustrated*'s Kenny Moore. "Thus, the Seoul Games were a showcase for American speed, Eastern European strength and Kenyan endurance."

In the men's competition, Americans won all three dashes and both hurdles, and took at least two medals in each event. Kenyans won the 800, the 1,500, the 3,000-meter steeplechase and the 5,000, and claimed medals in the 10,000 and marathon. Eastern Europeans won every throwing event but the javelin, which went to another European, a Finn.

For the record, the United States won the gold medal race, with 13, followed by the Soviet Union with 10 and the GDR with six. But the GDR, with a population of fewer than 20 million, won the overall medal race, once again proving its resourcefulness. The GDR collected 27 medals, outdistancing both superpowers (the USSR had 26; the United States 25). Nobody else was close, unless you want to count Great Britain, with eight, and the Joyner women, with six.

Flo-Jo, the unofficial star of these Games, won three gold medals and one silver and established two world and Olympic records in the 100- and 200-meter dashes. She won the 100-meter dash in 10.54 and the 200 in 21.34 and, with these times, changed women's sprinting forever. According to the International Amateur Athletic Federation (IAAF), Flo-Jo's 200-meter time is fast enough to stand as a national record in 69 countries—for men. One British publication wrote, "It took 25 years to lower the women's record for 100 meters a half-second . . . which is what Florence Griffith Joyner did in one afternoon . . . twice."

Flo-Jo was only slightly more successful than her sister-in-law, Joyner-Kersee, who won two gold medals and set two Olympic records and one world record. She won the heptathlon with a score of 7,291 points. It was the fifth time she has exceeded 7,000 points; no other woman has done it once. Joyner-Kersee returned later to win her favorite event, the long jump, with an Olympic record leap of 24' 3-1/2".

ABOVE / *The first couple of track, Florence Griffith Joyner and husband Al, revel in Flo-Jo's astonishing, world record-shattering performance in the 200-meter final.* (Michael Yada/LPI)

OPPOSITE / *Griffith Joyner runs with the pack early in the 100-meter final, but by race's end she would hold a giant .3 second lead over second-place finisher Evelyn Ashford.* (Bob Long/LPI)

OPPOSITE / *Flo-Jo carried the baton of world attention through most of the Games, but here in the 4x100-meter final she passes it on to Evelyn Ashford. Ashford started her final leg behind old rival Marlies Göhr of the GDR but caught and passed her in a thrilling battle down the straightaway in perhaps the meet's most exciting race . . .* (Dave Black)

ABOVE / *. . . But the baton of fame invariably returned to Griffith Joyner, this time passed from Valerie Brisco in the 4x400 final. Returning just 40 minutes after running her 100-meter relay leg, track's cover girl gave it her all, and it required a world record by Olga Bryzguina and her Soviet Union teammates to defeat the U.S. team. Flo-Jo's stunning Olympic report card: three golds, one silver.* (Michael Yada/LPI)

SHE RAN LIKE A MAN

Before 1988, Florence Griffith Joyner was just a good, but not great, sprinter. She won a silver medal in the '84 Games at 200 meters, but she didn't even run the 100, and, for that matter, rarely did in international meets. In truth, ''Flo-Jo,'' as she would come to be known, was more famous for her eccentricities than her sprinting. She raced in hooded or one-legged body suits of her own design, in Flo-rescent colors, and she grew her nails 6-1/2 inches, each sporting a different elaborate painting. Between races, she changed outfits and matching fingernail polish like a Vegas act.

Florence's career began to wane after the '84 Olympics. She worked as a bank secretary and some-time hairdresser and gained weight, and, by 1986, she had fallen completely out of the world and U.S. rankings. With some prodding from her coach, Bob Kersee, she recommitted herself to running and, in 1987, she won the silver medal in the 200 at the world championships.

Before Flo-Jo came along, the world record for the women's 100 meters was Ashford's 10.76, and it had stood for four years. In two months, Flo-Jo bested that six times—three times at the U.S. Olympic trials, where she set a world record of 10.49, a time that astounded track aficionados and three times at the Olympics. There are only a few men in the National Football League who can run that fast. Based on past performance improvements, women weren't supposed to run 10.65 until the year 2000.

Flo-Jo is 5' 6-1/2", 130 chiseled pounds, which is what comes from doing 1,000 situps daily and visiting the weight room four times weekly (she can squat 320 pounds). Says Flo-Jo, ''If you want to run like a man, you have to train like a man.'' □

The weather conditions, the fast new track in Seoul's Olympic Stadium and improving athletes combined to produce records and fast performances almost daily. Three men dipped under 10 seconds in the 100 (and a fourth was disqualified). Two men ran under 19.80 in the 200. Two men broke the magic 44-second barrier in the 400. Another man dipped under the 13-second mark in the high hurdles, a place where only one other man had been. Three men ran under 8:08 in the steeplechase. The list goes on. All told, 29 Olympic records and four world records were broken or equaled, and this is excluding the marks that fell in preliminary rounds that were bettered in the finals, or marks set in the individual events of the decathlon and heptathlon.

Not since the Olympics were held in Mexico City in 1968 had the world seen such speed, but this time there was no aiding 7,200-foot altitude.

And the most startling performance of them all will never count. Ben Johnson ran a mind-boggling 9.79 to win the men's 100-meter dash, breaking his own year-old world record of 9.83. Carl Lewis ran 9.92, the third fastest time in history—and he wasn't even close.

But three days later, the International Olympic Committee reported that Johnson had failed his post-race drug test. His urine sample showed traces of a banned anabolic steroid used to build muscle. Johnson was stripped of his medal and his world record, and Lewis was awarded the gold.

And what of Lewis anyway? The hero of the '84 Games was overshadowed in '88, and yet he won two gold medals and one silver. Nobody had a stranger Olympics than Lewis. First he was cheated, then vindicated, then beaten by DeLoach, then disqualified from the 4x100-meter relay and a sure gold medal before he ever stepped on the track. Ironically, though, Lewis seemed to win more fans in defeat than in victory, his perceived arrogance tempered by graciousness and a new vulnerability on the track. His place in Olympic track and field history is secure. So, too, is the memory of the '88 Games.

TRACK EVENTS

In every Olympic Games track and field competition there is a singular athlete (and sometimes more) who leaves his or her indelible mark on the Games for the ages. Jim Thorpe in 1912, Babe Didrikson in '32, Jesse Owens in '36, and, more recently, Wilma Rudolph in '60, Lasse Viren in '72, Alberto Juantorena and Bruce Jenner in '76, Carl Lewis in '84.

The Games of Seoul were Florence Griffith Joyner's.

Flo-Jo's mixture of beauty and power, combined with her historic racing, took center stage from start to finish in the Olympic Stadium. In the 100-meter dash, she broke the Olympic record twice in the heats, running 10.88 and 10.62—a time bettered by only one woman in history, herself. In the final, Flo-Jo opened up an early lead, and then seemed to lift into another stunning gear over the last 50 meters to beat a distinguished field. Her time was a wind-aided 10.54. Evelyn Ashford ran 10.83, a time bettered by only two other women in history, and the GDR's Heike Drechsler ran 10.85, but they finished far behind Flo-Jo.

"Only a man could run faster than she can," Ashford said.

The 200-meter dash was no less disheartening to Flo-Jo's rivals. In the semifinals, she dashed 21.56, smashing the nine-year-old world record of 21.71 first set by the GDR's Marita Koch and later tied by Drechsler. A few hours later Flo-Jo turned around and smashed her own record, running 21.34 in the final and winning by four meters over Jamaica's Grace Jackson, who clocked a superb time of 21.72.

ABOVE (TOP) / *Jackie Joyner-Kersee garnered the title "The World's Best Female Athlete." She unleashed the second longest jump in her career, under pressure near the end of the competition, to win the gold in the long jump . . .*

ABOVE / *. . . And that jump was accomplished on legs leaden from a recently completed world-record effort in the heptathlon, a grueling seven-event competition, including the javelin, over two days.* (both photos - Bob Long/LPI)

YOU'VE COME A LONG WAY, BABE

Like Flo-Jo, who grew up in a family of 11 children in the projects of L.A., Jackie Joyner-Kersee grew up in urban America, in a small house in East St. Louis. At age nine, Jackie and her pals used an empty potato chip bag to haul sand from a local youth center to build a jumping pit off the porch of Joyner's family home. She competed against Al, her older brother, and it was no contest; she beat him at everything. At 14, Jackie announced that she was going to be in the Olympic Games someday.

In high school, Jackie was both a cheerleader and an athlete, excelling at volleyball, basketball and track. When the time came, she went to UCLA, where one of her teammates was Florence Griffith (whom would later become her sister-in-law) and one of her coaches was Kersee (whom she later married). She starred in both basketball and track and field, and, after tinkering with the javelin throw, her weak event, she rose steadily to international stardom in the heptathlon.

Since winning the silver medal in the '84 Games, she has won all five heptathlons she has entered and set four world records. She could, if not for the demands of the heptathlon, excel elsewhere, as well. She often is compared to Babe Didrikson Zaharias, the former Olympic champion who has long been regarded as history's greatest all-around female athlete. Joyner-Kersee, 5'10-1/2", 155 pounds, tied the world record in the long jump in 1987 and the American record in the 100-meter hurdles in '88, and she plans to work on the 400-meter hurdles in '89. For the Olympics in Seoul, she settled on the heptathlon and the long jump and earned two golds, a world record in the former and an Olympic record in the latter. □

"She runs a different race than we do," Jackson said.

A short time later Flo-Jo returned to run the third leg of the winning 4x100-meter relay. She handed the baton to anchor Ashford, who exploded past East German Marlies Göhr on the straightaway to win the gold for the United States.

Flo-Jo returned again for her third race 40 minutes later, this time to run the anchor leg on the 4x400-meter relay. Flo-Jo, a late addition to the relay, ran 48.1, the fastest split on the team. Both teams beat the old work mark, but the United States had to settle for the silver medal behind the Soviets. Nevertheless, Flo-Jo was content. "It was more than I ever dreamed of," she said. "That silver is gold to me."

In any other Olympics, the story of the Games might well have been another American woman, Jackie Joyner-Kersee. She is sister-in-law to Flo-Jo by virtue of the latter's year-old marriage to Jackie's brother, Al, the '84 Olympic triple jump champion. To confuse matters, they were both coached at one time by Bob Kersee, who is also Jackie's husband. Meet the first family of the Seoul Olympics.

Joyner-Kersee's goal in the heptathlon was not so much to win—that was a given—but to set a world record. In the first event, the 100-meter hurdles, she ran 12.69, a time that would have earned the bronze medal in the open race. She was off to a fast start, but in the high jump, her next event, she strained a tendon in her left knee and cleared only 6' 1-1/4". With her knee taped, Joyner-Kersee managed 51' 10" in the shot put, a career-best. She finished the first day of competition by clocking 22.56 in the 200-meter dash, leaving her 103 points behind her world record pace.

After a night of ultrasound, ice and massage treatment, Joyner-Kersee opened the second day by soaring 23' 10-1/4" in the long jump, which would have been good enough for a gold medal and an Olympic record in the open long jump. She was now 11 points off record pace, but in the javelin—where she had to plant with a tender knee—she managed a throw of only some 10 feet off her normal distance. That meant she had to run 2:13.67 in the final event, the 800-meter run, to break the world record. Instead, she ran a personal-record 2:08.51 to total 7,291 points—which left her 394 points ahead of runner-up Sabine John of the GDR and 76 points ahead of her two-month-old world record.

Five days later, Joyner-Kersee returned to take on an impressive field in the long jump that included Drechsler, the former world record-holder, and Soviet Galina Tchistiakova, the current world record-holder. Understandably, Joyner-Kersee complained of tired legs, but something must have happened when she saw Drechsler leap 23' 8-1/4" on her fourth attempt to take the lead. Joyner-Kersee fouled her fourth attempt, but on her fifth jump she leaped 24' 3-1/2", which was worth another gold medal and an Olympic record.

In 1984 Carl Lewis won four Olympic gold medals, but not the expected adoration of the American public. He was perceived as aloof, arrogant, calculated, his image too polished and attended to. And hadn't he made it all look too easy?

By 1988 that was not a problem. Lewis was no longer invincible. In the 1987 World Championships, Ben Johnson ran away from Lewis in the 100-meter dash, lowering the world record from 9.93 to 9.83. Then, in the U.S. Olympic trials, Lewis was defeated by young Joe DeLoach in the 200-meter dash.

The rematch between Johnson and Lewis was the most eagerly anticipated event of the Games. Both were bent on victory. Lewis' father, Bill, had died of cancer the previous year. At the funeral, Carl placed the gold medal he had won in the L.A. Olympics 100 meters (it had been Bill's favorite event) in his father's hand. "Don't worry, I'll get another one," he told his mother, Evelyn. But Johnson was equally determined. "I don't care if I lose 100 races in a row to Carl Lewis, if I win this one," Johnson said. "The gold medal means everything to me."

The stage had been set when Lewis soundly defeated Johnson in Zurich on Aug. 17 in a 100-meter showdown. Now it was Johnson—who had been battling hamstring injuries all season—who was no longer invincible. Four days later he lost again, this time to Americans Calvin Smith and Dennis Mitchell in Cologne.

But a different Johnson turned up in Seoul. He coasted through the heats, as if to lull Lewis into a false sense of security, and then crushed him in the final with the astounding time of 9.79. As he crossed the finish line, Johnson turned his glowering look to Lewis and shot his index finger into the sky.

But if Lewis was no longer invincible in the sprints, that certainly wasn't the case in the long jump. The last time he lost a long jump competition was 1981. Still, no one had ever repeated as Olympic long jump champ—until now. Lewis produced the four longest jumps of the competition, the best being 28' 7-1/2" and led a U.S. sweep, with Mike Powell second and Larry Myricks third. It was Lewis' 56th straight victory in the long jump.

The next day, news of Johnson's drug test was made public. Lewis was awarded the gold, Great Britain's Linford Christie then received the silver and Smith, the bronze. Thus, Lewis had another crack at four gold medals with the 200-meter dash coming up next. Undoubtedly fatigued from seven races and the long jump, Lewis was run down by a fresh DeLoach late in the race. DeLoach clocked 19.75, which equaled Lewis' American record and broke his Olympic record. Lewis clocked 19.79.

"I hate that I was the one to stop Carl's dream," DeLoach said.

"Everyone competing against me is just getting better," said Lewis. " . . . It's getting more difficult to stay ahead of them."

Lewis' shot for a third gold medal ended when the United States botched a handoff in the semifinals of the 4x100-meter relay and ran out of the exchange zone to earn a disqualification.

At age 27, Lewis had bettered all three of his winning marks in the '84 Games, but he had fewer medals to show for it. Still, he might have won the one thing that eluded him in L.A. In defeat, he had been gracious, more personable and not quite so programmed—he was, as one writer noted, more human.

"I can't say I am really disappointed," Lewis told reporters. "I came here to have the best track meet of my career and I did . . . People tend to measure everything by winning or losing. I think that is wrong."

With all the wonders Seoul worked, the 400-meter dash produced still another. Steve Lewis, 19 years old, just one year removed from a California high school, won the Olympic gold medal and, en route, left recent world record-holder Butch Reynolds with second and UCLA teammate Danny Everett in third.

No one had seen it coming. Coming out of high school, Lewis' personal record had been 45.76. But at UCLA his times began to drop steadily. He ran 44.11 in the Olympic trials semifinals, but finished third in the finals. Given his youth and inexperience, he was expected to finish behind his two countrymen in the Olympics.

Reynolds, 23, and Everett, 21, went one-two at the U.S. Olympic trials, clocking 43.93 and 43.98 to become the first men ever to run under 44 seconds at sea level. A month later, Reynolds went after Lee Evans' legendary world record of 43.86, which had stood for 20 years. Reynolds took it down to an amazing 43.29, and left Everett, Lewis and the rest of the field far behind.

ABOVE / *The Griffith-Joyner-Kersee family affair overshadowed the performance of Carl Lewis, whose two golds and a silver strangely seemed to be a letdown after 1984's four-gold harvest. The favored Lewis finished second in this 200-meter final . . .* (Bob Long/LPI)

ABOVE / . . . and crossed the finish line (No. 1102) after the finger-pointing Ben Johnson of Canada in the meet's most-anticipated showdown, the 100 meters. Lewis eventually won the gold when Johnson's sensational world-record run of 9.79 was nullified after steroids were detected in his post-race drug test. (Bob Long/LPI)

In the Olympic final, Reynolds, the heavy favorite, had an ideal position in lane three. Everett was in lane four and Lewis would run blind in lane six. Strangely, Reynolds lagged through the first half of the race while Lewis opened a big lead, trailed by Everett. In the final turn, Reynolds still had not moved and, as they turned for home, he was six meters behind Lewis. Reynolds has a finish like no quartermiler in history, but even he could not make up so much ground. "I got too confident," he said later.

Given another meter or two, Reynolds might have caught Lewis, but he came up just short at the tape. Lewis clocked 43.87, Reynolds 43.93. Everett completed the U.S. medal sweep with a 44.09.

For all of the above reasons, the United States was a cinch to win the 4x400-meter relay, but the Americans wanted more—the world record of 2:56.16 set 20 years earlier in Mexico City. Everett opened with a 44.0 and Lewis contributed a 43.6 second leg. Kevin Robinzine ran 44.7 and then Reynolds, running alone, ran 43.7. They tied the world record, down to one one-hundredth of a second.

Since their stirring showing in the high-altitude Mexico City Olympics of 1968, Kenyan runners have continued to amaze and mystify the world of middle-distance and distance running, and yet no one was prepared for what happened in Seoul.

First, Paul Ereng, a man so unknown that NBC called him the wrong name all the way down the homestretch, burst through the pack coming off the turn and sprinted to victory in the 800 meters, clocking 1:43.45. In the process, Ereng relegated defending Olympic champion Joaquim Cruz of Brazil to second place, Morocco's great Said Aouita, loser of only two races in the past three years, to third, and American record-holder Johnny Gray to fifth. And Ereng, a 22-year-old University of Virginia student who had converted from the 400-meter dash only this year, isn't even Kenya's best half-miler.

The Kenyans were just warming up. In the 5,000 meters, John Ngugi, the two-time world cross country champion, delivered another victory. Having been outkicked at the end of 5,000 in the '87 World Championships, Ngugi moved early this time. After 1,000 meters, he tossed in a 58-second lap and eventually opened a 40-meter lead. Portugal's Domingo Castro gamely chased Ngugi late in the race, but he never could catch the Kenyan, and it probably cost him a medal. He faded to fourth on the homestretch, as West German Dieter Baumann and finally East German Hansjoerg Kunze passed him. Ngugi won by four seconds in 13:11.70.

In the 3,000-meter steeplechase, Kenyans Julius Kariuki, a student at Riverside Community College in California, and Peter Koech, a Washington State graduate, finished one-two in the fastest race in history. Kariuki clocked 8:05.51, an Olympic record and just .11 shy of the world record set by countryman Henry Rono a decade earlier. Koech was a few strides back, finishing in 8:06.79, history's third fastest time.

And then came the 1,500 meter final. With two laps to go, Peter Rono, a 21-year-old junior at Mount St. Mary's College in Maryland, moved from the back of the pack to the front, but surely he would be overtaken in the stretch. Aouita and Cruz had scratched from the heats, but Great Britain's Steve Cram, the world record-holder in the mile, was poised to strike, along with countryman Peter Elliott and the GDR's Jens-Peter Herold. As they hit the homestretch together, it seemed certain Cram would blow by them all; instead, Rono sprinted and pulled away, winning in 3:35.96, with Elliott second, Herold third and Cram fourth.

"It was tougher to win the Kenyan trials," Rono said. "We have many young talents back home and it is not easy to make the Olympic team. But a gold medal in my first Olympics—this must be a dream."

The Kenyans nearly claimed another gold medal in the marathon, but Douglas Wakiihuri, the '87 world champion, finished 15 seconds behind Italy's Gelindo Bordin and had to settle for the silver. Another Kenyan, Kipkemboi Kimeli, finished third in the 10,000, unable to keep pace with the strong finish of Morocco's Brahim Boutaib, who set an Olympic record of 27:21.46.

Add them up: Kenya won seven medals in six races—four golds, two silvers and one bronze. It surpasses their legendary Mexico City performance, in which they won three golds, two silvers and one bronze. It was a fine comeback for a country that had boycotted the '76 and '80 Games and didn't seem fully recovered in '84. What's more, two of Kenya's top runners weren't even in Seoul. Billy Konchellah, the defending 800-meter world champion, missed the Games with tuberculosis, and Paul Kipkoech, the '87 10,000-meter world champ, had malaria.

Few in the history of sport have ever dominated a sport like Edwin Moses. He has become such a force in the 400-meter intermediate hurdles that the event has become synonymous with his name. Coming into the Games, Moses had won all but two races during the past 11 years and, at one point, had won 122 consecutively. He had won two Olympic gold medals, in 1976 and 1984, and certainly would have won a third if not for the U.S. boycott in 1980. And so, at the age of 33, one of the oldest competitors in the track events, Moses came to Seoul in search of a historic third gold medal.

ABOVE / *Lewis' loss to not-so-friendly rival Johnson may have been harder to swallow than his defeat in the 200 at the hands of good friend and training partner, Joe DeLoach.* (George Long/LPI)

ABOVE / *After the heavily favored U.S. 4x100-meter relay team was eliminated for an illegal baton pass in a preliminary heat, the Soviet Union took advantage of the faux pas and won the gold.* (Bob Long/LPI)

But the man in lane six was equally driven. Andre Phillips, a 29-year-old American, came to Seoul hoping to erase the nightmare of 1984, when, hindered by flu, he had failed to make the U.S. Olympic team. He had been chasing Moses all his life and never once had beaten him.

Moses, in lane three, went out fast, as usual, but Phillips was out even faster. He held a slight lead down the backstretch, but Moses mounted his usual late rally. By the middle of the final turn they appeared to be even, and they were still even at the eighth hurdle. Phillips edged ahead at the top of the homestretch, and Moses couldn't close the gap. At the 10th hurdle Moses was struggling, and El Hadj Dia Ba of Senegal sprinted past him and nearly caught Phillips at the tape. Phillips was first in 47.19, Dia Ba, second, in 47.23 and Moses, third, in 47.56.

Like Lewis, Moses had run faster than he had in any Olympics, but it wasn't enough.

Since his surprising Olympic victory at Los Angeles in the 110-meter hurdles, the United States' Roger Kingdom had seldom been heard from. He had injured a hamstring in 1985 and, for the next two and one-half years, his performances went downhill until finally he dropped out of the world and U.S. rankings completely in 1987. With a great sense of timing, Kingdom returned to form in the summer of 1988, just in time for another Olympics.

In August, at Sestriere, Italy, Kingdom became only the second man in history ever to run under 13 seconds, clocking an altitude-aided 12.97, which was just over Renaldo Nehemiah's world record of 12.93. But could Kingdom repeat as Olympic champion? Only one hurdler in history, American Lee Calhoun, had ever managed that feat.

In the Olympic final, fellow American Arthur Blake got a flying start, but, by mid-race, Kingdom, wearing a hooded spandex racing suit, had taken charge. He slammed into the sixth hurdle, but Kingdom, a former University of Pittsburgh football player, barely noticed. "I ran the fastest last four hurdles of my life," said Kingdom, who clocked an Olympic record 12.98. He finished a full three meters ahead of Great Britain's Colin Jackson and the United States' Tonie Campbell.

While American women had their way in the short dashes between Flo-Jo and Ashford, the powerful East Germans and Soviets continued to dominate the rest of the track events as they always have. In the 400-meter dash, the USSR's Olga Bryzguina set an Olympic record of 48.65, leaving the GDR's Petra Mueller in second in 49.45 and Soviet Olga Nazarova third in 49.90. The Americans took the next three places. Valerie Brisco, the 1984 triple gold medalist, faded badly on the homestretch and finished fourth.

Tatiana Ledovskaia nearly claimed another gold for the Soviets in the 400-meter hurdles. She held a commanding lead down the homestretch, but then Australia's Debbie Flintoff-King found another gear—a gear that should have been burned up in oxygen debt. She had faded on the final turn, then held her own coming home, but suddenly she rallied. Over the last hurdle she caught and passed two rivals and then sprinted for the tape, gaining chunks of ground on Ledovskaia. They hit the tape together, and no one could be sure who was the winner. When Flintoff-King saw the scoreboard replay, she jumped up and down with her arms raised to the sky. A reading of the photo finish shown she had won by a lean in Olympic record time, 53.17 to Ledovskaia's 53.18.

The 100-meter hurdles, on the other hand, were only close until the gun went off. Then, Bulgaria's Jordanka Donkova took control to easily win in 12.38 for another Olympic record.

ABOVE / *Roger Kingdom of the United States leads a wave of runners over a hurdle in a 110-meter preliminary heat . . .* (R.L. Hagedohm/LPI)

RIGHT / *. . . while hooded Tonie Campbell enjoys the same advantage in his heat. In the final showdown between the two talented U.S. athletes, the hurdles proved to be Roger's kingdom; Campbell took the bronze.* (Bob Long/LPI)

ABOVE / *This proliferation of the Stars and Stripes celebrates the United States' 400-meter exploits of Steve Lewis (gold medal), Butch Reynolds (silver) and Danny Everett (bronze). It was one of just two American sweeps at the Olympics — the other came in the men's long jump.* (Bob Long/LPI)

LEFT / *Edwin Moses (No. 1114) enters his last straightaway as king of the 400-meter hurdles, an event he has dominated for more than a decade. By the finish line, the younger Andre Phillips of the United States and El Hadj Dia Ba of Senegal had pulled away from Moses.* (Bob Long/LPI)

In the 800-meter run, the favorites were a seemingly interchangeable pair. It's difficult to tell Christine Wachtel and Sigrun Wodars apart sometimes. Both have close-cropped hair, both are 5' 5-1/4", both are about 120 pounds, both are East Germans, both rank among, oh, say, the top two half-milers in the world, and both have personal records in the low 1:55s. Sometimes they're interchangeable. Wodars won the '87 World Championships, but Wachtel defeated her rival in several meets before the Olympic Games. When the big one rolled around, however, Wodars was once again the winner.

Wachtel took the early pace, with Wodars on her shoulder, and they covered the opening lap in a hot 56.4. At the bell, Wodars took the lead and held it until the final turn, when Wachtel again took the lead. But, at the top of the homestretch, Wodars pulled away from her rival to win the race with a time of 1:56.10. Wachtel was second in 1:56.64.

The only surprise of the race came from Kim Gallagher, the frail 101-pound American who had competed rarely since winning the silver medal in 1984 because of health problems. Despite the stiff early pace, Gallagher was in the race with 150 meters to go, but she was in trouble, if only temporarily. Boxed in a pack of five runners, Gallagher burst through a small gap on the inside lane coming off the final turn and chased Wodars and Wachtel to a third place finish with a time of 1:56.91, missing Mary Slaney's American record by .01.

The 3,000 meters was supposed to be Mary Slaney's just dues. After all her years of Olympic disappointment—boycotts, falls, injuries—at last she would win the Olympic medal that seemed only fitting, considering her brilliant career.

As always, Slaney sprinted to the front and forced a pace that seemed foolhardy, at best. She charged through the first lap in 63 seconds, which would be fast even for a 1,500-meter race. She reached 1,000 meters some 10 seconds ahead of world record pace. Said Slaney, "The idea was to run faster than anyone else was capable of." But it proved more than Slaney could handle as well. With four laps to go, she began to wilt and teammate Vicki Huber moved to her shoulder. A short time later, Slaney faded rapidly to the back of the pack and Huber took the lead. But behind Huber, looking relaxed and controlled, were Romania's Paula Ivan, the Soviet Union's Tatiana Samolenko and Great Britain's Yvonne Murray. With 500 meters to go, all three shot past Huber and pulled away from the field on the gun lap. It was now a matter of attrition. On the final backstretch, Ivan and Samolenko dropped Murray and, on the homestretch, Samolenko sprinted past Ivan to claim the gold medal. Samolenko was timed in 8:26.53 (an Olympic record) to Ivan's 8:27.15. Murray was third in 8:29.02.

As for Slaney, she finished 10th. Huber was sixth, with a time of 8:37.25, some nine seconds under her previous personal record. Perhaps it signaled a changing of the guard. Slaney, a dominant figure for a decade, is 30; Huber is 21, and her best days would seem to be ahead of her.

The 1,500 provided a rematch between Samolenko and Ivan, not to mention another chance for Slaney to claim an Olympic medal. It was the same cast of characters from the 3,000, but the results were different. This time Ivan ran away from everyone, Samolenko included. She beat her nearest opponent by six seconds and clocked 3:53.96, which was not only an Olympic record, but also the second fastest time in history. Soviet Lailoute Baikauskaite was second in 4:00.24, with Samolenko third in 4:00.30. Slaney was eighth in 4:02.49, which was considerably slower than the 3:58.92 she had run at the U.S. Olympic trials.

But perhaps Slaney will return to try another Olympics. After watching the 3,000, Slaney's husband, Richard, was overheard by one reporter to say, "Well, here we go, another four years."

Women have long been sold short by the Olympic Games. Until 1984, the Olympics held no women's race longer than 1,500 meters. In '84, the 3,000 and the marathon were added to the Olympic schedule, but it wasn't until '88 that the Olympics joined the modern world and added the 10,000.

The runaway favorite for the new event was the incomparable Ingrid Kristiansen of Norway, holder of world records in the 5,000, 10,000 and world best in the marathon. For all of her records, Kristiansen, like Slaney, had never won an Olympic medal and now, at 32, time was running out. She finished fourth in the marathon at the L.A. Games. This time she chose the 10,000—and the results were even worse.

Running from the front, Kristiansen suddenly winced and then stepped off the track just 1-1/2 miles into the race. This time she had been stopped by a foot injury.

In the meantime, Great Britain's Liz McColgan, who earlier in the summer had dealt Kristiansen her first loss ever at 10,000 meters, took the lead, followed closely by Soviets Olga Bondarenko and Elena Joupieva. Eventually this threesome pulled away from the field, then ran together through 8,000 meters then 9,000 meters. But Bondarenko, all of 5 feet and 90 pounds, blasted past McColgan on the gun lap and won in 31:05.21. McColgan was second in 31:08.44, and Joupieva third in 31:19.82

Francie Larrieu-Smith, a 35-year-old American, finished a surprising fifth, with a personal record time of 31:35.52. An American star since 16, she spent much of her career running the mile, a race that was probably too short for her. Alas, the addition of the Olympic 10,000 probably came too late in her career.

ABOVE / *Kenya's Paul Ereng placidly runs along while an all-star cast of runners — Morocco's Said Aouita (No. 733), Great Britain's Peter Elliott (418) and Brazil's Joaquim Cruz (115) — strain to keep pace with him. Ereng, in a major upset, held off his illustrious rivals down the stretch. (R.L. Hagedohm/LPI)*

ABOVE / *The Kenyans also prospered in the 3,000-meter steeplechase — all three are running with the front-runners at this point of the race. Eventually, Julius Kariuki (No. 653) won the race in Olympic record time and Peter Koech (No. 659) took second. Mark Rowland (No. 452) of Great Britain won the bronze.* (Bob Long/LPI)

With Kristiansen and defending Olympic champion Joan Benoit of the United States out of the race, Rosa Mota, a 5' 2", 99-pound Portuguese woman, was the clear favorite in the marathon. Since a third place finish in the '84 Games, she had won nine of 12 marathons she had entered, including the '87 World Championships in Rome.

Mota led throughout most of the race, but she was not without company. Australia's Lisa Martin, the GDR's Kathrin Doerre and the Soviet Union's Tatiano Polovinskaia pressed her late in the race, but Mota moved ahead in the final few miles, dropped her rivals and claimed the gold medal with a time of 2:25:40. Martin was second in 2:25:53 and Doerre, third, in 2:26:21.

Italy's Gelindo Bordin had no sooner crossed the finish line in the Olympic Stadium than he went to his knees and planted a kiss on the track. "It was like a war out there," he told reporters, but no one was sure if he was referring to the battle for the medals or the army that followed the race.

Bordin had to outkick the likes of Houssein Ahmed Saleh, the pre-race favorite from Djibouti, and Doug Wakiihuri, the 1987 world champion from Kenya, in the last three kilometers to win the marathon. Bordin clocked 2:10:32, finishing just ahead of Wakiihuri and Saleh, who finished second and third, respectively, with times of 2:10:47 and 2:10:59. It was the same threesome that had medaled in the '87 World Championships, but in a different order.

The men's marathon, the final event of the Games, completed another shutout of the Americans in the distance running events. The United States could do no better than Pete Pfitzinger's 14th place finish.

ABOVE / *Stamina is what prevails here in the 20-kilometer walk, and Jozef Pribilinec of Czechoslovakia had more of it than any other runner in this large pack — he broke the Olympic record by more than three minutes.* (Bob Long/LPI)

RIGHT / *Gelindo Bordin of Italy acknowledges the applause of the gathering Closing Ceremonies crowd after winning the event that epitomizes endurance, the marathon.* (R.L. Hagedohm/LPI)

FAR RIGHT / *After favorite Ingrid Kristiansen of Norway was felled by an injury early in the 10,000-meter final (she had set an Olympic record in the preliminary heat), Elizabeth McColghan of Great Britain (No. 231) and Olga Bondarenko of the Soviet Union (No. 514) took control (the runner in front of them is about to be lapped). Bondarenko outkicked McColghan on the final lap to win the gold, and smashed Kristiansen's recent record by about 40 seconds.* (R.L. Hagedohm/LPI)

OPPOSITE (TOP) / *Favored Rosa Mota, all 99 pounds of her, led the pack at the start of the marathon and at the end, outlasting Australia's Lisa Martin to win the gold by 13 seconds.* (Bob Long/LPI)

OPPOSITE (LEFT) / *Sigurn Wodars (left) breaks this mirror image in the 800-meter final stretch to edge her East German teammate, Christine Wachtel, by about a half second.* (Bob Long/LPI)

OPPOSITE (RIGHT) / *Olga Bryzguina of the Soviet Union propelled her powerful body one time around the track faster than any other woman in Olympic history — 48.65 seconds.* (Bob Long/LPI)

ABOVE / *Life seems a never-ending series of hurdles and, while some require years to conquer, the many here will only take about 13 seconds for these women to clear . . .* (R.L. Hagedohm/LPI)

RIGHT / *. . . And Jordanka Donkova of Bulgaria was graceful as a gazelle in finishing the task in 12.38 seconds, a new Olympic record.* (Bob Long/LPI)

SUCCEEDING PAGES / *Doing a limbo dance in reverse, American Hollis Conway jumps high over the bar on his way to a silver medal . . .*

(INSET) / *. . . But the best in the business this time was Soviet Guennadi Avdeenko, who juuuuuuust clears the bar here.* (both photos - Bob Long/LPI)

FIELD EVENTS

How does one explain the Eastern Europeans' dominance, not just in the throwing events, but in the field events, period? Why is it they can't run as fast as say, the Americans, yet they can jump, throw, hop and flop farther or higher than their rivals? Their dominance of the field events was complete in the '88 Games. Eastern European women won 14 of 18 medals in the field events and, on the men's side, Eastern Europeans won 12 of 19 medals in the field events.

There were, however, several breakthroughs, most of them keeping with tradition. For the 18th time in 21 Olympic long jump competitions, an American took the gold. Carl Lewis, Mike Powell and Larry Myricks made it a U.S. sweep.

Like the Americans and the long jump, the Finns have their own field event at which they excel—the javelin—and it is an event for which they have a special affinity. The Finns adore the javelin. Finnish children buy javelins like their American counterparts buy baseball gloves and, short of that, they cut down birch and pine saplings for use as temporary javelins. It's no wonder that Finland has produced seven Olympic javelin champions and six world record-holders.

Their latest Olympic champion and national hero is Tapio Korjus, who, on his sixth and final attempt, threw 276' 6" to edge Czechoslovakia's Jan Zelezny by a mere six inches. Another Finn, Seppo Raty, finished third, with a mark of 273' 2". It completed a remarkable year for 6' 5", 227-pound Korjus, who improved his personal record some 19 feet in one year.

In recent years, aside from Edwin Moses, there has been no more dominant figure in track and field than the Soviet Union's Sergei Bubka, who, at all of 25 years old, is already considered the greatest pole vaulter of all time. He has been ranked No. 1 in the world every year since 1985, raised the world record nine times, from 19' 2-1/2" to 19' 10-1/2", and won two consecutive world championships. All that had eluded him was an Olympic medal and then only because of the Soviet boycott in 1984. In Seoul, the question was not whether Bubka would win, but how high he would go. Was he ready to scale a historic 20 feet?

It is telling that Bubka didn't even enter the Olympic competition until the bar had been raised to 18' 8-1/4"—a height only three other vaulters managed to clear. Bubka missed his first attempt, made his second, and then passed until the bar was raised to 19' 4-1/4". Battling the swirling winds in the Olympic Stadium, Bubka missed his first two attempts at that height, and suddenly the great Soviet was facing an all-or-nothing proposition. A clearance would mean the gold medal, a Soviet sweep and an Olympic record; another miss would mean no medal—he would finish behind fellow Soviet teammates Radion Gataoulline, who had already cleared 19' 2-1/4", and Grigori Egorov (19' 0-1/4"), as well as Earl Bell, a 33-year-old American, who had cleared 18' 8-1/4". But Bubka, a proven clutch performer, literally screamed over the bar on his third attempt and the Soviet sweep was complete.

Now Bubka wanted more. With the medal competition finished, he could attempt 20 feet. He never got the chance. A mat was laid across the pole vault runway for the medal ceremonies, and, seeing this, Bubka threw up his arms and quit.

The pole vault was the second sweep for the Soviets in the track and field competition. Early in the meet, the Soviets, as expected, finished one-two-three in the hammer throw. Serguei Litvinov threw 278' 2", an Olympic record, to edge two-time Olympic champion and world record-holder Yuriy Sedykh, who threw 274' 10". Iouri Tamm completed the sweep with a mark of 266' 3".

The Soviets proved equally strong in the high jump and triple jump, claiming four more medals in those two events. Guennadi Avdeenko won the high jump with an Olympic record leap of 7' 9-3/4", then made a couple of unsuccessful tries at the

ABOVE / *The Soviet Union's Sergei Bubka is the world's best pole vaulter, so he always has the farthest to fall — either literally or figuratively. At the Olympics, he took home the expected gold and an Olympic record.* (George Long/LPI)

OPPOSITE / *Tapio Korjus of Finland, though hobbled by a leg injury, claimed victory in the javelin, an event his country traditionally dominates.* (pressfoto)

ABOVE / *Decathlete Christian Schenk of the GDR vaulted (and sprinted, jumped, threw, ran and hurdled) to the title as the best Jack-of-all-trades of athletics.* (Michael Yada/LPI)

OPPOSITE / *Natalia Akhremenko of the Soviet Union puts all of her muscle, heart and soul into this heave on her way to a seventh place finish in the shot put.* (Michael Yada/LPI)

vaunted eight-foot mark. Hollis Conway, a 21-year-old unheralded American, won the silver, based on fewer misses, and Soviet Roudolf Povarnitsyne tied Sweden's Patrik Sjöberg for third. All three cleared 7' 8-3/4".

It took an Olympic record to stop the Soviets in the triple jump. Hristo Markov, the defending world champion from Bulgaria, leaped 57' 9-1/2" to turn back a pair of Soviets—silver medalist Igor Lapchine (57' 5-3/4") and bronze medalist Alexandre Kovalenko (57' 2"). World record-holder Willie Banks, the 33-year-old American, could do no better than sixth.

Where the Soviets dominated the hammer, pole vault and high jump and triple jump events, the East Germans were equally dominating in the shot put and discus. The GDR had a formidable entry for each event—Ulf Timmermann and Jurgen Schult, both 6' 4" and 240 pounds, both world record-holders, both gold medal favorites.

Before the competition turned into an East-meets-West showdown, Timmermann had seemingly wrapped up the shot put competition. First he raised the Olympic record to 70' 1/2", then he took it to 73' 1-3/4" on his fifth throw. And where was Randy Barnes, the top American threat? After five attempts, the best he had managed was 69' 11", which left him in fourth place with one attempt remaining. "I was in awe of the situation," he later said. But not for long. On his final throw, Barnes wheeled and unleashed a heave of 73' 5-1/2", a startling improvement of nearly four feet and an Olympic record. For the first time since 1968, an American had finally won the Olympic shot put competition. Or so it seemed. Timmermann stepped into the ring for his final throw and delivered a huge, high-pressure throw of 73' 8-3/4" to win the gold medal and reclaim the Olympic record. For the third time in the last four Olympics that the United States has competed in, an American had been nudged into second place by an Eastern European. Switzerland's Werner Guenthoer was third at 72' 1-3/4".

A week later, it was Schult's turn in the discus. There he would face, among others, the United States' redoubtable Mac Wilkins, the 37-year-old 1976 Olympic champion and 1984 silver medalist. Wilkins had competed sparingly since '84, but the Olympic Games drew him back into the ring again. He won the U.S. Olympic trials, but there would be no more Olympic medals.

As expected, Schult won the gold with a throw of 225' 9", breaking Wilkins' 12-year-old Olympic record. The silver medal went to the Soviet Union's Romas Oubartas (221' 5") and the bronze to the FRG's Rolf Danneberg (221' 1"). Wilkins finished fifth with a throw of 216' 2".

Aside from Moses and Wilkins, there was another legend who was trying to return to form in the twilight of his athletic career. Great Britain's Daley Thompson, one of only two men ever to win the Olympic decathlon twice, had returned at age 30 to seek a third gold medal, just as he had planned eight years earlier. Before he had even claimed his first Olympic victory in the 1980 Games, Thompson sent a post card from Moscow to two-time Olympic decathlon champion Bob Mathias that said, simply, "I'm going for three."

But age, injuries and a couple of young East Germans were in his way. Thompson, unbeaten for nine years, was seemingly invincible until a ninth place finish in the '87 World Championships. The GDR's Torsten Voss and Christian Schenk had stepped to the forefront.

And yet, with one event to go in Seoul, Thompson was in third place, trailing Schenk by 78 points and Voss by 16. At the end of the longest day in decathlon history—13 hours—Thompson found himself running the 1,500 meters, with his left thigh heavily bandaged. Earlier in the day, in the pole vault, Thompson had snapped his pole midway through a vault and re-injured the abductor muscle of his thigh. Thompson

ABOVE / *Discus throwers Martina Hellman and Diana Gansky of the GDR share a gentle moment in the midst of winning gold and silver medals for their strength.* (Bob Long/LPI)

OPPOSITE / *American Louise Ritter pushes herself over the high jump bar by the barest of margins for an Olympic record and the gold medal. Perhaps no victory in the entire meet was as stunning as Ritter's upset of heavily favored Stefka Kostadinova of Bulgaria.* (R.L. Hagedohm/LPI)

never made a serious challenge in the 1,500. He labored to the finish line, clocking 4:45.11, which left him well behind his East German rivals. Schenk, 25, claimed the gold medal with a score of 8,488 points, and Voss was the silver medalist, with a score of 8,399. Canada's Dave Steen rallied in the 1,500 to take the bronze medal, with 8,328 points.

In the women's field events, there were two more breakthroughs in the Eastern European juggernaut, and one was a historic first, the other a major upset by the United States. American women have made great strides in catching the Eastern Europeans in the sprints in recent years, but they are still far behind in the field events, with at least two notable exceptions. Jackie Joyner-Kersee became the first American woman to win the long jump, leaping 24' 3-1/2", an Olympic record. That was no surprise, but Louise Ritter's win in the high jump was unexpected.

Ritter was given little chance of beating Bulgaria's Stefka Kostadinova, whose world record of 6' 10-1/4" was 2-1/4" higher than Ritter's American record. What's more, Ritter's luck in big meets was no secret: She had made the '80 Olympic team, but didn't compete because of the boycott; she made the '84 U.S. team, but finished only ninth, with a poor leap of 6' 3-1/4". In last year's world championships, she finished eighth. Her luck was no better in non-Olympic years—there had been surgery on her left ankle in 1977, 1980 and 1982, and arthroscopic surgery on her right knee in 1983 and 1985.

Now, at 30, Ritter was back for another Olympic Games, and, when the bar had been raised to 6' 8", only two women remained in the competition—Ritter and Kostadinova. They were tied for first, both having cleared 6' 7". At 6' 8", the bar defeated both jumpers on their first three attempts. So they held a jump-off; each would have one more attempt at 6' 8". Kostadinova went first, and missed. Ritter loped up to the bar, leaped and then arched over the bar, brushing it with her right thigh. The bar vibrated, but it didn't fall.

"I may have touched the bar, but that bar wasn't going anywhere," said Ritter, who leaped out of the pit and raised both arms in celebration. Thus, Kostadinova finished second, at 6' 7", and the Soviet Union's Tamara Bykova was third at 6' 6-1/4".

In the women's shot put, javelin and discus, the results were the same as the men's, if not even more pronounced. Natalia Lisovskaya, a 6' 2", 220-pound Soviet, not only won the shot put, but she also produced the six longest throws of the competition, the best being 72' 11-3/4". That was nearly four feet better than the rest of the field. Similarly, Petra Felke, the javelin world record-holder from the GDR, produced the three longest throws of the javelin final, with a best of 245' 0", which was an Olympic record and almost 15 feet better than her nearest rival. Another East German, Martina Hellmann, set another Olympic mark in the discus, with her throw of 237' 2".

Like any good movie, the track and field events in the Olympic Games left plenty of room for one or more sequels. Have the Olympic Games seen the last of Lewis, Moses and Thompson? How much more can an Olympic Games call out of an athlete, especially in light of the records and fast times of Seoul? Will the example of Ben Johnson serve as a drug deterrent in future Games? And what unknown Kenyan is out there now, running toward gold in '92? Tune in to Barcelona. □

BASKETBALL

I t was a nightmare. No, worse. It was a living nightmare. John Thompson could have been no prouder of his selection as U.S. Olympic basketball coach, no prouder to be given a once-in-a-lifetime opportunity to represent his country.

Now, here he was. After losing to the Soviet Union in the Olympic semifinals, in a jam-packed room in Seoul's Chamshil Gymnasium, he had to explain just how he and his team had let their country down.

"One thing I said all along is that our biggest problem is their (the Soviets') maturity . . .

"Sabonis creates a tremendous problem . . .

"On any given day . . ."

That was the low of Seoul. Thompson's team came back a day later to beat Australia and claim the bronze medal, but that was far from the gold it was almost required to carry back to the States. The game was born there, after all. The United States had lost only once before in the Olympics, and everybody knew that game was stolen in Munich in 1972.

Its saviors: the U.S. women.

For years, their international standing had been almost the reverse of the men's. The Soviets ruled and the Americans chased. But a Kay Yow-coached team had beaten the USSR twice in 1986, in the world championships and Goodwill Games, and Yow—back from cancer surgery only a year earlier—and nine holdover players were enough to do it again in Seoul. With conviction.

They beat the Soviets by 14 points in the semifinals, knocked off Yugoslavia a second time in the final, and claimed the United States' second consecutive gold medal in the Olympics—this one not devalued by a boycott.

"This is it," said center Anne Donovan, a hero off the bench in the final game. "I remember in '84, walking off the floor and everybody asking what would have

happened if the Soviets had been there. Now we know."

Both U.S. teams came to Seoul heavily favored. But Thompson had spent much of the spring and summer waving yellow caution flags.

A stunning loss to Brazil in the 1987 Pan American Games was proof, he said, that the rest of the world was catching up with the United States. He fussed about a system that puts an Olympic basketball team together in a matter of months, picking only from its pool of collegians, while other countries were fielding older, more mature teams that had played together for years.

To make matters worse, the National Basketball Association's Portland Trail Blazers had taken in Soviet superstar Arvidas Sabonis and given his injured Achilles' tendon four months of tender, loving care.

The Soviets and their 7'3-1/2" center looked awful in their opening game, a 92-79 loss to Yugoslavia.

The same day, the United States stormed out of the gate. Spain, the 1984 silver medalist in L.A., was supposed to be a respectable first-game opponent, but shot less than 33 percent against the Americans' relentless pressure defense and fell 97-53. After a summer of questions about his ability to come back from a year away from competition, center David Robinson had 16 points and 11 rebounds.

"If we play well one game, that's not indicative of consistency," Robinson cautioned.

That was evident in the second game as the United States struggled to overcome Canada, 76-70. Then, it was time to settle a year-old score with Pan Am gold medalist Brazil.

In Indianapolis, Brazilian forward Oscar Schmidt hit seven three-pointers, scored 46 points and became a celebrity.

This day, he ran into the United States' Dan Majerle. Then, Willie Anderson. Then, Mitch Richmond and Jeff Grayer. Thompson kept shuttling in fresh, in-

ABOVE / *At 6'2", American Katrina McClain isn't accustomed to looking up to other women, that is until she bumped into 6'10", 260-pound Zheng Haixia of China. McClain outjumps her far taller opponent here, and her U.S. teammates outran China, 94-79. (R.L. Hagedohm/LPI)*

ABOVE / *Vicki Bullett (No. 10) and Anne Donovan give each other a very high five-times-two, while other teammates pair off to celebrate their gold medal over Yugoslavia.* (R.L. Hagedohm/LPI)

spired defenders. Oscar hit two three-pointers, scored 31 points—nine below his Olympic average—and the United States rolled, 102-87.

The remaining preliminary-round games were academic. The United States trashed China, 108-57, and Egypt, 102-35, and it hardly seemed to matter that outside sharp-shooter Hersey Hawkins was lost for the rest of the Games with a strained knee.

The Soviets, meanwhile, continued to struggle. Sabonis sat out their second game, a victory against Australia. They needed overtime to beat Puerto Rico, and defeated the Central African Republic—appearing in its first Olympics—by only nine points.

"Maybe we are tired," Soviet guard Sharunas Marchulenis suggested. "We play many games before Olympics, and only three days' free time."

The Soviets squeaked by again in the quarterfinals, beating Oscar and Brazil, 110-105. The United States advanced with a 94-57 rout of Puerto Rico. And the long-awaited replay of the 1972 debacle in Munich, in which the USSR got three extra seconds to hand the United States its only previous loss in the Olympics, was at hand.

"Every day," Soviet coach Alexander Gomelsky said, "Russian people and Russian journalists and TV remember and talk about historic three seconds in Munich. This is good story. I like it same."

He got it. Without the taint.

The Soviets played a near-perfect game. They beat the United States back on the fast break, got the ball inside to Sabonis (13 points and 13 rebounds), and rained three-pointers—three by Marchulenis and four by guard Rimas Kurtinaitis.

The United States fell behind by eight, battled back behind Robinson to a 27-27 tie, then fell back again by eight, then by 10.

Star forward Danny Manning went scoreless. And shockingly, the feared pressure was no factor. In the final 2:41 alone, when the United States was trying desperately to pull even, the Soviets sprang loose for four uncontested lay-ups.

The USSR went on to win the gold medal, beating Yugoslavia, 76-63, as Sabonis—by now, the tournament's most valuable player—had 20 points, 15 rebounds and three blocked shots.

The United States finished with a 78-49 win over Australia, picked up its bronze and, a day later, took off for home and an uncertain reception.

"I think they (his players) gave all they could to represent their country," Thompson said, "and I think that's all their country can ask of them."

He wouldn't second-guess the team he picked or the style—heavy on defense and the running game, light on shooting—it was taught to play. "If somebody's going to criticize us for striving for excellence and not being able to achieve it," he said, "let it be."

For the U.S. women, there was absolutely no room for criticism. They dominated.

Actually, they started modestly, coming from behind to beat Czechoslovakia, 87-81, in their opener. Then, they dominated.

Yugoslavia was supposed to be one of the top three or four teams in the world. It fell 101-74 as Cynthia Cooper came off the U.S. bench to hit three, three-point shots and score 17 points. China featured 6'10", 260-pound Zheng Haixia. She scored 32 points, but 6'2" center Katrina McClain and 5'4" point guard Suzie McConnell countered with 27 and 18 points, and the Americans closed the preliminaries with a 94-79 victory.

The semifinals brought—guess who—the Soviets. But they were just one more overmatched opponent. The United States went on an early 18-4 run, led by as many as 19 points in the first half, and coasted to a rematch with Yugoslavia for the gold medal.

"We've beaten them by a large margin. They have a lot of incentive," Yow worried going in.

She needn't have. Donovan, an 11-year veteran of international competition and starter on the United States' gold medal team in 1984, had been relegated to the bench in Yow's conversion to Thompson-style quickness and speed. But the 6'8" center was inserted when McClain picked up her third foul late in the first half. Donovan scored six points and forced two Yugoslav turnovers in less than three minutes, and helped turn a two-point deficit into a 42-36 lead at halftime.

The rest was left to Teresa Edwards, one of the reasons the United States was able to lose Cheryl Miller to injury a year earlier and miss hardly a step. The former University of Georgia star scored 14 of her 18 points in the second half, and the United States increased its lead to as many as 17 points.

It had been only 24 hours since the men had seen their dream slip away. "But they were really encouraging," Cooper said. "They told us, 'Hey, go for the gold. Somebody has to bring it home.'"

Cooper had her medal only a few minutes, though, before she gave it up—to her mother, celebrating her 52nd birthday in Seoul.

"It's hers," Cooper said. "It's wonderful.

"What better present to give your mom on her birthday?" □

ABOVE / *You can't beat what you can't catch, and the sight of lightning-quick U.S. guards, such as Cynthia Cooper, streaking across open court for uncontested lay-ups was all-too-common for America's opponents.* (R.L. Hagedohm/LPI)

OPPOSITE / *Meanwhile, the U.S. men's team found itself in a bruising battle against Brazil. This game was a grudge rematch of the 1987 Pan American Games, when the Brazilians pinned a rare loss on the United States to win the gold. The Americans prevailed this time, 102-87.* (R.L. Hagedohm/LPI)

LEFT / *With superstar talent such as Danny Manning, the U.S. men's team seemed a good bet for the gold. But luck turned sour for the obviously unsuperstitious No. 13, first with this reluctant lay-in against Brazil, then later in the climatic game against the USSR, when he couldn't coax a single ball through the hoop . . .* (R.L. Hagedohm/LPI)

OPPOSITE / *. . . Not that 7' 3" Soviet center Arvidas Sabonis, who is perhaps headed for future showdowns with these Americans in the NBA, needed much help. Sabonis and his Soviet teammates played a technically masterful game in crafting an 82-76 victory over the United States in the long-awaited Olympic showdown between the two basketball superpowers.* (Michael Yada/LPI)

BOXING

The sport of boxing may be known as "the sweet science," but for almost everyone at the Olympic Games in Seoul, the boxing competition was overwhelmingly bittersweet.

There was suspect judging, overblown nationalism, protest, appeals and infighting. At times, it seemed as if there were as many fights outside the ring as there were inside.

But the American boxers came through the politics and squabbling remarkably well, rising supremely to the occasion as they pummeled the dismal pre-Olympic predictions of the "experts".

The U.S. team won three gold medals, three silvers and two bronzes. The six men who made the finals in Seoul equaled the U.S. record set in Montreal in 1976.

Light middleweight Roy Jones, the youngest member of the American team, was awarded the Val Barker Cup as the Most Outstanding Boxer of the Games.

"It's kind of nice," said Jones, 19, of Pensacola, Fla., "but if I'm the best boxer in the tournament how come I don't have a gold medal?" He did have a silver, although he had fought well enough to have won the gold. Only the third non-gold medalist to have won the Barker Cup, Jones battered Korea's Park Si-hun throughout their bout, which came on the last day of the Games.

The second round was especially telling as the stylish Jones, a protégé of Sugar Ray Leonard, hit Park almost at will. And in the third round, commentators of the host Korean Broadcasting System said Park would need a knockout to win.

The knockout blow was delivered by the judges: a 3-2 decision for Park, the hometown hero. Even Anwar Chowdry, the president of the International Amateur Boxing Association, said the decision had been unfair.

Although appeals were possible at the Los Angeles Olympics through a separate "scoring jury," the jury had been abolished by the international federation in 1986 and Jones was left with no alternative but to accept the decision.

Even his Korean opponent was astonished at the result, and Jones left the ring in tears. Deflated and disillusioned, he said he was considering quitting the sport.

Things went more smoothly in the only other U.S.-Korean final, which was between heavyweight Ray Mercer and Baik Hyun-man.

Mercer, at 27 the oldest member of the otherwise young U.S. team, is a sergeant in the Army stationed in the FRG. He had been largely unknown until he appeared at—and won—the U.S. championships earlier in the year.

None of his five Olympic fights went the distance, including the final against Baik. The Korean lasted 2 minutes, 16 seconds before Mercer knocked him out with a left hook, a punch that he had learned only weeks before the Nationals from Army coach Hank Johnson.

"I sort of figured I needed to stop the bout because if he was standing at the end of three rounds, he had a pretty good chance of winning," Mercer said. "The left hook is what took him out."

Another Army boxer, light heavyweight Andrew Maynard, also won a gold medal, scoring a decision over Nurmagomed Chanavazov in the only U.S.-Soviet final of the Games.

Maynard's toughest fight of the draw had been against Henryk Petrick of Poland, who knocked him down in the second round. But the Pole threw in the towel at the start of the third, sending Maynard into the final.

Although bantamweight Kennedy McKinney had left the Army, he had remained in Killeen, Texas, so he could work with the fighters and coaches at Fort Hood. After having had a tough time making the U.S. team over three-time national champion Michael Collins, McKinney more than earned his stripes in Seoul. He scored a 5-0 decision over

ABOVE / *Heavyweight Ray Mercer didn't want to take a chance on the boxing judges' decisions so he made his own decision, knocking out Korean opponent Baik Hyun-man in the first round to earn his gold.* (George Long/LPI)

OPPOSITE / *Light heavyweight champ Andrew Maynard gets draped then belted by an Olympic official, but this is a one-two combination where the recipient feels no pain.* (Michael Yada/LPI)

LEFT / *U.S. boxer Roy Jones hits Korean Park Si-hun with a solid left, and hit him again, and again, and again throughout their match. Yet, in a shocking 3-2 decision, the gold was awarded to Park. The decision was called a disgrace. IOC President Juan Antonio Samaranch even made a pointed reference to it in his closing remarks. . .* (Michael Yada/LPI)

ABOVE / *. . . Park, raises his arms in triumph after the decision was announced.* (Michael Yada/LPI)

veteran Alexander Hristov of Bulgaria, becoming the first U.S. medalist at 119 pounds since Oliver Kirk in 1904.

Hristov, 24, coincidentally also in the military, had been inadvertently involved in the major incident of the boxing competition. When the Bulgarian's 3-2 decision over Korea's Byun Jong-il was announced in an early round matchup, some of Byun's coaches and supporters jumped into the ring and assaulted the referee, Keith Walker of New Zealand.

Byun, 19, a student at Dongkuk University, staged a sit-in at the center of the ring for 67 minutes. When the arena lights were turned off, Byun finally ended his protest.

In the wake of the incident, the Korean coaches were banned from the Games. Kim Chong-ha, the president of the Korean Olympic Committee, resigned in humiliation. Walker, meanwhile, caught the first plane back to New Zealand that evening.

Extended coverage of the melee by NBC created some rancorous feelings between the Koreans and Americans: The hosts thought the network had been too aggressive in its reporting.

The result was that the impartiality of the judging was called into question as Korean boxers seemed to be given more and more decisions.

The U.S.-Korean rivalry had replaced the traditional one with the Soviet Union. The first U.S.-Soviet Olympic bout in 12 years had come in the third round of the 156-pound weight class, with Jones facing Evgeni Zaitsev and scoring a 5-0 win. The only other such matchups in Seoul were Maynard's gold medal victory and Riddick Bowe's unanimous third-round decision over Alexandre Miroshnichenko.

Bowe, 21, occasionally brilliant and always engaging, had rumbled through the super heavyweight class like he used to rumble through the streets of Brooklyn. His gold medal bout with Lennox Lewis of Canada promised to be a good one.

And it was . . . for two rounds. Lewis, 6'4'' and 220 pounds, won the gold medal when the referee stopped it at 43 seconds into the second round. Lewis, 23, the 1987 Canadian and North American champion, had knocked out heavily favored Uli Kaden of the GDR with his first punch in the first round of their bout. Lewis had lost to eventual U.S. gold medalist Tyrell Biggs in the quarterfinals of the 1984 Olympics in Los Angeles.

An eventual gold medalist at Seoul put an end to Romallis Ellis' Olympic dream in the 132-pound lightweight class. Ellis, of Ellenwood, Ga., lost a 5-0 decision to East German Andreas Zuelow in their semifinal bout and shared the bronze. He had beaten a tough Korean opponent, Lee Kang-suk, in his first Olympic fight.

Kenneth Gould of Rockford, Ill., also won a bronze after he was upset, 4-1, by Laurent Boudouani of France in the 147-pound welterweight semifinals. The rugged but stylish Gould had previously beaten the Frenchman, also by a 4-1 score, in the 1986 World Championships.

In the light welterweight final, 31-year-old Viatcheslav Janovsky of the Soviet Union won his country's only boxing gold medal when he slugged out a 5-0 decision over Grahame Cheney, a 19-year-old greenskeeper from Australia.

RIGHT / *American bronze medalist Romallis Ellis pounds away at his bloody, but unbowed, Korean opponent Lee Kang-suk in their early round lightweight match.* (Michael Yada/LPI)

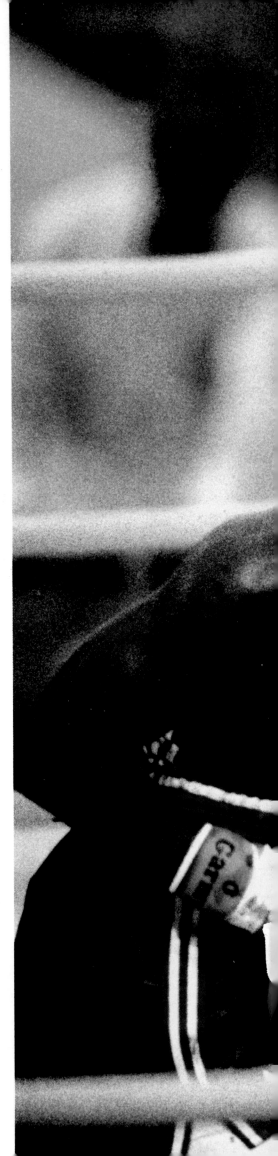

Todd Foster, the U.S. welterweight champion, had one of the stranger Olympic experiences in his second round fight against Chun Jin-chung. The Korean stopped fighting during their bout when he heard a bell in the adjoining ring. Foster, who had not responded to that bell, saw an opening and floored Chun and the referee counted the Korean out. After a protest was lodged, Foster was told he would have to fight Chun again, 90 minutes later. And he knocked him out again, at 2:25 of the second round. In his next bout, Foster, of Great Falls, Mont., lost to Cheney.

The highly partisan crowd had someone to cheer in the flyweight final as world champion Kim Kwang-sun, 24, defeated Andreas Tews of the GDR, 4-1. The single dissenting vote came from the American judge. Kim, a Korean folk hero who receives $425 a month from the government, decisioned American Arthur Johnson in a quarterfinal bout. Johnson, a budding broadcaster, is from Minneapolis.

Middleweight Henry Maske of the GDR won one of his country's two golds, decisioning Egerton Marcus of Canada in the final. Maske, 24, was the runner-up in the World Cup.

The middleweight division was a sore spot for the United States as the early going proved a bit rocky for the American squad. When Anthony Hembrick was kept off an overcrowded bus and U.S. coaches had miscalculated the fight schedule, Ha Jong-ho of Korea was awarded a walkover. Appeals and protests followed, of course, but to no avail. U.S. Olympic Committee president Robert Helmick even intervened with International Olympic Committee president Juan Antonio Samaranch, but the disqualification stood.

That was bad enough, but the featherweight division was its own little shop of horrors for the United States.

Italy's Giovanni Parisi would win the gold medal on a first-round knockout of Daniel Dumitrescu of Romania, but, earlier, when former world champion Kelcie Banks was knocked out in the first round of his first bout, things appeared dismal for the Americans.

But then came Michael Carbajal to the rescue.

The quiet, hard-working light flyweight scored an agonizingly close 3-2 decision over Oh Kwang-soo and thus energized the whole U.S. team. "That was a huge win for us," said Jim Fox, executive director of the USA Amateur Boxing Federation. "It was just like Paul Gonzalez's win in 1984. Michael set the tone for the whole rest of the tournament."

Gonzalez, a product of the barrio of East L.A. and also a light flyweight, won the gold medal and the Val Barker Cup in Los Angeles. Carbajal, who was trained by his brother Danny in a makeshift gym in the backyard of their Phoenix home, would not be so fortunate. But he did win the silver medal after a very close decision in the final bout to Bulgaria's Ivailo Hristov.

Carbajal's comments after the bout were indicative of the pride and determination with which the underdog U.S. team had carried itself throughout the tournament:

"I'm the Olympic silver medalist and that's not bad at all," he said. "I thought I'd won the gold medal and I'll always feel that way. I've achieved a lot in my career and I'm proud of what I've done." □

LEFT / *The ring seems barely big enough to hold the intimidating bodies of super heavyweights Lennox Lewis of Canada, right, and American Riddick Bowe. Bowe is about to bow out after being handed a second-round TKO compliments of Lewis.* (Michael Yada/LPI)

CANOE AND KAYAK

BARTON WINS DOUBLE GOLD

Greg Barton led the U.S. canoe and kayak team to its best performance ever in the Olympic Games. In a dramatic finish, Barton edged Australia's Grant Davies by 0.01 seconds to win the K-1 1,000-meter event. Ninety minutes later, Barton teamed with Norman Bellingham to win the K-2 1,000-meter gold medal as well.

The United States had not won an Olympic gold medal in canoe and kayak competition since Frank Havens captured the single canoe 10,000-meter race in 1952. Never before had an American won an Olympic kayak race.

Barton and Bellingham notwithstanding, the GDR, USSR and Hungary continued their traditional domination of the sport with nine, six and four medals, respectively.

The Han River Regatta Course on the outskirts of Seoul was an ideal setting. The man-made 2,200x140-meter pool assured reasonably calm water even on windy days; high tech equipment removed any doubt about results; and television monitors in the grandstand accentuated each start, every stroke and the exciting finishes for the thousands of spectators.

Hungarian Zsolt Gyulay was not to be denied Olympic gold by anyone. He finished 1.56 seconds ahead of the field in the K-1 men's 500-meter race. East German Andreas Staehle collected the silver and Paul MacDonald of New Zealand won the bronze. American

Mike Herbert finished fourth, only 0.27 seconds behind the bronze medalist.

An exciting finish and dramatic upset shook the women's kayak world in the K-1 500-meter race. If anyone came to Seoul as a sure gold medalist, it was Birgit Schmidt of the GDR. Schmidt had dominated women's kayak racing much like Edwin Moses had dominated the 400-meter hurdles. Whenever Schmidt entered a race, either in singles or in a team boat, the gold was virtually conceded to her. The rest would race for second.

Bulgarian Vania Guecheva, however, did not read the script. Guecheva started fast, but still trailed the confident Schmidt by 0.65 seconds at the 250-meter midpoint. Inexplicably, Schmidt slowed precipitously near the end, and Guecheva slipped by. Just across the line, Schmidt looked to her right from lane one and realized that she had been beaten. Her face registered shock and her body slumped in dismay.

Schmidt recovered quickly, however. With a vengeance, she and her teammates found their customary position at the top of the award platform in both of the women's team boat events. Guecheva affirmed her stature as well by leading her team to silver and bronze medals in the K-2 and K-4 events, respectively.

The last day of the kayak competition was Barton's day of triumph, but his singles victory did not come easily or with-

ABOVE / *Greg Barton, by a mere 0.01 second, captured the first kayaking gold ever for the United States, then, an hour later, he teamed with Norman Bellingham to win a second gold medal.* (Bob Long/LPI)

OPPOSITE / *Water dances in delicate, symmetrical arcs as kayaks knife their way down the Han River Regatta Course. In the foreground is Sweden's Gunnar Olsson, who finished fifth in the 1,000-meter race.* (Bob Long/LPI)

HE CONQUERED FOES AND ADVERSITY

Greg Barton is not just the premier kayak racer in the world; he is also the best of America personified. He was raised on a farm near the western Michigan town of Homer. His malformed legs and club feet might have kept an ordinary person out of athletics, but Barton isn't ordinary. In addition to kayaking, he is a proficient wrestler, runner and cross country skier.

The 28-year-old Barton, who graduated summa cum laude from the University of Michigan with a degree in mechanical engineering, is an engineer with Fluor Daniel in Newport Beach, Calif.

For the most part, he trains on his own and with a single-minded dedication and commitment to excellence. He has used his engineering mind to analyze and apply every detail of racing technique and strategy. His stroke is the picture of perfection, and his steady, solid and secure race pace usually builds to astonishing leads with 150 meters to go, virtually assuring victory. He did it twice in Seoul.

With all of these talents and achievements, he remains quiet, peaceful, introspective and always pleasant, respectful and modest.

Greg Barton is the definition of America at its best. □

out a few anxious moments. He was seventh after the first 250 meters, but he moved up to second by the midpoint. Paddling in lane eight, Barton was still second with 250 meters left. Hungary's powerful Ferenc Csipes held the lead in lane nine. Typically, however, Barton accelerated from the 250 mark.

As Barton surged, Csipes faded. Meanwhile, Andre Wohllebe of the GDR was also closing fast in lane five. Out of Barton's sight in lane one, Davies, the dark horse from Australia, was also slipping past the field. After leading at the start, Davies had appeared to have fallen out of contention. Yet, he mustered a finishing kick that took him from fifth to a dead heat for the lead. While Barton covered the final 250 meters in an impressive 1:00.43, Davies did it in an amazing 58.75. At the line, no one could be sure of the result. The television monitor indicated Barton by a few inches, but its camera was not mounted on the official line.

Grandstand spectators called it for Barton as well, but the scoreboard flashed Davies first by 0.37 seconds. U.S. team leader Bill Hanson shot up the finish tower to inspect the photo finish. There was a long delay with no official announcement. Barton had resigned himself to second place status, but neither the athletes nor the spectators knew the official result until the medal presentation.

Barton won by 0.01 of a second. An enlargement of the finish photo revealed a faint sliver of light between Davies' boat and the line. No light could be found from the bow in lane eight. Wohllebe was just 0.28 seconds back in third. For the first time in three and one-half decades, the Stars and Stripes fluttered majestically from the center pole as the Star-Spangled Banner filled the air at an Olympic canoe and kayak regatta.

The K-2 race followed a similar pattern. An exuberant Bellingham would comment after the race that "I just kept hoping he knew what he was doing!" Paddling in lane two, the grey U.S. boat trailed the defending champion New Zealand team of Ian Ferguson and MacDonald for 900 meters. The gap narrowed gradually, but consistently, all the way. When Barton put the pedal down, Bellingham was ready to hammer home. They won pulling away by three-tenths of one second.

The K-2 men's 500-meter race was expected to be the most hotly contested event of all, and it was. Eight boats finished within three seconds of the winning New Zealand team. Any of the finalists could have medaled on any given day. U.S. veterans Terry Kent and Terry White had to settle for eighth.

The men's K-4 team was the only U.S. kayak to miss the final. From their grandstand perch, they got a lesson in team boat perfection from Hungarians Csipes, Gyulay, Sandor Hodosi and Atilla Abraham. Csipes and Gyulay were distinguished singles racers, but in the K-4 they conformed perfectly to the team style. In unison, four blades hit the water and four shafts formed a precise plane on every stroke. On form alone, the Hungarians earned a 10. The Soviet and East German crews raced well for second and third, but the outcome was never in doubt.

U.S. entry Traci Phillips struggled through difficult heats, repechages and semifinal races just to reach the K-1 500-meter final. Once there, she had the race of her life to finish a very respectable sixth. She equaled the best U.S. finish in either Olympic or world championship competition since Marcia Smoke won a bronze medal in 1964. The U.S. women's K-2 and K-4 both reached the finals, but were never in serious contention for medals.

The only weakness in the U.S. program appeared to be in the canoes. The canoe requires a more specialized technique than the kayak, and the lack of early development programs in the States was reflected in the team's performance. None of the four canoe entries made the finals. In fact, none were particularly close.

Soviet single bladers, on the other hand, left the field in the wash. Three of the gold medals available went to the men in red. The only Soviet boat to miss the gold took home the silver. The GDR captured two silvers behind the Soviets and managed the only non-Soviet victory.

Soviet 1,000-meter champion Ivan Klementiev gave the most commanding performance of the entire regatta. His 3.18 second margin victory was the widest of all. Remarkably, the next two largest margins also belonged to Soviet canoeists. The C-2 team of Victor Reneiski and Nikolai Jouravski won the 500-meter event by 1.94 seconds and the 1,000-meter race by 3.08. By contrast, the average margin of victory in all of the kayak races was less than 0.72 seconds.

By all standards, the canoe and kayak competition in the 1988 Seoul Olympic Games was among the best in the history of the sport. Without doubt, it was the finest performance in international competition for any U.S. team. □

RIGHT / *Traci Phillips of the United States is the eye in this storm of colorful, swift-moving bodies in the women's 500-meter kayak race. Phillips finished sixth, the best American showing in the event since 1964.* (George Long/LPI)

CYCLING   EASTERN BLOC PUTS PEDALS TO THE MEDALS

Few cycling aficionados were surprised when the battle for Olympic cycling supremacy was a closely waged one between the Soviet Union and the GDR. Both countries yearly demonstrate their talents at the world championships, dominating events with the top three and even top four performers. While each country experienced an unexpected medal loss at the Games (the Soviets in the men's road race and the GDR in the kilometer event), when the Olympic medals were tallied, the Soviets narrowly edged the GDR by one medal. Perhaps even more impressive, of the nine countries that would earn medals, the Soviets and East Germans captured 13 of the 27 medals.

Australia, which has tailored its cycling program to that of the East Germans, showed how successful that model can be, taking home two silvers and two bronzes. The U.S. team, which had earned nine medals at the boycotted '84 Games, managed one medal, narrowly missing a second.

State-of-the-art cycling technology, which made its first Olympic appearance in '84, would not give the U.S. team any edge over the Soviets and East Germans. The radical changes in equipment and clothing seen in '84 had become status quo, and the technology in 1988 consisted of subtle refinements. The U.S. team bikes were made of carbon fiber, a very light and rigid material, with nearly perfect aerodynamics. Solid disk wheels made of Kevlar were used in time trial events such as the individual pursuit, team pursuit, kilometer and team time trial. The riders' rubberized "skinsuits" and teardrop-shaped helmets further aided in reducing wind resistance, which accounts for 80-90 percent of what slows the rider down.

In only one area did the U.S. team use a radical innovation—the team time trial. In this first event of the Games, the U.S. team rode bikes with Scott 100K handlebars, which are shaped like a Jew's harp, forcing the cyclists to keep their forearms together and extended over the front wheel. Although the team hoped

that the bars, which are approximately two minutes faster than the conventional "bullhorn" bars, would give them enough of an advantage to put them into medal contention, they finished a disappointing 10th. The GDR began its medal tally by acquiring the gold, followed by Poland and a surprising third place by Sweden, beating the favored Italians, Czechs and Soviets.

On the track, technology became less of an issue than good old leg power. The outdoor velodrome had a wood surface with 38-degree banking, making it the fastest outdoor, sea-level facility of its kind. The cyclists responded in kind, setting and resetting world records. In the qualifying rounds of the 4,000-meter team pursuit, the former world mark of 4:17.71 was bettered four times. The GDR clocked 4:17.61; France, 4:17.19; Australia, 4:16.32; and the Soviet Union, 4:16.10, to reclaim the world record. The U.S. pursuit team of Dave Lettieri, Mike McCarthy, Leonard Harvey Nitz and Carl Sundquist could not compete with these fantastic times, finishing ninth with a 4:22.96. With only the top eight teams advancing, the U.S. team was out of the competition by .32.

ABOVE / *Bicycles, uniforms and helmets are so high-tech these days, they almost appear alien. But underneath the helmets and racing skins are the very human and powerful foursome from the Soviet Union in the 4,000-meter team pursuit who took the gold as expected and in world-record time to boot.* (Michael Yada/LPI)

OPPOSITE / *East German Lutz Hesslich psyches himself up to some incredible feats. In the match sprint race he went full tilt for two of the race's three laps — three times the normal all-out sprinting distance. Needless to say, no one could touch him, or his gold.* (Dave Black)

EQUESTRIAN

THE FRG DIDN'T HORSE AROUND

There are times when teams do more than is expected of them. The FRG picked the best time to exceed its expectations—the Olympic Games.

The FRG, which had been expected to take only the dressage crown, made a clean sweep of all the team gold medals in equestrian sports in Seoul. The United States earned two silvers in its strongest discipline, show jumping.

Theoretically, the West Germans were weakest in jumping, but they had a decisive victory in the 16-team fray, with 17.25 faults. America came up with a 20.5 score, beating France, which logged 27.5 and was expected to be a contender for the gold.

In his second round of jumping, Joe Fargis, astride Mill Pearl, picked up only .25 faults to clinch the silver for him and his U.S. teammates, Lisa Jacquin (For the Moment), Anne Kursinski (Starman) and Greg Best (Gem Twist).

There was little doubt that 1984 Olympic individual gold medalist Mark Todd and his plucky Charisma, a 16-year-old, 7/8ths thoroughbred, had a great shot to repeat their title in the three-day eventing.

They led from the first phase, dressage, and with fellow New Zealander Tinks Pottinger (Volunteer), they logged the only penalty-free endurance efforts.

"I came here knowing the horse was in very good form," said Todd, thin and elegant like a character out of a Noel Coward play.

"But he hadn't done a three-day in nearly a year, because we saved him for this competition, and I wasn't sure how he would cope. He's such a wonderful little horse. He did one of the best dressage tests he ever did, and cross country, too."

Charisma's reward for his victory and 42.5 penalty score is semi-retirement to New Zealand, where he will do some light work, but no more eventing.

Ian Stark of Great Britain won the silver medal on Sir Wattie (52.8) and the bronze went to world champion Virginia Leng of Great Britain, who, riding Master Craftsman, logged 62 penalties—a mere 0.35 less than the FRG's team gold medalist Claus Ehrhorn (Justyn Thyme).

Eventing had yielded a team gold and individual silver for the United States in 1984, but the 1988 squad was less experienced, with half of the riders participating in their first championship-level meet at the Games.

Thirty-one-year-old Phyllis Dawson, America's highest finisher, was a respectable 10th with Albany II in her first Olympics. Two-time world champion Bruce Davidson, 38, finished 18th, but would have done better had his Dr. Peaches not lost a shoe and fallen two-thirds of the way through the cross country course.

Ann Sutton, riding Tarzan, met her donnybrook at the 16th fence. Tarzan jumped into the middle of the hilltop spread obstacle instead of across it, pinning himself between the two elements and throwing his rider over the back rail. A second attempt ended the same way in a heart-stopping instant replay, and Sutton's Olympic Games were scuttled.

After a fall from The Optimist over the straight-downhill fourth fence, Karen Lende twice suffered the same fate as Sutton and was eliminated. Since three members of a squad must complete the event—which still had the stadium phase to go—that was it for the United States.

"I don't know what happened," said team manager Michael Page. "Everybody was so up and enthusiastic. We had a good team and great team spirit. Everyone felt prepared—it just didn't work."

Meanwhile, a steady effort from the West Germans gave them 225.95 penalties to beat the heavily favored British, who settled for the team silver with 256.8. Third place went to New Zealand with 271.2.

ABOVE / *Kyra Kyrklund and Matador are stately as they strut through their individual dressage performance. The Finnish duo finished fifth.* (pressfoto)

OPPOSITE / *This idyllic spot was the setting for the gritty cross country course — a test of speed and stamina — in the three-day eventing. But idyllic it was not on this day, as many a rider tumbled, head first, into the drink.* (Tish Quirk)

There was no defeating the West Germans in the team dressage, as they earned 4,302 points to take the gold for the second Olympic Games in a row. Switzerland was second with 4,164 and Canada gained its first Olympic medal in the European-dominated sport with 3,969.

The youngest person ever to win the individual dressage gold, Nicole Uphoff, 21, of the FRG, earned 1,521 points with her impressive, light-stepping Rembrandt 24. Second was European champion Margitt Otto-Crepin of France (Corlandus, 1,462), while Switzerland's Christine Stueckelberger (Gauguin de Lully Ch.) won the bronze with 1,417.

Dressage, traditionally the United States' weakest discipline, yielded no medals and hardly anyone had expected it to. There were, however, signs of progress. Robert Dover and Jessica Ransehousen, the stalwarts of the team that wound up sixth of 12, both made it through to the individual ride-off, the grand prix special.

Dover was 13th in dressage with the stylish Federleicht (1,320 points), and the 49-year-old Ransehousen, riding in her second Olympics after 24 years, was 17th with Orpheus (1,282), a bay stallion she had taken from rebellion to a working partnership.

"It was a good effort. We haven't had two riders in the Special for 12 years. It shows we're on the move up," said the 32-year-old Dover.

After two qualifying classes at the Seoul Equestrian Park sliced the field from 74 to 37 riders, the individual show jumping competition moved to the Olympic Stadium on the final day of the Games. There, the favorites rapidly fell by the wayside. World Cup champion Ian Miller of Canada knocked down rails with an obviously tired Big Ben. Great Britain's Nick Skelton, the most successful rider in the world in 1988, got very little out of his big, white-faced Apollo and ended up far from the medal range.

The one entry whose form did hold up was that of European champion Pierre Durand, whose sprightly Jappeloup was the best in the finals. The Frenchman won the competition with a mere 1.25 faults.

But the real drama of the day centered on the tiebreaker between Best and West German Karsten Huck. In show jumping, the round with the fewest number of faults wins, though in the event of an equal number of faults, the faster trip wins.

"I can get from point A to point B faster than anyone else," said Best, adding that the big question in that process is "whether I can leave the fences up."

Best's strategy was to outrun Huck. But a rail went down, leaving him with a four-fault penalty.

As Huck took his turn, Best paced nervously along the sidelines. When Huck dropped a rail, too, Best was assured the silver, having posted the faster time.

"To be a silver medalist is a great feeling," Best said. "I was hoping that if by 1992 I got my act together, I'd have a shot then.

"I'm four years ahead of schedule," he grinned.

OPPOSITE / *Greg Best of the United States, aboard the stunning white steed Gem Twist, is a striking sight for the Olympic Stadium crowd gathering for Closing Ceremonies. They won a silver for this performance.* (Michael Yada/LPI)

SECOND BEST IN SEOUL

It started off as an absurd idea, really, the thought that a young man with less than two seasons in grand prix show jumping could make the U.S. Olympic team.

America has the world's toughest competition in the sport, and every one of the serious contenders for the squad had at least twice as much experience as the 24-year-old Greg Best.

But this was a dream that did not shatter when it bumped up against reality. Best not only made it to the Games, but he also won two silver medals in Seoul.

Best didn't win by himself, however. A decade or so before, his mother, Maxine, decided he should be trained by the best talent available, though the family didn't have much money.

Living a few miles from the Bests' Flemington, N.J., home, however, was Frank Chapot, former captain of the U.S. equestrian team and a six-time Olympian. He became Maxine's target. The horseman was reluctant to take on young Best, but a mother's persistence would not be denied.

Chapot happened to have a horse named Gem Twist, a sleek gray thoroughbred who was a son of Good Twist, the stallion who carried Chapot to many of his international victories. Gem Twist became Best's mount and together they've come a long way.

As he watched the medal ceremonies, Chapot remembered his own Olympic career: "I was fourth once and fifth once. But this feels doubly good, not just because I bred and trained the horse, but because of the boy, too."

"He's been with me a lot of years," reflected Chapot, who at such a moment still envisions Best as the eager youth who first came to him so long ago. "It's almost like having a son do it." □

ABOVE / *With the flame at Olympic Stadium in the background, American Anne Kursinski, aboard Starman, are both intent as they clear a hurdle in the individual jumping competition. They wound up in a tie for fourth.* (Tish Quirk)

OPPOSITE / *New Zealand's Mark Todd and Charisma are both legends in equestrian circles, and they again made a big splash in this competition, winning the individual three-day eventing.* (Lori Adamski-Peek)

FENCING

The West Germans, fencing as they always do—as if possessed—dominated the competition (particularly in women's events) at the Olympic Games in Seoul.

Of the 24 medals at stake, seven were captured by the FRG, including a medals sweep in the women's individual foil event. Next was the resurgent Soviet Union with five medals, followed by Italy with four, France and Hungary with three each, and Poland and the GDR with one each.

Fencing at the Olympic Games, though, was really another chapter in the continuing saga of West German coach Emil Beck. The three winners in the women's individual foil—Anja Fichtel, Sabine Bau and Zita Funkenhauser—were all disciples of Beck. All were members of his fencing club in Tauberbischofsheim, a town of 12,000.

Beck is to fencing what workaholic George Allen was to professional football and then some. His philosophy about his work, as described by *Sports Ilustrated*'s Gary Smith, is simple:

"Man was born to work. Without work, he could not exist. I work 14 to 18 hours a day. Seven days a week. Vacations? They are an invention of modern times. Man doesn't need a holiday."

Apparently, according to Beck, he doesn't need hospitalization, either. After the '84 Olympics in Los Angeles, he had a stroke on his way to work. He was hospitalized until the doctor left. Then Beck left.

But if winning is where it's at—and the $12 million complex the West German government has built for Beck indicates it is—then Beck's method has been extremely successful.

The sweep by Fichtel, Bau and Funkenhauser was the first medal sweep in any sport by the FRG. Fichtel defeated Bau in the final, 8-5. And those three medalists combined with Annette Klug and Christiane Weber to take the gold in the women's team foil event.

The West German men's team had one gold medal winner, Arnd Schmitt in the epée, who edged Philippe Riboud of France, 10-9, in the finals.

Italy upstaged the FRG in the men's individual foil. Stefano Cerioni defeated Mathias Gey, the reigning world champion from the FRG, as well as five-time world champion Alexander Romankov of the USSR, before beating Udo Wagner of the GDR in the gold medal match.

The Soviets proved their mettle in men's team foil. The West Germans were favored and were impressive en route to the finals, downing Italy, 9-6, and the GDR, 9-3. The Soviets downed China, 9-5, but struggled against Hungary, as both countries finished the match, 8-8. The Soviets earned the win, however, as they had six more touches during the match. In the gold medal showdown, the USSR soundly defeated the FRG, 9-5.

The Hungarians got back at the Soviets in team sabre competition. In a remarkable display of swordsmanship, Hungary rallied after trailing 7-2 to tie the Soviets, 8-8, in the gold medal match. This time, with three more touches than the USSR, Hungary won the tiebreaker.

It was France's turn to break the FRG's domination in the team epée event. France defeated Hungary, 8-7, and the Soviet Union, 9-5, to reach the finals, while the West Germans got there by topping Korea, 8-6, and Italy, 8-7. With the gold medal on the line, the Frenchmen prevailed, 8-3.

In the individual sabre event, Frenchman Jean François Lamour defended his Olympic title with a 10-4 gold medal victory over Poland's Janus Olech.

The best U.S. finish was in women's team foil where Caitlin Bilodeau, Elaine Cheris, Sharon Monplaisir, Mary Jane O'Neill and Molly Sullivan combined to finish sixth. Bilodeau took 11th in women's individual foil, the highest U.S. women's finish in 12 years.

For the men, the highest finish came in team sabre, where Robert Cottingham, Paul Friedberg, Michael Lofton, Steve Mormando and Peter Westbrook combined for seventh place. □

ABOVE (TOP) / *Everybody loves a winner, Janusz Olech of Poland finds out after losing his gold medal sabre match . . .*

ABOVE (BOTTOM) / *. . . while not far away, Olech's conqueror, France's Jean François Lamour, has all the company he needs for an uplifting victory celebration.* (both photos - R.L. Hagedohm/LPI)

OPPOSITE / *Poland's Olech (No. 196) would be a dead man if this were an honest-to-goodness sabre duel, but here it takes 10 "hits scored" to eliminate your opponent, and the loser lives to fight another day. Olech went on to edge eventual bronze medalist Giovanni Scali of Italy, 10-9, in this match.* (R.L. Hagedohm/LPI)

FIELD HOCKEY

Heading into the 1988 Olympic women's field hockey competition, the question was not which team would win the gold, but which teams would take the silver and the bronze. Holland was heavily favored to repeat as the Olympic champion, leaving the other seven teams in the tournament with the leftovers.

But someone forgot to pass the word onto Australia.

In a tournament full of surprises (only one team actually finished where it was seeded prior to the start of the competition), Australia defeated host Korea, 2-0, to win the gold medal. The team from The Netherlands, which had not lost a major international title since 1980, including an Olympic and two World Cup titles, had to settle for the bronze.

The men's tournament also had its share of surprises. Top-seeded Australia failed to medal as Great Britain earned the gold medal with a 3-1 victory over the FRG. In the bronze medal game, Holland defeated the Australians by a 2-1 count. Pakistan, the 1984 gold medal team, finished the tournament fifth.

The makeup of the women's semifinal match was a bit of a surprise. In 1984, Korea was not seeded among even the top 10 teams in the world but came from nowhere in 1986 to win the Asian Games, and earn the third seed in the Olympic tournament. Strengthened by the partisan crowds and their knowledge of the Olympic turf, the Koreans managed to win their pool ahead of Australia.

Korea's semifinal opponent, Great Britain, earned its Olympic berth (and eighth seed) the hard way. Great Britain had qualified in a playoff against the Soviet Union in December, and quickly proved that it deserved the spot by beating Argentina and tying the United States in pool play to finish second and advance to the medal round. In a tough semifinal, Korea edged Great Britain, 1-0.

When Australia and Korea met in the preliminary round, they played to a 5-5 tie. The stakes were much higher the second time around. Korea was looking for its second team gold medal in Olympic history, after its women's team handball squad had sent the Korean fans into a frenzy just one day earlier by winning its tournament. Australia's defense would not give in during the final, however, shutting out the host country, 2-0. The gold more than made up for the bronze medal the Australians narrowly missed in 1984, when the Americans claimed third place on penalty strokes in sudden death.

The U.S. team, which was seeded fifth in the tournament after earning a silver medal at the 1987 Pan American Games, suffered from its lack of international experience. After winning the 1984 Olympic bronze, only three players remained and the team had to start virtually from scratch in 1985. The United States had to rely heavily on the Olympic and international experience of midfielders Beth Beglin and Sheryl Johnson and back Marcy Place von Schottenstein. In the game for seventh and eighth place, the United States took a 1-0 lead over Argentina on a goal by Christy Morgan but lost in overtime, 3-1. □

ABOVE / *Great Britain (in red) and the FRG scramble for a loose ball in front of the goal in rapid-fire, athletic action that may dash some perceptions that this is a sport only for high school girls. Great Britain won the gold.* (GES)

OPPOSITE / *Goalkeeper Donna Lee of the United States stretches as far as her bulky pads will allow to snare a shot on her goal. Try as she and her American teammates might, they could manage but an eighth place in the tournament.* (George Long/LPI)

GYMNASTICS

Leonid Arkayev, architect and coach of the Soviet Union's masterful men's gymnastics team, seldom uses superlatives to describe the achievements of his well-tuned athletes. Because he has grown accustomed to precision and daring by his gymnasts, Arkayev is not easily impressed.

But, after witnessing the heights to which his beloved sport was raised during the 1988 Olympic Games in Seoul, Arkayev's immunity to excitement suddenly disappeared. The legacy of the talented gymnasts who competed in Seoul, he suggested, will be that of pioneers who led the way into a new, more exciting era and redefined perfection.

"This will go on," said Arkayev, after the eight perfect scores of 10 were awarded to his pupils. "As the technique is perfected, gymnastics will become an even more spectacular sport than it is today."

It is difficult to imagine what might have been more spectacular than the Soviet Union's trio of Vladimir Artemov, Valeri Lioukine and Dmitri Bilozertchev, who for only the third time in Olympic history secured a sweep of the men's all-around medals by one nation. They wore the same uniforms, but there was no confusing them. Each gymnast left a stamp of distinction in leading the Soviet Union to the team gold medal and individual honors in the all-around and event finals. The handsome Artemov, heartthrob of young Korean girls who often surrounded him for photographs, never seemed to notice the pressurized atmosphere of the Games. He won a total of four gold medals, the most by a male in Olympic competition in 28 years. The elfish Lioukine, an alpine skier in his free time, was co-gold medalist on the horizontal bar and living proof that a small man (Lioukine is just 5' 5") can be someone to look up to. And, finally, there was Bilozertchev, the incredible hulk of the Soviet team and perhaps its most courageous member. Although he yielded his 1987 all-around title to Artemov in Seoul, Bilozertchev used his massive upper body strength—the prod-

uct of exhaustive weight training following a 1985 car accident that shattered his left leg—to win a pair of gold medals (pommel horse and rings).

To the delight of spectators who packed Seoul's 15,000-seat Olympic Gymnastics Hall, the Soviet men represented just one of the Games' tantalizing sub-plots.

Nineteen-year-old Elena Shoushounova, the broad-shouldered Soviet female gymnast, captured the women's all-around title with one of the competition's most memorable vault routines. On her second of two tries, she scored a perfect 10 when no other mark would do, finishing ahead of Romania's Daniela Silivas by the slimmest margin in Olympic history. But that was not the last word from the 18-year-old Silivas, who came back with determination in the event finals to win three of the four women's gold medals, achieving her own level of perfection on the uneven bars.

As past Olympiads have demonstrated, heroic roles are rarely limited to the front-runners. This was evident again in Seoul when the U.S. women's team emerged as more than a resolute collection of underdogs but as legitimate challengers to the medal winners from the Soviet Union, Romania and the GDR. The U.S. squad that was assembled at

ABOVE / *In a competition where perfection became almost routine, the Soviet Union's Sergei Kharikov settled for a mere 9.975 in this floor exercise to edge the field for a gold.* (Michael Yada/LPI)

OPPOSITE / *Tiny Chen Cuiting of China is a blur as she whirls on the uneven bars during the women's team competition. The Chinese finished sixth.* (R.L. Hagedohm/LPI)

ABOVE / This well-muscled, graceful paragon of precision was also judged the world's best all-around male gymnast at this Olympics: Vladimir Artemov of the USSR. (Bob Long/LPI)

OPPOSITE / American Brandy Johnson stretches to the limit in the uneven bars. The 15-year-old placed 10th in individual all-around, the best U.S. showing in the event. (Michael Yada/LPI)

RIGHT / Still another in the seemingly endless line of precision-minded Soviet gymnasts is Dmitri Bilozertchev, who carted home medals in the pommel horse, rings, all-around and team competitions. This routine earned him a 10. (Bob Long/LPI)

SUCCEEDING PAGES / The new queen of gymnastics, Romania's Daniela Silivas, had nothing to kick about over her Olympic performance — golds in the floor exercise, balance beam, and uneven bars; a bronze in the vault, a silver with her team, and a silver in all-around. (Michael Yada/LPI)

the Olympic trials in Salt Lake City appeared to have just the right blend of youthful enthusiasm and experience, but no one could have predicted what it would achieve after journeying across the Pacific. In Phoebe Mills, Kelly Garrison-Steves and Hope Spivey, the United States was blessed with proven performers, gymnasts who had risen beyond athletic obstacles in the past. Mills, a strong-willed 15-year-old from Northfield, Ill., was often described by her coach, the dynamic Bela Karolyi, as "a kid who's not going to give up easily, a fighter." By winning the 1988 U.S. championships and Olympic trials events, Mills finally had overcome the label of promising but injury-prone. Oklahoma's Garrison-Steves, 21, a two-time NCAA champion and 1984 Olympic team alternate, had become a shining example of persistence and durability by remaining in the sport long after her peers had stepped aside. Spivey, 17, of Allentown, Pa., among the top five all-around finishers in three consecutive U.S. championship meets, carried the distinction as the team's most reliable and consistent competitor.

Adding to expectations was Salt Lake City's Melissa Marlowe, 17, who arrived in Seoul with renewed confidence after advancing from 11th overall in the U.S. rankings into the sixth and final spot on the Olympic team in a span of just one month. Finally, the United States would call upon two rising Karolyi trainees, 15-year-olds Brandy Johnson and Chelle Stack, unproven but also unflappable.

Although the U.S. women had placed sixth in team competition at the 1987 World Championships, it was clear from the start that they would be more formidable in Seoul. Mills and Johnson set the tone with one solid routine after another, lifting the United States into third place after the team compulsory exercises. The celebration was to be a brief one, however. During the uneven bars competition, the GDR's Ellen Berger, head of the women's technical committee within the International Gymnastics Federation, rose from her seat to notify judges of a possible rule violation by the U.S. squad. Berger insisted that the presence of team alternate Rhonda Faehn on the raised competition surface (known as the podium) was inappropriate. Faehn had been instructed by Karolyi to stand near the bars and remove the springboard after her teammates mounted the apparatus.

After the judging panel conferred with Berger, it deducted five-tenths of a point from the U.S. total, ruling that Faehn was obstructing the view. Suddenly, the United States no longer was in third place and trailed the East Germans by almost one point (.975).

There was little indication that the U.S. team was distracted by the incident two nights later when the remaining 50 percent of team scores were decided in the optional exercises phase. Mills was awarded a pair of 9.9s for her balance beam and floor exercise routines, while Johnson scored a 9.9 on uneven bars and 9.825 in floor exercise. On both occasions, she followed a teammate who had faltered slightly. But Johnson responded to the task of keeping the United States in the race. When the final scores were tabulated, the United States had fallen short of a team bronze medal—by just three-tenths of a point behind Berger's East Germans.

Powerless to change the judges' minds or their scoring sheets, the U.S. delegation decided, instead, to emphasize the significance of placing fourth among the 12 teams that qualified for the Olympics. At the 1984 Games, the U.S. women captured the team silver medal, but had done so in the absence of the Soviet and East German squads who stayed away because of a political boycott. From an historical point of view, what the '88 squad achieved in Seoul was unprecedented by an American team.

"This shows me, yes, we can do it," Karolyi said. "These girls can be just as good as anybody else in the world. There should be no more questions about the mysterious way the Russians and Romanians prepare their kids. Honestly, they are no different in desire and aggressiveness than we are."

Mike Jacki, the U.S. Gymnastics Federation's executive director, described the fourth place finish as "a moral victory" and insisted that "everyone knows we are the third-best team in the world, including the East Germans."

A similar discovery was yet to be made when the women's competition progressed into its final day on Sept. 25. Through three events in the individual finals, no U.S. woman had won a medal, although Johnson placed fifth in vault, prompting Karolyi to call her one of the "best vaulters in the world." The competition moved to the balance beam, where most U.S. observers considered Mills the team's best hope for a medal. Always resilient, Mills had dismissed a fall from the beam two nights earlier (during the all-around phase) as a fluke. Needing a flawless routine this time, Mills eyed the beam and sprung atop its narrow surface. What followed was a confident display of skill and well-defined movement.

The 90-pound Mills had cried on Karolyi's shoulder after placing 15th among the all-around qualifiers. But after scoring a 9.962 in the beam final, she was beaming as Karolyi approached to smother her with a warm hug. Mills' score tied her with Romania's Gabriela Potorac for the bronze and, more importantly, gave her the distinction of becoming the first U.S. woman to medal in an Olympics where the strongest teams competed together.

"Phoebe will bring out a new generation of athletes by showing that an average kid can make it," Karolyi said. "This type of performance will bring those little individuals out from their homes and into the gyms."

While members of the Soviet men's team won a total of 11 individual medals in Seoul, including five collected by Artemov, the American squad's primary objective was met when three of its developing stars qualified for the 36-man all-around field. Charles Lakes, 24, of Newhall, Calif., emerged with a 19th place finish, followed by Kevin Davis, 22, of Lincoln, Neb. (34th), and promising Lance Ringnald (35th), a wide-eyed 18-year-old from Albuquerque, N.M. Along with teammates Scott Johnson, 27, of Lincoln, Neb., Wes Suter, 24, of Reston, Va., and Dominick Minicucci, 19, of Staten Island, N.Y., they'd managed an 11th place finish in team competition.

For younger team members, the experience of participating in the Games became an invaluable motivational tool. Having witnessed the world's finest gymnasts competing at their peaks, the team was anxious to return home and go to work. U.S. coach Abie Grossfeld, himself a two-time Olympian (1956, '60), concluded that "the level of these athletes was better (than in 1984) and the consistency of our guys was improved in relation to the other teams."

Lakes, who scored a 9.95 on horizontal bar during the all-around phase, viewed developments in Seoul as an indication that he should remain in training. With his routines embedded in the memories of the world's judging community, Lakes expects higher scores and the opportunity to become a medal contender when the Games of the XXVth Olympiad are contested in Barcelona, Spain.

"In four more years," he said, "I think I'll be able to challenge for the Olympic gold medal. That's my prediction. It was nice to be on the receiving end of some outrageously high scores for a change."

Taking his final bow at the '88 Games was seven-year U.S. national team member Johnson, who attacked his team compulsory routines with abandon and paid for it. "I popped into my dismount on rings higher than I'd ever gone before," he said. "I was so far up there that I misjudged my landing." After a disastrous afternoon plunged the American team into last place in the 12-team field, it was determined to move

ABOVE / *The women's all-around title went to Elena Shoushounova of the Soviet Union, who edged out Romanian Silivas by soaring to scores of 9.9 or higher on the four apparatus.* (Michael Yada/LPI)

PICTURE-PERFECT GYMNAST

Even the world's greatest male gymnast needs a hobby. On those rare occasions that find the Soviet Union's Vladimir Artemov contemplating something other than floor exercises and parallel bars, the boyish looking 24-year-old athlete is likely to be peering through a camera lens.

"This is a good way of keeping memories," says Artemov's coach, Leonid Arkayev, who apparently approves of his student's other interests.

And while Artemov searches for the perfect frame in his leisure time, it is, ironically, the camera that finds a perfect subject in Artemov. Within the boundaries of the viewfinder is a complete gymnast, strong yet expressive.

The vivid images of Artemov's dominance of the Summer Games are likely to linger, even without the help of photos. After leading the Soviet men's team to the Olympic title and winning his first gold medal, Artemov might have been content to bask in victory, but he was not. He upstaged teammate Dmitri Bilozertchev to win the men's all-around title, scoring two perfect 10s, one on parallel bars, the other on the horizontal bar.

In the event finals, two more gold medals were placed around his neck in addition to a silver. Ironically, the individual best qualified to appreciate Artemov's four gold-medal performance just happened to be among the spectators at Olympic Gymnastics Hall. In 1960, Boris Stakhlin also won four gold medals as a member of the Soviet gymnastics team. Today, he is an International Gymnastics Federation judge. Until Artemov, no one had managed to match Stakhlin's performance in Rome, 28 years ago.

"I must say I feel great pleasure in doing these exercises," the modest Artemov said.

At the Seoul Olympics, Artemov shared his pleasure with the world. □

up a notch or two by hitting consistently during team optionals. Johnson, who moved to Orlando, Fla., to pursue a career in restaurant management after the Games, led the way two days later. In the end, the United States had moved past West Germany and into 11th.

By "showing the judges we are tough," Johnson, a 1984 Olympic gold medalist, was content to close his career and hang on to the memories of competing with some of the best his sport could offer. "I definitely believe that just being in the atmosphere of the Olympics is an enjoyable, happy experience," he said.

When the battle for the women's all-around title reached its conclusion on Sept. 23, the showdown between the Soviet Union's Shoushounova and Romania's Silivas provided a rare opportunity to watch two of the finest female competitors of their generation. For once, there was nothing else going on in the Olympic Gymnastics Hall to distract anxious spectators. All eyes were on the vault, and two tiny, confident warriors sharing the dream of a gold medal and the coveted all-around title.

Entering the day's final event, Silivas had built a narrow lead over her Soviet rival. The young Romanian already had surprised some experts by upstaging teammate Aurelia Dobre, the 1987 all-around world champion. Dobre, 15, had dropped out of contention for a medal, however, with a 9.85 floor exercise. Her right knee, injured earlier in the year, was not fully recovered, and it was too fragile to allow Dobre to attack her routines as she had done in Rotterdam.

With perfect 10s on uneven bars and floor exercise, Silivas went into the vault event with a scoring total of 69.687, while Shoushounova, the spunky veteran of the Soviet squad, had accumulated a 69.662 total. Like Silivas, Shoushounova already had scored a perfect 10 on floor exercise.

The would-be gold medalists were thus separated by the smallest fraction imaginable—.025.

"During the competition, I never thought of the scores of other gymnasts," Silivas said, whose innocent smile veils a killer instinct.

With her thoughts uncluttered by Shoushounova's challenge, Silivas took her position at the end of the runway, prepared to sprint toward a roundoff entry and, perhaps, her first Olympic title. Seconds later, it was over. Silivas landed without incident, raising her arms and flashing a radiant smile. She had assaulted the horse with 90 pounds of gracious fury. The judges' reward: 9.95.

"After my last vault," Silivas said, "I thought maybe I should be champion."

But the stoical Shoushounova had something else in mind. It was obvious to everyone in the packed arena that Shoushounova needed perfection if she hoped to surpass Silivas and become the Soviet Union's first Olympic all-around champion in eight years.

The dramatic moment evoked instant flashbacks to the 1984 Games, when U.S. star Mary Lou Retton, a physical mirror image of Shoushounova, needed a 10 on the vault to secure her gold medal. Retton had succeeded. Now it was Shoushounova's turn to win or to settle for the silver medal.

As she waited for Silivas' score to appear, Shoushounova sat motionlessly, eyes closed. She was thinking, no doubt, of the many years of training and discipline that were about to be condensed into one, pivotal vault. In an instant, Shoushounova was darting over the runway, bounding toward the springboard. The Soviet wobbled slightly as her feet hit the mat, but she held the landing without a step.

A few more tense moments followed, then the verdict flashed on the giant scoreboard: 10.000. Suddenly, the narrow margin had swung in Shoushounova's favor and she

PHOEBE'S PHABULOUS

The balance beam must have been invented with a gymnast like Phoebe Mills in mind. It demands equal doses of fluid movement, precision and, most of all, guts.

By no coincidence, those words are frequently used to describe Mills, the Illinois native who arrived in Seoul as the U.S. and Olympic trials champion. Upon her broad but delicate shoulders, Mills carried the burden of being a nearly universal choice to win a medal for the U.S. team.

After placing 15th in the all-around phase, during which Mills fell off the beam trying a back handspring, Bela Karolyi's determined student was left with one more chance. It came in the event finals, during the last hour of competition at Olympic Gymnastics Hall. And, as expected, it would require one final battle with the beam, described by Karolyi as ''the event of the devil.''

''I was nervous,'' said Mills, who turned 16 on Nov. 2. ''But I tried to visualize my whole routine, and I visualized myself doing it well.''

What followed in the next 90 seconds was ''probably the best beam I've ever done,'' and the judges agreed, awarding Mills a 9.962. She received the second-highest beam score of the day to put her on the awards podium. Afterward, a proud Karolyi called Mills the sport's ''new American idol.''

With her confidence restored, she suggested that the balance beam has not seen the last of Phoebe Mills.

''I'm going back to the gym,'' said Mills, looking to the future. ''I'm going to keep working and see what happens.'' □

OPPOSITE / Phoebe Mills of Northfield, Ill., became the first American woman to medal in apparatus competition during a full-field Olympics with her bronze medal in the balance beam. Her medal-winning routine, highlighted by this creative touch, was rated at 9.962. (Michael Yada/LPI)

was Seoul's all-around champion with a 79.662 total. Silivas was the silver medalist with 79.637, .025 shy of Shoushounova. The Romanian was a victim of the closest finish in the history of the women's Olympic all-around. The Soviet Union's Svetlana Boguinskaia took the bronze (79.400).

''I tried only to think of the exercise,'' Shoushounova said later. ''I had to do it. Only work will achieve results. And maybe a little luck.''

Although Shoushounova wore the gold, the intrigue of the women's event finals quickly shifted to Silivas. Only one other gymnast had managed to receive a perfect total score of 20.000 on one apparatus in Olympic competition. Nadia Comaneci, a legend in Romania, achieved the feat at the 1976 Games in Montreal with two 10s on the bars during team competition and a third 10 in the apparatus final.

With two 10s of her own entering the final, Silivas had a chance to enhance Romania's legacy once more. Moving confidently from bar to bar, Silivas completed her entertaining routine without a break and descended softly to await judgment, already assured of her first gold medal of the day. In a few seconds, Romania's new Nadia was awarded the 10 to match Comaneci's long-standing record.

Two more 10s were awarded on the bars, one to silver medalist Dagmar Kersten of the GDR, another to Shoushounova, the bronze medalist.

On the balance beam, Silivas upstaged Shoushounova yet again with a 9.987 mark to win her second individual gold. Shoushounova was the silver medalist, finishing just ahead of co-bronze medalists Mills and Potorac.

Later, a giggle and a smile were to be Silivas' only response to a difficult question: ''Who is the best female gymnast in the world?'' That answer was provided, instead, by U.S. coach Karolyi, who had guided Comaneci's career before leaving his native Romania in 1981 and starting a new life in Houston.

''The Soviet kid (Shoushounova) is a strong athlete with a strong will and, yes, she is the Olympic champion,'' Karolyi said. ''But I believe the best overall is Silivas. She has better technical accuracy, she is more of a stylist.''

When Silivas was a five-year-old, it was Karolyi who selected her to train in his famous Deva Gymnastics school in Transylvania. Even 13 years ago, ''you could see the spark,'' he said. After his defection, Silivas was left in the hands of Karolyi assistant Adrian Goreac, now the Romanian Olympic coach.

The Soviet Union also showed its strength in the rhythmic portion of the gymnastics competition in Seoul, taking both the gold and bronze medals. The USSR's Marina Lobatch earned two perfect scores of 10 in the preliminaries and another four 10s in the individual event finals (rope, hoop, clubs and ribbon) to snare the gold medal with a perfect total of 60.000, while Bulgaria's Adriana Dounavska, who also earned four perfect marks in the final, finished second with a close 59.950. The bronze medal went to Lobatch's teammate, Alexandra Timochenko, who also earned perfect marks in each of her four event finals. After a total of 18 perfect 10s were awarded (including 16 in the final) during this competition in Seoul, everyone agreed that scoring changes will be necessary in the future, in order for the sport to continue to grow.

The two American rhythmic gymnasts, Michelle Berube and Diana Simpson, finished 22nd and 26th, respectively, in the competition, a significant improvement from a sport on the rise in the United States and a good sign for the future. □

BELOW / *Soviet bronze medalist Alexandra Timochenko has body-bending skills a contortionist would long for.* (Michael Yada/LPI)

JUDO

The 1988 men's Olympic judo competition opened to seven days of sellout crowds at Seoul's Changchuong Gymnasium. Throughout the week throngs of spectators filled the crowded gym, jostling for better views. Korean cheerleaders complete with pompons, electric megaphones and drums orchestrated the crowd, often bringing them to near-frenzy levels. In a land where martial arts sports are nurtured at youth, judo clearly held a favored spot in the hearts of the Koreans.

An expected rematch in the extra-lightweight (60 kg) division between 1984 Olympic champion Shinji Hosokawa of Japan and 1987 world champion Kim Jae-yup of Korea set the tone for the competition. Each had defeated the other to win his particular title and were the favored pairing for the gold medal match. Kim progressed easily to the final, but there was a spoiler in the wings for Hosokawa—American Kevin Asano in the semifinals. Asano, who hails from Hawaii, was a 1987 World bronze medalist. Asano capitalized on his speed and precision to pound out a strong decision, upset the Japanese, and become the first American to reach the judo finals in a full-field Games. Asano and Kim were well-matched, but a minor penalty in Kim's favor gave him the match and the gold.

Surprising upsets of champions and favorites continued to be the theme at the judo venue. In the half-lightweight (65 kg) event, Japanese world champion Yosuke Yamamoto was thrown to his back by Janusz Pawlowski of Poland in the semifinals. Then, Iouri Sokolov of the Soviet Union, the co-favorite, was soundly beaten by France's Bruno Carabetta. The Frenchman later lost his semifinal to Lee Kyung-keun of Korea, who, in the end dominated Pawlowski to take the gold.

The favorites fell again in the half-heavyweight (95 kg) event. Robert Van de Walle of Belgium, the 1980 gold medalist, has garnered a reputation as the exemplary warrior. He's not the best technically, but he is considered the toughest of the tough. Van de Walle eliminated 1984 gold medalist Ha Hyung-ju of Korea and another favorite, newcomer Vladimir Poddoobnyi of the Soviet Union. But in a stunning upset, Marc Meiling of the FRG routinely disposed of the reputable warrior. The final pitted underdogs Aurelie Miguel of Brazil against Meiling, with the Brazilian capturing the gold.

Japan's Hitoshi Saito and the Soviet's Grigori Veritchev were the virtual shoo-ins for the gold medal match in the heavyweight (over 95 kg) division. Saito, the 1984 Olympic champion, advanced to the final despite some uncharacteristic, lackluster judo from this 320-pound behemoth. Veritchev, on the other hand, failed to get past Henry Stoehr of the GDR. The disappointing final, marred by stalling penalties, matched Saito and Stoehr with the Japanese claiming his second Olympic championship.

In the lightweight (71 kg) event, a surprising drug incident in the traditionally clean sport of judo gave the United States its second medal. Michael Swain, the only American male to win a world judo championship, defeated Steffen Stranz of the FRG in the repechage, but lost a decision to Great Britain's Kerrith Brown. When Brown, however, was disqualified after testing positive for use of a banned substance, Swain received one of the bronze medals. East German Sven Loll, whom Swain lost to in the closing seconds of the quarterfinal, lost the final match and the gold medal to Marc Alexandre of France.

In the other divisions, Waldemar Legien of Poland threw the 1984 Olympic champion Frank Wieneke of the FRG to claim the gold in the half-middleweight (78 kg) event. In the middleweight (86 kg) division, Austria's Peter Seisenbacher, another 1984 Olympic champion, soundly defeated Soviet Vladimir Chestakov for the gold.

In the end, no country was a clear winner. Instead, it was the sport that won. Where once the competition was dominated by as few as six countries, the 28 medals in Seoul were shared by 13. □

ABOVE (TOP) / *Shinji Hosokawa of Japan falls heels over head for U.S. silver medalist Kevin Asano.* (David Finch)

ABOVE / *Japan's Hitoshi Saito repeated as heavyweight champ.* (David Finch)

OPPOSITE / *Though it might not look it, Waldemar Legien of Poland did take this match with Soviet Bachir Varaev seriously. He won.* (David Finch)

MODERN PENTATHLON   YOUTH PREVAILS IN THIS AGE-OLD SPORT

The sport of modern pentathlon is a century-old test of skill and stamina. And never was the factor of youth more apparent than during the 1988 Olympic Games in Seoul.

For the Americans, the hope for a medal rested on the back of 40-year-old Bob Nieman, the oldest competitor in the field. Nieman had come back to the sport after a two-year hiatus, primarily to earn enough money in his chosen profession of architecture to train full-time for the Olympics. Nieman won the 1979 World Championships to become the first American ever to win a gold medal in the sport. He was relying on the skills acquired from over 15 years of competition to counter the youthful stamina of his competitors.

It wasn't quite enough.

In the end, it was the youngest athlete, Hungarian Janos Martinek, who would prevail after a three-day battle for the gold with the Soviet Union's newest protégé, Vakhtang Iagorachvili. At 23 years of age, Martinek became the youngest gold medalist ever in pentathlon and signaled the beginning of an era in which strength would count as much as skill and strategy.

Not that Martinek was lacking any prowess in the skill sports—shooting, riding and fencing. He and his Hungarian teammates, Attila Mizser and Laszlo Fabian, would prove by the end of the five days of competition why pentathlon is practically the national sport of Hungary.

There was some doubt, however, about Martinek being able to withstand the rigors of competing in the Olympic Games. As much as physical stamina is a part of pentathlon, so is the mental strength necessary to remain calm and hold steady in a sport that can have an athlete soaring to the top one day and plummeting to the bottom the next. Martinek not only managed to withstand the pressure but stayed near the top all five days.

The only drop in performance he suffered was in the shooting, the next to the last of the events, when he shot a score of 868, putting him in second place overall behind Iagorachvili.

On the final day of the competition, Iagorachvili, 24, held only a nine-second advantage in the staggered start of the 4,000-meter cross country run, not enough to hold off Martinek.

The course, however, would prove to be too much for Nieman.

The former Army captain, in fourth place going into the final day, had built a point total of 4,124, just 64 points behind Martinek. But Nieman could not hold off the youthful competitors behind him and eventually faded to an 18th place finish.

Americans Rob Stull and Mike Gostigian, both competing in the Olympics for the first time, were not able to overcome disastrous rides on the first day of competition. In the riding, Stull recorded a score of 470 and Gostigian had a zero ride. They finished the competition in 48th and 59th, respectively.

The ride is really the event that can set the pace for the overall competition and it did just that in Seoul. The low scores on the first day eliminated the United States from medal contention in the team competition and, in the end, plummeted the Americans to 16th place.

Luck plays as much a role in the ride as anything else. The athletes do not know which horse they will be riding until about 30 minutes before the competition and then have only a 20-minute period in which they can get acquainted with the horse.

The course also tends to cause problems. It is 600 meters long and includes 15 obstacles at a set height. But in the Olympics, the jumps appear larger because of the way they are decorated for the competition and often the horse and rider are overwhelmed by the trappings.

The Americans weren't the only ones who had trouble in the ride. Overall there were 16 riders who scored under 900 points and six zero rides.

ABOVE / *Rob Stull may have been the U.S. Olympic team's busiest athlete. He competed in the modern pentathlon, a five-day, five-event combo plate of riding, fencing, swimming, shooting and running before switching full-time as an epee-wielding member of the fencing squad.* (R.L. Hagedohm/LPI)

Martinek started his run for the gold with a fourth-place ride and a score of 1,066.

In fencing the next day, the Hungarians came on strong, tallying a team total of 2,888, 153 points ahead of the Soviets and the Americans, who tied for second in the event.

Frenchman Christophe Ruer won the swimming competition the next day with the two Soviets, Iagorachvili and Anatoli Avdeev, finishing close on his heels. Iagorachvili, now in second, still trailed Martinek by 81 points. That, however, would change on the fourth day in the shooting competition.

While neither Martinek nor Iagorachvili placed in the top 10 in the shooting, Iagorachvili's 978 points were enough to move him ahead of a poor-shooting Martinek.

By the end of the day, it was apparent that the cross country course would be the battlefield for the gold. And what a battlefield it was: a hilly course described as brutal by many.

By the 2,000-meter mark, Martinek had erased his nine-second handicap, passed Iagorachvili, and was on his way to gold. Martinek's point total of 5,404 in the five events paced the Hungarian team to the gold medal with a total of 15,886 points.

As Iagorachvili began to fade, a familiar Italian appeared, 1984 Olympic bronze medalist Carlo Massullo. Massullo, who started the run in third place about 25 seconds behind Iagorachvili, passed the Soviet in the final 1,000 meters and crossed the finish line second for the silver medal. A tired Iagorachvili finished third to win the bronze.

Massullo's second place finish lifted the Italians to second place overall in the team competition and gave Italy its second medal in the history of this Olympic event (Italy won the team gold in 1984).

Strong finishes in the cross country run for Great Britain gave the Brits the bronze, beating the French team by a narrow eight-point margin. □

ROWING

If most of the fans at the Han River Regatta Course were unfamiliar with the national anthem of the German Democratic Republic at the beginning of Olympic rowing competition, by Sunday afternoon they knew it by heart. The rowing federation in the GDR had announced in July that its 1987 World Championship silver medal men's eight had failed to make time standards and would not compete in Seoul. It appeared that the GDR would send only those crews capable of winning a medal.

The appearance became reality during the first week of the Olympic Games, as East German rowers dominated one event after another. Their consistent, impressive performances earned them 10 total medals, including eight golds, one silver and one bronze. For the United States, it was the end of a long, difficult summer.

It had begun May 15, 1988—the day Anne Marden won the women's single sculls trials to become the first U.S. rower named to the 1988 Olympic team. Eight trials, six selection camps and four months later, the 61-member U.S. team headed for Seoul.

Hopes were high—1987 had yielded the first men's eight world championship gold medal in 13 years, the women's eight had garnered an impressive silver and American crews had dominated the Pan American Games. The talent was deep and the primary task appeared to be sorting the right people into the appropriate boats. But accomplishing that task took time—the last members of the U.S. team were selected a mere two weeks prior to departure for Seoul.

After early competition, the U.S. potential looked promising. Following the three-day process designed to narrow the field to the top six boats in each category, nine U.S. boats, five women's and four men's remained. It was a remarkable performance, especially for the American women. For them, Seoul was only the second time U.S. oarswomen had competed against the entire world in an Olympic Games.

But while the U.S. chances looked promising, finishing promising is what counts. And the East Germans were into reality, not sentimentality.

The East Germans made that clear in the women's double sculls as Birgit Peter and Martina Schroeter dispatched the best the United States and every other country had to offer with a time of 7:00.48. While the U.S. team of Cathy Tippett and Monica Havelka finished sixth and therefore out of the medals, they certainly fared well in the "overcoming adversity" sweepstakes.

For Tippett, her trip to Seoul was her fourth time on a U.S. Olympic team. She had spent the past four years regaining her strength after being diagnosed as having Epstein-Barr Syndrome. Havelka, a former schoolteacher, had tripped over her mother's labrador and broken both of her arms in January of this year. "I'm rather amazed just to be rowing," she said after the trials in June.

The East Germans again scuttled the chances of the United States and others for gold in the women's four with coxswain and women's eight, taking the golds in both events. Romania finished second and China third in the four, with those two countries trading places in the eight.

Jutta Begrendt continued the GDR's domination in the single sculls, winning the gold by more than three seconds

ABOVE / *The top three finishers in the single sculls have winning smiles at their medal ceremony: Peter Michael Kolbe of the FRG (left, silver medal), Thomas Lange of the GDR (center, gold) and Eric Verdonk of New Zealand (right, bronze).* (R.L. Hagedohm/LPI)

ABOVE | *A coxswain is on board for his head, not his body, but U.S. pair rowers Robert Espeseth and Jonathan Fish will still need to explain where they stashed the rest of Daniel Lyons. The trio was eliminated in the semifinals.* (Michael Yada/LPI)

with a time of 7:47.19. The United States did get a medal, though, as Marden passed defending world champion Magdalena Gueorguieva from Bulgaria in the last 500 meters to take the silver with a time of 7:50.28.

The men's competition centered around the single sculls, featuring longtime rivals Pertti Karppinen of Finland and Peter Michael Kolbe of the FRG.

It was in 1976 the two first met—in the Olympic finals at Montreal. Kolbe had a seemingly insurmountable eight-second lead at the halfway point, but Karppinen stunned Kolbe and the rest of the field, charging past Kolbe with 100 meters to go to win by 2.64 seconds. Since then Kolbe has won four world championships to Karppinen's two, but the Finn had won their other Olympic matchup in 1984 in Los Angeles (Karppinen also won the gold in Moscow in 1980, but Kolbe didn't compete because of the boycott).

This dramatic matchup of the two 35-year-old rowing greats didn't even make it to the finals, however, as the 6'7'', 230-pound Karppinen finished dead last in his semifinal heat, 31 seconds behind the victorious 6'4'', 200-pound Kolbe. In the other semifinal heat, the GDR's Thomas Lange, who defeated both Kolbe and Karppinen at the world championships in Copenhagen last summer, held off Andy Sudduth of the United States, beating him by one second.

In the finals, it was Lange who was the easy victor, passing Kolbe in the second half of the race to win by 4.9 seconds. Sudduth, who wasn't feeling well, struggled and finished sixth.

Great Britain's dynamic duo—Andrew Redgrave and Steven Holmes—entered both pairs events, winning the gold in the pair and the bronze in the pair with coxswain. The gold in that event went to the equally legendary Italian brothers, Carmine and Guiseppe Abbagnale.

For America, in addition to Sudduth, three other men's boats made the finals: both men's fours—with coxswain and without—and the eight. The men's four with coxswain, easily the largest U.S. boat in terms of athlete size, performed consistently throughout the competition. But so did the East Germans, who won. The U.S. crew finished fifth.

The West Germans, who were favored in the men's eight, took a while to assume command, as the United States led for the first half of the race. First the West Germans and then, in the closing seconds, the Soviets, passed the U. S. crew, who settled for the bronze.

It was—who else?—the East Germans who thwarted the United States in the four without coxswain. The U.S. team of Dave Krmpotich, Tom Bohrer, Raoul Rodriguez and Richard Kennelly, doggedly pursued the East Germans throughout the race. While the team wasn't able to catch the GDR, it was able to hold off the West Germans to take the silver medal.

Kris Korzeniowski, technical advisor for the United States, said it was evident the sport of rowing was growing rapidly because "the semifinals here (Seoul) are like finals" in past Olympiads. □

LEFT / *Though just a practice run, it's still serious business for East German eight coxswain Daniela Neunast, who barks out commands to her crew. Her intensity no doubt helped bring the team its eventual gold medal.* (Michael Yada/LPI)

A LASTING IMPRESSION

On a rare occasion, two can finish last and celebrate the moment. Such was the case with Mara Keggi and Barb Kirch, who seven weeks before the women's pair without coxswain race had never rowed together.

They finished a remarkable sixth overall, albeit last, in the final, at the Han River Regatta Course at the Olympic Games in Seoul.

Keggi and Kirch were the final two athletes named to the U.S. Olympic team on Aug. 28. Their victory at Mercer County Park in New Jersey was particularly sweet, as it was their last chance to go to Seoul as Olympians. A 1984 Olympian in pairs, Kirch hoped to make the U.S. team in the quadruple sculls. But the 28-year-old University of Pennsylvania graduate, who medaled with the 1982 and 1987 U.S. national teams, saw her bid turned away.

Meanwhile, Keggi was trying to make the Olympics in the women's eight. A 1984 graduate of the University of Wisconsin, Keggi was on the 1985 and 1986 national teams, and also rowed in the Moscow Goodwill Games in 1986. But, like Kirch, Keggi was cut from the selection camp.

After agreeing to get together over the phone, Keggi and Kirch went to Boston, where Holly Hatton, coach of the Boston Rowing Center was eager to help. Her task, though, was not an enviable one. Hatton had just 18 days to make them into a team of Olympic caliber. "It was one huge rush to Seoul," she remarked.

The dedication of all three paid off as Keggi and Kirch made it to the finals in Seoul. That in itself was a triumph. They didn't medal but finished as one of the top six pairs in the world. □

RIGHT AND INSET / *Practice makes perfect and U.S. rowers Mara Keggi (front) and Barb Kirch did a remarkable job finishing sixth in Seoul with only seven weeks rowing experience together.* (both photos-Michael Yada/LPI)

SHOOTING

Shooting experienced probably its biggest and most exciting year in the sport's long Olympic history in 1988. Final round shoot-offs, instituted by shooting's international federation in 1986, drew hundreds of spectators, and attendant media, to the Taenung International Shooting Range during the sport's week-long competition.

Shooting's 39 medals were divided among 19 countries; more nations went home with something to show for their efforts than in any other sport. And those medals were won in incredibly stiff competition. Olympic records were broken in nine of the 13 events, and two world marks were tied or broken.

Men's air pistol made its Olympic debut in Seoul, and U.S. shooter Erich Buljung of Fort Benning, Ga., stepped to the forefront, tying the world record 590 out of 600 in qualification. By the last shot in the 10-shot final, however, the 44-year-old U.S. Army Marksmanship Unit (USAMU) master sergeant was a slim.7 points ahead of Bulgaria's Taniou Kiriakov. The last shot told the story; Kiriakov fired a 9.8, Buljung a 9.1. The tie was broken in favor of the Bulgarian by virtue of his higher shoot-off score. Buljung's silver stood as one of the United States' finest performances of the Games and its only shooting medal in Seoul. China's Xu Haifeng, the 1984 Olympic free pistol gold medalist, moved from fourth during the final to grab the bronze.

In the rapid-fire pistol event, where shooters fire five-shot series in progressively shorter time limits from eight to four seconds, John McNally, a USAMU captain, totaled a fantastic 597 out of 600 in the preliminaries. Soviet shooter Afanasi Kouzmine eclipsed that score by one point, setting an Olympic record. He then went on to fire a perfect 100 in the final to capture the gold. McNally faltered and dropped from medal contention. Ralf Schumann shot a 99 to claim the silver for the GDR, and Zoltan Kovacs of Hungary bolted from his sixth-place ranking to win the bronze.

Free pistol competition found world champion Igor Bassinski of the USSR holding a four-point lead over the field going into the final. But in the last 10 shots he was caught by Sorin Babii, who fired a 94 in the shoot-off to win the gold for Romania. Bassinski managed a bronze, while five-time Olympian, 54-year-old Ragnar Skanåker of Sweden added another silver to his collection of one gold (' 72) and one silver (' 84).

This year was the second time for women's sports pistol in the Olympics. The first part of the competition, fired with.22 caliber pistols, is the precision stage; the second is rapid-fire. In the preliminary round, Nino Saloukvadze of the Soviet Union and Yugoslavia's Jasna Sekaric set Olympic records at 591. Saloukvadze prevailed in the final, shooting a 99 to win the gold. Sekaric's 95 dropped her to third, while Tomoko Hasegawa moved into second place with a final tally of 99 to give Japan its first medal of these Games.

The women's air pistol, held two days later, staged a rematch between Saloukvadze and Sekaric. This time it was Sekaric grabbing the gold, outpacing the Soviet in the final. Saloukvadze held on for the silver and teammate Marina Dobrantcheva won the bronze.

The first medal of the Seoul Olympics was awarded in the women's air rifle event. No fewer than six of the athletes surpassed the Olympic mark of 393, including U.S. shooter Launi Meili. The Soviet Union's unheralded Irina Chilova went on to win the gold medal. Silvia Sperber of the FRG, burst from her seventh-place ranking to capture the silver. Another Soviet, Anna Maloukhina, won the bronze.

Meili competed again in the women's standard rifle, fired at 50 meters with.22 caliber rifles, and again she broke an Olympic record to get there—topping the old mark by one point with a 582 out of 600. She finished seventh in the final, which was won by Sperber, her second medal of the Games.

Men's rifle, too, saw the fall of Olympic records, starting with the english match event in which a number of shooters cohold the world record of a perfect 600. Those scores went through the roof—

ABOVE / *It was a proud and emotional Erich Buljung who stood on the awards platform. The Olympic debut of men's air pistol saw a close match between Buljung and Bulgaria's Taniou Kiriakov, with Kiriakov edging the American by virtue of his higher shoot-off score. Buljung's silver medal was well earned; his 590 in the qualification equaled the world record.* (Scott Rupp)

ABOVE / *Gunslinger Arimatti Nummela of Finland placed eighth in the Olympic trap competition.* (Hannu Vierula)

the two shooters who "only" equaled the Olympic record of 589 tied for 12th place. Eleven athletes broke that mark, and three of those sat on the sidelines for the final. Goran Maksimovic of Yugoslavia held the top spot with a 594 out of 600; Nicolas Berthelot of France followed at 593 and the FRG's Johann Riederer was third at 592. All three held their respective positions through the 10-shot final. U.S. shooter Bob Foth Springs finished fourth.

In the men's free rifle event, where competitors shoot 40 shots each in the prone, standing and kneeling position with.22 caliber rifles, it was two Britons shooting it out for the gold. Defending Olympic gold medalist Malcolm Cooper, who trailed Alister Allan by one point in the preliminaries, edged his countryman in the final to become the first shooter to win two smallbore free rifle gold medals.

Trap consisted of two 75-target days followed by 50 clays on the last day for the shooters who'd made the cut. The top six shoot a 25-target final to determine medals. The gold medal race saw Dmitri Monakov of the Soviet Union and Czechoslovakia's Miloslav Bednarik tied after the final with 222—197s in qualification and perfect 25s in the final. They entered a "miss and out" tiebreaker similar to football's sudden death. Bednarik missed his eighth claybird and watched his competitor's next shot intently. Monakov turned his eighth claybird into a cloud of fluorescent orange dust and won the gold medal.

Dan Carlisle made U.S. Olympic history as the first athlete to shoot both trap and skeet. The 1984 bronze medalist in trap did not qualify for that final, but the 32-year-old shooting instructor found himself in skeet's shoot-off. Carlisle was in third place going into the final 25 targets, but equipment problems led to two missed claybirds that dropped him from the medals. In the shoot-off for the gold, a triumphant Axel Wegner of the GDR prevailed over Chile's Alfonso de Iruarrizaga.

The Games of the XXIVth Olympiad also marked the end of the running game target event as it has been known. Gone will be the "pig" target, replaced instead by a round bull's-eye. A host of other changes have also been made in hopes of improving participation in this event. Norway's Tor Heiestad won the gold and, along with bronze medalist Guennadi Avramenko, set an Olympic record of 591 that will stand for all time. □

SOCCER

The participation of the U.S. Olympic soccer team in the 16-team final tournament in the 1988 Summer Games was a perfect example of just how far the United States had progressed in this most international of sports—and just how far it has yet to go in order to be considered one of the world's major soccer powers.

This national team put together by U.S. head coach Lothar Osiander and his assistant, Len Roitman, was the best prepared of any U.S. Olympic soccer team in history.

The U.S. team wasn't the only one that was well prepared, however. The Soviet Union, Brazil, Italy and the FRG all brought strong teams to the Games. That would become quite evident as the tournament progressed to the medal round. And the host nation, Korea, had a feisty team that would prove difficult for the Americans to deal with.

The 1988 Games marked the ninth time since 1924 that the United States had qualified for the soccer tournament in the Olympics and the fourth time since 1972. Only perennial Olympic soccer medal candidate Yugoslavia (11) and Italy (10) have been to the final Olympic tournament more than the United States since the 1924 Games in Paris.

In the weeks before the trip to Korea, Osiander and Roitman felt it would take a total of three points—based on the internationally accepted practice of awarding two points for a win, one for a tie and none for a loss—for the United States to advance to the second round. Osiander & Company "planned" on earning two points from the opening contest with Argentina and then hoped to get a tie from one of their two remaining preliminary games against either the host Koreans or the Soviets in order to advance.

Armed with what Osiander would later call "a perfect tactical approach" for Argentina, the American team completely outplayed their South American counterparts before a largely pro-U.S. crowd of 18,500 at Taegu's main stadium.

For 80 minutes the United States outclassed one of the world's greatest soccer nations, taking a 1-0 lead on a picture-perfect goal by Mike Windischmann off a pass from Brian Bliss. But, in the last 10 minutes, Argentina—the nation of Maradona and the current world champions—scrambled in the tying goal on a penalty shot. They then successfully stalled the final moments to gratefully secure a tie it had little hope of claiming for most of the night.

The United States next faced the Koreans in Pusan on Sept. 20, knowing they now had to probably earn two points from either of its final first-round games to qualify for the second round.

Three U.S. players—forward Peter Vermes, midfielder Murray and Windischmann, hero of the Argentina game—sat out the Korea match battling stomach pains from pizza they ate the evening before. Without that trio, the United States was forced to use Brent Goulet as its lone attacker against Korea and enter into what Osiander called "a bunker mentality."

The Koreans swarmed and swooped the entire game, but could not score. But neither could the United States, and the game ended in a 0-0 tie.

Korea, wary in the first half, launched almost non-stop offensives in the second. "It was an all-out onslaught, a non-stop barrage," U.S. goalie David Vanole said. "They came at us at 100 miles an hour with no letup."

Worn down by Korea's offensive strategy (and 22,000 partisan fans) and without Murray's power in the U.S. midfield and Vermes' non-stop running up front, Osiander's troops survived, barely. The United States had held on grimly even though defender Paul Krumpe was ill. Defender John Doyle—one of three collegians on a U.S. squad dominated by professional players—played well after coming on as a second-half reserve. But playmaker Bliss, one of the stalwarts in the first U.S. game, was given little room to work and was not a factor.

ABOVE / *Romario Farias of Brazil celebrates his goal in the soccer final against the USSR, but in the end the Soviets were doing the jumping after a 2-1 overtime victory.* (Michael Yada/LPI)

ABOVE / *The level of action rises a notch as two U.S. players try to use their heads in a skirmish with goalie Luis Alberto Islas of Argentina. The United States earned a 1-1 tie in this game, but its 0-1-2 record didn't earn a ticket to the medal round.* (George Tiedemann/Sports Illustrated)

All alone up front, Goulet had few chances although his blistering shot against the grain in the game's final moments ironically could have won the game.

It was a different situation two days later in Taegu against the Soviets. The Americans went into their final game knowing a win or a tie would put them into the second round.

A string of defensive mistakes handed the Soviets an early lead, 3-0 at halftime, that stretched to 4-0 early in the second half. That lead was cut in half midway through the second half on goals by Goulet and defender Doyle, but the United States' chances had, in essence, evaporated in the first 20 minutes.

"We made some really silly, amateurish mistakes out there," said a subdued Osiander after the game. "Today, nerves and over-enthusiasm on our part killed us. Maybe we aren't ready for this kind of team. Against some teams in our CONCACAF region you can make mistakes like we made today and not get punished, but against a really good team like the Soviets, they punish you for your errors and end up winning this kind of game."

"We were under a lot of pressure to do well," Vanole said, "and I was so intense, so uptight, I made a few mistakes early. I was over-anxious and not concentrating.

"There were a lot of guys running free, like on their fourth goal, and the second goal was a defensive error when a ball wasn't cleared. There were a lot of mistakes made, including mine," Vanole added.

Ahead by four, the Soviets allowed the United States to score two goals. Goulet finished off a great pass from Davis with an arching shot off his right foot into the right corner to make it 4-1. Twenty minutes later, Doyle used his height to beat two Soviet defenders to a ball in the air. The surprised Soviet defense watched it roll untouched into their goal for the final 4-2 tally.

In the other group play, a revitalized Argentina upset Korea, 2-1, to advance to the quarterfinal round, but they were soon disposed of by the Brazilians, 1-0, in their matchup in Seoul. Meanwhile, the Soviets remained unbeaten, toppling Australia—the surprise second place finisher in Group D—3-0. Group A winner Sweden lost, 2-0, to a young Italian team, who were runners-up in Group B. And a strong West German squad came back from its loss to Sweden in group play to hammer African entrant Zambia, 4-0.

Thus, the semifinals paired the Brazilians with the West Germans, and the Italians with the Soviets. Brazil advanced to its second straight gold medal match by nipping the FRG on penalty kicks, 2-1. The Soviets slipped past the energetic Italians, going into overtime to do so for a final score of 3-2. The Soviets again relied on its dynamic trio of Igor Dobrovolski, Arminas Narbekovas and Alexei Mikhailitchenko for its three goals.

In the tournament's championship game, Brazilian midfielder Romario Farias gave his team a first half 1-0 lead before a sellout crowd of 70,000 at the Olympic Stadium in Seoul, but Dobrovolski tied it for the Soviets in the second half and Iouri Savichev scored with 13 minutes left in overtime to give the Soviets their fourth soccer medal in the last five Olympiads and their first gold medal since the 1956 Games in Melbourne. □

RIGHT / *Brazil's Jose Ferreira finds himself outnumbered by Soviet players as he attempts to advance the ball in the tense, tightly played gold medal game.* (Michael Yada/LPI)

SWIMMING AND DIVING   The Superstars Were Super

If you wanted records, you didn't have to go to a music shop in Seoul to find them. The swimming venue did quite nicely. And, in an Olympics packed with drama and intrigue, the swimming and diving venue made as big a splash as any of the competitions.

From there came the arguably single most dramatic moment of the 1988 Games in Seoul—the final dive of Greg Louganis.

Earlier, in the springboard competition, Louganis hit the diving board before he hit the water on a reverse 2-1/2 somersault dive, the result being not only a lousy dive (the seven judges gave him scores between 0.0 to 1.0), but a nasty gash on the head and fear of a serious injury.

He had overcome that to win the gold medal. Now, to win the platform diving competition and a unique place in Olympic history, he had to make a near-perfect dive to take the gold from a remarkable 14-year-old Chinese diver, Ni Xiong. Louganis' final dive—the most difficult one in his repertoire, a 2-1/2 somersault in tuck position—was nearly perfect, allowing him to edge Ni by a mere point to win the gold.

It took near perfection to upstage swimming's stars—Kristin Otto of the GDR and Matt Biondi and Janet Evans of the United States. Those three accounted for 14 gold medals.

By the time she was finished, the Amazonian Otto (she's 6' 1", 150 pounds) had enough gold to open her own Fort Knox in her native land. She went to the starting blocks six times and touched the end of the pool first six times (actually, relay teammates touched it twice for her).

Her six gold medal performance was the best ever for an Olympic female swimmer, topping countrywoman Kornelia Ender's five medal achievement (four golds, one silver) at the 1976 Olympics in Montreal.

Actually, Otto received even more gold. She was selected as the outstanding athlete of the Seoul Olympics, receiving a crown made of 20 ounces of 20-karat

ABOVE / *Bodies arch outward in near unity at the start of a preliminary 200-meter backstroke race. But after entering the water, some swimmers turned to a new technique — a "dolphin kick" that propelled them underwater at least 30 meters. It paid off for two swimmers — the gold for Japan's Daichi Suzuki and the silver for American David Berkhoff.* (Michael Yada/LPI)

OPPOSITE / *The GDR's Kristin Otto (center) visits over the back fence with Jill Sterkel of the United States after their 50-meter freestyle final. Otto dominated women's swimming, winning this race and five others, while Sterkel tied for the bronze.* (Norbert Schmidt)

SEVEN MEDALS AND RETIREMENT

One look at Matt Biondi and you knew he was an athlete. "It's nice to go home to Berkeley to be known as a student," he once said. "A tall student who looks like a basketball player," he added.

Actually, he was a swimmer who seemed sculpted for the sport—tall (6'8"), solid (210 pounds), with broad shoulders, big hands, narrow waist and hips, slender legs and size 14 feet. On the ground, he loped like one of those U.S. marshals that John Wayne used to play. In the water, he swam with a long, gentle, textbook stroke.

He started swimming at 10, relatively late. As a virtual novice, he made the 1984 Olympic team and won a gold medal in the 400-meter freestyle relay.

Then his career took off. At the University of California, he made All-America four years in swimming and four years in water polo. He won eight individual and five relay titles in national collegiate championships and broke world and/or American freestyle records at 50, 100 and 200 meters and yards.

In the 1986 World Swimming Championships in Madrid, he won a record total of seven medals (three golds, one silver, three bronzes). In the Seoul Olympics, in the same seven events, he won five golds, one silver and one bronze.

At Berkeley, Biondi majored in the political economics of industrial societies. He became active in environmental causes and several times swam with dolphins off the coast of Florida. "They helped me be aware of how water moves over my body," he said.

After his final race in Seoul, he retired as a swimmer, though he said he intended to continue with water polo. He planned to fix up his pickup truck and drive across America.

"I've traveled everywhere in the world and seen nothing, but pools and hotel rooms," he said. □

BY FRANK LITSKY

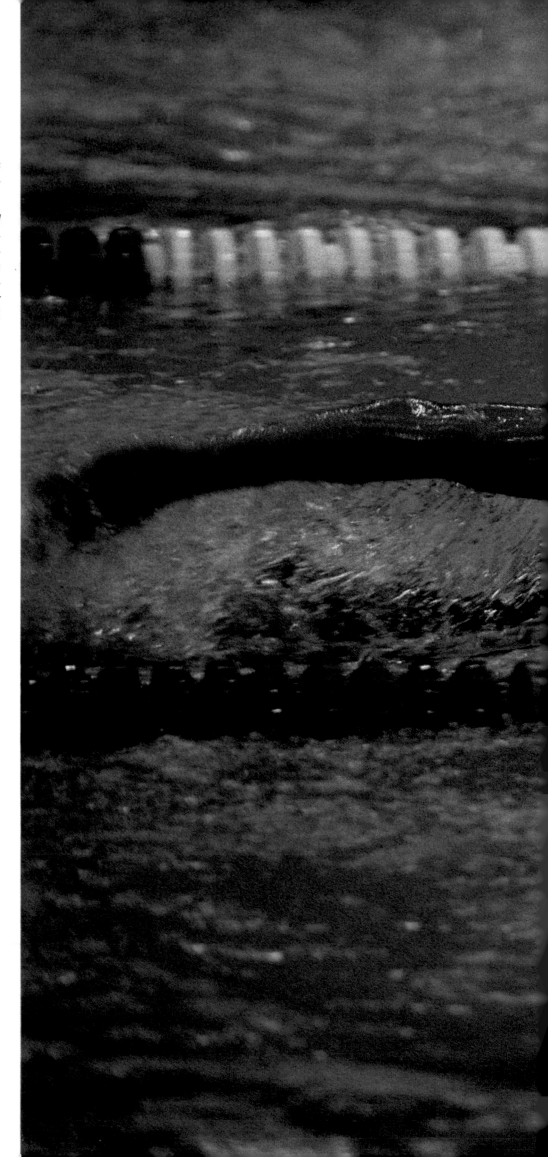

RIGHT / *Seventeen-year-old Janet Evans won golds in all three of her races, setting records in two of them . . .*

(INSET) / *. . . and she accomplished this feat with a sleek, almost fragile-appearing body frame, seemingly better suited to distance running than distance swimming, and she was invariably surrounded by imposing, muscular opponents.* (both photos - Michael Yada/LPI)

ABOVE / Hungary's Jozsef Szabo attacks the water with karate-like strokes en route to his gold medal swim in the 200-meter breaststroke. (Norbert Schmidt)

OPPOSITE / Michael Gross of the FRG gets a pat on the back from second place finisher Benny Nielsen of Denmark after Gross' record-setting victory in the 200-meter butterfly. (Nobert Schmidt)

"Enterprising neighbors had organized a barbecue, complete with banners and balloons, in her honor . . . as the Evans' car turned onto Brookhaven Avenue in Placentia, a police motorcycle escort joined them, and when the motorcade turned onto Brower, children from the elementary school at the end of the block fell in behind on foot and bicycle. Before long, 500 people were milling around on the street in front of No. 424, and Janet, still in her traveling clothes, was signing autographs and taking the little ones upstairs to show them her medals."

Another athlete worthy of a big homecoming was Hungary's Tamas Darnyi. Outside of Otto, Biondi and Evans, he may have had the best Olympics for a swimmer.

He won both the 200- and 400-meter individual medleys in world record time. In both events he had to beat America's gold medal hopeful, David Wharton. Darnyi proved to be too strong, with his record-setting times of 2:00.17 and 4:14.75, respectively.

The 1988 Olympics served as the final race for one of distance swimming's top performers—Vladimir Salnikov of the Soviet Union. Because of the boycott of the '84 Games, Salnikov was not able to defend the 1,500-meter title he won in Moscow. It was during his Moscow Olympic gold medal performance that he became the first swimmer to break the 15-minute mark as he broke the world record with a time of 14:58.27. At Seoul, the 28-year-old Salnikov swam slightly slower, 15:00.40, but it was enough to take the gold.

Other men's champions were Uwe Dassler of the GDR in the 400-meter freestyle (3:46.95, a world record); Adrian Moorhouse of Great Britain in the 100-meter breaststroke (1:02.04); Joszef Szabo of Hungary in the 200-meter breaststroke (2:13.52); Michael Gross of the FRG in the 200-meter butterfly (1:56.94, an Olympic record); and Igor Polianski of the Soviet Union in the 200-meter backstroke (1:59.37).

Women's winners included Friedrich in the 200-meter freestyle (1:57.65); Tania Dangalakova of Bulgaria in the 100-meter breaststroke (1:07.95); Silke Hoerner of the GDR in the 200-meter breaststroke (2:26.71); Kathleen Nord of the GDR in the 200-meter butterfly (2:09.51); 14-year-old Krisztina Egerszegi of Hungary in the 200-meter backstroke (2:09.29); and Daniela Hunger of the GDR in the 200-meter individual medley (2:12.59).

The United States finished second in gold medals (eight) and total medals (18) in swimming to the GDR, which had 11 golds and 28 total medals. Of the 11 world records that fell in the 31 events, six were broken by Americans.

One of those broken by the United States came in one of the heats of the 100-meter backstroke by David Berkoff.

Berkoff was one of the Games' more intriguing figures. He was a bona fide revolutionary with his unorthodox start. While most backstrokers stay under water only a short time after they push off before surfacing to pinwheel their arms and propel themselves with a flutter kick, Berkoff looks like he's on an assignment for Jacques Cousteau. By the time he rejoins the air-breathing world, he's 30 to 35 meters into the race, or only 15 meters before it's time to make the turn.

And, instead of a flutter kick, Berkoff borrows from the butterfly and uses a dolphin kick. So, here's a man who starts his races with his arms extended and uses a dolphin kick upside down while five feet underwater against the rest of the field.

He was supposed to beat the rest of the field. He established two world records at the U.S. Olympic trials and then lowered his record to 54.51 seconds in a heat.

But those who live by the start apparently die by the start—at least that was the case with Berkoff. Whereas he'd gotten an excellent start in his heat, he had a terrible

ABOVE / American Michele Mitchell came up just short in her quest to improve on 1984's silver medal-winning performance on the platform, but earned another silver medal to match the last one. (Michael Yada/LPI)

OPPOSITE / One of China's up-and-coming young divers, Li Deliang, cuts an arrow-true figure on one of his springboard efforts. Li won the bronze. (Michael Yada/LPI)

one in the final and finished second to Japan's Daichi Suzuki, who won the gold medal with a time of 55.05.

"It was a quick gun," U.S. coach Richard Quick explained.

Berkoff, a 21-year-old Harvard senior who had taken a year's leave of absence to prepare for the Olympics, had to have a strong finish to medal.

"I was expecting the gold. When I look back on this in five years I'll be really happy. I'm happy now just to medal. With 10 meters to go I didn't think I would," he said.

Berkoff did get a gold to go with his silver in the 400-meter medley relay, putting the United States one second under world record pace after his leadoff leg.

Like high jumping's Fosbury Flop, which gained notoriety at the 1968 Games in Mexico City, courtesy of Dick Fosbury, the Berkoff Burrow may be common by the Barcelona Games in 1992. Others, including former American Olympic champion Jesse Vassallo, had tried it as early as the 1960s, but Berkoff is the one who perfected it.

Another American gold medalist, Chris Jacobs, was certainly a candidate for the biggest comeback story. He was a member of the winning 400-meter freestyle and medley relays and the silver medalist in the 100-meter freestyle.

Jacobs had overcome some tremendous personal problems to get to Seoul. "Making the Olympic team sort of validated everything I've done in the last two years," he said. "I don't have to look back and reflect on my past anymore."

Two of America's top women swimmers, Mary T. Meagher and Jill Sterkel, who'd had a glorious past, came out of retirement for the Seoul Olympics. Meagher, 23, a world record-holder at both the 100- and 200-meter butterfly, got a medal on the last day of the swimming competition, finishing third in the 200 butterfly. Sterkel also won a medal, tying for third in the 50-meter freestyle.

DIVING

It was fitting that the drama centered on Greg Louganis. After all, that's what the 28-year-old diving great is planning to go into. By the time the 1992 Olympics are held in Barcelona, he's hoping his golden smile will be seen on a movie screen near you.

And, don't be too surprised if one day he's the subject of a movie. His performance at the Games was something more out of Hollywood than Seoul.

Consider:

As the favorite in both the springboard and platform events, he was not only expected to do well, but to win the gold medals. The silver in either event would surely be seen as a disappointment. A group of talented Chinese divers and a frightening injury nearly proved to be insurmountable.

The jovial Louganis was in cruise control during the springboard qualifying. The top 12 divers in qualifying make the finals. No problem for the Boca Raton, Fla., resident. He was in first place with just a few dives remaining when he tried a reverse 2-1/2 dive in pike position, a dive difficult for most, but routine for Louganis.

It wasn't routine this time. As he spun backward the second time, it became apparent he hadn't jumped far enough off the board. It became particularly apparent to his head, which struck the board. The symmetrical dive suddenly turned into one you see all the time at the local plunge, arms and legs out of sync as the diver, in this case Louganis, enters the water.

ABOVE / *Whether by springboard, as it is here, or by platform, the image of Greg Louganis flawlessly descending to a crisp, clean entry into the water never changes. Rebounding from a near-disastrous accident when he hit his head on the springboard, Louganis courageously held off a competitor half his age with a clutch final dive in the platform that completed his unprecedented sweep of both gold medals in two consecutive Olympics. (Michael Yada/LPI)*

FAREWELL TO A LEGEND

His early life was a nightmare. His later life made athletic history.

Greg Louganis was born in California to unmarried 15-year-olds. When he was eight-months old, he was adopted by Peter and Frances Louganis.

At 1-1/2, he started dance lessons. He also took gymnastics and drama classes. At nine, he started diving.

He grew up stuttering, insecure and introverted. Schoolmates taunted him because he was dark skinned (his birth father was of Samoan heritage). They taunted him because he had difficulty reading, not knowing the problem was caused by dyslexia, a learning disorder.

Diving became his outlet, and he became the greatest diver in history. He won an Olympic silver medal in 1976 at age 16, both diving gold medals in 1984, and both golds again in 1988. He won world championships in 1982 and 1986 and accumulated a record total of 47 U.S. titles indoors and outdoors.

Louganis considered himself an entertainer rather than an athlete. His dives seemed balletic and effortless, and good or bad he always smiled.

His proudest accomplishment, he said, was when he quit smoking.

"I smoked from the time I was eight," Louganis explained. "When I was 23, I saw a 12-year-old diver smoking at poolside. I asked him why he was smoking, and he said, 'I want to be just like you.' It really had an impact. It finally hit me that I have a responsibility to other people. So I stopped smoking right then."

After the Seoul Olympics, at age 28, he retired from diving to concentrate on his acting career. Ron O'Brien, his coach, was sad.

"We'll never see another like him in our lifetime," O'Brien said. □

BY FRANK LITSKY

He was not hurt as badly as first expected, though four stitches were needed to close the gash in his head. "I think my pride was hurt more than anything else," he said.

Physically, he was okay to continue diving. But what about mentally? How easy is it to come back after hitting your head soundly on the board?

Louganis provided the answer one half-hour later. There he was, laughing and smiling as he approached his next dive, on which he would record the highest score of the day. Louganis had passed the test and then some.

He also passed all the divers the next day, easily taking the gold medal, with Tan Liangde of China, who had beaten him twice earlier in the year, taking the silver.

Louganis' head wasn't the problem in platform diving. It was Ni, the 5' 3", 105-pound tyke from China.

Ni wouldn't let Louganis take a comfortable lead as the two exchanged the lead throughout the 10-dive final. If he was feeling any pressure, the stoic Ni wouldn't let it show—in or out of the water. Leading going into his final dive, Ni did a masterful job on an inward 3-1/2 somersault in a tuck position.

Two things saved Louganis. One, his final dive, a reverse 3-1/2 somersault in tuck position, was the most difficult dive from the platform and, as such, could score more points than Ni's last dive. Two, he executed it to near perfection to get one 9.0, five 8.5s and one 8.0 from the judges. Louganis had defeated Ni by less than two points—638.61 to 637.47.

The tears he cried as he fell into coach Ron O'Brien's arms after climbing from the pool were probably from relief as well as joy. With the dive he became the first man to win both diving gold medals in successive Olympics.

The double-double had been achieved by an American woman, Pat McCormick, in 1952 and 1956. Coincidentally, McCormick's daughter, Kelly, won the bronze medal in the women's springboard in Seoul. Eighteen-year-old Gao Min of China won the gold with 580.23 points and 15-year-old Li Qing of China took the silver with 534.33, edging McCormick, who had 533.19.

In the women's platform competition, the United States surprisingly won two of the three medals. Xu Yanmei of China won the gold with 445.20 points. Michele Mitchell, repeating her silver medal-winning performance in Los Angeles, followed with 436.95, and Wendy Lian Williams, the U.S. indoor and outdoor champion, captured the bronze with 400.44. □

SYNCHRONIZED SWIMMING SOLELY IN SYNC AND DOUBLE TAKES

The sport of synchronized swimming, which made its Olympic debut in 1984, saw some new faces in Seoul, Korea. For the first time, Korea, China and the Soviet Union entered synchronized swimming teams in Olympic competition. Though not yet medal contenders, it was clear that it won't be long before their technical expertise is matched with experience, giving these teams high hopes for Barcelona.

There were some familiar faces, too. Canada's 1984 Olympic silver medalist Carolyn Waldo returned to meet the United States' 1984 double gold medalist, Tracie Ruiz-Conforto.

In 1984, Ruiz-Conforto, the United States' star synchronized swimmer, retired from the sport. But, after two years, she confessed feeling a void and returned to competitive synchronized swimming in late 1986.

"With the solo competition being added so suddenly to the 1984 Olympics, I felt I hadn't given my best because I didn't have time to prepare," explained Ruiz-Conforto. "I needed to give myself a chance to be better than I was in 1984."

Canada's Waldo showed she was better, too. She was good enough to go from silver in 1984 to gold in 1988. Waldo, Ruiz-Conforto and others demonstrated that the sport of synchronized swimming is an electric mix of graceful art and powerful athleticism. Waldo was the best at combining the two, taking the gold medal with 200.15 points. Ruiz-Conforto was next at 197.63. And Japan's Mikako Kotani, at 191.85, was decorated with the bronze.

The heavily-weighted compulsory figures competition played the major role in determining the winner where technical precision is key. Results in this part of the competition account for 55 percent of the final score. The routine, a more physical and entertaining event, accounts for the remainder of the score.

Waldo put in a strong effort in compulsories, scoring 101.15 points. Ruiz-Conforto, who earned 98.63 in the compulsories, knew that the gold was too far out of reach.

"I came here to be the best I can be, and perform the ultimate routine," said the gracious Ruiz-Conforto. "I just want to have the swim of my life."

Her performance was laced with difficulty and risk. Holding her breath for at least half of the 3-1/2-minute routine, Ruiz-Conforto executed a complicated series of sustained twists, spins and waist-high body boosts. Then, she surfaced for air and glided dramatically through the water to the sound of Stravinsky's "Firebird," her charm captivating the crowd.

Acknowledging Ruiz-Conforto's leadership in the sport, Waldo said, "When Tracie came back I was excited. I didn't feel winning would mean as much if I couldn't compete against the greatest athlete in our sport."

Two days after winning the solo event, Waldo and partner Michelle Cameron won the gold medal in the duet competition. They needed—and received—a high score in compulsories to fend off the U.S. tandem, 24-year-old twins Karen and Sarah Josephson.

The Josephsons, graduates of Ohio State University in biochemistry, took a four-year break from their books and the pursuit of medical degrees to chase a long-awaited Olympic dream.

Their 18 years of training together were reflected in the routine competition where they demonstrated synchronization of breath-taking spins, intricate legwork and energetic choreography. For the performance, they earned four perfect 10s and the rest 9.9s for an average of 99.6, slightly higher than the Canadians' 98.60 total.

Japan earned its second medal as Miyako Tanaka and Kotani took the bronze.

"We did our best in the figures. Carolyn just had a great day and it pulled their figure average up," Sarah Josephson said.

Karen added, "We thought we could make up over one point in the routine. It was really disappointing that we didn't, but at least we had a great swim and know that we won the routine competition fairly." □

ABOVE / A familiar face, and gold medal winner from the 1984 Olympics, Tracie Ruiz-Conforto took two years off from the sport, but returned in fine style in '88 to win the silver in Seoul. (R.L. Hagedohm/LPI)

OPPOSITE / Karen and Sarah Josephson take the idea of synchronization literally — they're identical twins from Bristol, Conn. And yes, it is possible to beat a team that matches precisely not only in motion, but in size and appearance: the twins took second. (Michael Yada/LPI)

TABLE TENNIS

The world's most popular racket sport, table tennis, made its long overdue entrance into the Olympic arena at the Summer Games in Seoul, Korea. Sixty-four men and 48 women, selected through zonal trials, played to standing-room only audiences throughout the competition.

The 5,000-seat Seoul National University Gymnasium was the theater for a table tennis drama of roaring nationalism, major upsets and revenge. The drama started before the Games when China replaced two of their original Olympic women qualifiers with two new names. How could the current world champion and still the number one woman in the world, He Zhili, be told to stay home from the Olympics? Why was the number three-ranked woman in the world, Dai Lili, taken off the team? Their substitutes, Chen Jing and Li Huifen, were ranked in the international top 10, but still below the Korean favorite, Yang Young-ja.

Political intrigue or coaching genius? Whatever the reason, the results cannot be denied: Chen over Li in the finals and teammate Jiao Zhimin over Marie Hrachova of Czechoslovakia to complete a Chinese sweep in the women's singles.

Although he lost to Korea's Nam Kyu-yoo in the 1988 Asian Championships, Jiang Jialiang of China, winner of two world championships, was a clear favorite to win the gold in the men's singles in Seoul. This personable young man, a hero and role model for China's youth—and a pretty good disco dancer—understandably succumbed to the pressure of being number one. He lost in the quarterfinals to Eric Lindh of Sweden, which marked the beginning of upsets to come.

Jiang's teammate, Chen Longcan, the third-ranked player in the world in 1988, confidently walked onto the court to battle the aging Hungarian, long ago world doubles champ Tibor Klampar. Klampar, whose footwork is known as the Klampar Shuffle, brought a cunning strategy and steady backhand into play, de-

feating the favored Chen. It was not just an upset, but an "up-and-downset" defying all the right thinking of the experts. Chen, however, came back with partner Nei Qingguang to take the men's doubles competition.

The semifinals surprises, Klampar and Lindh, found themselves pitted against not only Koreans Kim Ki-taik and Nam, respectively, but what must have seemed like all of South Korea loudly packed into the National University Gym. There were to be no more upsets, only a final match that assured Korea of the gold (Nam) and the silver (Kim).

Three Americans made their way to these Olympics through the circuitous route of a zonal qualifying tournament, which allowed only two men and three women from all of North America to travel to Seoul.

Sean O'Neill (men's singles) and Insook Bhushan and Diana Gee (women's singles and doubles) went to Seoul looking for personal bests in the competition, knowing that medals were only a distant glimmer. O'Neill, was also looking to even an old score.

"Two months prior to the Olympics, Carlos Kuwai from Brazil, beat me in the finals of the under 22 age division at the U.S. International Open. It was an event I really wanted to win," he said. "When I saw the draw sheet for the Olympics, he and I were in the same round robin. It couldn't have been better. The match was two-out-of-three and we split the first two games, and I found myself down 20 to 17 in the third . . . I scored the next five points and closed it out. It was a rush to see on the scoreboard: Sean O'Neill, USA, vs. Carlos Kuwai, Brazil, 3-2. It was fantastic!"

In the women's doubles, Gee and Bhushan proved to be a powerful team extending eventual quarterfinalists Hrachova and Renata Kasalova of Czechoslovakia to a fifth game in their match. Losing at 21-17 ended their hope of advancing to the medal rounds. In the end, the Korean team of Hyun Jung-hwa and Yang Young-ja won the gold. □

ABOVE / *Sean O'Neill of McLean, Va., sends the ball flying and spinning toward his opponent. This Olympic sport was dominated by Koreans and Chinese, but provided the 21-year-old O'Neill with valuable experience.* (George Long/LPI)

ABOVE / *Hyun Jung-hwa of Korea is seen here by herself, but the gold medal came with the help of doubles teammate Yang Young-ja.* (COLOS)

TEAM HANDBALL

Yo-bo-se-yo! Korea greeted the rest of the handball world with two surprising finishes at the 1988 Olympics. Backed by sold-out partisan crowds, the women's team won the gold medal and then a silver in the men's competition battling the Soviet Union, the goliath of this popular European sport.

Led by Kim Choon-rye, Kim Hyun-mee, and Sung Kyung-hwa, the Korean women surprised the top-rated Soviet Union, 21-19, at Suwon Gymnasium. Korea rallied from a first-half deficit to win the game and send the crowd into a frenzy. It was Korea's first gold medal in team handball.

Meanwhile, the Korean men defeated the GDR in the final five seconds. And they beat Czechoslovakia on a seven-meter penalty shot with time expired in the game to send them to the gold medal match with the Soviets.

Led by the acrobatic shooting of Kang Jan-won, the leading scorer of the tournament with 49 goals, and Lee Sang-hyo, who notched 31 tallies, the diminutive Koreans were nonetheless manhandled by the Soviet team. The Soviets, averaging 6'6'' and 225 pounds, seemed to toy with the Koreans, defeating them, 32-25, in the gold medal game. It marked a regained supremacy for the Soviet Union, which dominated the sport in the late '70s and early '80s before faltering in the 1986 World Championships.

The U.S. men's and women's teams finished quite the opposite of their hosts, as the men finished 12th (last) overall and the women seventh (second to last) overall. But the United States, the only representative from the Western Hemisphere, was a surprise just to make the Olympics.

After losing six consecutive games at Seoul, men's captain Joe Story said, "Qualifying by winning the Pan American Games may have been the peak of team handball in the United States. We've never done better and it doesn't look like we will do much better in the near future."

U.S. Team Handball Federation executive director Mike Cavanaugh said, "It took almost 10 years to build this Olympic team and look what happens. This was going to be our turn to do well."

So what happened to the gold medal-winning team from the 1987 Pan American Games? It lost its two top players, Tom Schneeberger and Bob Djockovich, to retirement, changed coaches, and lacked international experience.

Schneeberger was the team's prolific scorer and lead player. Djockovich, says Story, was the team's emotional leader and floor general. " 'Jock' likes to win and we needed that leadership skill," said Peter Lash, who was the team's second top scorer behind Steve Goss in Seoul.

Story said the team realistically thought it could defeat Iceland, Sweden and Algeria in its preliminary rounds and advance to the final round game for fifth place. Instead, the United States lost to defending world champion Yugoslavia, 31-23; Iceland, 22-15; Sweden, 26-12; Soviet Union, 26-14; and African champion Algeria, 20-17. In the final game for 11th and 12th place, Japan defeated the United States, 24-21.

Things were not much brighter for the women's team. The United States' only win came against African champion Ivory Coast, 27-16, on the final day.

Earlier in the tournament, the United States lost to Czechoslovakia, 33-19; China, 31-22; Korea, 22-18; and Yugoslavia, 19-18.

The bright spot for the U.S. team was Leora "Sam" Jones. Jones scored 35 goals, second behind China's Sun Xiulan, who tallied 36. Jones was one of the many U.S. players who entered the tournament with hopes of a medal.

"We had defeated the Soviet Union and Korea earlier in the year," Jones said. "And we tied Norway and Czechoslovakia. We put a lot of pressure on ourselves. But we thought we could win a medal judging by our play up to the Olympics. Here we just fell apart." □

ABOVE / *Despite the imposing presence of Leora "Sam" Jones, widely considered one of the best female team handball players in the world, the U.S. squad managed just one victory in six matches in Seoul.* (R.L. Hagedohm/LPI)

OPPOSITE (TOP) / *The American men's team, defending their goal here against Yugoslavia, fared about the same as the U.S. women's squad, going winless in six games.* (R.L. Hagedohm/LPI)

OPPOSITE (BOTTOM) / *Czechoslovakia's Alena Damitsova attracts plenty of attention as she powers in for a shot against the United States. The Czechs won the match, 33-19.* (R.L. Hagedohm/LPI)

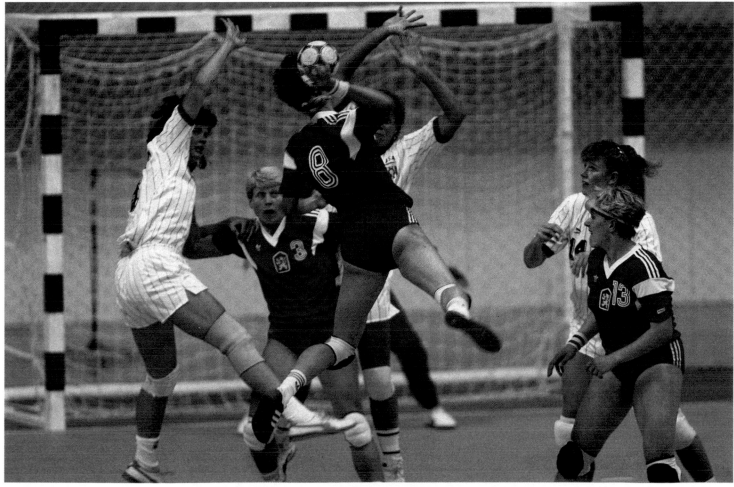

TENNIS

Steffi Graf of the FRG arrived in Seoul for the Games of the XXIVth Olympiad with the cheers of her U.S. Open victory in New York still echoing in her ears. At 19, she had just become the fifth player in tennis history to win the Grand Slam: a sweep of the Australian, French, Wimbledon and U.S. championships in one calendar year. The only others to accomplish this feat were Don Budge (1938), Maureen Connolly (1953), Rod Laver (1962 and 1969) and Margaret Court (1970). With tennis back in the Olympics as a medal sport for the first time since 1924—it had been a demonstration sport at Mexico City in 1968 and Los Angeles in 1984—Graf had the opportunity for an unprecedented achievement. The "Golden Slam," people called it.

"That would probably be the ultimate for a tennis player," said Chris Evert, 33, who also looked forward to an Olympic medal as "frosting" on her distinguished 17-year career. She was seeded No. 2 to Graf in the women's singles draw of 48 in Seoul, but was upset in the third round by Rafaella Reggi of Italy, who had never taken a set from her before.

Graf, who had won the demonstration gold medal in L.A., was drained from the Slam and lost a set to Larissa Savchenko of the Soviet Union in the quarterfinals, but then routed American Zina Garrison in the semis and Gabriela Sabatini of Argentina in the gold medal match.

"I'm very excited that I have achieved this now," Graf said, beaming with relief and satisfaction. "I think it's something that not many people after me will achieve."

It was a new experience for the wealthy pros of tennis to be in what had long been the last bastion and supreme showcase of amateur sports, but anybody who wondered if medals would mean anything to millionaires should have seen Graf, men's singles champion Miloslav Mecir of Czechoslovakia, and the doubles champs from the United States—Ken Flach and Robert Seguso,

and Garrison and Pam Shriver. They glowed with the Olympic flame.

When Garrison served out a 4-6, 6-2, 10-8 victory over Helena Sukova and Jana Novotna of Czechoslovakia on the sixth match point of a final that Shriver called "traumatic," the winners bear-hugged and danced to the victory stand. Shriver sang "The Star-Spangled Banner," laughed, cried and kept looking at her medal.

"I hadn't seen one up-close. I'd seen a bronze and a demonstration one, and I'd hoped the real thing was better—and it is. It's much nicer, and heavier than I thought," said Shriver, 26, who has won a Grand Slam in doubles with Martina Navratilova and close to $4 million in prize money. "If I do nothing else in tennis, this will be the highlight of my career. It's been five or six years since I got such a kick out of winning a match."

Garrison, who received a bronze medal for singles, was also on an emotional cloud when she ascended the top tier of the victory podium. "It was really strange, hearing your national anthem and all the U.S. people here cheering for you," she said. "It's just a special moment in your life."

Flach and Seguso were so psyched to win the gold that Flach played through a painful torn shoulder muscle that made it hard for him to serve out the men's doubles final over Spaniards Emilio Sanchez and Sergio Casal, 6-3, 6-4, 6-7, 6-7, 9-7. "It'll be something I'll always cherish," Flach said.

Mecir—who beat Wimbledon champion and 1984 gold medalist Stefan Edberg of Sweden in the semis and tied American Tim Mayotte in knots in the men's singles final, 3-6, 6-2, 6-4, 6-2—spoke for many players, especially the East Europeans, when he said: "It's a great feeling to forget about the money for a couple of weeks and to play for the sporting spirit of the Olympics . . . I was very happy I could come here, see the other sports, feel the atmosphere . . . I think in Czechoslovakia, the Olympic Games is the biggest sporting event and this is the best thing I could do for them." □

ABOVE (TOP) / *West German Steffi Graf completed an unprecedented quintuple in 1988 — winning the Grand Slam, then adding an Olympic gold medal. She reached these heights . . .*

(BOTTOM) / *. . . largely on the strength of a high-powered serve, shown here, and above, in triplicate. Graf defeated Gabriella Sabatini of Argentina, 6-3, 6-3, in the final.* (both photos - R.L. Hagedohm/LPI)

ABOVE / *American Pam Shriver allows her emotion to spill after she and doubles partner Zina Garrison finally clinched their gold medal with a tense, tight victory over Czechoslovakia's Jana Novotna and Helena Sukova.* (Michael Yada/LPI)

VOLLEYBALL

The Olympic Games are almost larger than life in America's sporting consciousness. Victory at the Olympics establishes athletic greatness. Anything less, unfortunately, is often viewed by the public as failure.

Members of the U.S. men's Olympic volleyball team knew that as they prepared for the '88 Games. They knew that their gold medal of 1984, their World Cup title in 1985, the world championship they won in 1986, and the Pan American Games title of 1987 — their domination of the sport for the past four years— would mean little if they lost in Seoul.

So, leaving nothing to chance, the American men pushed and pounded their way through the Olympic competition with a perfect record, defeating the USSR in the final, 13-15, 15-10, 15-4, 15-8, to capture the gold and establish themselves as an amateur sports dynasty.

The United States isn't the biggest, fastest or strongest volleyball team in the world, it's just the best. The Americans have perfected all phases of the game to the point where they have no weakness. Combine their technical brilliance with endless hours of pre-game preparation and they are ready for anything the opposition might try.

"Volleyball is so interactive in nature," U.S. coach Marv Dunphy said. "In volleyball, in order for you to hit, I need to pass, and someone else has to set. You need each other much more. I feel like our guys really complement each other."

The man who complemented all others was 27-year-old U.S. captain Karch Kiraly. An outside hitter with a 41-inch vertical jump, Kiraly is considered the greatest player in the world. He was at his best in Seoul and was honored as Most Valuable Player of the tournament.

But, as Dunphy noted, it is impossible for one player to carry a team in volleyball, and Kiraly had plenty of support. Middle blocker Craig Buck and outside hitter Steve Timmons, both members of the '84 Olympic team, are among the best in the world at their positions. The three other starters—setter Jeff Stork,

middle blocker Doug Partie and outside hitter Bob Ctvrtlik—each turned in strong performances at the Games. A deep bench was led by '84 veteran Dave Saunders, defensive specialist Eric Sato, setter Ricci Luyties and middle blocker Scott Fortune.

The United States needed every bit of talent available throughout a grueling two weeks of competition in Seoul. In the tougher of the two six-team pools, the Americans faced difficult challenges in all but one of their seven matches.

Playing in fits and starts, the United States was 5-0 in pool play. The key early on was a come-from-behind win against Argentina. Stork, nursing an injured back, provided a big lift when he came off the bench to get the United States back on track after it lost the first two games.

As the winner of its pool, the United States moved on to a semifinal match with Brazil, a team that defeated the Americans in preliminary competition at the '87 Pan Am Games.

This time, however, the South Americans were no match for a U.S. team that had its golden goal in sight, falling 15-3, 15-5, 15-11. The Soviets beat Argentina in the other semifinal to set up a much anticipated showdown between the world's two best teams.

While the United States clearly has been No. 1 since 1984, the USSR has been No. 1A. Raimond Vilde is the team's top hitter and an international superstar. The Soviets are a bigger, stronger team than the United States, but they lack the crisp passing and quickness of the Americans. Regardless, either team was more than capable of beating the other.

For a time, it seemed this would be the Soviets' day. Game one of the gold medal confrontation lasted 45 minutes, with the USSR prevailing, 15-13. But the Americans began to click toward the end of the first game and, in game two, Timmons got hot and sparked a 15-10 victory. Game three also went to the United States, 15-4, in just 16 minutes.

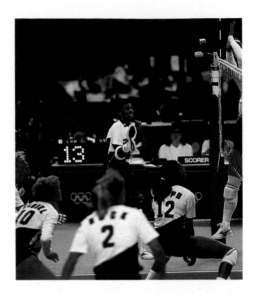

ABOVE / There's strength in numbers, and five U.S. players converge on the net, led by high-kicking Kim Oden, in an attempt to drive the ball past China's defense. But more strength lies in the number appearing in the background, showing the Chinese with nearly enough points to win. They did win this game and the match. (Bob Long/LPI)

OPPOSITE / Karch Kiraly watches from the lofty vantage of a prodigious vertical leap as one of his usually deadly spikes heads for an unusual destination — returned to sender. Holland won this encounter, but overall was no match for the eventual gold medal winners. (Bob Long/LPI)

From there it was just a matter of time as the intense, emotional Americans cruised to a 15-8 victory to close out the match, capture the gold medal and earn a place in volleyball history as, arguably, the greatest men's team of all time.

The women's side of the Olympic tournament was incredibly well-balanced.

Coming in, China was considered the favorite since the world's top-rated team, Cuba, chose to stay away from the Games. The Chinese women had a record as remarkable as the American men this decade, winning the world championship in 1982 and '86, and the Olympic gold in 1984. In the final of the '84 Games, China defeated the United States and several players from that team continued another four years in hopes of repeating.

The same wasn't true for the United States. All but one member of the '84 Olympic team retired after the Games, leaving new coach Terry Liskevych with a major re-building project.

After some tough times in 1985 and '86, the new U.S. team started to jell in '87 and, as the Olympics approached, it was considered no worse than the fifth-ranked team in the world.

The problem the Americans faced in Seoul was a difficult draw. They were in the tougher pool with China, third-seeded Peru, and Brazil, the seventh seed.

The U.S. women took on China in the opener and showed their youth and inexperience, falling 3-0. But, in the second match against Brazil, the United States came back strong and scored a hard-fought victory in five games, 14-16, 15-5, 15-13, 12-15, 15-7. Captain Kim Oden and reserve outside hitter Angela Rock led the way.

That set up the key match of the tournament. With a victory over Peru in the final game of the preliminary round, the Americans could tie Peru and China at 2-1 in pool play. However, in order to advance to the semifinals, the United States was faced with the unenviable task of not only beating the Peruvians, but beating them in three straight games *and* holding their point total to 32 or less. All that was necessary because of a tiebreaker procedure based on games and points won.

For a while it looked like the Americans just might pull off the impossible. Playing inspired volleyball at an emotionally gut-wrenching level, they hammered out 15-12 and 15-9 victories in the first two games. One more win by a score of 15-11 or better, and they would advance with China to the medal round.

It wasn't to be.

Peru got its act together and the U.S. women—tensing up as points slipped away— were unable to make the magic last a little longer. Peru jumped to the lead and, at 12-2 in game three, the opportunity to advance vanished.

"We played two great games against Peru with all the pressure in the world on us," Liskevych said. "I thought we responded well and played well. That's as well as we played in the tournament. It would have been a great Olympic story if we had won."

The disappointed U.S. women ended up losing the match in five games and went on to the consolation bracket. Down and discouraged, they were upset by the GDR, then recovered to knock off Korea and take seventh place.

In the medal round, Peru trounced Japan in one semifinal, while the Soviets pulled a major surprise by blasting China in three straight. The USSR held China to just 11 total points in the match. The Soviets then rallied in a memorable gold medal match to beat Peru, 10-15, 12-15, 15-13, 15-7, 17-15. □

ABOVE / *Kiraly alights on Earth long enough to join his teammates in celebration of their gold medal victory over the Soviet Union.* (Bob Long/LPI)

OPPOSITE / *Overshadowed by its heavy-hitting attack, the U.S. team's defense also performed at gold medal levels, often sending four, or even six, arms high over the net to block oncoming spikes.* (Bob Long/LPI)

WATER POLO

In water polo, that rugged aquatic sport that combines swimming, throwing and underwater wrestling, it became a tournament to remember, or is that re-remember, for Yugoslavia and the United States, the two teams that fought for the gold medal in Los Angeles.

U.S. standout goalie Craig Wilson reclined at the post-game press conference after the 1988 gold medal game in water polo. He was flanked by seven-year teammate Terry Schroeder and Igor Milanovic, Yugoslavia's top player, while he aired his opinion of the 1988 Olympic water polo tournament: "By far this was the toughest tournament I've ever played in. Any one of the seven teams could have won the gold medal. It was who ever got the right breaks."

Yugoslavia seemed to draw the lucky straw and "received a couple of good breaks," according to U.S. coach Bill Barnett, and defeated the United States, 9-7, in overtime to win the gold medal. The United States settled for the silver medal for the second consecutive time. The Soviet Union captured the bronze medal by defeating the FRG, 14-13.

The U.S.-Yugoslavia game was almost a replay of the 1984 gold medal match in which the United States and Yugoslavia tied, 5-5. Yugoslavia won the gold medal on a goal-differential tiebreaker. After 1984, ties were abolished from Olympic competition, and a medal round was instituted, with the top four teams from the two round-robin brackets advancing. The new system seemed to work fine, even for the frustrated Americans.

"All we know is that we didn't want the gold medal determined on a goal differential or anything else," Barnett said. "We wanted to control our destiny, and I think that happened."

The road of destiny had many crossroads en route to the gold medal game. In its first preliminary game, James Bergeson scored with five seconds remaining to lift the United States to a 7-6 win over Yugoslavia. The win eventually gave the United States a first place finish in its bracket and advancement into the medal round.

In game two, the following day, Spain upset the United States, 9-7. The loss followed an emotional letdown, Barnett said. "When we got the draw for the Olympics and I saw that we played Spain after Yugoslavia, it scared the hell out of me. No matter how much you try to prepare your team, you are always going to have a letdown after a big game. Our passes were bad and our mental errors—not so much the physical errors—killed us," he added.

Barnett's fiery comments apparently propelled the team in its next two matches. The United States dismantled Asian champion China, 14-7, and Greece, 18-9, setting up a dramatic preliminary-round finish with Hungary. Heading into the game against Hungary, the United States had to win in order to advance to the medal round.

Never a dull team, Schroeder scored with three seconds remaining with two players hanging on him to give the United States a 10-9 victory and a trip to the medal round. After the game Schroeder said, "In the last 15 seconds, all that was running through my mind was that if we didn't score, all the hard work and sacrifice from the past four years would be flushed down the toilet."

The following night, behind the brilliant play of Wilson, who recorded eight heart-stopping saves, the United States defeated the Soviet Union, the pre-Olympic favorite, 8-7, to advance to the gold medal game. Wilson ended with a tournament-high 68 saves. It was the first Soviet-American matchup in the Olympics since the bronze medal game in 1972.

It was then deja vu for the U.S. team. Like 1984, the United States faced Yugoslavia in the gold medal game (except this time the U.S. team had filtered its way through the powerful Eastern European countries that were missing from the 1984 Games). Like 1984, the Americans took a commanding 5-2 lead. Like 1984, Yugoslavia rallied back on some

ABOVE / *Three-time Olympian Terry Schroeder not only captained the U.S. water polo team to the silver medal, he was also named to carry the American flag and represent his country's delegation in the Closing Ceremonies.* (Bob Long/LPI)

OPPOSITE (TOP LEFT) / *Considered one of the two best goalies in the world, Craig Wilson spends many of his out-of-the-water hours programming computers, not opponents' shots.* (Bob Long/LPI)

OPPOSITE (TOP RIGHT) / *In the tip of this iceberg of action in the gold medal game pitting the United States against Yugoslavia, American Jody Campbell looks for a friendly cap to pass to.* (Bob Long/LPI)

questionable officiating calls. Like 1984, the United States tired late in the game. And, like 1984, the teams were tied at the end of regulation. Unlike 1984, there was overtime and Yugoslavia outscored the United States, 3-1, in two three-minute extra periods to win.

Schroeder, one of five U.S. players along with Wilson, Jody Campbell, Peter Campbell and Kevin Robertson, once again had to settle for silver. All five players, along with four others on the 13-man team, announced their retirement after the game.

A disappointed and shaken Jody Campbell, who ended with a team-high 12 goals during the Olympics, said before the first round, "I've come here to win the gold medal."

Typical of most of the team's players, Campbell, awakened at 5:30 a.m., swam for two hours at a local pool near Los Angeles and then worked 10 hours a day before driving an hour to practice an additional three hours, finally getting to bed at 10:30 p.m. Because of that kind of Olympic dedication, silver gave little consolation to many players like Campbell.

As the Yugoslavs celebrated their win by dunking each other in the pool and popping open champagne bottles, Campbell sat motionless for 12 minutes with his head in his hands looking down, only to be disrupted finally by a teammate who extended a handshake, a pat on the back and said, "Overall, it was a good four years."

Though gold is glorious, silver is not bad. □

WEIGHTLIFTING

TURKEY'S NEWEST NATIONAL TREASURE

Seoul had the honor of hosting the Olympic Games after 12 years marred by boycotts and, just as in other Olympic events, weightlifting in 1988 will be remembered by stunning performances and stunning developments.

At the top of the performance list was weightlifting's media sensation, Naim Suleymanoglu, the proud Turk who brought glory to his new homeland. Known as "Pocket Hercules," the five-foot Suleymanoglu obliterated six world records en route to the gold medal in the 60 kg category.

The competition was expected to be between the Bulgarians, the acknowledged leaders, and the Soviets, who have followed closely on the heels of their western neighbor for the past several years. While the Bulgarians had little trouble handling weights, they had big trouble handling the drug tests, the same trouble they ran into at the 1976 Olympics when two of their best lifters tested positive for steroids. After the Montreal fiasco, the Bulgarians promised to swear off steroids in favor of acceptable training practices. They apparently held true to their promise about steroids, but another banned substance cropped up in the drug tests to deflate the Bulgarians' global dominance. After two Bulgarian gold medalists, Mitko Grablev (56 kg) and Angel Guenchev (67.5 kg), were disqualified for using a diuretic, the distraught Bulgarian delegation pulled the remainder of its team out of the Olympics.

Hungary also lost a medal when Andor Szanyi tested positive for stanozolol, the same steroid that resulted in the disqualification of Canada's Ben Johnson in the 100 meters.

The lightest category, 52 kg, saw Sevdalin Marinov of Bulgaria in superb shape, but China's favored He Zhuoqiang was out of sync. He, coming in as the owner of all the world records in this division, managed only a bronze. Marinov snatched two world records from He with a 120 kg snatch and 270 kg total. The silver medal went to Chun

Byung-kwan of Korea who lifted a total of 260 kg.

The competition, which started out with a hot surge, cooled abruptly following the disqualification of Guenchev and Grablev. Guenchev, who lost 17 pounds to qualify for his 67.5 kg category also lost the world records he established: 160 kg in the snatch, 202.5 kg in the clean-and-jerk and 362.5 kg total. Guenchev's loss was Joachim Kunz's gain. The ecstatic East German lifted 340 kg, 22.5 kg less than the Bulgarian, to take the gold. The Soviets chalked up another medal with Grablev's elimination. Oxen Mirzoian hoisted a total of 292.5 kg—five kilograms less than Grablev—to become champion.

After the Bulgarians pulled out, the Soviets took total command and from 82.5 kg up they swept the remaining five classes.

The 60 kg division was the most talked about event of the competition. It was here that Suleymanoglu put on a dazzling display. The 20-year-old weightlifter, who had made a daring defection from Bulgaria to Turkey two years ago, was finally released by the National Olympic Committee to participate in the Olympics at Seoul, but at a hefty price of over $1 million, which was footed by the Turkish government. Suleymanoglu proved to be worth his weight in gold.

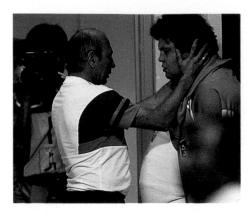

ABOVE / *Jiri Zubricky of Czechoslovakia, at 363 pounds easily the largest Olympic weightlifter, tries to compose himself before returning for a third attempt at 185 kg in the snatch. He failed and was eliminated from the competition.* (Michael Yada/LPI)

LEFT / *Martin Zawieja of the FRG won a bronze for what he lifted in the over 110-kilogram category, but he won a gold as the crowd favorite for his demonstrative failures and, in this case, successes.* (Michael Yada/LPI)

OPPOSITE AND INSET / *Bulgarian-turned-Turk Naim Suleymanoglu, or Pocket Hercules if you prefer, is considered pound-for-pound the best weightlifter in the world. He didn't disappoint, breaking world records in the clean-and-jerk and overall weight lifted.* (both photos - Bob Long/LPI)

IN THE SHADOW OF SUCCESS

The fate of American weightlifting once rested solely on the mighty shoulders of a man who was regarded by some experts as the strongest man who ever lived—Paul Anderson.

His chest, the size of a 55-gallon oil drum was accentuated by pinnate thighs which measured three feet in circumference. His arms and neck measured 24 inches and at 5'10", 362 pounds, he was an imposing sight.

By the time the 1956 Melbourne Olympics rolled around, his fame was known globally and he was a heavy favorite to win the gold medal. But it was a weakened Anderson that arrived in Melbourne, having lost over 60 pounds due to infected tonsils.

Anderson had been pushed to the limit and the coveted gold medal hinged on one final lift. The silent and foreboding yellow barbell waited—187.5 kg (413 1/4 lbs.) of cold unyielding iron. The Soviets, who had expected defeat, hovered around the stage like vultures anticipating the fall of the U.S. goliath.

Every fiber and sinew strained as the weight froze on massive quivering arms that lifted it overhead. Bedlam erupted at his feat and a tired, but elated, 23-year-old stood on the podium as the strains of the Star-Spangled Banner filled the cold Melbourne night.

America's last Olympic champion came four years later in Rome when Chuck Vinci, 26, repeated his success from Melbourne by winning his second gold medal.

After more than two decades, there are some indications that America is ready to reassert itself as a medal contender in weightlifting. Mario Martinez, the 1984 silver medalist, led the way in Seoul, finishing just out of the medals, as he placed fourth in the super-heavyweight category. He and others may put the United States in position to win some medals in Barcelona. □

Six times the Pocket Hercules obliterated world records. He snatched 150 kg and then 152.5 kg and jerked 188.5 kg, then 190 kg, to give him two total records as well—first 338.5 and then 342.5 kg. He annihilated former teammate Stefan Topurov by 30 kg. It was the first gold medal for Turkey in any sport in 20 years and its first ever in weightlifting. The news media reported that Suleymanoglu announced his retirement after Seoul—a move which may allow his family in Bulgaria to join him in Turkey.

The USSR's Israil Arsamakov, a former junior world champion, lifted 15 kg below his best but still won the 82.5 kg class by 7.5 kg. His winning total was 377.5 kg, well behind the Olympic record of 400 kg established in Moscow (1980) by fellow Soviet Yuri Verdanyan.

Without the Bulgarians, it was a foregone conclusion at 90 kg that the defending world champion, Anatoli Khrapatyi of the Soviet Union, would win. But without the threat of challenge, the spark needed to break his world record wasn't there. His 225 kg opening clean-and-jerk lift followed by 187.5 kg snatch won the gold. Two subsequent tries at 237.5 kg and a new world record in the clean-and-jerk failed, but Khrapatyi ended the competition having set three Olympic records.

The Soviet Union's Pavel Kouznetsov coasted to an easy 425 kg victory in the 100 kg division, also setting three Olympic records in the process. Like his compatriot in the 90 kg division, Kouznetsov's attempt at the clean-and-jerk world record (243 kg) also failed.

The world record drought for the previous four weight classes ended abruptly when another Soviet, Yuri Zakharevitch, showed he was in a class of his own at up to 110 kg. The victim of a severe elbow injury five years ago, Zakharevitch has returned as a dominant competitor after extensive surgery and artificial ligaments. Zakharevitch popped two world records in the snatch lift—205 kg and then 210.0 kg with his ultra wide grip and tremendous shoulder strength. His 245 kg jerk won the gold and, with it, bumped his world record total mark up another notch to 455 kg.

An anticipated clash of the titans never took place in the super heavyweight category. Joining Bulgaria's Antonio Krastev on the sidelines was another pre-Olympic favorite, Leonid Taranenko of the Soviet Union. That left Taranenko's countryman, Alexandre Kourlovitch, as the expected—and eventual—winner. Kourlovitch snatched 212.5 kg and jerked 250 kg after missing once, barely enough to stay ahead of the previous class winner Zakharevitch. Nevertheless, he had a 462.5 kg total to easily defeat runner-up Manfred Nerlinger of the FRG, who lifted 430 kg. Mario Martinez, the 1984 U.S. Olympic silver medalist, jerked 232.5 kg for a U.S. record and made a stab at the bronze at 242.5. He failed to catch the weight on his chest, but his fourth place finish was the best ranking by a U.S. weightlifter in these Games. □

OPPOSITE / *Mario Martinez, one of only three Americans to earn medals in weightlifting since 1960 (a silver in '84), again was the best U.S. finisher. But his fourth place meant another medal-less Olympics for the United States in a sport it once dominated in the 1950s and '60s. (Michael Yada/LPI)*

WRESTLING: A SOVIET SHOW AGAIN

It was supposed to be America's best showing in Olympic wrestling history. Freestyle coach Jim Humphrey was predicting eight or nine medals for his experienced squad, and Greco-Roman coach Pavel Katsen was anticipating a top-four finish for his improving band.

But instead, it was the same old show. The Soviet Union has dominated world wrestling for the past two decades, and it flexed its muscles once again in Seoul. In freestyle, the Soviets captured four gold medals and nine medals overall in the 10 weight divisions. They rang up 80 points to 47 for the second place U.S. team. Bulgaria, finishing third in the 64-team field, scored 36 points.

Greco-Roman is a rugged discipline, far more restrained than freestyle, allowing no holds below the waist and no use of the legs for anything other than standing. The USSR boasts an estimated 10,000 Greco-Roman wrestlers to America's 200, and that advantage showed clearly in Seoul. While the U.S. captured one bronze medal and placed 11th out of 51 countries, the Soviets finished first by a 72-54 margin over runner-up Bulgaria. They returned home with six Greco-Roman medals, including four golds.

FREESTYLE. The Soviet gold medals in freestyle were won by Sergeui Beloglazov (57 kg), Arsen Fadzaev (68 kg), Makharbek Khadartsev (90 kg) and David Gobedjichvili (130 kg).

Japan had a pair of freestyle champions in Takashi Kobayashi at 48 kg and Mitsuro Sato at 52 kg. The other two freestyle gold medals went to Korea's Han Myung-woo at 82 kg, and Romania's Vasile Puscasu at 100 kg.

Despite the disappointment of not pressing the Soviets harder, the American performance was punctuated with some very bright spots.

"In freestyle, John Smith, 62 kg, and Ken Monday, 74 kg, were superb," said Greg Strobel, national teams director for USA Wrestling. "Both had extremely tough draws, and still won gold medals with

great efforts. And in Greco-Roman, we had a wonderful moment: Dennis Koslowski became the first medal winner in a full Olympics in American history, placing third at 100 kg."

Smith, a senior last year at Oklahoma State University, turned in one of the grittiest performances in Olympic wrestling history. The 23-year-old was a marked man after winning the Goodwill Games in 1986, the Pan-American and world titles in 1987, and two NCAA championships. The Soviets, determined to crack his string of successes, searched their 15 provinces to find a wrestler who could beat him. Their choice was Stepan Sarkissian, 1987 European champion at 68 kg. To face Smith, the muscular Soviet pared down from his normal weight class; for all his effort, he was blanked 4-0 in the gold medal bout.

Smith won despite a series of nagging injuries. After several unsuccessful attempts to drain blood from Smith's ear, it was taped to prevent a cauliflower from forming. His swollen fingers were bandaged, too, and his nose had been fractured in an early match with Bulgaria's Simeon Chterev.

"This has been the biggest goal of my life and tonight it just came true for me," Smith said.

En route to the finals, Smith scored victories over Jozsef Orban of Hungary (11-4), Chterev (6-3), Marian Skubacz of Poland (4-2), Mika Lehto of Finland (16-6), Giovanni Schillaci of Italy (fall in 5:34) and Avirmed Enhe of Mongolia (12-7).

America's only other gold medalist also did his wrestling and training at OSU. Monday, who was 104-0-1 in high school, never quite hit his stride in college despite winning one NCAA title. But this year was his. He defeated 1983 world and 1984 Olympic champion Dave Schultz in a classic showdown to make the team, and then defeated 1987 world champion Adlan Varaev of the Soviet Union in the finals. But he had to go overtime to do it.

ABOVE / *Dennis Koslowski of St. Paul, Minn., had a leg up on most of his 100-kilogram Greco-Roman wrestling opponents, winning a bronze — the only U.S. Greco-Roman medal in Seoul.* (R.L. Hagedohm/LPI)

OPPOSITE / *In this Greco-Roman clash of the titans, blue-clad Alexandre Kareline of the USSR squeezed out a win over Hungary's Laszlo Klauz. The bottom line: Kareline went on to win gold in 130 kilograms.* (R.L. Hagedohm/LPI)

He and Varaev were locked in a fierce struggle late in the final period, with Monday trailing 2-1. With the Soviet clinging desperately to his ankle, Monday gained a reverse in the final seconds to tie the match at 2-2. That sent the match into sudden-death overtime, with the gold medal going to the first man to score.

Forty-two seconds later, Monday caught Varaev in one of his patented body locks and threw the world champion straight to his back. The three-point move ended the bout the second they hit the mat, and gave Monday a 5-2 triumph.

If Smith and Monday provided the most exhilarating moments of the wrestling competition for the Americans, heavyweight Bruce Baumgartner provided the most perplexing moment in taking the silver medal. Baumgartner had been considered—at least by Americans—the best heavyweight in the world the past two years. He was Olympic champion in 1984, and captured titles at the Goodwill Games in 1986 and the world tournament in 1986. Even though he was upset in the 1987 world tournament and wound up third, most Americans were convinced he would get sweet revenge in Seoul.

But Gobedjichvili, who had beaten Baumgartner in the 1985 world meet before losing to him in the 1986 world championship, wrestled a strategically perfect match. The tall and lanky Gobedjichvili scored two quick takedowns and coasted to a 3-1 triumph. Baumgartner, who has not lost to an American since 1982, was simply unable to untrack Gobedjichvili's high-powered offense.

The U.S. team suffered other tough losses along the way. At 68 kilograms, muscular Nate Carr, a three-time NCAA champion at Iowa State, was considered a serious threat to the Soviet Union's great Arsen Fadzaev, who has never lost internationally.

In Seoul, he was sailing along with a series of big wins, and then dropped a controversial 3-2 match to Korean Park Jang-soon. Humphrey appealed the decision and won. The official who worked the match was downgraded two levels, and the mat crew was banned for one year. But the victory for Park stood, relegating Carr to the bronze medal bout, where he scored a lackluster 5-1 victory over Japan's Kosei Akaishi.

But arguably the most numbing loss—''a nightmare,'' Humphrey said—occurred at 90 kg. There, Jim Scherr, one of the twin brothers from Mobridge, S.D., held a commanding lead over Japan's Akira Ota in the fifth round when he shot in for another takedown and was pinned with less than one minute left in the match.

Scherr, a gold medal hope going into the competition wound up fifth. His brother Bill, world champion at 90 kg in 1985, earned a bronze medal at 100 kg. He lost just one match, and pinned the GDR's Uwe Neupert in 3:31 in their battle for third place.

The United States suffered another blow in the opening round at 82 kg. There, Mark Schultz, 1984 Olympic champion and world champion in both 1985 and 1987, was pitted against old nemesis Alexander Nanev of Bulgaria. Nanev edged Schultz in the finals of the world meet in 1986, and lost to Schultz in the 1987 finals.

But, because the Olympics has no seeding and is a blind draw, world champions can meet in the first round. This time Schultz scored a 4-0 win, but severely injured a knee in the process. He won three more matches before losing to the Soviet Union's Alexandre Tambouvtsev in the sixth round, 7-3, and to Turkey's Necmi Gencalp, 14-0, in the seventh. Considered a very strong title favorite coming into the meet, Schultz wound up sixth.

Another unpleasant surprise came at 57 kg with Barry Davis, three-time NCAA champion for the University of Iowa, 1984 Olympic silver medalist and 1987 world runner-

ABOVE / *Gold medalist Takashi Kobayashi of Japan is lifted into ecstasy and one of those truly great moments of life — knowing that on this day he became the best 48 kg freestyle wrestler in the world.* (Michael Yada/LPI)

OPPOSITE / *In the 90-kilogram final. Makharbek Khadartsev (in blue) of the Soviet Union wrestles his opponent, Akira Ota of Japan, to the ground. Khadartsev won the freestyle gold.* (Michael Yada/LPI)

Opposite / *U.S. freestyle wrestler John Smith was a marked man from the start. Soviet wrestling officials conducted a specific nationwide search for a man who could beat him. But Smith grittily clawed his way to first place, defeating the designated Soviet "hit man," Stepan Sarkissian, in the 62 kg final.* (Michael Yada/LPI)

up. Davis won his first match over Josef Schwendtner of Czechoslovakia, 11-2, but lost in the second round to Ahmet Ak of Turkey, 11-5. He was knocked from the tournament when he was pinned in the third round by Bela Nagy of Hungary.

"We knew Barry needed a good draw, because he gets a lot tougher as a tournament wears on," Strobel said. "It was a very tough break for him and the team."

Veteran Tim Vanni gave one of the finest performances of his career, and took fourth at 48 kg. Ken Chertow, the only current collegian (Penn State) on the team, dropped his first two matches at 52 kg and was eliminated.

GRECO-ROMAN. Just as in freestyle, no other country dominated Greco-Roman like the Soviet Union, who added four Olympic champions to its growing roster in the record books: Kamandar Madjidov at 62 kg; Levon Djoulfalakian at 68 kg; Mikhail Mamiachivli at 82 kg; and Alexandre Kareline at 130 kg. It took six different countries to wrestle the Olympic crown from the Soviets in the other divisions. Sharing the honor of Olympic champion with the Soviets were Italy's Vincenzo Maenza at 48 kg, Norway's Jon Ronnigen at 52 kg, Hungary's Andras Sike at 57 kg, Korea's Kim Young-nam at 74 kg, Bulgaria's Atanas Komchev at 90 kg, and Poland's Wronski at 100 kg.

Because the United States has far less Greco-Roman practitioners than do European countries, the United States has never fared well internationally. But the appearance of coach Katsen on the American scene in the 1980s has raised expectations considerably. Katsen was born and raised in the Soviet Union and became an expert Greco-Roman wrestler. He emigrated to the United States in 1979, acquired his citizenship in 1984, and became head coach of the U.S. team this Olympiad.

Under Katsen's tutelage, America has made great progress in Greco-Roman, going from 18th to sixth in the world over the past four-year period. In Los Angeles, the United States captured its first Olympic medals ever—two golds, one silver and one bronze.

Still, the American wrestling fraternity was eager to earn its first Greco-Roman medal in a full-field Olympics, and Katsen felt his charges had closed the gap enough to win several in Seoul. As it was, only Koslowski, a chiropractor from Minneapolis, competing at 100 kilograms, was able to fulfill Katsen's dream.

The ruggedly handsome Koslowski, who was once tested for a role in a Sylvester Stallone movie, won three straight matches, then lost a 5-4 decision to the Soviet Union's defending world champion, Couran Guedekhouri. He then dropped a 1-0 match to Andrzej Wronski of Poland, the eventual gold medalist, but rebounded with a 2-0 victory over Jozef Tertei of Yugoslavia to advance to the bronze medal bout. There, he defeated Illia Gueorguiev of Bulgaria for a 6-0 victory and a place in American history.

The second best effort by an American in Greco-Roman was Isaac Anderson's sixth at 62 kg. Also placing were John Morgan, seventh at 82 kg, and Duane Koslowski, Dennis' twin, who was eighth at 130 kg. □

and Soviets Larissa Moskalenko and Irina Tchounikhovskai, who picked up the silver and bronze, respectively.

In the Star class, a larger, heavier keelboat, the U.S. men were not so fortunate. Mark Reynolds, a 32-year-old sailmaker from San Diego, had campaigned for an Olympic berth for over nine years. This time, he finally had it and, going into the last race, it looked like he and crewmate Hal Haenel had the gold as well. But the wind gods wouldn't have it. Their boat's mast broke, sending them to the dock early, and leaving them with the silver while a dark horse team from Great Britain won the gold.

Others reveled in the high winds and for the U.S. trio of John Kostecki, Bob Billingham and Will Baylis, competing in the largest boat, the Soling, it was a chance to battle their only real competition in the 26-boat fleet, the GDR. It was almost an America's Cup-style match race for the two teams, the East Germans winning in the end by a tiny margin over the United States.

In the men's 470 division, Americans John Shadden and Charlie McKee blasted through the fleet in the last race to narrowly grab the bronze—the second Olympic medal in the McKee family since Charlie's brother, Jonathan, had sailed to a gold in 1984.

"I can do very well in survival conditions," claimed 22-year-old U.S. boardsailor Mike Gebhardt. Gebhardt, who earlier in the regatta was awarded compensation points for a defective sailboard provided by the Koreans, finished third behind Bruce Kendall of New Zealand (the '84 bronze medalist) and Jan D. Boersma, who brought home the Netherlands Antilles' first medal.

The yachting events provided the U.S. Virgin Islands with their first Olympic medal as well when Peter Holmberg sailed the single-handed Finn dinghy to the silver, behind Spain's Jose Luis Doreste. New Zealand's John Cutler took the bronze.

Only two other U.S. entries failed to medal. Paul Foerster and Andrew Goldman, newcomers to the complex, highly technical Flying Dutchman boat, placed 11th in a fleet dominated by the Danes and the Norwegians. Pete Melvin and Patrick Muglia, hampered by breakdowns and a disqualification in one race, finished 14th in the Tornado catamaran division, which was won before the last race was over by the duo of Jean-Yves Le Deroff and Nicholas Henard from France, who wore aerodynamic speed suits specially designed for the event. New Zealand's Chris Timms and Rex Sellers, gold medalists in '84, won the silver. □

LEFT / *In the men's 470 class competition, the choppy and unpredictable waters of Suyong Bay left one man overboard and others resorting to survival-level sailing tactics.* (George Lean-Vercoe)

EAST MEETS WEST

The United States demonstrated how the sport of baseball should be played and took the gold medal in what was probably the most popular of the demonstration sports at the Games of the XXIVth Olympiad in Seoul.

And it was appropriate that the Koreans dominated taekwondo, its second choice for a demonstration sport and one that originated in their land.

BASEBALL GOLD— MISSION ACCOMPLISHED

The mission began in Millington, Tenn., on June 12. It ended in Seoul, Korea, on Sept. 28 with a gold medal.

Paced by first baseman Tino Martinez's two home runs and backed by the seven-hit pitching of Jim Abbott, the U.S. Olympic baseball team downed Japan, 5-3, to win the gold medal in Seoul. The win gave the United States its first Olympic baseball gold medal and ended baseball's run as a demonstration sport at the Games. Beginning with the 1992 Games in Barcelona, Spain, baseball will be a full-medal Olympic sport.

The United States began its march to the gold by beating Korea, 5-3. The United States next took on Australia and posted a 12-2 win in a game called after seven innings by the international 10-run rule. The United States nursed a 4-2 lead for six innings before exploding for eight runs in the seventh to end the contest.

Having assured themselves of advancing to the medal round, U.S. head coach Mark Marquess elected to use ace lefty Abbott for only three innings in the team's final round robin game against Canada. Although Abbott departed with a 4-1 lead, the bullpen was unable to hold it as the Canadians battled back to post an 8-7 win.

Marquess tabbed pitcher Ben McDonald to face Puerto Rico in the semifinal matchup and the righty responded in fine fashion. For the second straight game, McDonald went the distance, scattering nine hits and striking out seven as the United States moved on to the finals with a 7-2 win.

The final staged a rematch of the 1984 gold medal game as the United States took on Japan, who posted a 3-1 winner over Korea in the other semifinal. In 1984, Japan upset the United States, 6-3, and Marquess hoped history would not repeat itself. To ensure that it wouldn't, Marquess sent Abbott to the mound to face Japan's top pitcher, Takehiro Ishii.

A second inning RBI groundout by Yasushi Matsumoto gave Japan an early 1-0 lead. The United States, however, took the lead for good in the fourth. Martinez drove Ishii's first pitch 425 feet over the center field fence for a 2-1 U.S. lead. Following singles by Ted Wood and center fielder Tom Goodwin, shortstop Dave Silvestri lined a single to left to make it 3-1. Martinez then made it 4-1 with a RBI single to right in the fifth.

Abbott had a touch of wildness in the sixth, enabling Japan to close to 4-3. He walked Atsuya Furuta with the bases loaded to force in one run and gave up a run-scoring grounder to Kenji Tomashino.

Martinez led off the eighth with his second homer of the game to make it 5-3. Abbott used that extra cushion to his advantage as he retired the Japanese on three straight ground balls in the ninth to start a mad celebration on the mound. And underneath all the chaos were Abbott and catcher Doug Robbins.

"I'm a little sore after that," Abbott confessed. "Everyone was on top of Doug and me and my face was in the dirt. It felt great."

United States 5, Japan 3. Mission accomplished.

TAEKWONDO MAKES ITS OLYMPIC DEBUT

The ancient martial art of taekwondo made a dramatic initial Olympic appearance in the land where the sport was conceived more than 5,000 years ago and, as expected, its native sons and daughters dominated competition in the eight respective weight categories for men and women.

ABOVE / *Sharon Hedrick of Urbana, Ill., puts all she has into the final moments of her 800-meter wheelchair race. Hedrick won the gold.* (Bob Long/LPI)

OPPOSITE / *American catcher Scott Servais has just made the critical tag that saved his team a run. The U.S. baseball team defeated the hometown favorites 5-3 on its road to a gold medal.* (R.L. Hagedohm/LPI)

Korea, where 90 percent of the children practice taekwondo, captured nine gold medals, four silvers and three bronzes in this demonstration sport.

The sport of taekwondo, which involves 80 percent kicking and 20 percent punching, and awards points by the severity of blows to an opponent, drew capacity crowds throughout its four days of competition. The only country that occasionally upstaged the Koreans seemed to be the United States, which, ironically, was coached by Master Sang Lee, a native of Seoul and a 13-time Korean national welterweight champion. Lee moved to the United States in 1979 and helped build America into an international power in taekwondo.

Arlene Limas of Chicago started the U.S. gold rush on the first day of competition, capturing first place in the women's welterweight division. Dane Hee of Redwood City, Calif., followed with the women's lightweight title. For an encore, three-time world champion Lynnette Love added another gold medal to her collection in the women's heavyweight division.

Four days prior to men's heavyweight competition, 21-year-old Jimmy Kim had been confined to bed with the flu. Fighting off sickness, the young American fought his way to the gold medal bout and won in the last minute on an ax kick to the head of challenger Kim Jong-suk of Korea. It was Korea's only loss and the United States fifth medal (one gold, one silver, three bronzes) in the men's competition.

* * *

In addition to baseball and taekwondo, Korea hosted one demonstration event, women's judo; two exhibition sports, badminton and bowling; and exhibition wheelchair events for men and women.

WOMEN'S JUDO. Only the top eight women in the world were invited to compete in this demonstration event, with the medals being awarded to competitors from Europe, Australia, Asia and North America. Surprisingly, Great Britain won two gold medals, compliments of Sharon Rendle at 52 kg and Diane Bell at 61 kg.

Among the medalists were two U.S. women. Lynn Roethke of Nassau, N.Y., couldn't repeat her gold medal performance from the 1987 World Championships, but did come away with the silver medal at Seoul in the 61 kg division.

Margaret Castro-Gomez of Groton, Conn., lost to the eventual champ Angelique Seriese from Holland in her second match, but won a bronze medal in the heavyweight division.

BADMINTON. As you travel around Korea, you're liable to find groups young and old playing not baseball but badminton. It came as no surprise, therefore, that the Far East countries dominated the sport at Seoul. Korea took the gold medal in two events and China the gold in the remaining two. Hwang Hye-young of Korea took the gold in women's singles and the Korean tandem of Kim Yun-ja and Chung So-young did likewise in women's doubles. Yang Yang of China won the men's singles and Yohbo Li and Bingyi Tian of China took the men's doubles title.

BOWLING. Again, the Koreans took at least one of the top honors, as Yul Keon-jong won the gold medal in the men's competition. For the women, Arianne Cerdena won the first gold medal in any Olympic event (demonstration or medal) for the Philippines.

WHEELCHAIR. The 800-meter and 1,500-meter events for women and men, respectively, proved to be as exciting as much of the track competition. The United States went one-three in the women's division with Sharon Hedrick of Urban, Ill., taking the gold and Candace Cable-Brooks of San Luis Obispo, Calif., the bronze. Denmark's Connie Anee-Hansen was the silver medalist. Mustapha Badid of France came on strong at the end to win the men's competition. Belgium's Paul Van Winkel took the silver and Craig Blanchette of Eugene, Ore., the bronze. □

SEATTLE HAD TO WAIT

Every young baseball player dreams of playing professional baseball. Tino Martinez is no exception. But back in June he had a decision to make. Does he start his professional career with the Seattle Mariners, who made him their first pick in the draft, or does he play for the U.S. Olympic baseball team and delay that pro career? To Martinez the decision wasn't that difficult.

"I knew I wanted to play in the Olympics," said the Tampa, Fla., native. "I had a great experience playing at the Pan American Games last year and many of the same guys were coming back. We all became great friends and I didn't want to miss out."

Martinez certainly didn't miss out. In fact, without him the U.S. team may have missed out. The 6' 2", 190-pound first baseman from the University of Tampa saved his best for last as he blasted a two-run home run in the fourth inning, singled in a run in the fifth and capped his day with a solo homer in the eighth, to lead the U.S. to a 5-3 victory over Japan and the Olympic baseball gold medal.

Martinez finished the tournament with a .471 average, two homers and eight RBI. But that just capped a great season for Martinez. In the U.S. team's 53-game schedule (including Seoul), Martinez hit .402 (third on the team), drove in 70 runs (second best) and set a U.S. team record with 20 home runs. That broke the previous record set by the 1984 Olympian Will Clark.

"It was a great feeling catching the last out," Martinez said. "When they put the medal around my neck, it was the greatest feeling I ever had in my life. Winning the gold medal was worth delaying my pro career. Not many people have a gold medal."

Tino Martinez does. □

ABOVE / *Lynnette Love, left, connects with a rather unusual right-right combination to the face of her Korean opponent, Jang Yoon-sung, in their taekwondo gold medal showdown. Love was one of 11 American medal-winners in the Korean-originated sport.* (George Long/LPI)

CLOSING CEREMONIES

BACKGROUND / *The host nation could proudly give itself a gold medal during the spectacular Closing Ceremonies that again had a bit of everything . . .* (Leonora V. Goldberg)

OPPOSITE (TOP) / *. . . the endearing Hodori and Barcelona friend Kobi . . .* (Leonora V. Goldberg)

(MIDDLE) / *. . . a colorful Korean dance . . .* (Bob Long/LPI)

(BOTTOM) / *. . . a traditional red-lantern sendoff . . .* (Michael Yada/LPI)

RIGHT / *. . . a last hurrah among the 160 nations . . .* (Bob Long/LPI)

SUCCEEDING PAGES / *. . . and a final farewell of fireworks.* (Michael Yada/LPI)

CALGARY

CALGARY

Calgary sits by itself in the Canadian West, 200 miles north of Missoula, Mont., and 55 miles east of the Rocky Mountains. It is the largest city in the province of Alberta.

A century before, Calgary was a trading post. Now it is Canada's oil and natural gas capital, a city of 640,000 with computer and technology clusters and gleaming glass skyscrapers. It blossomed during the oil boom of the 1970s and survived the oil crash of the 1980s.

But it has never pretended to be sophisticated. It is the proud home of the Calgary Stampede, an annual July rodeo and wild civic party. It revels in its reputation as a cowtown, a Western outpost where men wear cowboy hats and many main thoroughfares are called not streets or avenues, but trails.

In 1988, Cowtown became Big Town. From February 13 to 28, Calgary staged the XVth Olympic Winter Games with sincerity and love. Except for the interruptions caused by high winds and spring-like temperatures, these Winter Olympics became a human, artistic and financial success.

The Canadian Olympic budget allowed construction of impressive venues for the Olympic sports. It has left the city with such permanent facilities as the $98 million (U.S. $79 million) Saddledome, the home of the Calgary Flames of the National Hockey League; the $72 million (U.S. $58 million) Canada Olympic Park

for ski jumping, bobsledding and luge; the $40 million (U.S. $32 million) enclosed oval for speedskating; the $27 million (U.S. $22 million) Nakiska complex for alpine skiing and the $17 million (U.S. $14 million) Canmore Nordic Centre for cross country skiing.

The budget also provided $6 million (U.S. $5 million) for the Olympic Plaza, the downtown park and skating rink where Olympic medal ceremonies were conducted each night. The area is paved with 20,000 inscribed bricks, each financed by a $19.88 (U.S. $16.12) donation from local residents. The proceeds will be used for future upkeep.

The total Olympic budget of $500 million (U.S. $405 million) produced a $22 million (U.S. $18 million) surplus that will aid Canadian amateur sports. Most of the income came from ABC, which paid $309 million American dollars for U.S. television rights. Other money came from corporate sponsors, ticket sales and the Canadian and provincial governments. The governments were willing allies because the Olympics pumped an estimated $1.2 billion (U.S. $973 million) into the Canadian economy.

The Olympics attracted more than 1,400 athletes from 57 nations. They brought 180,000 visitors to Calgary, including 21 members of European royalty.

Calgary had bid unsuccessfully for the Winter Olympics of 1964, 1968 and 1972. It bid for the 1988 Games against

PRECEDING PAGES / *The rugged Canadian Rockies at Nakiska, 55 miles west of Calgary, are veiled in blowing snow, an appropriate way to remember the breathtaking, but wind-shaken, venue for alpine skiing.* (LPI)

ABOVE / *Calgary burst at the chance to show the world its sparkling stuff for 16 Olympic days—and nights.* (LPI)

OPPOSITE (TOP LEFT) / *Robyn Perry, a 12-year-old Calgary seventh-grader, ignites a life-long memory as she lights the eternal Olympic flame.* (LPI)

OPPOSITE (RIGHT) / *The flagbearers of superpowers USSR and United States share the pride of being chosen to lead their delegations. Lyle Nelson, a 39-year-old biathlete, competed in his fourth Olympics.* (pressfoto)

PAGES 172-173 / *What's more Canadian than a mountie? Calgary's Opening Ceremonies just had to include a precision performance on horseback by Canada's finest, the Royal Canadian Mounted Police . . . as well as a bit of everything from everywhere, including these Tibetans in native dress . . . all to the utter delight of 60,000 eyewitnesses, including these two bundled-up youngsters.* (all photos - Lori Adamski-Peek)

Cortina d'Ampezzo, Italy, the 1956 host, and Falun, Sweden. In 1981, the International Olympic Committee chose the Cowtown.

Despite problems caused by ticket allotments, warm and windy weather and little snow, Calgary moved ahead. When the organizers sought 9,400 volunteers for Olympic jobs, more than 22,000 people applied. Local residents created an "Adopt a Parent" program, which brought 450 families from 18 nations to watch their sons and daughters, brothers and sisters compete in the Olympics.

Olympic rules require organizers to stage an arts festival showcasing primarily national talent. Calgary allocated $10 million (U.S. $8 million) for a five-week festival of theater, ballet, opera, symphony and chamber music concerts, a folk festival, a writers' festival, a book fair, sculpture, crafts, paintings and even a poetry contest. And in a city famous for its annual Stampede, the arts festival included a rodeo.

While the arts festival affected only Calgarians and their visitors, the torch relay touched a nation. It brought a rare patriotic surge to a nation often torn by diverse cultures, languages and regional interests.

On November 15, 1987, in Olympia, Greece, the home of the ancient Olympic Games, a torch was lit from the reflected rays of the sun. Two days later, the flame arrived by air in St. John's, Newfoundland, in easternmost Canada. From there, it began an odyssey through Canada that lasted 18,000 kilometers (11,160 miles) and 88 days.

Petro-Canada, a government-owned oil company, funded the torch relay that took the flame from the Atlantic to the Pacific, from southernmost Ontario to the Eskimo town of Inuvik, north of the Arctic Circle. In temperatures that dropped to 53 degrees below zero Fahrenheit, the flame traveled by airplane, helicopter, snowmobile, dogsled, snowshoes, skis, boat and ferry.

It also traveled by foot, carried by approximately 7,000 volunteers. Petro-Canada asked those who wanted to carry the torch one kilometer (three-fifths of a mile) to send in their requests, and 6,500 torchbearers would be chosen by lot. Petro-Canada received six million replies, including 4,000 from one man. In addition, the relay organizers reserved the remaining relay legs for Canadian Indians, Eskimos, handicapped, Canadian sports heroes and Olympic champions.

The flame arrived in Calgary in time for the Opening Ceremonies of the Olympics. In the early afternoon of February 13, a capacity crowd of 60,000 jammed the expanded McMahon Stadium on the University of Calgary campus. It was a cold, biting day, and spectators were warned to bundle up. Though it snowed during the ceremonies, there was no snow on the field, so the organizers trucked in white sand from British Columbia to cover the field and give the appearance of snow.

The ceremonies began with Indians from Alberta's five aboriginal tribes racing into the stadium on horseback at full gallop. There was entertainment from 6,000 performers, dancers, singers and musicians.

When the spectators arrived, they found colored parkas attached to their seats, souvenirs of the occasion. When the people on one side of the stadium put on their parkas, the colors formed a Canadian maple leaf. The multicolored arrangement of parkas on the other side of the stadium formed the five Olympic rings.

The athletes marched into the stadium behind the flags of their nation. The American flag was carried by Lyle Nelson, a 39-year-old West Point graduate from Essex, Vt., competing in his fourth Olympic biathlon. The Canadian flagbearer was Brian Orser, who would go on to win the silver medal in men's figure skating. The U.S. Virgin Islands team marched in wearing down parkas and flower-laden straw hats.

Then the flame was carried into the stadium by speedskater Cathy Priestner and alpine skier Ken Read, two Canadian heroes of recent years. They handed the torch to Robyn Perry of Calgary, a 12-year-old, seventh-grade student and a junior figure skating champion. The organizers said they chose her because she represented the youth of Canada.

She ran up the stairs of a 10-story-high steel-girder tepee that framed a massive unlit torch. When the youngster ignited the large torch with hers, church bells and sirens sounded across the city and 1,000 pigeons were released.

The two-hour extravaganza ended with nervous and excited anticipation of the coming weeks of competition. The world would be watching Calgary.

The Closing Ceremonies also were held in McMahon Stadium, the first Olympic Closing Ceremonies ever staged outdoors.

The 1-1/2 hour ceremonies featured a three-part ice show on a double-sized artificial rink painted blue to reduce glare for television cameras. The 300 skaters included past Olympic medalists Dorothy Hamill of the United States and Toller Cranston of Canada. Finally, the Olympic flame was extinguished, a fireworks display erupted and athletes danced with performers. The Calgary Olympics had ended.

Calgary had produced, said Juan Antonio Samaranch, the president of the International Olympic Committee, "the best organization of the Olympic Winter Games ever."

"The City of Calgary," Mayor Ralph Klein said, "has forever changed because now we are a city of the world." The Cowtown had become a "big" town. □

RIGHT / *Calgary's McMahon Stadium is awash with color during a climatic moment in the Opening Ceremonies. Even the audience got into the act, donning colored parkas to form the Olympic rings and, on the near side, a Canadian maple leaf.* (LPI)

BIATHLON

ROETSCH IS KING OF THE MOUNTAIN

Few American competitors at the Winter Games had as much riding on their performance as Josh Thompson, the soft-spoken biathlete from Gunnison, Colo. He had galvanized the nordic sports world the year before by winning a world championship silver medal in the 20-kilometer individual race. As the Olympics neared, the pressure intensified. Thompson was thrust into the limelight, and he knew all too well that a strong Olympic performance would give his beloved but obscure sport all the publicity and support it needed.

Biathlon, the dual sport of cross country skiing and rifle marksmanship, requires incredible endurance and mental strength. Competitors race hard for several kilometers before they must stop, still their slamming hearts enough to steady their .22-caliber rifles, and squeeze off five shots at small targets 50 meters away. There are two prone and two standing stations in the 20 km race, and each miss costs one minute. A miss at either the prone or standing station in the 10 km or the 4x7.5-km relay means one lap on the penalty loop. It takes years of training to master the delicate balances of this sport: To win, the biathlete must maintain a fast pace while avoiding anaerobic levels and shoot at cadence with discerning accuracy.

Cautious U.S. coaches and trainers danced around the word "medal," but clearly thought a top-five or at least a top-10 finish was a surety. Thompson matched eventual winner Frank-Peter Roetsch at the first three shooting stations of the 20 km. And, despite what he later called a "too-hard start," Thompson was in fourth place coming into the final stage. Then it came apart. He missed three targets. "Josh Thompson doesn't even shoot two-for-five in practice," exclaimed a team spokesman. The U.S. biathlon hopeful finished in 25th place with tears streaming down his face. Three days later, in the 10 km, Thompson slumped again in shooting and finished 27th.

It was up to Roetsch, the 23-year-old policeman from the GDR, to provide the dazzle of the competition, just as he had at the '87 World Championships, where he was on the gold medal relay team as well. In Calgary, his performance was just as legendary. He swept both individual events, the first man to do so since the 10 km became an Olympic event in 1980. He bettered his 1984 silver medal performance in the 20 km with a time of 56:33.3, hitting 17 of 20 targets. The Soviet Union's Valeri Medvedtsev won the silver in 56:54.6, and Italy's Johann Passler took the bronze in 57:10.1.

In the 10 km, Roetsch shot nine for 10 and skied to his second gold in 25:08.1, and Medvedtsev took another silver with clean shooting and a time of 25:23.7. Serguei Tchepikov, another Soviet, took the bronze with perfect shooting and a time of 25:29.4.

The rest of the U.S. performances provided no surprises. Lyle Nelson from Essex, Vt., was the proud and well respected four-time Olympian who was elected to carry the flag for the U.S. delegation at the Opening Ceremonies. At 39, he did well to finish 30th—three places behind Thompson—in the 10 km. Willie Carow of Putney, Vt., 29, who had placed 21st at Sarajevo, finished 49th in both races at Canmore. Twenty-year-old newcomer Curt Schreiner of Day, N.Y., finished 50th in the 10 km and 52nd in the 20 km. And Darin Binning, another young national champion at 21, from Pinedale, Wyo., took 42nd place in the 20 km.

In the 4x7.5-km relay, the Soviet team of Dmitri Vassilev, Tchepikov, Alexandre Popov and Medvedtsev took the gold in 1:22:30. The team from the FRG was second in 1:23:37.4, and the Italian team, which included Passler, was third in 1:23:51.5. The U.S. team of Nelson, Schreiner, Binning and Thompson placed ninth in 1:29:33.0.

Only two members of the U.S. team have retired. Josh Thompson, the rookie at Sarajevo and the hopeful at Calgary, should be the veteran with a vengeance at Albertville. □

ABOVE / *The race begins for Frank-Peter Roetsch of the GDR; he would cross the same line 20 kilometers later as the gold medalist in biathlon, a sport that combines nordic skiing and shooting skills. Roetsch became the first person ever to sweep the two Olympic individual biathlon events by winning the 10-kilometer race three days later.* (Lori Adamski-Peek)

OPPOSITE / *Top U.S. biathlete Josh Thompson, pegged before the Olympics by* Sports Illustrated *to win a gold medal in the 20 km race, had problems with his shooting and finished 25th. He finished an equally disappointing 27th in the 10 km.* (R.L. Hagedohm/LPI)

BOBSLED

Bobsledding at the Olympics had all the dramatic ingredients a Hollywood producer could yearn for.

There was the Jamaican bobsled team, with exactly four months sledding experience, which did a booming business selling T-shirts and had its own theme song. There was royalty, Prince Albert of Monaco, plus a professional football player as a last-minute addition as first alternate to the U.S. squad. There were the Chinook winds, which sent temperatures into the 60s, dumped sand on the track, forced postponements and prompted protests.

Bobsledding by its nature perhaps attracts such drama. It is a sport of raw speed, somewhat akin to auto-racing on ice—without brakes. Driver and riders shove off in a sprint start, hop in, and the driver pilots the sled down a labyrinth of icy curves at speeds reaching 90 mph. Each competition has four heats, and there are four-man and two-man categories.

The U.S. team began its quest to medal in Calgary at the Olympic trials in Winterberg, FRG, in October 1987. The competition among the 10 teams was stiff and, with the exception of Brent Rushlaw, the top spots were decided in the last of six races—actually in the last heat of the final race. The U.S. team accumulated over 100 training and competition runs during the October trials, equal to two years of sliding in Lake Placid.

It wasn't until two days before the Olympic competition that the top two positions among the three competitive U.S. teams were decided in a race-off. Drivers Rushlaw and Matt Roy of Lake Placid, prevailed over Randy Will of Endwell, N.Y., and earned the right to represent the United States in Calgary.

When the winds relented and the sand cleared, it was the East Germans and Soviets who dominated. Ianis Kipours, piloting USSR I, turned in a 3:53.48 for the gold medal in the two-man. The GDR's Wolfgang Hoppe was second

with 3:54.19, and Hoppe's countryman Bernhard Lehmann in GDR II took third with 3:54.64. Roy, tired after the demanding pre-Olympic racing schedule, finished 16th of 41 in 3:59.34, and a trailing Rushlaw withdrew after three runs with reports of a pulled back muscle.

It was in the four-man competition, the last weekend of the Games, that the cagey Rushlaw came to the forefront. The 36-year-old Rushlaw had slimmed down and shaped up to qualify for his fourth Olympics, but no one could claim he had the pushing power of his teammates, Hal Hoye, Mike Wasko and Bill White. So Rushlaw tried hopping in the sled three steps sooner while his powerful teammates provided the push, and the strategy worked fine. Rushlaw, an enormously skilled driver, sizzled in the first run, but in the second, bumped a wall slightly. His third run was good and his fourth was the best of the heat, but Kipours nipped Rushlaw by two one-hundredths of a second to take the bronze in 3:48.26. Hoppe, who had won double golds in 1984, nailed down the silver in 3:47.58, and Switzerland's Ekkehard Fasser, competing in his last Olympics, claimed the gold in 3:47.51, the smallest winning margin ever.

Roy, in USA II, was 16th once again. Prince Albert finished up in 25th place in two-man, and, in the four-man, the Jamaicans performed a frightening upside-down skid that left some wondering if the Olympics were the place for rookies, charming though they might be.

Rushlaw's fourth place made history as the best U.S. finish since 1956 and marked the return of the U.S. bobsled teams as serious contenders in this sport. Financial support and boosted recruiting efforts have helped fueled the United States' comeback in bobsledding.

"We have achieved more in the last quadrennium than in the previous three," said David Heim, the executive director of the U.S. Bobsled Federation, "and, because of the continuing support, we foresee a bright future in terms of international placings." □

ABOVE / *Bobsledding is not exactly the national pastime of Jamaica, so the sight of this black ice rocket from the sun-drenched Caribbean island nation was a genuine, and popular, oddity. This two-man team finished 30th of 37 entries but won a following around Calgary rivaled perhaps only by ski jumping's Eddie "The Eagle" Edwards.* (LPI)

OPPOSITE / *Brent Rushlaw, Hal Hoye, Mike Wasko and Bill White, who made up the four-man USA I team, perfect their starting strategy in a practice run. The team finished fourth in the final, only a blink—.02 second—from winning a bronze medal.* (courtesy of U.S. Bobsled Federation)

FIGURE SKATING

Brian Boitano was caught in the crossfire. "When I stepped on the ice," he said, "there was a voice saying, 'This is it, this is it.' And then there was another voice saying, 'Just treat it like another competition.' It was a kind of a fight, a tug of war, an exhausting fight."

It was hardly another competition. It was the free skating final event of the Olympic figure skating for men, 4-1/2 minutes of glory or gloom.

For 10 years, the 24-year-old Boitano of Sunnyvale, Calif., and the 26-year-old Brian Orser of Penetanguishene, Ontario, had been rivals. They were also good friends. Now they were meeting for Olympic gold. Orser, the Canadian champion for eight consecutive years and the silver medalist at Sarajevo, was a slight favorite because he had beaten Boitano in the 1987 World Championships and was skating now before an adoring home crowd.

As it turned out, Orser faltered, Boitano did not and Boitano won. Except for that, the favorites won the other three gold medals in the figure skating events at Calgary—Katarina Witt of the GDR in women's singles, 16-year-old Ekaterina Gordeeva and Serguei Grinkov of the Soviet Union in pairs, and Natalia Bestemianova and Andrei Boukine of the Soviet Union in ice dancing.

Witt's expected battle with Debi Thomas of San Jose, Calif., disintegrated. Witt skated well enough to win, but there was room for Thomas to beat her. But when Thomas made three errors in her four-minute long program, she emerged with the bronze medal.

MEN. The competition started with the three compulsory figures, tracings of continuous circles of variations on the figure eight, which counts for 30% of the final score. The nine judges checked closely, brushing away ice shavings with a little broom, reviewing how well each skater formed the figures and how accurately each was traced. It is not as boring as it sounds, but, as Orser learned

in Sarajevo, any skater who falls too far behind in the figures may never catch up.

When the compulsory figures had been completed, Aleksandre Fadeev of the Soviet Union led, Boitano was second and Orser third; the battle lines were drawn. Fadeev was the acknowledged master of figures, but he usually faded in the freestyle. All three men were world champions at one time or another.

Next came the two-minute short program, 20% of the final score, in which each skater had to execute seven required elements—jumps, spins and footwork.

Orser won the short program and moved into second place overall. Boitano was second in the short and took the overall lead. Fadeev faded to third.

"We knew coming in here it would be whoever won the long," Orser said.

Boitano, at 5' 11", is tall for a singles skater. Athletically and technically, Boitano was superb, but in the past he had been considered weak in musical interpretation. The 5' 6" Orser was more artistic, which could give him a slight edge.

ABOVE / *Canada's Brian Orser bobbled ever-so-slightly in his free skating program before an adoring audience of his countrymen. He skated well enough to win a gold medal on almost any night . . .*

OPPOSITE / *. . . but not quite well enough to beat good friend and rival Brian Boitano of the United States, who rose to the occasion with the performance of a lifetime—but then doesn't his ecstatic expression as he finishes the performance give it away? The electrifying "Battle of the Brians," one of the highlights of this Olympics, was won by Boitano by the narrowest of margins.* (both photos - LPI)

SUCCEEDING PAGES / *Elfin Ekaterina Gordeeva and lanky Serguei Grinkov are a physical mismatch—until they glide in effortless, mirrored harmony across the ice. The Soviet team, as expected, won the pairs skating competition, quite a feat for a 90-pound, 16-year-old young lady!* (LPI)

Both were performing programs with military themes, and the leaders skated in the last group of six. Of the 24 skaters, the blind draw had Boitano skating 19th and Orser 21st. Boitano skated as well as he ever had. He cleanly hit all eight triple jumps, including two in combination and two triple axels. The mostly Canadian crowd gave him a standing ovation.

"It was the ultimate artistic performance of his life," said Linda Leaver, his coach.

Boitano later watched a television replay and said, "For the first time in my life, it looked better than it felt."

The nine judges gave each skater two scores—one for technical merit (based on the difficulty and technical accuracy of the skater's program) and one for artistic impression (for presentation and style). Boitano received high marks, mostly 5.8s and 5.9s. The judges left room for Orser to score higher, but he had to be almost faultless.

He was not. Of his eight planned triple jumps, he landed six. He lost the landing on a triple flip and omitted another, changing a triple axel to a double.

Orser's scores, like Boitano's, were mostly 5.8s and 5.9s, with one perfect score of 6.0 for artistic impression. But the only thing that mattered was how the judges ranked the skaters against each other.

When the scores were tabulated and the technical mark tie-breaking procedure used, five judges had ranked Boitano first in the free skating and four had Orser first. By that narrow margin, Boitano had won the gold medal.

"I went out and nailed it," a proud Boitano said. "I really didn't care so much about the medal or the color of it. I wanted to prove to myself that I could do well under this extreme type of pressure and hold it together."

WOMEN. The women's competition appeared to have many role players but only two principals—Witt and Thomas. Witt was 22 years old, the winner of three world (1984, 1985 and 1987) and six European championships. She was an artistic showperson who combined personal and skating beauty.

Thomas, at 20 years old, had won the 1986 World Championship, handing Witt her only loss in five years, and she was twice U.S. champion. She had taken a one-year leave from her pre-med studies at Stanford to train for the Olympics.

To remedy a skating style that was athletic but not really elegant, Thomas enlisted the help of Mikhail Baryshnikov, the ballet dancer. He brought in George de la Pena, a former soloist with the American Ballet Theater, who worked with Debi on choreography and artistic presentation.

Thomas was the first black skater to win a world singles championship and, if she won in Calgary, would become the first black athlete to win a medal in the Winter Games.

In second place after the compulsory figures, Thomas jumped and spinned, rocked and rolled to a driving disco beat in a flawless two-minute short program. Sleek and powerful in a black unitard, she won the favor of the hand-clapping audience but less easily impressed the judges, who marked her lower on artistic performance than Witt. In a trademark performance — graceful, smooth and engaging—Witt won the short program, moving her into second overall with Thomas in first.

Like the men's competition, the long program would decide the gold medalist. Ironically, Witt and Thomas planned to skate to music from Bizet's opera "Carmen." One difference was the end: "Witt's Carmen dies, mine doesn't," Thomas quipped.

Skating first, Witt turned in a good, but conservative, performance. Though she succeeded on four triple jumps, she scaled back a fifth to a double. The door was open for Thomas.

Thomas was the last skater of the night. The key to her program was a combination of two consecutive triple toe loops 15 seconds after the start. Before the competition, she said, "For some reason, if I hit that, I feel I can do anything."

Instead of hitting it cleanly, she landed on both feet, a major flaw. Later, she missed a triple loop and a triple salchow.

"Well, back to school," a disappointed Thomas said. "It wasn't there. What a nightmare. I'm not going to make any excuses. I tried. I'm not ashamed. I'm still alive."

While the Witt-Thomas battle fizzled before the capacity crowd at the Saddledome, two skaters, Midori Ito of Japan and Elizabeth Manley of Ottawa, brought back the fire. The irrepressible 18-year-old Ito wowed the crowd with an amazing athletic display and seven triple jumps. The bubbly 22-year-old Manley, skating to music from "Irma La Douce" and "Canadian Concerto," landed five perfect triple jumps, brought the ecstatic home crowd to its feet and snagged first place in the free skating competition.

In the final results, Witt won the gold medal, Manley slipped past Thomas for the silver and Thomas was awarded the bronze. Jill Trenary and Caryn Kadavy, who train together in Colorado Springs, Colo., were regarded as potential medalists. Trenary placed fourth overall while Kadavy, coming into the long program in seventh place, was forced to withdraw with a 102-degree fever.

PAIRS. Standing five feet, she was doll-like, an enchanting study of natural grace and blossoming beauty of a 16-year-old girl. Her partner, provided a startling contrast: a lanky six-footer, he was the silent leading man who lifted and threw his 90-pound partner to spectacular heights. They were none other than Ekaterina Gordeeva and Serguei Grinkov, the Soviet Union's latest pearl of figure skating pairs in a string of champions.

They were the heavily favored pair for gold in Calgary having won the 1986 and 1987 world titles, and they did not disappoint. Their performance was studded with heart-stopping jumps and effortless landings. Their breathtaking unison in spins and jumps endeared the audience, impressed the judges and outscored the competition.

The silver medal went to Elena Valova and Oleg Vassiliev, also of the Soviet Union and the 1984 Olympic gold medalists. Jill Watson of Bloomington, Ind., and Peter Oppegard of Knoxville, Tenn., bronze medalists in the 1987 World Championships, finished the short program in a solid third place, followed closely by Gillian Wachsman of Riverside, Conn., and Todd Waggoner of Schaumburg, Ill. The battle for America's first medal of the Games was between the current and former national pairs champions.

Watson and Oppegard had just begun their long program when a photographer dropped a camera on the ice and a volunteer walked out to retrieve it while they were skating! Despite this, a fall by Watson on side-by-side double axels was the

ABOVE / *American Debi Thomas whirls flawlessly to a disco beat during her short program, but the much-anticipated gold medal showdown between she and Katarina Witt of the GDR was dashed when Thomas made several errors during her free skating performance. She still earned the bronze medal.* (LPI)

OPPOSITE / *Suzanne Semanick and Scott Gregory cut a handsome and romantic image during their ice dancing performance. Though Gregory skated in pain from a ruptured spinal disc, the pair placed sixth.* (R.L. Hagedohm/LPI)

ABOVE / *Jill Watson circles millimeters above the ice in a death spiral, with only a tenuous grip connecting her to partner Peter Oppegard. Watson, happily, survived, and the duo went on to win a bronze medal in pairs skating.* (R.L. Hagedohm/LPI)

LEFT / *Midori Ito of Japan may not have won a medal (she placed fifth), but she won hearts with her energetic free skating program and childlike ebullience. Watch for her in 1992.* (R.L. Hagedohm/LPI)

OPPOSITE / *Canadian Elizabeth Manley did win a medal— the silver, after she dazzled a delighted audience with what the judges rated as the competition's best free skating routine in the women's singles event.* (R.L. Hagedohm/LPI)

THE ICE KING IN CALGARY

A young Brian Boitano spent five hours a day roller skating, trying all kinds of jumps and tricks.

"I liked the speed," he recalled, "things that go fast. My parents started worrying I might crack my skull when I began jumping in the air, trying to do axels. But I started thinking, 'I've got the speed. Now I've got to fly'."

At age eight, he made the big move. He gave up Little League baseball and went to see Linda Leaver, a young figure skating coach in the San Francisco Bay area.

"After the very first lesson I gave Brian," Leaver said, "I came home and told my husband I was teaching someone who could be world champion someday."

In 1986, still coached by Leaver, Boitano did become world champion. In 1987, he lost the title to Brian Orser of Canada. As it turned out, he said, losing helped.

"I learned a lot," he said. "I wouldn't be where I am today. I wouldn't have taken a different route and been a better skater and competitor if I hadn't lost the world championship last year. I know myself as a person and skater more now. I'm a lot more clear on life as a whole."

In April 1987, the month after Boitano lost his world title, he started working with Sandra Bezic. She was a figure skating choreographer who once held the Canadian pairs title. She was not happy with what she found in her new pupil.

"I didn't know his artistic scope, what he had inside emotionally," she said. "He seemed to be like a robot, a bionic man."

But soon, Boitano began to embrace music rather than hear it. The self-styled "technical robot" started to skate with emotion, and he beat Orser for the 1988 Olympic gold medal. □

only flaw in an otherwise dynamic program with original lifts. They held onto their position for the bronze medal.

Wachsman and Waggoner had minor difficulties, catching a rut in the ice on a pair of spread eagles and dropped to fifth overall. The Marion, Ind., sister and brother team, Natalie and Wayne Seybold, finished 10th, delighting the Calgary audience to music from Copeland's "Rodeo."

ICE DANCING. Natalia Bestemianova and Andrei Boukine, known in skating as B&B, had won three world and four European championships and the silver medal in Sarajevo. Here, they swept the first-place votes in the three compulsory dances (30 percent of the final score), the original set pattern dance (20 percent) and the free dancing (50 percent).

The silver medal went to husband and wife, Marina Klimova and Serguei Ponomarenko of the Soviet Union, 1984 Olympic bronze medalists. Canada's Tracy Wilson and Rob McCall took the bronze to the roaring approval of the Canadian audience.

Suzanne Semanick of Bridgeville, Penn., and Scott Gregory of Skaneateles, N.Y., 1987 U.S. dance champions, finished a creditable sixth, considering Gregory skated all events in a special orthopaedic brace and in pain from a ruptured spinal disc. Susan Wynne of Camillus, N.Y., and Joseph Druar of Amherst, N.Y., finished 11th out a field of 20.

The greatest excitement and controversy was provided by the avant garde dancing of the French sister-brother team of Isabelle and Paul Duchesnay, who finished eighth. Their non-traditional jungle routine was choreographed by Olympic and world gold medalist Christopher Dean.

With one gold and two bronzes, American figure skaters brought home half of the U.S. medals from Calgary. □

KATARINA THE GREAT

In a nation in which ordinary people may wait a lifetime to buy a car or get a larger apartment, 22-year-old Katarina Witt has an expensive Soviet-made car, a three-room apartment, a Western wardrobe, and freedom to travel and do just about anything she wants. Those are her rewards for winning Olympic gold medals in figure skating in 1984 and 1988 and bringing glamour to people whose lives usually offer little excitement.

She has beauty and charm and a wonderful ability to project them as she communicates with her audience through skating. This ability did not happen by accident. It is a result of her relationship with Jutta Müller, her 59-year-old coach.

Witt was brought up in Karl-Marx-Stadt. Her father is a department director at a plant and seed co-operative and her mother is a physical therapist who once danced with a folk-dancing group.

Witt started skating at age five. Müller first saw her at 10 and has coached her since. Witt, who spends more time with Müller than with her parents, has blossomed under her coach's tutelage. A coach for 33 years, Müller supervises Witt's choreography, hairdo, lipstick color, makeup and costumes. Müller believes in style. She does not believe — at least for Witt — in ice cream (Witt loves chocolate), boyfriends and late-night discos.

At Calgary, Witt became the first Olympic singles champion to repeat since Dick Button in 1952, and the first woman since Sonja Henie in 1932. Now she intends to retire from skating, take acting classes and become a movie star.

"I do not want people to come up to me one day," she said, " and say, 'Aren't you that skater who used to be famous?' I am, and I will be, much more than that." □

ABOVE / Katarina Witt's "Carmen" died dramatically, but Witt herself merely retired, at 22, as the undisputed champion of women's figure skating. (R.L. Hagedohm/LPI)

OPPOSITE / Soviet ice dancers Natalia Bestemianova and Andrei Boukine, better known as B&B, were dashing as they won a medal to match the trim on their costumes—gold. (R.L. Hagedohm/LPI)

It was as odd an ice hockey tournament as the Olympics had ever seen. The Finns upset the Soviets, yet fell to the Swiss. The Poles tied the world champion Swedes. The Americans scored on their first three shots against the Czechs—and still couldn't win. The West Germans surprised the Americans, then lost their next game by eight goals.

Yet, after 45 games had been crammed into 16 days, nothing changed at the top. The Soviets prevailed, just as they did in 1984 and in five of seven other Olympics.

This was supposed to have been the year that the rest of the world caught up with the Red Helmets. The Soviets had lost their world title to the Swedes and fallen to the Canadians at their own Izvestia Cup two months before the Games. Their goalkeeping was undistinguished, their motivation questioned, their coach under fire. "There has been a lot of criticism about the national team," admitted Viktor Tikhonov, who stood to lose his coaching job if the Soviets came home without the gold.

That seemed possible. For the first time, the Soviets' rivals were able to use National Hockey League (NHL) professionals alongside their customary amateurs. That rule change was supposed to benefit the United States and Canada, who theoretically had dozens of current and former players from whom to choose. But it didn't.

The Canadians, who used sensational amateur Sean Burke in the goal, did fill their roster with NHL veterans but most were borderline players whose clubs deemed them expendable. The Gretzkys and Lemieuxs and Bourques were simply untouchable. "It's one thing to talk about who is eligible," said Canadian coach Dave King. "Who's available is another thing."

The Americans, who wanted only players who could train with their squad from the beginning, used but two professionals. "We couldn't get players from Canadian clubs," said U.S. team manager Art Berglund, "and we couldn't get anybody who ranked among the top 10 on their respective team."

So the United States went with their usual group of energetic young collegians willing to take a year off from classes to climb Mount Olympus. They didn't make it to the medal round (expanded from four to six teams), but the Americans delighted spectators with a gambling style which produced goals—both for and against them—in bunches.

The Yanks were the most entertaining team in the Saddledome by a mile, playing hockey the same way the University of Nevada-Las Vegas played basketball—high octane, fifth gear and no brakes. "Call us the Running Rebels," Berglund said. "We run and shoot."

The Americans scored goals by the half dozen. Problem was, they yielded them by the half dozen, too. Austria, which managed only 12 goals in the tournament, scored half of them against the U.S. team in a wild 10-6 opener.

No deficit was too large for the Americans to overcome; no advantage was too great to squander. They had the Czechs dead and buried (3-0) after six minutes, but lost 7-5 on two shorthanded goals. Then, they scared the Soviets to death two nights later.

Nobody had beaten the USSR since the Americans did it at Lake Placid in 1980, and they nearly managed it again, coming from four goals down to within a ricocheted slapshot of tying the game. The U.S. team finally bowed 7-5 on an empty-net goal, but not without a fight.

With two losses in four matches, the United States needed to defeat the FRG by two goals to advance to the medal round. Since the West Germans could lose and still advance, they were content to muscle the attacking Americans and wait for a chance to counterpunch. Once the FRG took a 2-0 lead, though, the rest —and the 4-1 final—was irrelevant.

So the West Germans advanced with the Soviets and Czechs, and the Americans found themselves playing the Swiss for seventh place. There was no disgrace there, U.S. coach Dave Peterson said. The U.S. team hadn't been expected to

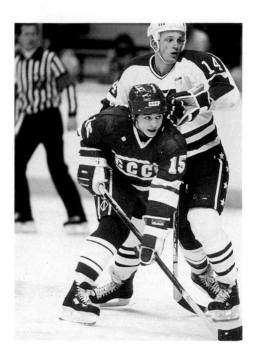

ABOVE / *U.S. forward Scott Young struggles for position with Andrei Khomutov of the Soviet Union. The hoped-for repeat of the "Miracle of Lake Placid" never came about as the powerful Soviets defeated the Americans, 7-5, but the two teams did provide one of the tournament's most exciting games.* (Dave Black)

OPPOSITE (TOP) / *The FRG's Dieter Hegen pokes the puck just past the outstretched glove of U.S. goalie Mike Richter for a 1-0 first-period lead that would eventually become a 4-1 West German victory. The loss relegated the Americans to the consolation, rather than medal, round; they wound up seventh in the 12-team tournament.* (LPI)

OPPOSITE (BOTTOM) / *Switzerland's Fredy Luethi (in red) sends Kai Suikkanen of Finland careening into the boards during the Swiss' 2-1 upset victory over the eventual silver medalists.* (Dave Black)

SUCCEEDING PAGES / *Finnish and Soviet players intensely pair up while Finland goalie Jukka Tammi scrambles for a loose puck all-too-close to his goal. Finland won the tournament's concluding game, 2-1, but the Soviets had long since wrapped up their expected gold medal.* (pressfoto)

beat the Soviets or Czechs, and the West Germans traditionally gave them trouble. "The history is that our ranking normally is sixth," Peterson said. "We usually play the West Germans for sixth."

Sweden and Finland, bolstered by former NHLers from their own pro leagues, played more cautiously than the Americans and both won medals, the Finns for the first time in Olympic history. But the predicted scramble for the gold never happened. The Soviets won their first seven games, and wrapped up the title before they lost a meaningless match to their Finnish neighbors.

The Soviets might have played listlessly in a couple of major tournaments, but they still had the world's top line in Serguei Makharov, Igor Larionov and Vladimir Krutov, as well as its best pair of defensemen in Vyacheslav Fetisov and Alekesei Kasatonov. Once Evgeni Beloshieken began playing solidly for them in the goal, the Red Helmets rolled—6-1 over the Czechs, 8-1 over the Austrians, 5-0 over the Norwegians, 6-3 over the West Germans.

Only the Americans gave them trouble in their qualifying group, and that was after the Soviets had piled up a 6-2 lead. "We forgot that the Americans fight to the very end," assistant coach Igor Dmitriev said.

The Soviets took nobody else lightly until they'd already clinched the gold medal. They blitzed Canada 5-0, scoring two goals early in the second period, and knocked out the Swedes with four goals in the first 15 minutes.

Their loss to Finland, only the fourth in 125 meetings, meant nothing. "I'm absolutely certain that if the medal had been at stake," Dmitriev said, "you would have seen a different team."

The Soviets may have been predictable, but nobody else was. The Swedes, who had won their first world title in 25 years in 1987, were lifeless in their group games, tying three matches and struggling to beat the Swiss.

The Czechs, who'd won the silver medal at Sarajevo, were humbled by the West Germans in their opener, then battered by the Soviets, Canadians and Swedes. Then, after their medal hopes were gone, the Czechs smacked down Finland by three goals.

The West Germans played magnificently in victories over the Czechs and Americans and creditably in a loss to the Soviets. Then, on the verge of winning their first medal in 12 years, they lost 8-0 to Finland and then 8-1 to Canada and expired.

Strangest of all were the Finns. They lost to the Swiss, then shocked Canada and tied Sweden. Later, with everyone expecting a gold medal duel between them and the Soviets, the Finns fell meekly to the Czechs. Resigned to the bronze medal—or none at all—they then rose up against the Soviets and took the silver.

Peterson had insisted all along that the European teams were underrated, that they were all capable of startling their betters on a given night. Except for the overmatched French, whom one writer dubbed 'Les Miserables,' it was true. The Swiss, most of whom played in a casual professional league back home, overturned the Finns and lost to the Swedes and Canadians by only two goals.

The Poles, who said they would be happy to finish eighth, tied Sweden and lost only 1-0 to Canada. And the West Germans beat the astonished Czechs, who finished last in the medal round.

Olympic expectations were high in Prague, but there were even loftier in Moscow. When the Soviets won their gold medal, their faces showed as much relief as jubilation.

"Everything is measured by first place," said Tikhonov, who kept his job after all. "Second place is considered a failure. For any team and any coach that is an incredible burden." □

LUGE

THE U.S. TEAM GOES FOR A RECORD

Eight years ago, in 1980, Bonny Warner won a chance to carry the Olympic torch on its route to the XIIIth Olympic Winter Games in Lake Placid, N.Y. During her two weeks at the Games, the 17-year-old Californian attended every Olympic event except luge. But Warner was curious about the fast-paced sport, where competitors ride a four-foot sled feet-first down an icy track. So when the U.S. Luge Association held an introductory camp after the Olympics, the adventurous high school field hockey player stuck around to give luge a try.

"After that," she said, "I was hooked."

Warner traveled to Europe where the West Germans taught her the subtleties of steering and the art of sled preparation. Four years later, she was a member of the U.S. luge team at the Olympic Winter Games in Sarajevo.

The luge competition that week was dominated by the GDR, but Americans took notice of the plucky 21-year-old who gave the East Germans a run for their money. Warner was in eighth place after two of her four runs, but she crashed in her third heat and finished 15th.

Warner came to Calgary determined to beat the United States' best Olympic luge finish, a ninth place in the 1984 doubles competition, but she knew she would face stiff competition from the GDR. In the men's race, the Europeans wasted no time asserting their dominance when 22-year-old Jens Mueller of the GDR rocketed down the 3/4-mile track in 46.301 seconds, setting a new course record. Mueller went on to win the gold, leading a corps of Europeans so strong that they allowed only one American to break into the top 12 during the race. U.S. veteran slider Frank Masley had a poor start on his fourth run, but held on to capture 12th place, his best finish in three Olympic Games. Americans Duncan Kennedy and Jon Owen finished 14th and 23rd, respectively.

One day after Masley's record performance, Warner took to the track to try for a record of her own. The GDR women, however, were less than cooperative: young hotshot Cerstin Schmidt and 1984 bronze medalist Ute Oberhoffner took control of the race before their teammate Steffi Walter, 1984's defending gold medalist, charged by them to take the lead.

"No one's going to move into the top three unless the East Germans make a mistake," said U.S. coach Ron Rossi after the second heat. But no mistakes were made and, after two heats, Warner was languishing in eighth place.

In the meantime, even mother nature couldn't slow the East Germans. When gusts up to 20 mph caused the second day of competition to be postponed, only the East German women seemed unaffected.

Walter went on to win the gold, her second in four years, and was followed by Oberhoffner in second and Schmidt in third. Americans Cammy Myler and Erica Terwillegar finished in ninth and 11th place, respectively. And Warner poured it on in her last two runs to move up two places overall and claim America's best-ever Olympic finish in luge.

The East Germans competed their sweep of the gold medals when Jorg Hoffmann and Hochen Pietzsch won the men's doubles competition by narrowly defeating their countrymen Stefan Krausse and Jan Behrendt. West Germans Thomas Schwab and Wolfgang Staudinger won the bronze. Americans Miroslav Zajonc and Tim Nardiello finished in 11th place, and the U.S. team of Joe Barile and Steve Maher finished 16th.

But for the Americans, their new record was as good as gold, and the new record-holder was already looking toward a medal in 1992.

"This year, I improved nine places over last time," said a jubilant Warner. "Next time, I just have to improve three places. I can do it." □

ABOVE / U.S. coach Wolfgang "Wolfie" Schadler (in blue) watches as Bonny Warner begins her run down the 14-turn, 3,543-foot luge course. Warner, who had never climbed aboard a luge until just after the 1980 Winter Games at Lake Placid, N.Y., finished sixth at Calgary, the best Olympic performance ever by a U.S. athlete in this sport. (Nancie Battaglia)

ABOVE / *Duncan Kennedy demonstrates how little separates luge riders from the cold, hard world around them as they streak downhill at speeds up to 75 mph. The U.S. athlete placed 14th in the men's singles competition. (LPI)*

RIGHT / *A surrealistic image seemingly hung in defiance of gravity, Steffi Walter of the GDR slickly rounds a nearly vertical turn on her way to the gold medal in women's singles. (LPI)*

SKIING

ALPINE

A SWISS AFFAIR

After the 1984 Sarajevo Olympics, Europe's alpine skiing powers were embarrassed by their showing. Of the six medal events available, Switzerland had won four medals, France three and Austria, once the world's best, only one. The United States, which had struggled for years, had been the most successful nation, winning three gold medals and two silvers.

That surely would change in the Calgary Olympics, where Switzerland, coming off a hot 1986-87 season, was ready to run off with almost every honor. Furthermore, Pirmin Zurbriggen of Switzerland seemed ready to make Olympic history. He had won two gold and two silver medals in the 1987 World Championships. Now he was about to ski all five events at Calgary, and he had a chance to sweep all five.

Well, the Swiss did well and Zurbriggen did well, though they did not shut out the opposition. Switzerland won 11 medals (three golds, four silvers and four bronzes); Austria was next with six (three golds, three silvers).

For the first time since 1968, the United States won no medals in alpine skiing. In fact, plagued by injuries and misfortune, Americans finished only 22 times in their 39 starts. Their only top-10 finish was ninth place in the women's super giant slalom by Edith Thys of Squaw Valley, Calif. The best men's finish was a 12th in the giant slalom by Gale "Tiger" Shaw of Stowe, Vt.

MEN. The first event of Olympic alpine skiing was the men's downhill, the glamour race, and the 25-year-old Zurbriggen was favored over his outspoken teammate, Peter Mueller.

The alpine competition was held at the Nakiska ski area at Mount Allan, on the eastern slope of the Rocky Mountains, 55 miles west of Calgary. On the day the race was scheduled, winds of 98 mph swirled around the top of the

course and forced a one-day postponement.

The best skiers go down the course first, with the exact order determined by lot. Zurbriggen had drawn the fifth spot and Mueller 11th, but when the race was postponed a new drawing was held. This time, Mueller would start first and Zurbriggen 15th.

That upset Mueller. Two inches of new snow had fallen the night before the rescheduled start, and the first few skiers would struggle to find the proper course line. Mueller had won 17 World Cup downhills, but none when he had skied first.

Besides, Mueller did not like the course. He was a pure downhiller who skied best on straightaways. The top of the course had a 79-degree incline and sharp turns, which favored a giant slalom type of skier such as Zurbriggen.

With all that, Mueller raced down the course and then watched challenger after challenger fail to match his time. Then Zurbriggen skied. He beat Mueller's time by just over a half-second, won the gold medal and relegated Mueller to the silver medal for the second straight Olympics.

ABOVE / *Surviving Nakiska's windy, treacherous downhill course merited at least a purple heart. These women settled for medals of different hues: Marina Kiehl of the FRG (center), the gold, Brigitte Oertli of Switzerland (right), the silver, and Karen Percy of Canada, the bronze. (Lori Adamski-Peek)*

OPPOSITE / *American Edith Thys is poised to explode from the starting gate for her downhill run. She ended up 18th, the top American finisher in this event. (Lori Adamski-Peek)*

NICE GUYS FINISH FIRST

Pirmin Zurbriggen is almost too good to be true.

His skiing feats are legendary—world junior champion at 17, world downhill champion in 1985 (three weeks after arthroscopic knee surgery), World Cup overall champion in 1986 and 1987, winner of four World Cup season titles and two world championships in 1987, Olympic downhill champion in 1988. He earned $2 million in 1987 and earned even more in 1988.

He is 25 years old and disciplined to the point of blandness. He arises at 6 a.m. and gets to sleep by 9:30 p.m. He trains six hours a day, spends some time in the family hotel he owns in the Swiss mountains and tries to spend time with his parents. He leads the social life of a monk.

"I go out once or twice a year," he said.

He was born 20 yards from the hotel ski lift. He was given the name Pirmin, which in Swiss means "first." Like all youngsters in the Swiss mountains, he started skiing soon after he started walking.

"I had the feeling he had talent," said his father, Alois, "when we first put him on skis and he didn't fall over."

He is tall, blond and wholesome. He is also reserved and detached, shy and serious. He is deeply religious, a former altar boy who still prays twice a day and has made five visits to Lourdes. His hero is Pope John Paul II.

"Being a champion doesn't mean I have to live the life of a rock star," he said. "Yes, it is true I go home whenever I can. It is also true that I help my mother do the dishes, that I play the trumpet, that I pray in the morning, even at midday with my parents before a meal, and that I go to church on Sundays. God doesn't forget me. And I don't forget Him." □

OPPOSITE / *Pirmin Zurbriggen led Switzerland's resurgence in alpine skiing by winning one gold and one bronze and only an unlucky fall kept him from another gold in the combined event. (LPI)*

ABOVE (TOP) / *Jack Miller listens to U.S. coach George Capaul. Miller's succeeding fate typified the misfortune that haunted the entire American ski team—he fell on his second slalom run. (Lori Adamski-Peek)*

ABOVE / *American Beth Madsen, an 11th-place finisher in the slalom, makes her contribution to a young fan's impressive T-shirt collection. (Lori Adamski-Peek)*

"It was my biggest goal," Zurbriggen said. "Now I have won a gold. I am more relaxed."

Mueller had no more events in the Olympics. Zurbriggen had four more events, four more opportunities to win gold medals. The most gold medals any alpine skier had ever won in an Olympics were three—by Toni Sailer of Austria in 1956 and Jean-Claude Killy of France in 1968. Could Zurbriggen win five?

"I don't think so," he said. "It's nice when I can win one medal."

His next event was the alpine combined, a new Olympic event that consisted of a special downhill one day and a special slalom the next. The results were combined into one standing.

Zurbriggen won the downhill portion by almost a half-second. On the first of two runs in the slalom, he tied for sixth place.

His major competitors were out of the running, so all he had to do on his second slalom run was stay on his feet. He did not reach the finish. He was approaching the 39th of the 57 gates, only 16 seconds from the finish line, when he hooked a control gate with his right ski. His right leg went flailing out, he lost his balance and rolled over.

"I was trying not to make any mistakes or take any risks," Zurbriggen said. "I was totally surprised when I found the gate between my skis.

Hubert Strolz of Austria, fifth in the downhill and seventh in the slalom, won the gold. His Austrian countryman Bernhard Gstrein won the silver medal with a 15th place finish in the downhill and a third place in the slalom. The bronze went to Switzerland's Paul Accola, who won the slalom and placed 24th in the downhill.

Still, there were more opportunities for Zurbriggen, starting with the super giant slalom. This was also a new Olympic event, a cross between the all-out downhill and the more controlled giant slalom. It also became the first Olympic race in the career of Alberto Tomba, the flamboyant 21-year-old from Italy.

It was not a happy race for Zurbriggen or Tomba. In fact, the rugged course, rock hard and icy and marked with tough dips and turns, defeated a third of the field of 100 skiers.

Zurbriggen tied for fifth place and called it "a hard blow to absorb." Tomba lasted only six seconds before he lost his balance, hooked a gate and did not finish. "A stupid mistake," he said. Franck Piccard of France, who had never won a World Cup race, broke his helmet when he hit a gate near the top of the course, but he won anyway with a time of 1:39.66. Helmut Mayer of Austria, who only two days earlier had entered the super GS after beating a teammate in a training race, was second, and a surprised Lars-Boerje Eriksson from Sweden won the bronze.

Now the men were down to two races—the giant slalom and the slalom—Tomba's two specialties. Earlier in the season, he won seven of his 12 World Cup races in these disciplines. Now he was ready to make his mark in the Olympics.

On the first of his two runs, Tomba took a lead of 1.14 seconds, a huge margin. On the second run, he skied cautiously and won with a combined total of 2:06.37. Strolz garnered his second Olympic medal with a second place finish in 2:07.41. Zurbriggen, almost one second behind, took the bronze. Italian fans knocked down the fence at the finish line and mobbed Tomba.

"Oh, my God, I did it," he said. "I am the strongest in the world."

Two days later came the slalom. Tomba felt good, saying, "It will be easier than in the giant slalom, trust me."

ABOVE / *Austria's Hubert Strolz won the combined gold by taking fifth in downhill and seventh in slalom.* (LPI)

OPPOSITE / *Only the camera can still Switzerland's Vreni Schneider—to the rest of the women's slalom field she was a blur, blowing past them to win by nearly two seconds.* (R. L. Hagedohm/LPI)

SUCCEEDING PAGES / *Dashing Alberto Tomba of Italy skied with bravado to golds in the slalom and giant slalom.* (LPI)

It was not easier. It was the closest men's slalom in Olympic history. On the first of the two runs, Frank Woerndl of the FRG led and Tomba, slowed by a course that had become rutted, was third. On the second run, Tomba blasted down the course and won the gold medal in 1:39.47, six one-hundredths of a second over Woerndl. Liechtenstein's Paul Frommelt took the bronze in 1:39.84. Zurbriggen, in his weakest event, finished seventh.

WOMEN. The glamourous Maria Walliser and the temperamental Michela Figini, Swiss teammates and rivals, had opportunities to win three gold medals each. As it turned out, it was the quiet and unassuming Vreni Schneider whose two gold medals made her the most successful Swiss skier, male or female, at Calgary. Still, her Swiss teammates rallied: Walliser won two bronzes, Figini one silver and their teammate, Brigitte Oertli, two silvers.

When the downhill started, the first skier was Oertli. She was blown off the course by winds of 72 mph, and the officials decided to postpone the race for 24 hours and allow her to restart.

In the rescheduled race, Marina Kiehl of the FRG, who had never won a major downhill, took the gold medal by three-quarters of a second over Oertli in a time of 1:25.86. Karen Percy of nearby Banff finished one one-hundredth of a second behind Oertli and gained the bronze medal, Canada's first medal in these Olympics. Figini, the 1984 Olympic gold medalist at 17, placed ninth.

In the alpine combined, Oertli finished first in the slalom portion, but Anita Wachter of Austria put together a third place in the downhill and a second in the slalom to win the gold medal. Oertli settled for another silver while teammate Maria Walliser took the bronze.

In the super giant slalom, Figini seemed headed for a gold medal until Sigrid Wolf of Austria overtook her by one second. Percy won the bronze medal.

Austrians had won two of the first three gold medals. Time was running out for the Swiss, but they had a potential winner waiting in Schneider. She had been winning half of her giant slalom races, but in the giant slalom here she was only fifth after the first of the two runs. The leader was Blanca Fernandez Ochoa, Spain's one-woman team. However, Fernandez Ochoa fell 20 seconds into her second run, and Schneider won by almost one second. Two days later in the slalom, Schneider decimated the field. Schneider was the only one to break 49 seconds for the first run and 48 seconds for a slightly different second run, and she won the gold medal by almost two seconds. Yugoslavia's Mateja Svet was second and Christa Kinshofer Guetlein of the FRG third.

U.S. TEAM. An incredible series of injuries restricted some of the best Americans and kept others out of the Olympics. For example, the women's giant slalom was probably the strongest event for the United States. Its entries included Debbie Armstrong of Seattle, the 1984 Olympic champion; Diann Roffe of Williamson, N.Y., the 1985 world champion, and Tamara McKinney of Olympic Valley, Calif., the only American medalist in the 1987 World Championships.

McKinney was still not fully recovered from a hairline fracture of the left ankle, and this was her first international competition of the winter. Armstrong was slowed by a dislocated bone in the left leg. Roffe bruised a thigh so badly in the U.S. championships just before the Olympics that she could not compete there.

In the Olympic giant slalom, Roffe finished 12th and Armstrong 13th. McKinney fell.

At least Armstrong, Roffe and McKinney competed. Pam Fletcher of Acton, Mass., the main American hope in the women's downhill, was skiing down a warm-up area two hours before the race was scheduled to start. She collided with a course worker and broke her right leg. □

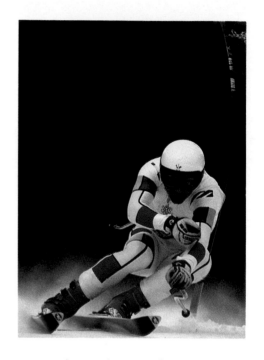

ABOVE / *Franck Piccard is a compact package as he rounds a gate on an icy super-G course that made just getting to the bottom an art. Piccard was the best at conquering adversity and won the gold for France.* (R.L. Hagedohm/LPI)

OPPOSITE (TOP) / *A growling Tiger Shaw attacks the giant slalom course on his way to the best finish of any American male alpine skier in Calgary—a 12th.* (R.L. Hagedohm/LPI)

OPPOSITE (BOTTOM) / *A.J. Kitt of the United States, who finished 20th in the downhill portion of the combined event, catches a gate and seals his unlucky fate on the second run of the combined slalom.* (LPI)

bobsled and luge runs). The 70-meter jumping event went off without incident but it was the last time a jumping event was held as planned; the last medal event, nordic combined, was telescoped from two days into one—the final day—because of winds at COP. By the Games' end, cynics maintained the initials COP really meant "Canceled or Postponed."

Finland's birdman, Nykänen, and the Swedish men's relay team were the lone gold medalists from Sarajevo to repeat in 1988. The Thin Finn, who won the 90-meter gold medal in 1984, took the 90 m again, won the 70 m and led Finland to the 90-meter team competition title. Svan, who won the 15 km event and three other medals in 1984, outran a late-arriving snow storm to capture the 50 km crown in Canmore and once again was part of the winning relay team.

If Nykänen's triumphs and the strong showings by Svan and the Soviet men's and women's cross country squads were expected, the unexpected tally would have to include the nordic combined team event, which turned into a central European picnic as the FRG, Switzerland and Austria were 1-2-3. Then a Swiss and an Austrian took the gold and silver, respectively, in the individual event of the nordic combined. And even the Czech men were at a loss to explain how they finished third in the 4x10-km relay, ahead of powers such as Norway and Finland.

A closer look at the nordic events:

CROSS COUNTRY. The Soviets—who looked so disorganized, so lackluster at the '87 Worlds when they won four individual medals and two team medals—captured 13 Olympic medals (11 individual), including five golds.

Tamara Tikhonova, looking more like Huck Finn than Mother Russia with her freckles and strawberry blonde hair, was part of the winning "Sovi-jet" 4x5-km relay unit, won the 20 km, earned silver in the 5 km and placed fifth in the 10 km. Her ageless teammate, Raisa Smetanina, who had planned to retire after Sarajevo yet came back year after year, earned her record ninth Olympic medal in her fourth Games. She finished third in the 20 km as the Soviet women collected all three medals.

On the other side of the coin, Norway—which had gone to Calgary as the only competing nation besides the United States to have won only one gold in the nordic events since the Winter Games began in 1924—got little help from its vaunted cross country skiers. Pål Mikkelsplass and Vegard Ulvang picked up one silver and one bronze medal, respectively, in the men's 15 km and 30 km, and the women's relay squad got the silver but that was it. Oddvar Braa, who turned 37 two weeks after the Games ended, was an amazing fourth in the men's 15 km.

Marja-Liisa Kirvesniemi (née Hämäläinen) of Finland, who won all three individual cross country gold medals in 1984, came out of retirement for the '88 season but was stymied in her bid for another individual medal. Marjo Matikainen, the Finn with the sunshine smile, was the only skier to break the Soviet women's grip; she won the 5 km sprint and took the bronze in the 10 km. And she joined with Kirvesniemi to gain the relay bronze for the Finns.

The U.S. team's top individual cross country result was turned in by Dorcas Denhartog of Lebanon, N.H., who was 23rd out of 52 finishers in the women's 20 km. Leslie Thompson of Stowe, Vt., followed in 25th. Betsy Youngman of Cleveland was 42nd and Nancy Fiddler of Crowley Lake, Calif., was 43rd. In both the women's 5 km and the 10 km, Leslie Krichko of Portland, Ore., was the top American, placing 31st among 53 finishers in the 5 km and 36th among 51 finishers in the 10 km. The U.S. women's 4x5-km relay team of Denhartog, Thompson, Fiddler and Krichko raced to an eighth place finish in that event.

ABOVE / *Mikhail Deviatiarov earned a gold in the men's 15 kilometers, one of 13 medals (including five golds) his powerful nordic team took back to the Soviet Union.* (Esa Pyysalo)

OPPOSITE (TOP) / *Gunde Svan of Sweden is king of this hill in cross country skiing's equivalent of the marathon—the 50 kilometers . . .*

(BOTTOM) / *. . . and the world's best long distance skier, whose 1987 season had been watered down with illness, returned to win the gold by more than one minute. He also led his Swedish teammates to victory in the relay, giving him six medals in just two Olympics.* (both photos-pressfoto)

THE SWEDE WITH SPEED

Gunde Svan was a troubled man. The incomparable king of the cross country World Cup ski scene for three seasons had something wrong with his engine during the 1987 World Championships. He sputtered through the 30-kilometer and 15 km races, ran poorly in the 4x10-km relay and skipped the 50 km completely.

Gunde the Great didn't compete in another World Cup race during the 1987 season. Doctors checked and rechecked him, prescribed rest, and combed through medical tests.

"It was some kind of flu. It normally stops people for maybe a week and a half but it stopped me for a month and a half," he said later. "I got back on skis in late March, which really meant I started preparations for the Olympics seven or eight weeks early."

Svan trained carefully and was in prime condition when the 1987-88 season opened. He won a World Cup race despite ankle-deep rain in the tracks in Davos, Switzerland, shortly before Christmas. "This was very important for me because it shows I'm really back in good form," he said.

But trouble set in during the first race of the Olympics, the 30 km classical-style (diagonal stride) event. He and his Swedish mates used the wrong wax and finished way off the Soviet pace. Three days later, wax spelled more problems for the Swedes in the 15 km.

Things turned, though, in the relay as Svan and Torgny Mogren lifted Sweden to its first cross country gold medal. And Svan crushed everyone in the 50 km.

"In the 50, I wanted to ski easily in the early part and see how everyone was doing but after the first 15 km, I saw I was building a lead, so I didn't hold back any more," Svan said. He won by more than one minute.

His two gold medals gave Svan a total of six in two Olympics. □

ABOVE / *Marjo Matikainen of Finland collapses moments after completing her frantic dash to the gold medal in the 5-kilometer race. She edged the Soviet Union's Tamara Tikhonova by 1.3 seconds.* (Chris Wilkins)

OPPOSITE / *The best U.S. cross country performance was turned in by Dorcas Denhartog of Lebanon, N.H., who finished 23rd in the 20-kilometer race.* (Ned Bonzi)

In the men's 15 km and 30 km, Dan Simoneau, 29, took top honors for the Americans. In the 15 km he placed 29th out of 85 finishers, and in the 30 km Simoneau placed 49th out of 87 finishers. Kevin Brochman of Stillwater, Minn., was the top American finisher in the 50 km, placing 47th out of 61 finishers in 2:19:45.5. The U.S. men's squad of Todd Boonstra, Simoneau, Bill Spencer and Joseph Galanes placed 13th in the 4x10-km relay, finishing in 1:50:27.6.

JUMPING. Nykänen and Edwards were truly the Odd Couple: Nykänen winning the crowd with his matchless gift for flying, Edwards becoming the overwhelming favorite with his gritty futility. On the first day of the Games, Nykänen set a hill record with back-to-back jumps of 89.5 meters for 229.1 points in the 70-meter jump. Pavel Ploc, bronze medal winner in the 90-meter jump at Sarajevo, took the silver with Czech teammate Jiri Malec the surprise bronze medalist.

In the 90-meter competition, originally set for February 20 and finally held on the 23rd after wind-caused delays, was another impressive victory for Nykänen, who set a hill mark of 118.5 meters on his first jump and settled in safely at 107 meters on his second. Erik Johnsen of Norway was second, with Yugoslavia's unheralded Matjaz Debelak taking the bronze. The best American result was Mark Konopacke's 18th in the 70 m. Nykänen and former Olympic medalist Jari Puikkonen sparked the Finns to victory one day later in the 90-meter team competition. It was the first time this event had been held in the Olympics. The team competition features four skiers on each team with the three best jumps in each of the two rounds tallied.

NORDIC COMBINED. The FRG has owned this event since taking the title at the 1985 World Championships. This country has dominated the team competitions and, although Torbjorn Loekken of Norway took the 1987 world title and World Cup championship, the West Germans have been too strong for everyone else. And, despite the absence of team leader Hermann Weinbuch because of oral surgery, they did it again in Canmore in the team event. The Soviets were sidelined by stomach problems, but the disappearance of the Norwegians and the Finns was a little puzzling, as the Austrians and Swiss earned the other medals.

In the individual event, there was an even bigger surprise. For one thing, the winds kicked up and officials were forced to jam everything into one frantic day—the last one—with athletes jumping at 8 a.m. at COP and then sprinting by car to Canmore for the 15 km race. "When we were done jumping, everyone threw everything into the car and we raced to Canmore," U.S. skier Joe Holland said. "There was no time to rest," Austrian Klaus Sulzenbacher added.

Loekken, known in some areas as "The Norwegian Rocket" because of his high-speed talent, had two bad jumps and was too far back to truly challenge the leaders. Hippolyt Kempf of Switzerland overtook Sulzenbacher at the 12.7 km mark and won. Sulzenbacher happily took the silver medal while a wobbly Levandi, battling stomach pain, held on to earn the bronze. Holland was the top Yank, finishing 19th in the field of 41 skiers. □

ABOVE / *Eddie "The Eagle" Edwards of Great Britain was most un-eagle-like in taking last place (easily) in both jumping events, but each of the clumsy, yet safe, landings was greeted by wild cheering . . . and international folk hero status followed for this house plasterer.* (Lauri Kautia)

OPPOSITE / *The view is spectacular for U.S. ski jumper Mark Konopacke as he begins his approach for a safe landing on an icy runway far below. Konopacke finished 42nd in the 90-meter event and 18th in the 70 meters.* (Dave Black)

SUCCEEDING PAGES / *Finland's Matti Nykänen, "The Flying Finn," dominates his sport as few others do, or ever have. He didn't disappoint at the 1988 Olympics, nailing three of his four jumps with machine-like perfection and winning both the 70- and 90-meter events by wide margins.* (pressfoto)

THE FLYING FINN

Matti Nykänen, Finland's talented but troubled ski jumper with the truckload of medals and trophies, entered the 1987-88 season as a changed athlete. He was going to be all business.

Nykänen, who had dropped out of school to practice ski jumping, had accumulated a hefty collection of prizes since winning the 1981 World Junior Jumping Championship: among them, three World Cup titles, 30-plus World Cup victories, a couple of world ski-flying championships, Olympic gold and silver medals in Sarajevo, and a few medals from the world championships of 1982, 1985 and 1987.

But the airborne brilliance of The Thin Finn always coexisted with a dark side. He was a bad drinker. He created turmoil on the team with his undisciplined style. He was suspended from the team during each of the last two seasons.

Now, though, he said marriage and fatherhood had helped him to mature and he was putting his surliness and unruly ways behind him.

And he did.

And he put everyone else behind him, too. Wa-a-a-ay behind him.

He had won seven more World Cup meets going into the Olympics and simply dominated every event. "Matti was jumping so far," said U.S. coach Greg Windsperger, "that officials had to make the starting point on the in-run lower to slow him down so he wouldn't out jump the hill. But that simply made it tougher for everyone else because they couldn't get the speed, and Matti continued to fly so well."

At the Olympics, while the winds at Canada Olympic Park interrupted training and pestered everyone, Nykänen calmly fine-tuned his technique.

In the end, Nykänen said, "I came here to win three gold medals and now I have them." A slight flu and stomach problems hobbled him in his bid for two golds at Sarajevo, "but I am completely happy now," he said. □

SPEEDSKATING

The pre-Olympic form sheet was clear. The United States had a chance to win the men's 500-meter and 1,000-meter speedskating events with Dan Jansen of West Allis, Wis., and Nick Thometz of Minnetonka, Minn., and the two women's sprints with Bonnie Blair of Champaign, Ill. Otherwise, the East Germans would sweep the other three races for women and the Dutch and Norwegians would dominate the three other races for men.

It did not work out that way. Jansen's older sister died a few hours before his first race, and he fell in both of his races. Thometz, weakened by a blood disorder, finished eighth in the 500 and 18th in the 1,000. The Dutch men won four medals, but no golds. The Norwegians won no medals. The East Germans took 10 of the 15 medals for women, but only one gold, Christa Rothenburger's at 1,000 meters.

The 23-year-old Blair did live up to her promise. She finished with the gold medal and world record of 39.10 seconds in the women's 500, the bronze medal and an American record of 1:18.31 in the 1,000, and a fourth place finish in the 1,500.

The big winners were 23-year-old Yvonne van Gennip of the Netherlands and 28-year-old Tomas Gustafson of Sweden. Between them, they won half of the 10 gold medals.

Four years before, van Gennip dropped her medical studies to train for skating. Two months before these Olympics, she underwent surgery on her right foot. Still, she said she hoped to win a silver or a bronze medal.

Instead, she won gold in the three longest races—at 1,500 meters (2:00.68, an Olympic record); at 3,000 meters (4:11.94, a world record); and at 5,000 meters (7:14.12, a world record). That was the most gold medals for a female speedskater in a Winter Olympics since Lydia Skoblikova of the Soviet Union won four in Innsbruck in 1964, three months before van Gennip was born.

Van Gennip was especially proud that she had beaten Karin Enke Kania and Andrea Ehrig, the renowned East Germans. In fact, van Gennip credited Blair, whose earlier win in the 500 broke the GDR stronghold and fizzled the anticipated rivalry between Rothenburger and Kania, with giving her the confidence to beat the GDR powerhouses.

"They are the best," van Gennip said, "and when you beat them you are very good also."

In the 1984 Sarajevo Olympics, the GDR won all four gold medals, all four silvers and one bronze (the 5,000 meters was not skated in the Olympics until Calgary). This time, Kania and Ehrig won three medals each, and Kania retired at age 26 with a record eight Olympic speedskating medals.

In Sarajevo, Gustafson won the gold medal at 5,000 meters and the silver at 10,000. In the years since, he overcame knee surgery and meningitis. In Calgary, he won the 5,000 with a furious last lap, finishing in 6:44.63. Four days later, he won the 10,000 in 13:48.20. Both were world records.

"How can you describe such happiness," he asked after the 5,000. "I must write a poem."

He did, and after the 10,000 he read it to reporters. There was no happiness and no poem, however, for Geir Karlstad of Norway, who was favored in both distance races. Instead, he finished seventh in the 5,000 and fell in the 10,000.

"I am 24 years old," Karlstad said after the 10,000. "The last time I fell in a race, I was 11."

The United States, which had hoped for as many as eight or nine medals, won just three—Blair's two and Eric Flaim's silver in the 1,500 meters. The 20-year-old Flaim, from Pembroke, Mass., also finished fourth in his three other races—the 1,000, 5,000 and 10,000. He had a chance for the bronze in the 1,000 until he caught his skate on his racing skin, slipped and had to put his hand on the ice on the last turn to keep his balance.

ABOVE / *Yvonne van Gennip of the Netherlands streaked to three speed-skating gold medals, and to some very fast times, in the 1,500 (Olympic record), 3,000 (world record) and 5,000 meters (world record) . . . (Lehtikuva Oy)*

OPPOSITE / *. . . but there were nothing but sad times for gold medal favorite Dan Jansen of the United States, who, though learning of his sister's death hours before his 500-meter race, decided to race on in her honor. He fell, and fell again four days later in his other specialty event, the 1,000 meters. (Lori Adamski-Peek)*

In the 1,500, Flaim set a world record of 1:52.12. Six minutes later, Andre Hoffmann of the GDR finished his heat in 1:52.06, so by the margin of six one-hundredths of a second Flaim missed the gold medal. His time was an American record, and he set another American record of 6:47.09 in the 5,000.

Hoffmann, along with Jens-Uwe Mey, became the first GDR men to win gold medals in Olympic speedskating. Mey won the 500 meters in 36.45 seconds, a world record. The gold medal in the men's 1,000 meters went to Nikolai Guliaev of the Soviet Union, who won in 1:13.03, an Olympic record.

One star of the speedskating was the gleaming new $32 million Olympic Oval, the first 400-meter indoor facility built in North America. The organizers decided on an indoor rink because they feared that the spring-like temperatures that often swept into Calgary in February would leave an outdoor ice rink slushy.

An indoor facility eliminated wind resistance which meant faster times. And the times were fast. World records were broken in eight events and the Olympic records were surpassed in all 10.

Fast times were certainly expected of the American sprinters. In 1987, Thometz and Blair won the World Cup series championships at 500 and 1,000 meters, and each broke the world record at 500 meters.

At Calgary, Thometz's illness switched the burden to Jansen, and Jansen seemed ready to handle it. A week before the Olympics, he won the World Sprint Championship at the Wisconsin Olympic Ice Rink in Milwaukee.

Then Jansen's Olympic dream blurred. His 27-year-old sister, Jane Jansen Beres, had taken a turn for the worse after a 13-month bout with leukemia. The day of Dan's biggest race of his life, his sister died.

Jansen, who months earlier had dedicated the Olympics to Jane, raced that night in the 500 meters, an all-out sprint of one lap plus a straightaway. The skaters race against the clock, two at a time.

Jansen started from the inside lane. He made a false start, a rarity for him and perhaps an indication that his concentration was not right. Then the race started, and he seemed to have trouble gripping the ice with his skates.

On the first turn, he lost his footing. He fell on his left side, slid across the ice, knocked down Yasushi Kuroiwa of Japan (who was allowed to reskate) and slammed into a padded restraining wall. He bounced up and threw his arms in the air in disbelief. Then he slapped his thighs in disgust and buried his head in his hands.

Four days later, Jansen had a chance to redeem himself. The shock of his sister's death behind him, or at least seemingly under control, Jansen said he was ready for his race in the 1,000. In the 1,000-meter race, at every timing point, Jansen was faster than anyone who had preceded him. Less than 200 meters remained, and, Jansen would say later, "I thought I was home free."

He was not. His right skate caught an edge. He fell to his knees, spun around and slammed into a restraining wall. Incredibly, he had fallen again. He cried.

"I feel a slight sense of relief that this is over," he said later.

The world embraced Jansen and the U.S. Olympic Committee honored him, presenting Jansen with the Olympic Spirit Award, sponsored by Maxwell House Coffee, an award given to the U.S. Olympian who best exemplifies the Olympic ideal at either the Summer or Winter Games.

It was at the World Cup finals in Inzell, FRG—held almost two weeks after the end of the Winter Games—that the U.S. men's speedskating team rallied. Jansen, back

ABOVE / *Tomas Gustafson of Sweden took advantage of Calgary's sleek, indoor speedskating oval by racing to world-record victories in the 5,000 and 10,000 meters.* (Dave Black)

OPPOSITE / *Imagine a track athlete achieving world-class excellence in both sprints and distance runs . . . that's precisely what American Eric Flaim has done in speedskating. The versatile American competed in four of five Olympic events, winning a silver in the 1,500 and just missing three other medals with fourths in the 1,000, 5,000 and 10,000 meters.* (Dave Black)

AN OLYMPIC FLAIM

"When I saw Eric Heiden with all five gold medals at Lake Placid in 1980," said Eric Flaim, the American record-holder in the 1,500, 5,000 and 10,000 meters, "it was a great inspiration for me. To be that versatile and that strong was really something."

In the Calgary Olympics, his first Olympics, Flaim was almost that versatile, skating in four of the five races (everything but the 500 meters). And his success—a silver medal in the 1,500 meters and fourth places in the 1,000, 5,000 and 10,000—led to the inevitable comparisons with Heiden.

Flaim was simultaneously flattered and annoyed: "It's like being a batter and being compared to Babe Ruth just because you hit a couple of home runs."

But Flaim is unique. Since the Heiden days, the sport has become more specialized and speedskaters are either sprinters or distance skaters. Flaim is solid at both.

When Flaim was growing up in Pembroke, Mass., near Boston, he played hockey. But he feared he would not grow big enough for the sport.

"I found myself sitting on the bench in hockey and thinking about how I'd really like to be out there skating all by myself," he said. "That's when I started skating on the short tracks around Boston."

Now, at 20, he is 5'6" and 156 pounds, a bit small for hockey but plenty big enough for speedskating. In fact, Calgary's Olympic Oval, because of its tight corners and no wind, favors smaller skaters.

One week after the Olympics, in Alma Alta, USSR, Flaim won the Overall All-Around World Championship, finishing second in both the 500 and 1,500, 14th in the 5,000, and fourth in the 10,000. The last American to take that title was Eric Heiden in 1979.

In 1992, Flaim wants to skate all five races in the Albertville Olympics.

"Eric Heiden set the precedent," he said. "It can be done." □

to his pre-Olympic form, clinched the 1988 World Cup title in the 1,000 meters and placed second in the 500 meters. Thometz, with 123 points to Jansen's 124, claimed second in the 1,000 and third in the 500. One week after the Olympics, Flaim repeated his success at Calgary, capturing the Overall All-Around World Championship in Alma Alta, USSR. And Dave Silk, whose best finish at Calgary was sixth place in the 5,000, won the 1,500 in 1:53.66 to claim third in the all-around.

After the men had skated their five races the first week in Calgary, the women skated their five the next week in the oval. The pressure was on the Americans to win a gold.

In the first race, the 500 meters, the favorites were Blair and Rothenburger. They had split the two 500-meter races in the World Sprint Championships, with Blair's victory coming in a rare head-to-head pairing of the two top contenders. Still, Rothenburger was the world record-holder and the Olympic defending champion.

At Calgary, Rothenburger was the first of the two to skate and lowered her world record to 39.12 seconds.

"I really didn't watch her skate," Blair said, "but I did see her time. I knew before the race I had to go in world-record time."

Blair did just that. Fueled by a peanut butter and jelly sandwich, she skated two one-hundredths of a second faster—about the length of a skate blade—and won the gold medal.

"When I crossed the finish line," Blair said, "I looked at the scoreboard, and it brought tears to my eyes. I think it was the happiest moment of my life. When they played the national anthem, I think it was the second." □

CHAMPAIGN BONNIE

In 1964, Eleanor Blair was about to give birth in Cornwall, N.Y., to her sixth and last child. Her husband, Charlie, dropped her off at the hospital. Then he drove to nearby Yonkers, where his five other children would compete in a speedskating meet and he would be a timer.

A few hours later, the public-address system gave the news to Charlie Blair and everyone else.

"Well," intoned the announcer, "the Blair family has just added another female skater."

They named her Bonnie, and like her brothers and sisters she became a speedskater. All but one won national titles. Bonnie became the most successful, winning a gold and a bronze medal in the 1988 Calgary Olympics.

At 23, 5'5" and 125 pounds, Bonnie Blair was the best technical skater on that U.S. Olympic team, according to her coach Mike Crowe. She certainly had been skating long enough.

When she started at two, her parents could not find a skate small enough, so she had to wear shoes inside her skates. At four, when she competed in peewee races, she often skipped the finals and took a nap instead.

She has lived most of her life in Champaign, Ill., where the Patrolmen's Benevolent Association became her chief financial supporter. She started skating there in short-track pack races. In 1979, a friend talked her into trying an Olympic-size 400-meter track.

In her debut on the large track, at the age of 15, she qualified for the finals of the 1980 U.S. Olympic trials. In her next race, she finished seventh (the first five made the 1980 Olympic team). In 1984, she made the Olympic team and finished eighth in the 500 meters. In 1988, she won it.

"Not everybody gets to win," she said. "I'm really one of the lucky ones. In a way, it's a relief that it's over, but in a way it's a little sad." □

OPPOSITE / *Fueled by a peanut butter and jelly sandwich and funded by the Patrolmen's Benevolent Association of Champaign, Ill., Bonnie Blair edged the GDR's Christa Rothenburger by the length of a skate blade to win the 500-meter gold in world-record time . . .* (Dave Black)

ABOVE / *. . . but Rothenburger returned to top form in the 1,000 meters, also in world-best time, while Blair took third.* (Dave Black)

HOW ABOUT A DEMONSTRATION?

In the Winter Olympics, the host nation is allowed to include one demonstration sport to showcase a sport unique to itself.

Canada chose curling as its demonstration sport, a sport whose popularity in that country rivals baseball in the United States. In addition, there were two demonstration events—freestyle skiing and short-track speedskating and one exhibition event — disabled skiing.

CURLING. This game, developed in Scotland about 400 years ago, has become Canada's favorite participation team sport. It was a demonstration sport in the first four Winter Olympics, starting in 1924.

Curling is an ice sport of finesse and strategy and includes elements of shuffleboard, lawn bowling and bocce. It is played on an indoor ice sheet that is 146 feet long and 15 feet wide. Champion curlers, like champion golfers, must display a fine touch and have great mental toughness.

One member of a four-member team slides a 20-kilogram (44-pound) granite stone toward a bull's-eye, called the "house," frozen into the ice near the far end. The slider's teammates use brooms to vigorously sweep the ice in front of the moving stone to make it travel farther and straighter or, in other words, "curl" less.

The idea of the game is to place more stones closer to the center of the house than the opponents do. As in shuffleboard, knocking away an opponent's stone, called a take-out, is part of the strategy and fun. A team gets one point for each stone closer to the house than the opponent's closest stone.

A curling match generally lasts two to two and one-half hours and has 10 ends or innings. In each end, each player delivers two stones, with the teams alternating deliveries.

The sport attracts participants of all ages. The U.S. men's team included Bob Christman, Tom Locken, Bob Nichols and Bud Somerville, aged 45, 45, 40 and 50, respectively. On the other hand, Erika Brown on the U.S. women's team

turned 15 years old three weeks before the Olympics. Carla Casper, Lori Mountford and Lisa Schoenberg rounded out the women's team.

The Olympic men's competition consisted of an eight-team round-robin tournament, followed by playoffs; a similar format was used for women. Canada was favored to win both gold medals.

The men's round-robin ended with Switzerland and Canada leading with 5-2 records. Because Switzerland had beaten Canada in the round-robin, it moved directly to the final. The semifinal matched Canada against the winner of the tiebreaker games involving the United States, Norway and Sweden, all with 4-3 records. Norway won the tiebreakers, then defeated Canada, 8-5, in the semifinal and Switzerland, 10-2, in the final.

A disappointed Canadian team, the same team that had won the 1986 World Championships, settled for the bronze.

In the women's round-robin, Sweden and Canada led with 5-2 records, and Sweden drew a bye into the final. The United States, the FRG and Norway finished with 4-3 records, with the Norwegian women, like the Norwegian men, winning the tiebreaker competition.

ABOVE / *Short-track speedskating, sort of a stock-car race on skates, lent plenty of chilling, spilling excitement to the 1988 Winter Games. Here the three medalists in the 1,000-meter race lead the pack into an always eventful turn.* (R.L. Hagedohm/LPI)

OPPOSITE / *Didlier Meda of France will fly, flip, twist, contort, and who knows what else, and do it stylishly, before alighting on snow again. Meda won the silver in the men's freestyle skiing aerial event, witnessed by 60,000 spectators.* (LPI)

Canada then struggled to a 6-5 victory over Norway in the semifinal and a 7-5 victory over Sweden in the final. Canada won the final with two points in the final end, the equivalent of sinking a 15-foot birdie putt on the 18th hole in golf to win.

FREESTYLE SKIING. When this competition first surfaced in the 1960s, it was known as hot-dog skiing and its participants often were undisciplined exhibitionists. In 1979, the event came under the umbrella of the International Ski Federation and became more sophisticated.

Scoring is subjective and based generally on how difficult the maneuvers are and how well they are performed. There are three types of competition in freestyle skiing:

Aerials—The skiers ski one at a time down a steep slope onto a sharply pitched ramp and then perform somersaults and twists while airborne. The aerials are the most spectacular and most dangerous of the freestyle events, with jumps as complex as a triple somersault with four twists.

Moguls—The skiers race one at a time down a steep hill, about 200 meters long and studded with treacherous mounds, called moguls, up to six feet high. They perform two aerial maneuvers en route. Speed also enters into the scoring of this event.

Ballet—Performing one at a time to music—like figure skaters on short skis—the competitors ski to a choreographed routine down a gentle slope.

The women's and men's gold medalists in freestyle skiing at the Games were Melanie Palenik of Littleton, Colo., and Jean-Marc Rozon of Sherbrooke, Quebec, in aerials; Tatjan Mittermaier of the FRG and Håkan Hansson of Sweden in moguls; and Christine Rossi of France and Herman Reitberger of the FRG in ballet. Of the 18 medals, the United States won one gold, two silvers and one bronze.

SHORT-TRACK SPEEDSKATING. In Olympic-style speedskating competition, skaters race against the clock, two at a time, over a 400-meter oval. In short-track speedskating, the skaters race in packs of four to six over a 122-yard oval laid on the surface of a hockey rink. Short-track skating was invented in the late 19th century when indoor rinks were introduced, and it has spawned such successful Olympic large-oval medalists as Bonnie Blair and Eric Flaim.

The sport has elements of stock-car racing and roller derby. Though body or elbow checks are illegal, there is considerable contact and there are many spills. The skaters wear helmets, knee pads and shin guards. Their $700 skates, custom-made of fiberglass and leather, have razor-sharp blades.

The Olympic program in Calgary had four individual races and a relay for both men and women. The biggest winners were the Canadians, who won a medal in every event—one gold, six silvers and three bronzes. The U.S. men's 3,000-meter relay team came the closest to winning one of the 30 medals when it placed fourth overall, the best U.S. finish.

Sylvie Daigle of Canada won four medals—one gold (in the women's 1,500 meters, two silvers (1,000 and 3,000 m) and one bronze (3,000-m relay). Earlier that month, she had regained her world overall championship.

The only double winner was Wilfred O'Reilly, a 23-year-old business student from Great Britain. He won the men's 500 meters in 44.80 seconds and the 1,000 meters in 1:33.44, both world short-track records.

DISABLED SKIING. There were two exhibition competitions each for men and women in Calgary—a 5,000-meter cross country race for blind skiers and a modified giant slalom over a three-quarter mile course for above-the-knee amputees.

In the cross country skiing, which involved 10 men and five women, each skier was led by a sighted guide. The guides skied just in front of the competitors and advised them of the course conditions and upcoming terrain.

ABOVE / *Fifteen-year-old Erika Brown, the "third" on the U.S. curling team, prepares, in the sport's parlance, to shoot a rock toward the house. Though curling is largely unfamiliar to people in the United States, the sport played to capacity audiences throughout the Olympics in Calgary.* (courtesy of Steve Brown)

OPPOSITE / *This American ski team swept its event: gold medal-winner Diana Golden, center, is joined by silver medalist Catherine Gentile, left, and Martha Hill on the victors' platform after their winning—in more ways than one—performances in women's disabled alpine skiing.* (LPI)

SKIING'S GOLDEN GIRL

Diana Golden started skiing at age five. At 12, she contracted bone cancer, and her right leg was amputated above the knee.

"The first thing I asked the doctor," the 24-year-old Golden recalled, "was if I could ski. He said yes. I said O.K. I was a mediocre, rockabout skier, but I loved it."

She became the world's most successful amputee skier. She won eight U.S. disabled championships, four gold medals in the 1986 World Disabled Championships and two golds in the 1988 World Winter Games for the Disabled. At Calgary, Golden won the gold medal in the modified giant slalom for amputees, an Olympic exhibition event.

She has campaigned for regular World Cup and national championship races for world-class disabled skiers. Not surprisingly, Golden has competed regularly in races in the Northeast for non-disabled skiers.

"She throws her body down the hill with reckless abandon," said Jack Benedick, the competition director for the U.S. disabled ski team, "no different than any elite able-bodied athlete."

At age 24, Golden has earned a degree in English literature from Dartmouth and holds a firm vision of herself and her role.

"People are always telling me how brave I am," she said. "I don't consider myself brave. It's too easy to excuse yourself if you think of yourself as brave. This is an experiment, a journey. No one has tested the limits. I hope I'll have the energy to stick with this at least a couple more years and see how far I can go."

"I would not trade the last 12 years for anything. If my leg magically reappeared down the road, great. But I miss the leg like I miss a tooth." □

The winners were Hans Anton Aalien of Norway among the men and Veronika Preining of Austria among the women. Their gold medals were etched in Braille.

John Novotny, a 28-year-old mental health therapist from Brekenridge, Colo., finished sixth among the men. He lost his sight at age two from cancer of the retina. His guide was Craig Ward of Aspen, Colo., a former member of the U.S. cross country ski team.

"People say, 'You can't ski. You're blind,' " Novotny said. "That's one of the greatest feats in being here."

"This is an exhibition event for exceptional athletes who happened to be disabled, not for disabled athletes," Ward said.

In the modified giant slalom, most of the skiers used one ski with two outrigger ski poles to help keep their balance. Diana Golden of Lincoln, Mass., used two ordinary ski poles and won the five-women competition handily, while teammates Catherine Gentile of Vail, Colo., and Martha Hill of Winter Park, Colo., were second and third, respectively.

The winner in the field of 13 men was Alexander Spitz of the FRG, with American Greg Mannino of Yorba Linda, Calif., taking the silver. □

1988 RESULTS

XVth OLYMPIC WINTER GAMES

Calgary, Alberta, Canada
February 13 - 28, 1988

WR = World record   DNS = Did not start
OR = Olympic record   DNF = Did not finish
T = Tie   DQ = Disqualified

BIATHLON

10 KILOMETERS / February 23

No. of countries: 22   No. of entries: 72
No. of finishers: 72

RANK	CTRY	ATHLETE	TIME
1	GDR	ROETSCH, Frank-Peter	25:08.1
2	URS	MEDVEDTSEV, Valeri	25:23.7
3	URS	TCHEPIKOV, Serguei	25:29.4
4	GDR	ANDERS, Birk	25:51.8
5	GDR	SEHMISCH, Andre	25:52.3
6	GDR	LUCK, Frank	25:57.6
7	FIN	PIIPPONEN, Tapio	26:02.2
8	ITA	PASSLER, Johann	26:07.7
27	USA	THOMPSON, Josh	27:27.7
30T	USA	NELSON, Lyle	27:34.3
49	USA	CAROW, Willie	28:19.6
50	USA	SCHREINER, Curtis	28:19.9

20 KILOMETERS / February 20

No. of countries: 21   No. of entries: 71
No. of finishers: 68

RANK	CTRY	ATHLETE	SKI TIME	PENALTIES	TOTAL
1	GDR	ROETSCH, Frank-Peter	53:33.3	3	56:33.3
2	URS	MEDVEDTSEV, Valeri	54:54.6	2	56:54.6
3	ITA	PASSLER, Johann	55:10.1	2	57:10.1
4	URS	TCHEPIKOV, Serguei	56:17.5	1	57:17.5
5	URS	KASHKAROV, Yuri	55:43.1	2	57:43.1
6	NOR	KVALFOSS, Eirik	54:54.6	3	57:54.6
7	GDR	SEHMISCH, Andre	55:11.4	3	58:11.4
8	FIN	PIIPPONEN, Tapio	55:18.3	3	58:18.3
25	USA	THOMPSON, Josh	56:29.4	5	1:01:29.4
42	USA	BINNING, Darin	59:54.8	4	1:03:54.8
49	USA	CAROW, Willie	1:00.10.1	5	1:05:10.1
52	USA	SCHREINER, Curtis	1:00.22.7	5	1:05:22.7

4×7.5-KILOMETER RELAY / February 26

No. of countries: 16   No. of entries: 16
No. of finishers: 16

RANK	CTRY	ATHLETES	TIME
1	URS	VASSILIEV, Dmitri / TCHEPIKOV, Serguei POPOV, Alexandre / MEDVEDTSEV, Valeri	1:22:30.0
2	FRG	REITER, Ernst / HOECK, Stefan ANGERER, Peter / FISCHER, Friedrich	1:23:37.4
3	ITA	KIEM, Werner / TASCHLER, Gottlieb PASSLER, Johann / ZINGERLE, Andreas	1:23:51.5
4	AUT	LENGAUER STOCKNER, Anton / HOFSTAETTER, Bruno / SCHULER, Franz / EDER, Alfred	1:24:17.6
5	GDR	WIRTH, Juergen / ROETSCH, Frank-Peter JACOB, Matthias / SEHMISCH, Andre	1:24:28.4
6	NOR	EINANG, Geir / LOBERG, Frode FENNE, Gisle / KVALFOSS, Eirik	1:25:57.0
7	SWE	SJODEN, Peter / LOFGREN, Mikael WESTLING, Roger / ANDERSSON, Leif	1:29:11.9
8	BUL	BOJILOV, Vassil / VELITCHKOV, Vladimir VIDENOV, Krassimir / VODENITCHAROV, Hristo	1:29:24.9
9	USA	NELSON, Lyle / SCHREINER, Curtis BINNING, Darin / THOMPSON, Josh	1:29:33.0

BOBSLED

TWO-MAN / February 22

No. of countries: 22   No. of entries: 41
No. of finishers: 38   4 runs/elapsed time

RANK	CTRY	ATHLETES	TIME
1	URS-I	KIPOURS, Ianis / KOZLOV, Vladimir	3:53.48
2	GDR-I	HOPPE, Wolfgang / MUSIOL, Bogdan	3:54.19
3	GDR-II	LEHMANN, Bernhard / HOYER, Mario	3:54.64
4	SUI-II	WEDER, Gustav / ACKLIN, Donat	3:56.06
5	AUT-I	APPELT, Ingo / WINKLER, Harald	3:56.49
6	SUI-I	HILTERBRAND, Hans / KISER, Andre	3:56.52
7	FRG-I	FISCHER, Anton / LANGEN, Christoph	3:56.62
8	AUT-II	KIENAST, Peter / MARK, Christian	3:56.91
16	USA-II	ROY, Matt / HERBERICH, Jim	3:59.34
DNF	USA-I	RUSHLAW, Brent / ALJOE, Mike	—

FOUR-MAN / February 28

No. of countries: 17   No. of entries: 26
No. of finishers: 25   4 runs/elapsed time

RANK	CTRY	ATHLETES	TIME
1	SUI-I	FASSER, Ekkehard / MEIER, Kurt FAESSLER, Marcel / STOCKER, Werner	3:47.51
2	GDR-I	HOPPE, Wolfgang / SCHAUERHAMMER, Dietmar / MUSIOL, Bogdan / VOGE, Ingo	3:47.58
3	URS-II	KIPOURS, Ianis / OSSIS, Gountis TONE, Iourin / KOZLOV, Vladimir	3:48.26
4	USA-I	RUSHLAW, Brent / HOYE, Hal WASKO, Mike / WHITE, Bill	3:48.28
5	URS-I	POIKANS, Maris / KLIAVINCH, Olafs BERZOUPS, Ivars / IAOUDZEMS, Iouris	3:48.35
6	AUT-I	KIENAST, Peter / SIEGL, Franz MARK, Christian / TEIGL, Kurt	3:48.65
7	AUT-II	APPELT, Ingo / MUIGG, Josef REDL, Gerhard / WINKLER, Harald	3:48.95
8	GDR-II	RICHTER, Detlef / FERL, Bodo JAHN, Ludwig / SZELIG, Alexander	3:49.06
16	USA-II	ROY, Matt / PLADEL, Scott HERBERICH, Jim / SHIMER, Brian	3:51.23

FIGURE SKATING

CF = Compulsory Figures / SP = Short Program
FS = Free Skating / FP = Factor Placement

WOMEN'S SINGLES / February 27

No. of countries: 24   No. of entries: 31
No. of finishers: 30

RANK	CTRY	ATHLETE	CF	SP	FS	FP
1	GDR	WITT, Katarina	3	1	2	4.2
2	CAN	MANLEY, Elizabeth	4	3	1	4.6
3	USA	THOMAS, Debra	2	2	4	6.0
4	USA	TRENARY, Jill	5	6	5	10.4
5	JPN	ITO, Midori	10	4	3	10.6
6	FRG	LEISTNER, Claudia	6	9	6	13.2
7	URS	IVANOVA, Kira	1	10	9	13.6
8	URS	KONDRACHEVA, Anna	9	7	7	15.2
DNF	USA	KADAVY, Caryn	7	5	—	—

MEN'S SINGLES / February 20

No. of countries: 21   No. of entries: 28
No. of finishers: 24

RANK	CTRY	ATHLETE	CF	SP	FS	FP
1	USA	BOITANO, Brian	2	2	1	3.0
2	CAN	ORSER, Brian	3	1	2	4.2
3	URS	PETRENKO, Victor	6	3	3	7.8
4	URS	FADEEV, Alexandre	1	9	4	8.2
5	POL	FILIPOWSKI, Grzegorz	7	4	5	10.8
6	URS	KOTIN, Vladimir	5	6	8	13.4
7	USA	BOWMAN, Christopher	8	5	7	13.8
8	CAN	BROWNING, Kurt	11	7	6	15.4
10	USA	WYLIE, Paul	12	8	9	19.4

PAIRS / February 16

No. of countries: 8   No. of entries: 15
No. of finishers: 15

RANK	CTRY	ATHLETES	SP	FS	FP
1	URS	GORDEEVA, Ekaterina GRINKOV, Serguei	1	1	1.4
2	URS	VALOVA, Elena VASSILIEV, Oleg	2	2	2.8
3	USA	WATSON, Jill OPPEGARD, Peter	3	3	4.2
4	URS	SELEZNEVA, Larissa MAKAROV, Oleg	6	4	6.4
5	USA	WACHSMAN, Gillian WAGGONER, Todd	4	5	6.6
6	CAN	BENNING, Denise JOHNSTON, Lyndon	5	7	9.0
7	GDR	SCHWARZ, Peggy KOENIG, Alexander	11	6	10.4
8	CAN	HOUGH, Christine LADRET, Doug	8	8	11.2
10	USA	SEYBOLD, Natalie SEYBOLD, Wayne	10	10	14.0

ICE DANCING / February 23

CD = Compulsory Dance / OSP = Original Set Pattern Dance / FD = Free Dance

No. of countries: 14   No. of entries: 20
No. of finishers: 20

RANK	CTRY	ATHLETES	CD	OSP	FD	FP
1	URS	BESTEMIANOVA, Natalia BOUKINE, Andrei	1	1	1	2.0
2	URS	KLIMOVA, Marina PONOMARENKO, Serguei	2	2	2	4.0
3	CAN	WILSON, Tracy McCALL, Robert	3	3	3	6.0
4	URS	ANNENKO, Natalia SRETENSKI, Guenrikh	4	4	4	8.0
5	AUT	BECK, Kathrin BECK, Christoff	5	5	5	10.0
6	USA	SEMANICK, Suzanne GREGORY, Scott	6	6	6	12.0
7	HUN	ENGI, Klara TOTH, Attila	7	7	7	14.0
8	FRA	DUCHESNAY, Isabelle DUCHESNAY, Paul	8	8	8	16.0
11	USA	WYNNE, Susan DRUAR, Joseph	11	11	11	22.0

ICE HOCKEY

No. of countries: 12   No. of entries: 12
No. of finishers: 12

OVERALL RANK	CTRY	WON	TIED	LOST	PTS	USA GAME SCORES	
1	URS	4	0	1	8	USA vs. AUT	10-6
2	FIN	3	1	1	7	USA vs. TCH	5-7
3	SWE	2	2	1	6	USA vs. URS	5-7
4	CAN	2	1	2	5	USA vs. NOR	6-3
5	FRG	1	0	4	2	USA vs. FRG	1-4
6	TCH	1	0	4	2	USA vs. SUI	8-4
7	USA	-	-	-	-		
8	SUI	-	-	-	-		

	URS	FIN	SWE	FRG	CAN	TCH
URS	–	1-2	7-1	6-3	5-0	6-1
FIN		–	3-3	8-0	3-1	2-5
SWE			–	3-2	2-2	6-2
FRG				–	1-8	2-1
CAN					–	6-3
TCH						–

LUGE

WOMEN'S SINGLES / February 18

No. of countries: 14   No. of entries: 24
No. of finishers: 24   4 runs/elapsed time

RANK	CTRY	ATHLETE	TIME
1	GDR	WALTER, Steffi	3:03.973
2	GDR	OBERHOFFNER, Ute	3:04.105
3	GDR	SCHMIDT, Cerstin	3:04.181
4	FRG	BILGERI, Veronika	3:05.670
5	URS	ANTIPOVA, Ioulia	3:05.787
6	USA	WARNER, Bonny	3:06.056
7	CAN	DOYON, Marie Claude	3:06.211
8	URS	DANILINA, Nadejda	3:06.364
9	USA	MYLER, Cameron	3:06.835
11	USA	TERWILLEGAR, Erica	3:07.291

MEN'S SINGLES / February 15

No. of countries: 18   No. of entries: 38
No. of finishers: 36   4 runs/elapsed time

RANK	CTRY	ATHLETE	TIME
1	GDR	MUELLER, Jens	3:05.548
2	FRG	HACKL, Georg	3:05.916
3	URS	KHARTCHENKO, Iouri	3:06.274
4	GDR	JACOB, Thomas	3:06.358
5	GDR	WALTER, Michael	3:06.933
6	URS	DANILINE, Serguei	3:07.098
7	FRG	SCHETTEL, Johannes	3:07.371
8	ITA	RAFFL, Hansjorg	3:07.525
12	USA	MASLEY, Frank	3:07.943
14	USA	KENNEDY, Duncan	3:08.472
23	USA	OWEN, Jonathan	3:11.464

MEN'S DOUBLES / February 19

No. of countries: 11   No. of entries: 18
No. of finishers: 18   2 runs / elapsed time

RANK	CTRY	ATHLETES	TIME
1	GDR	HOFFMANN, Joerg / PIETZSCH, Jochen	1:31.940
2	GDR	KRAUSSE, Stefan / BEHRENDT, Jan	1:32.039
3	FRG	SCHWAB, Thomas / STAUDINGER, Wolfgang	1:32.274
4	FRG	ILSANKER, Stefan / HACKL, Georg	1:32.298
5	AUT	FLUCKINGER, Georg / MAZENREITER, Robert	1:32.364
6	URS	MELNIK, Vitali / ALEXEEV, Dmitri	1:32.459
7	ITA	BRUGGER, Kurt / HUBER, Wilfried	1:32.553
7	URS	BELOOUSSOV, Evgueni / BELIAKOV, Alexandre	1:32.553
11	USA	ZAJONC, Miroslav / NARDIELLO, Tim	1:33.320
16	USA	BARILE, Joseph / MAHER, Steve	1:34.963

SKIING

ALPINE

WOMEN'S DOWNHILL / February 19

No. of countries: 14   No. of entries: 37
No. of finishers: 28   Did not start: 2

RANK	CTRY	ATHLETE	TIME
1	FRG	KIEHL, Marina	1:25.86
2	SUI	OERTLI, Brigitte	1:26.61
3	CAN	PERCY, Karen	1:26.62
4	SUI	WALLISER, Maria	1:26.89
5	CAN	GRAHAM, Laurie	1:26.99
6	AUT	KRONBERGER, Petra	1:27.03
7	FRG	MOESENLECHNER, Regine	1:27.16
8	AUT	KIRCHLER, Elisabeth	1:27.19
18	USA	THYS, Edith	1:28.53
20	USA	KRONE, Kristin	1:29.13
DNF	USA	LINDH, Hilary	—

NOTE: American Pam Fletcher was originally entered in this event, but was injured in a practice run and withdrew before the first race was held.

WOMEN'S SLALOM / February 26

No. of countries: 26   No. of entries: 60
No. of finishers: 28   Did not start: 3

RANK	CTRY	ATHLETE	1ST RUN	2ND RUN	TOTAL
1	SUI	SCHNEIDER, Vreni	48.81	47.88	1:36.69
2	TCH	SVET, Mateja	49.21	49.16	1:38.37
3	FRG	KINSHOFER GUETLEIN, Christa	49.84	48.56	1:38.40
4	AUT	STEINER, Roswitha	50.43	48.34	1:38.77
5	ESP	FERNANDEZ OCHOA, Blanca	49.89	49.55	1:39.44
6	AUT	LADSTAETTER, Ida	49.71	49.88	1:39.59
7	ITA	MAGONI SFORZA, Paoletta	50.42	49.34	1:39.76
8	FRA	MOGORE TLALKA, Dorota	50.28	49.58	1:39.86
11	USA	MADSEN, Beth	51.09	50.09	1:41.18
15	USA	ROFFE, Diann	51.74	51.14	1:42.88
DNF	USA	McKINNEY, Tamara	—	—	—
DNF	USA	VOELKER, Heidi	—	—	—

WOMEN'S GIANT SLALOM / February 24

No. of countries: 26   No. of entries: 64
No. of finishers: 29

RANK	CTRY	ATHLETE	1ST RUN	2ND RUN	TOTAL
1	SUI	SCHNEIDER, Vreni	1:00.53	1:05.96	2:06.49
2	FRG	KINSHOFER GUETLEIN, Christa	59.98	1:07.44	2:07.42
3	SUI	WALLISER, Maria	1:00.57	1:07.15	2:07.72
4	YUG	SVET, Mateja	1:00.95	1:06.85	2:07.80
5	FRG	MEIER, Chistine	1:00.43	1:07.45	2:07.88
6	AUT	MAIER, Ulrike	1:01.41	1:06.69	2:08.10
7	AUT	WACHTER, Anita	1:00.23	1:08.15	2:08.38
8	FRA	QUITTET, Catherine	1:01.11	1:07.73	2:08.84
12	USA	ROFFE, Diann	1:01.75	1:08.94	2:10.69
13	USA	ARMSTRONG, Debbie	1:01.73	1:08.99	2:10.72
DNF	USA	VOELKER, Heidi	1:02.10	—	—
DNF	USA	McKINNEY, Tamara	—	—	—

WOMEN'S SUPER GS / February 22

No. of countries: 20   No. of entries: 48
No. of finishers: 41   Did not start: 2

RANK	CTRY	ATHLETE	TIME
1	AUT	WOLF, Sigrid	1:19.03
2	SUI	FIGINI, Michela	1:20.03
3	CAN	PERCY, Karen	1:20.29
4	FRG	MOESENLECHNER, Regine	1:20.33
5	AUT	WACHTER, Anita	1:20.36
6	SUI	WALLISER, Maria	1:20.48
7	ITA	MARZOLA, Micaela	1:20.91
7	SUI	HAAS, Zoe	1:20.91
9	USA	THYS, Edith	1:20.93
18	USA	ARMSTRONG, Debbie	1:21.87
26	USA	LINDH, Hilary	1:23.11
32	USA	KRONE, Kristin	1:24.51

WOMEN'S COMBINED / February 20 (Downhill) / February 21 (Slalom)

No. of countries: 14   No. of entries: 40
No. of finishers: 26   Did not start: 1

RANK	CTRY	ATHLETE	DOWNHILL	SLALOM	TOTAL POINTS
1	AUT	WACHTER, Anita	1:17.14	1:22.97	29.25
2	SUI	OERTLI, Brigitte	1:18.37	1:20.71	29.48
3	SUI	WALLISER, Maria	1:16.98	1:25.92	51.28
4	CAN	PERCY, Karen	1:18.22	1:24.00	54.47
5	TCH	KEBRLOVA, Lenka	1:18.43	1:24.38	60.87
6	TCH	MEDZIHRADSKA, Lucia	1:18.62	1:24.35	63.56
7	CAN	McKENDRY, Michelle	1:17.58	1:26.44	64.85
8	CAN	LEE, Kerrin	1:18.15	1:25.43	65.26
15	USA	MADSEN, Beth	1:21.31	1:24.78	108.64
17	USA	KRONE, Kristin	1:18.80	1:30.19	114.81
23	USA	LINDH, Hilary	1:19.27	1:35.31	164.57
DNF	USA	THYS, Edith	1:18.38	—	—

MEN'S DOWNHILL / February 15

No. of countries: 18   No. of entries: 51
No. of finishers: 45

RANK	CTRY	ATHLETE	TIME
1	SUI	ZURBRIGGEN, Pirmin	1:59.63
2	SUI	MUELLER, Peter	2:00.14
3	FRA	PICCARD, Franck	2:01.24
4	AUT	STOCK, Leonard	2:01.56
5	AUT	PFAFFENBICHLER, Gerhard	2:02.02
6	FRG	WASMEIER, Markus	2:02.03
7	AUT	STEINER, Anton	2:02.19
8	GBR	BELL, Martin	2:02.49
26	USA	KITT, A.J.	2:04.94
28	USA	OLSON, Jeff	2:05.09
32	USA	LEWIS, Doug	2:06.25
DNF	USA	HUDSON, Bill	—

MEN'S SLALOM / February 27

No. of countries: 36   No. of entries: 114
No. of finishers: 54   Did not start: 5

RANK	CTRY	ATHLETE	1ST RUN	2ND RUN	TOTAL
1	ITA	TOMBA, Alberto	51.62	47.85	1:39.47
2	FRG	WOERNDL, Frank	50.99	48.54	1:39.53
3	LIE	FROMMELT, Paul	51.69	48.15	1:39.84
4	AUT	GSTREIN, Bernhard	51.87	48.21	1:40.08
5	SWE	STENMARK, Ingemar	52.71	47.51	1:40.22
6	SWE	NILSSON, Jonas	51.44	48.79	1:40.23
7	SUI	ZURBRIGGEN, Pirmin	52.05	48.43	1:40.48
8	ITA	TOTSCH, Oswald	52.44	48.11	1:40.55
DNF	USA	MILLER, Jack	55.00	—	—
DNF	USA	McGRATH, Felix	—	—	—
DNF	USA	WILLIAMS, Alexander	—	—	—
DQ	USA	ORMSBY, Robert	—	—	—

MEN'S GIANT SLALOM / February 25

No. of countries: 38   No. of entries: 120
No. of finishers: 69   Did not start: 3

RANK	CTRY	ATHLETE	1ST RUN	2ND RUN	TOTAL
1	ITA	TOMBA, Alberto	1:03.91	1:02.46	2:06.37
2	AUT	STROLZ, Hubert	1:05.05	1:02.36	2:07.41
3	AUT	ZURBRIGGEN, Pirmin	1:05.57	1:02.82	2:08.39
4	ITA	CAMOZZI, Ivano	1:05.86	1:02.91	2:08.77
5	AUT	NIERLICH, Rudolf	1:05.75	1:03.17	2:08.92
6	LIE	WENZEL, Andreas	1:05.65	1:03.38	2:09.03
7	AUT	MAYER, Helmut	1:06.32	1:02.77	2:09.09
8	FRG	WOERNDL, Frank	1:06.10	1:03.12	2:09.22
12	USA	SHAW, Tiger	1:06.71	1:03.52	2:10.23
13	USA	McGRATH, Felix	1:06.79	1:03.81	2:10.60
34	USA	ORMSBY, Robert	1:10.07	1:05.78	2:15.85
DNF	USA	MILLER, Jack	—	—	—

MEN'S SUPER GS / February 21

No. of countries: 34   No. of entries: 100
No. of finishers: 57   Did not start: 6

RANK	CTRY	ATHLETE	TIME
1	FRA	PICCARD, Franck	1:39.66
2	AUT	MAYER, Helmut	1:40.96
3	SWE	ERIKSSON, Lars-Boerje	1:41.08
4	AUT	STROLZ, Hubert	1:41.11
5	SUI	ZURBRIGGEN, Pirmin	1:41.96
5	AUT	MADER, Guenther	1:41.96
7	FRA	ALPHAND, Luc	1:42.27
8	AUT	STOCK, Leonard	1:42.36
18	USA	SHAW, Tiger	1:44.26
24T	USA	OLSON, Jeff	1:45.46
30	USA	HUDSON, Bill	1:47.29
DQ	USA	KITT, A.J.	—

MEN'S COMBINED / February 16 (Downhill) / February 17 (Slalom)

No. of countries: 21 No. of entries: 57
No. of finishers: 26 Did not start: 1

RANK	CTRY	ATHLETE	DOWNHILL	SLALOM	TOTAL POINTS
1	AUT	STROLZ, Hubert	1:48.51	1:27.31	36.55
2	AUT	GSTREIN, Bernhard	1:50.20	1:25.82	43.45
3	SUI	ACCOLA, Paul	1:51.27	1:24.93	48.24
4	FRA	ALPHAND, Luc	1:49.60	1:28.47	57.73
5	TCH	JURKO, Peter	1:50.29	1:27.61	58.56
6	FRA	CRETIER, Jean-Luc	1:50.04	1:28.52	62.98
7	FRG	WASMEIER, Markus	1:49.32	1:29.84	65.44
8	TCH	BIRES, Adrian	1:50.24	1:28.94	68.50
DNF	USA	KITT, A.J.	1:50.42	—	—
DNF	USA	McGRATH, Felix	1:53.35	—	—
DNF	USA	HUDSON, Bill	—	—	—
DNF	USA	OLSON, Jeff	—	—	—

NORDIC

WOMEN'S 5 KM CLASSICAL / February 17

No. of countries: 18 No. of entries: 56
No. of finishers: 53 Did not start: 1

RANK	CTRY	ATHLETE	TIME
1	FIN	MATIKAINEN, Marjo	15:04.0
2	URS	TIKHONOVA, Tamara	15:05.3
3	URS	VENTSENE, Vida	15:11.1
4	NOR	JAHREN, Anne	15:12.6
5	FIN	KIRVESNIEMI, Marja-Liisa	15:16.7
6	NOR	NYBRATEN, Inger Helene	15:17.7
7	SWE	WESTIN, Marie Helene	15:28.9
8	URS	NAGUEIKINA, Svetlana	15:29.9
31	USA	KRICHKO, Leslie	16:31.1
39	USA	THOMPSON, Leslie	16:58.5
41	USA	FIDDLER, Nancy	17:05.4
47	USA	YOUNGMAN, Elizabeth	17:32.6

WOMEN'S 10 KM CLASSICAL / February 14

No. of countries: 17 No. of entries: 53
No. of finishers: 51 Did not start: 1

RANK	CTRY	ATHLETE	TIME
1	URS	VENTSENE, Vida	30:08.3
2	URS	SMETANINA, Raisa	30:17.0
3	FIN	MATIKAINEN, Marjo	30:20.5
4	URS	NAGUEIKINA, Svetlana	30:26.5
5	URS	TIKHONOVA, Tamara	30:38.9
6	NOR	NYBRATEN, Inger Helene	30:51.7
7	FIN	MAATTA, Pirkko	30:52.4
8	SWE	WESTIN, Marie Helene	30:53.5
36	USA	KRICHKO, Leslie	33:25.1
40	USA	DENHARTOG, Dorcas	34:26.1
41	USA	FIDDLER, Nancy	34:31.1
45	USA	THOMPSON, Leslie	35:17.7

WOMEN'S 20 KM FREE TECHNIQUE / February 25

No. of countries: 18 No. of entries: 55
No. of finishers: 52

RANK	CTRY	ATHLETE	TIME
1	URS	TIKHONOVA, Tamara	55:53.6
2	URS	REZTSOVA, Anfissa	56.12.8
3	URS	SMETANINA, Raisa	57:22.1
4	SUI	GILLI-BRUEGGER, Christina	57:37.4
5	GDR	OPITZ, Simone	57:54.3
6	ITA	DI CENTA, Manuela	57:55.2
7	GDR	MORING, Kerstin	58:17.2
8	NOR	DAHLMO, Marianne	58:31.1
23	USA	DENHARTOG, Dorcas	1:00:48.6
25	USA	THOMPSON, Leslie	1:01:04.1
42	USA	YOUNGMAN, Elizabeth	1:03:31.3
43	USA	FIDDLER, Nancy	1:03:57.5

WOMEN'S 4 × 5-KM RELAY / February 21

No. of countries: 12 No. of entries: 12
No. of finishers: 12

RANK	CTRY	ATHLETES	TIME
1	URS	NAGUEIKINA, Svetlana / GAVRILIUK, Nina TIKHONOVA, Tamara / REZTSOVA, Anfissa	59:51.1
2	NOR	DYBENDAHL, Trude / WOLD, Marit JAHREN, Anne / DAHLMO, Marianne	1:01:33.0
3	FIN	MAATTA, Pirkko / KIRVESNIEMI, Marja-Liisa MATIKAINEN, Marjo / SAVOLAINEN, Jaana	1:01:53.8
4	SUI	THOMAS, Karin / PARPAN, Sandra KRATZER, Evi / GILLI-BRUEGGER, Christina	1:01:59.4
5	GDR	MORING, Kerstin / OPITZ, Simone BRAUN, Silke / GREINER PETTER, Simone	1:02:19.9
6	SWE	FROST, Lis / FRITZON, Anna-Lena LAMBERG-SKOG, Karin / WESTIN, Marie Helene	1:02:24.9
7	TCH	BALAZOVA, Lubomira / KLIMKOVA, Viera RADLOVA, Ivana / HAVRANCIKOVA, Alzbeta	1:03:37.1
8	USA	DENHARTOG, Dorcas / THOMPSON, Leslie FIDDLER, Nancy / KRICHKO, Leslie	1:04:08.8

MEN'S 15 KM CLASSICAL / February 19

No. of countries: 33 No. of entries: 92
No. of finishers: 85 Did not start: 2

RANK	CTRY	ATHLETE	TIME
1	URS	DEVIATIAROV, Mikhail	41:18.9
2	NOR	MIKKELSPASS, Pål	41:33.4
3	URS	SMIRNOV, Vladimir	41:48.5
4	NOR	BRAA, Oddvar	42:17.3
5	GDR	BELLMANN, Uwe	42:17.8
6	ITA	DE ZOLT, Maurilio	42:31.2
7	NOR	ULVANG, Vegard	42:31.5
8	FIN	KIRVESNIEMI, Harri	42:42.8
29	USA	SIMONEAU, Dan	44:53.8
40	USA	SPENCER, Bill	45:59.6
53	USA	BOONSTRA, Todd	47:21.8
58	USA	GALANES, Joseph	48:05.2

MEN'S 30 KM CLASSICAL / February 15

No. of countries: 32 No. of entries: 91
No. of finishers: 87 Did not start: 1

RANK	CTRY	ATHLETE	TIME
1	URS	PROKOUROROV, Alexei	1:24:26.3
2	URS	SMIRNOV, Vladimir	1:24:35.1
3	NOR	ULVANG, Vegard	1:25:11.6
4	URS	DEVIATIAROV, Mikhail	1:25:31.3
5	ITA	VANZETTA, Giorgio	1:25:37.2
6	NOR	MIKKELSPLASS, Pål	1:25:44.6
7	ITA	POLVARA, Gianfranco	1:26:02.7
8	ITA	ALBARELLO, Marco	1:26:09.1
49	USA	SIMONEAU, Dan	1:35:21.4
51	USA	ENGEN, Jon	1:35:41.9
56	USA	BROCHMAN, Kevin	1:37:07.1
DNF	USA	GALANES, Joseph	—

MEN'S 50 KM FREE TECHNIQUE / February 27

No. of countries: 25 No. of entries: 74
No. of finishers: 61 Did not start: 4

RANK	CTRY	ATHLETE	TIME
1	SWE	SVAN, Gunde	2:04:30.9
2	ITA	DE ZOLT, Maurilio	2:05:36.4
3	SUI	GRUENENFELDER, Andy	2:06:01.9
4	NOR	ULVANG, Vegard	2:06:32.3
5	GDR	BAUROTH, Holger	2:07:02.4
6	SWE	OTTOSSON, Jan	2:07:34.8
7	FIN	RISTANEN, Kari	2:08:08.1
8	GDR	BELLMANN, Uwe	2:08:18.6
47	USA	BROCHMAN, Kevin	2:19:45.5
56	USA	SPENCER, Bill	2:25:22.6
DNF	USA	ENGEN, Jon	—
DNF	USA	SIMONEAU, Dan	—

MEN'S 4 × 10-KM RELAY / February 22

No. of countries: 16 No. of entries: 16
No. of finishers: 16

RANK	CTRY	ATHLETES	TIME
1	SWE	OTTOSSON, Jan / WASSBERG, Thomas SVAN, Gunde / MOGREN, Torgny	1:43:58.6
2	URS	SMIRNOV, Vladimir / SAKHNOV, Vladimir DEVIATIAROV, Mikhail / PROKUROROV, Alexei	1:44:11.3
3	TCH	NYC, Radim / KORUNKA, Vaclav BENC, Pavel / SVANDA, Ladislav	1:45:22.7
4	SIU	GRUENENFELDER, Andy / CAPOL, Jurg GUIDON, Giachem / WIGGER, Jeremias	1:46:16.3
5	ITA	BARCO, Silvano / WALDER, Albert VANZETTA, Giorgio / DE ZOLT, Maurilio	1:46:16.7
6	NOR	MIKKELSPASS, Pal / BRAA, Oddvar ULVANG, Vegard / LANGLI, Terje	1:46:48.7
7	FRG	KUSS, Walter / FISCHER, Georg BEHLE, Jochen / FRITZENWENGER, Herbert	1:48:05.0
8	FIN	LAUKKANEN, Jari / KIRVESNIEMI, Harri RASANEN, Jari / RISTANEN, Kari	1:48:24.0
13	USA	BOONSTRA, Todd / SIMONEAU, Dan SPENCER, Bill / GALANES, Joseph	1:50:27.6

INDIVIDUAL NORDIC COMBINED / February 28

No. of countries: 13 No. of entries: 44
No. of finishers: 41 Did not start: 2

RANK	CTRY	ATHLETE	70 M JUMP POINTS	15 KM SKI TIME
1	SUI	KEMPF, Hippolyt	217.9	38:16.8
2	AUT	SULZENBACHER, Klaus	228.5	39:46.5
3	URS	LEVANDI, Allar	216.6	39:12.4
4	GDR	PRENZEL, Uwe	207.6	38:18.8
5	SUI	SCHAAD, Andreas	207.2	38:18.0
6	NOR	LOKKEN, Torbjorn	199.4	37:39.0
7	TCH	KOPAL, Miroslav	208.7	38:48.0
8	GDR	FRANK, Marko	209.4	39:08.2
19	USA	HOLLAND, Joseph	210.4	41:01.8
40	USA	WILSON, Todd	180.1	42:07.9
41	USA	CRAWFORD, Gary	135.8	43:54.7
DNS	USA	JOHNSTONE, Hans	—	—

TEAM NORDIC COMBINED / February 23 (70 M JUMP)
February 24 (3x10-KM RELAY)

No. of countries: 10 No. of entries: 10
No. of finishers: 10

RANK	CTRY	ATHLETES	70 M JUMP POINTS	3 × 10-KM SKI TIME
1	FRG	POHL, Hans / SCHWARZ, Hubert MUELLER, Thomas	629.8	1:20:46.0
2	SUI	SCHAAD, Andreas / KEMPF, Hippolyt GLANZMANN, Fredy	571.4	1:15:57.4
3	AUT	CSAR, Guenther / ASCHENWALD, Hansjoerg / SULZENBACHER, Klaus	626.6	1:21:00.9
4	NOR	BOGSETH, Hallstein / BREDESEN, Trond / LOKKEN, Torbjorn	596.6	1:18:48.4
5	GDR	PRENZEL, Thommas / FRANK, Marko PRENZEL, Uwe	571.6	1:18:13.5
6	TCH	PATRAS, Ladislav / KLIMKO, Jan KOPAL, Miroslav	573.5	1:19:02.1
7	FIN	SAAPUNKI, Pasi / PARVIAINEN, Jouko YLIPULLI, Jukka	561.3	1:19:56.3
8	FRA	BOHARD, Jean / GIRARD, Xavier GUY, Fabrice	541.0	1:19:45.4
10	USA	HOLLAND, Joe / WILSON, Todd JOHNSTONE, Hans	516.9	1:23:42.9

70-METER SKI JUMPING / February 14

No. of countries: 19 No. of entries: 58
No. of finishers: 58

RANK	CTRY	ATHLETE	DISTANCES		POINTS
1	FIN	NYKÄNEN, Matti	89.5	89.5	229.1
2	TCH	PLOC, Pavel	84.5	87.5	212.1
3	TCH	MALEC, Jiri	88.0	85.5	211.8
4	YUG	TEPES, Miran	84.0	83.5	211.2
5	TCH	PARMA, Jiri	83.5	82.5	203.8
6	AUT	KUTTIN, Heinz	87.0	80.5	199.7

(Continued)

70-METER SKI JUMPING (Continued)

RANK	CTRY	ATHLETE	DISTANCES		POINTS
7	FIN	PUIKKONEN, Jari	84.0	80.0	199.1
8	SWE	TALLBERG, Staffan	83.0	81.0	198.1
18	USA	KONOPACKE, Mark	83.5	79.0	188.2
33	USA	HOLLAND, Michael	79.5	74.5	174.6
43	USA	McGRANE, Dennis	78.0	73.0	169.8
54	USA	MEWBORN, Rick	75.0	74.0	158.6

90-METER INDIVIDUAL SKI JUMPING / February 23

No. of countries: 19   No. of entries: 58
No. of finishers: 55   Did not start: 3

RANK	CTRY	ATHLETE	DISTANCES		POINTS
1	FIN	NYKÄNEN, Matti	118.5	107.0	224.0
2	NOR	JOHNSEN, Erik	114.5	102.0	207.9
3	YUG	DEBELAK, Matjaz	113.0	108.0	207.7
4	FRG	KLAUSER, Thomas	114.5	102.5	205.1
5	TCH	PLOC, Pavel	114.5	102.5	204.1
6	AUT	FELDER, Andreas	113.5	103.0	203.9
7	CAN	BULAU, Horst	112.5	99.5	197.6
8	SWE	TALLBERG, Staffan	110.0	102.0	196.6
32	USA	HOLLAND, Michael	105.0	92.0	170.6
42	USA	KONOPACKE, Mark	100.0	96.0	160.2
49	USA	HASTINGS, Chris	94.0	93.0	145.1
50	USA	LANGLOIS, Tad	95.0	90.0	142.8

90-METER TEAM SKI JUMPING / February 24

No. of countries: 11   No. of entries: 11
No. of finishers: 11

RANK	CTRY	ATHLETES	POINTS
1	FIN	NIKKOLA, Ari Pekka / NYKÄNEN, Matti YLIPULLI, Tuomo / PUIKKONEN, Jari	634.4
2	YUG	ULAGA, Primoz / ZUPAN, Matjaz DEBELAK, Matjaz / TEPES, Miran	625.5
3	NOR	EIDHAMMER, Ole / KJORUM, Jon FIDJESTOI, Ole / JOHNSEN, Erik	596.1
4	TCH	DLUHOS, Ladislav / MALEC, Jiri PLOC, Pavel / PARMA, Jiri	586.8
5	AUT	VETTORI, Ernst / KUTTIN, Heinz STANNER, Guenter / FELDER, Andreas	577.6
6	FRG	BAUER, Andreas / ROHWEIN, Peter KLAUSER, Thomas / HEUMANN, Josef	559.0
7	SWE	TALLBERG, Par Inge / DAUN, Anders BOKLOV, Jan / TALLBERG, Staffan	539.7
8	SUI	BALANCHIE, Gerard / LEHMANN, Christoph PIAZZINI, Fabrice / HAUSWIRTH, Christian	516.1
10	USA	LANGLOIS, Tad / KONOPACKE, Mark McGRANE, Dennis / HOLLAND, Mike	496.8

SPEEDSKATING

WOMEN'S 500 METERS / February 22

No. of countries: 15   No. of entries: 30
No. of finishers: 30

RANK	CTRY	ATHLETE	TIME
1	USA	BLAIR, Bonnie	39:10 WR
2	GDR	ROTHENBURGER, Christa	39:12
3	GDR	KANIA, Karin	39.24
4	GDR	STAHNKE, Angela	39.68
5	JPN	HASHIMOTO, Seiko	39.74
6	CAN	RHEAD, Shelley	40.36
7	FRG	HOLZNER-GAWENUS, Monika	40.53
8	JPN	FUSANO, Shoko	40.61
12	USA	CLASS, Katie	40.91
23	USA	BADER, Leslie	41.57
25	USA	TALBOT, Kristen	41.71

WOMEN'S 1,000 METERS / February 26

No. of countries: 12   No. of entries: 28
No. of finishers: 26   Did not start: 1

RANK	CTRY	ATHLETE	TIME
1	GDR	ROTHENBURGER, Christa	1:17.65 WR
2	GDR	KANIA, Karin	1:17.70
3	USA	BLAIR, Bonnie	1:18.31
4	GDR	EHRIG, Andrea	1:19.32
5	JPN	HASHIMOTO, Seiko	1:19.75
6	GDR	STAHNKE, Angela	1:20.05
7	USA	BADER, Leslie	1:21.09
8	USA	CLASS, Katie	1:21.10
24	USA	SWIDER-PELTZ, Nancy	1:24.81

WOMEN'S 1,500 METERS / February 27

No. of countries: 13   No. of entries: 29
No. of finishers: 28   Did not start: 1

RANK	CTRY	ATHLETE	TIME
1	HOL	VAN GENNIP, Yvonne	2:00.68 OR
2	GDR	KANIA, Kania	2:00.82
3	GDR	EHRIG, Andrea	2:01.49
4	USA	BLAIR, Bonnie	2:04.02
5	URS	LAPOUGA, Elena	2:04.24
6	JPN	HASHIMOTO, Seiko	2:04.38
7	GDR	KLEEMANN, Gunda	2:04.68
7	POL	RYS-FERENS, Erwina	2:04.68
10	USA	BADER, Leslie	2:05.53
13	USA	CLASS, Katie	2:07.30
18	USA	GOLDMAN, Janet	2:08.72

WOMEN'S 3,000 METERS / February 23

No. of countries: 16   No. of entries: 29
No. of finishers: 28

RANK	CTRY	ATHLETE	TIME
1	HOL	VAN GENNIP, Yvonne	4:11.94 WR
2	GDR	EHRIG, Andrea	4:12.09
3	GDR	ZANGE, Gabi	4:16.92
4	GDR	KANIA, Karin	4:18.80
5	POL	RYS-FERENS, Erwina	4:22.59
6	URS	BOIKO, Svetlana	4:22.90
7	JPN	HASHIMOTO, Seiko	4:23.29
7	URS	LAPOUGA, Elena	4:23.29
11	USA	GOLDMAN, Janet	4:25.26
19	USA	DOCTER, Mary	4:29.93
20	USA	BADER, Leslie	4:30.09

WOMEN'S 5,000 METERS / February 28

No. of countries: 14   No. of entries: 25
No. of finishers: 25

RANK	CTRY	ATHLETE	TIME
1	HOL	VAN GENNIP, Yvonne	7:14.12 WR
2	GDR	EHRIG, Andrea	7:17.12
3	GDR	ZANGE, Gabi	7:21.61
4	URS	BOIKO, Svetlana	7:28.39
5	URS	LAPOUGA, Erwina	7:28.65
6	JPN	HASHIMOTO, Seiko	7:34.43
7	GDR	KLEEMANN, Gunda	7:34.59
8	SWE	KROHN, Jasmin	7:36.56
10	USA	GOLDMAN, Janet	7:36.98
11	USA	DOCTER, Mary	7:37.00
22	USA	SWIDER-PELTZ, Nancy	7:52.12

MEN'S 500 METERS / February 14

No. of countries: 15   No. of entries: 37
No. of finishers: 36

RANK	CTRY	ATHLETE	TIME
1	GDR	MEY, Jens-Uwe	35.45 WR
2	HOL	YKEMA, Jan	36.76
3	JPN	KUROIWA, Akira	36.77
4	URS	FOKITCHEV, Serguei	36.82
5	KOR	BAE, Kitae	36.90
6	URS	GELEZOVSKY, Igor	36.94
7	CAN	THIBAULT, Guy	36.96
8	USA	THOMETZ, Nick	37.19
15	USA	HENRIKSEN, Eric	37.50
22	USA	PIERCE, Marty	37.76
DNF	USA	JANSEN, Dan	—

MEN'S 1,000 METERS / February 18

No. of countries: 16   No. of entries: 40
No. of finishers: 36

RANK	CTRY	ATHLETE	TIME
1	URS	GOULIAEV, Nikolai	1:13.03 OR
2	GDR	MEY, Jens-Uwe	1:13.11
3	URS	GELEZOVSKY, Igor	1:13.19
4	USA	FLAIM, Eric	1:13.53
5	CAN	BOUCHER, Gaetan	1:13.77
6	AUT	HADSCHIEFF, Michael	1:13.84
7	CAN	THIBAULT, Guy	1:14.16
8	GDR	ADEBERG, Peter	1:14.19
17	USA	CUSHMAN, Tom	1:14.68
18	USA	THOMETZ, Nick	1:14.71
DNF	USA	JANSEN, Dan	—

MEN'S 1,500 METERS / February 20

No. of countries: 20   No. of entries: 40
No. of finishers: 39   Did not start: 1

RANK	CTRY	ATHLETE	TIME
1	GDR	HOFFMAN, Andre	1:52.06 WR
2	USA	FLAIM, Eric	1:52.12
3	AUT	HADSCHIEFF, Michael	1:52.31
4	URS	GELEZOVSKY, Igor	1:52.63
5	JPN	AOYANAGI, Toru	1:52.85
6	URS	ALEXANDER, Klimov	1:52.97
7	URS	GULIAEV, Nikolai	1:53.04
8	GDR	ADEBERG, Peter	1:53.57
11	USA	GREENWALD, Mark	1:54.64
15	USA	SILK, David	1:55.26
20	USA	BASKFIELD, John	1:55.88

MEN'S 5,000 METERS / February 17

No. of countries: 18   No. of entries: 38
No. of finishers: 38

RANK	CTRY	ATHLETE	TIME
1	SWE	GUSTAFSON, Tomas	6:44.63 WR
2	HOL	VISSER, Leo	6:44.98
3	HOL	KEMKERS, Gerard	6:45.92
4	USA	FLAIM, Eric	6:47.09
5	AUT	HADSCHIEFF, Michael	6:48.72
6	USA	SILK, David	6:49.95
7	NOR	KARLSTAD, Geir	6:50.88
8	GDR	FREIER, Roland	6:51.42
9	USA	GREENWALD, Mark	6:51.98

MEN'S 10,000 METERS / February 21

No. of countries: 19   No. of entries: 32
No. of finishers: 30

RANK	CTRY	ATHLETE	TIME
1	SWE	GUSTAFSON, Tomas	13:48.20 WR
2	AUT	HADSCHIEFF, Michael	13:56.11
3	HOL	VISSER, Leo	14:00.55
4	USA	FLAIM, Eric	14:05.57
5	HOL	KEMKERS, Gerard	14:08.34
6	URS	KLIOUEV, Iouri	14:09.68
7	ITA	SIGHEL, Roberto	14:13.60
8	GDR	FREIER, Roland	14:19.16
14	USA	SILK, David	14:25.56
25	USA	KLAIBER, Jeffrey	14:38.60

CURLING (DEMONSTRATION SPORT)

No. of countries: 8   No. of entries: 8
No. of finishers: 8

WOMEN / February 20

RANK	CTRY	GAMES* WON	LOST	USA GAME SCORES	
1	CANADA	7	2	USA vs. SWE	2-10
2	SWEDEN	5	3	USA vs. CAN	5- 7
3	NORWAY	6	4	USA vs. DEN	9- 2
4	FRG	4	4	USA vs. NOR	5- 9
5	UNITED STATES	4	4	USA vs. SUI	9- 6
6	DENMARK	3	4	USA vs. FRG	5- 3
7	SWITZERLAND	2	5	USA vs. FRA	6- 5
8	FRANCE	1	6	Tiebreaker:	7-10
				USA vs. NOR	

* Includes tiebreakers, semifinals and final games

MEN / February 18

RANK	CTRY	GAMES* WON	LOST	USA GAME SCORES	
1	NORWAY	8	3	USA vs. DEN	6-5
2	SWITZERLAND	5	3	USA vs. CAN	5-9
3	CANADA	5	3	USA vs. SWE	10-6
4	UNITED STATES	4	4	USA vs. GBR	7-6
5	SWEDEN	4	4	USA vs. SUI	4-7
6	DENMARK	3	4	USA vs. FRG	6-7
7	FRG	3	4	USA vs. NOR	9-3
8	GREAT BRITAIN	0	7	Tiebreaker:	
				USA vs. NOR	3-6

* Includes tiebreakers, semifinals and final games.

FREESTYLE SKIING
(DEMONSTRATION EVENT)

WOMEN'S AERIALS / February 21

No. of countries: 8   No. of entries: 9
No. of finishers: 9

RANK	CTRY	ATHLETE	POINTS
1	USA	PALENIK, Melanie	268.83
2	FRG	REICHART, Sonja	267.03
3	SWE	HERNSKOG, Carin	245.98
7	USA	QUINTANA, Maria	203.88

WOMEN'S BALLET / February 25

No. of countries: 5   No. of entries: 6
No. of finishers: 6

RANK	CTRY	ATHLETE	POINTS
1	FRA	ROSSI, Christine	45.8
2	USA	BUCHER, Jan	44.0
3	SUI	KISSLING, Conny	43.2
6	USA	PALENIK, Melanie	34.1

WOMEN'S MOGULS / February 22

No. of countries: 6   No. of entries: 6
No. of finishers: 6

RANK	CTRY	ATHLETE	POINTS
1	FRG	MITTERMAYER, Tatjana	36.16
2	FRA	MONOD, Raphaelle	34.91
3	SUI	KISSLING, Conny	34.07
6	USA	PALENIK, Melanie	28.64

MEN'S AERIALS / February 23

No. of countries: 10   No. of entries: 14
No. of finishers: 14

RANK	CTRY	ATHLETE	POINTS
1	CAN	ROZON, Jean-Marc	410.93
2	FRA	MEDA, Didlier	380.77
3	CAN	LANGLOIS, Lloyd	377.97
4	USA	FEDDERSEN, Kris	376.24
14	USA	HASLOCK, Christopher	181.56

MEN'S BALLET / February 25

No. of countries: 9   No. of entries: 12
No. of finishers: 12

RANK	CTRY	ATHLETE	POINTS
1	FRG	REITBERGER, Herman	46.6
2	USA	SPINA, Lane	45.6
3	USA	KRISTIANSEN, Rune	44.0
6	USA	BOLESKY, Bruce	42.6

MEN'S MOGULS / February 22

No. of countries: 9   No. of entries: 13
No. of finishers: 13

RANK	CTRY	ATHLETE	POINTS
1	SWE	HANSSON, Håkan	39.56
2	NOR	ENGELSEN EIDE, Hans	39.37
3	FRA	GROSPIRON, Edgar	37.71
5	USA	DESOVICH, Steve	35.16
10	USA	CARMICHAEL, Nelson	27.94

SHORT TRACK SPEEDSKATING
(DEMONSTRATION EVENT)

*   Quarterfinal time; did not advance to semifinals.
**   Semifinal time; did not advance to final.
\#   Did not advance past heats.
\#\#   Did not advance past quarterfinals.

WOMEN'S 500 METERS / February 22

No. of countries: 11   No. of entries: 32
No. of finishers: 32

RANK	CTRY	ATHLETE	TIME
1	HOL	VELZEBOER, Monique	48.28
2	CAN	DONATELLI, Eden	48.34
3	CHN	LI, Yan	48.84
12	USA	LASZLO, Tara	51.00 *
#	USA	PETERSON, Amy	
#	USA	MANE SAN FELIPPO, Becky	
#	USA	STENNES, Tricia	

WOMEN'S 1,000 METERS / February 25

No. of countries: 11   No. of entries: 31
No. of finishers: 29

RANK	CTRY	ATHLETE	TIME
1	CHN	LI, Yan	1:39.00
2	CAN	DAIGLE, Sylvie	1:41.15
3	HOL	VELZEBOER, Monique	1:43.10
15	USA	STENNES, Tricia	1:48.01 *
#	USA	MANE SAN FELIPPO, Becky	
#	USA	PETERSON, Amy	
#	USA	LASZLO, Tara	

WOMEN'S 1,500 METERS / February 23

No. of countries: 11   No. of entries: 31
No. of finishers: 31

RANK	CTRY	ATHLETE	TIME
1	CAN	DAIGLE, Sylvie	2:37.61
2	HOL	VELZEBOER, Monique	2:37.77
3	CHN	LI, Yan	2:37.92
#	USA	MANE SAN FELIPPO, Becky	
#	USA	PETERSON, Amy	
#	USA	LASZLO, Tara	
#	USA	STENNES, Tricia	

WOMEN'S 3,000 METERS / February 24

No. of countries: 11   No. of entries: 29
No. of finishers: 29

RANK	CTRY	ATHLETE	TIME
1	JPN	SHISHII, Eiko	5:25.44
2	CAN	DAIGLE, Sylvie	5:25.82
3	ITA	CANDIDO, Maria Rosa	5:25.89
#	USA	LASZLO, Tara	
#	USA	STENNES, Tricia	
#	USA	MANE SAN FELIPPO, Becky	
#	USA	PETERSON, Amy	

WOMEN'S 3,000-METER RELAY / February 23

No. of countries: 6   No. of entries: 6
No. of finishers: 6

RANK	CTRY	ATHLETES	TIME
1	ITA	CANDIDO, Maria Rosa / SCIOLLA, Christina MONTEDURO, Gabriella / MUSSIO, Barbara	4:45.88 WR
2	JPN	TAKEUCHI, Hiromi / YAMADA, Nobuko YAMADA, Yumiko / SHISHII, Eiko	4:46.91
3	CAN	LAMBERT, Nathalie / DAIGLE, Sylvie DONATELLI, Eden / PERREAULT, Maryse	4:49.77
5	USA	MANE SAN FELIPPO, Becky / PETERSON, Amy LASZLO, Tara / STENNES, Tricia	4:52.25 **

MEN'S 500 METERS / February 23

No. of countries: 10   No. of entries: 32
No. of finishers: 30

RANK	CTRY	ATHLETE	TIME
1	GBR	O'REILLY, Wilfred	44.80 WR
2	CAN	VINCENT, Mario	45.15
3	JPN	ISHIHARA, Tatsuyoshi	45.37
9	USA	ARSENEAU, Brian	45.76 *
15	USA	MOORE, Patrick	1:00.65*
#	USA	GABEL, Andy	
#	USA	BESTEMAN, David	

MEN'S 1,000 METERS / February 24

No. of countries: 10   No. of entries: 32
No. of finishers: 28

RANK	CTRY	ATHLETE	TIME
1	GBR	O'REILLY, Wilfred	1:33.44 WR
2	CAN	DAIGNAULT, Michel	1:33.66
3	FRA	BELLA, Marco	1:34.45
18	USA	ARSENEAU, Brian	2:01.13 #
##	USA	GABEL, Andy	
##	USA	BESTEMAN, David	
DQ	USA	MOORE, Patrick	

MEN'S 1,500 METERS / February 22

No. of countries: 10   No. of entries: 32
No. of finishers: 30

RANK	CTRY	ATHLETE	TIME
1	KOR	KIM, Ki Hoon	2:26.68
2	CAN	GRENIER, Louis	2:26.99
3	ITA	FAGONE, Orazio	2:27.16
12	USA	MOORE, Patrick	2:51.21
16	USA	ARSENEAU, Brian	2:51.08 **
#	USA	BESTEMAN, David	
#	USA	GABEL, Andy	

MEN'S 3,000 METERS / February 25

No. of countries: 10   No. of entries: 32
No. of finishers: 31

RANK	CTRY	ATHLETE	TIME
1	KOR	LEE, Joon-Ho	5:21.63
2	HOL	VELDHOVEN, Carolus	5:22.39
3	CAN	DAIGNAULT, Michel	5:30.68
11	USA	GABEL, Andy	5:35.30 **
#	USA	BESTEMAN, David	
#	USA	MOORE, Patrick	

MEN'S 3,000-METER RELAY / February 25

No. of countries: 6   No. of entries: 6
No. of finishers: 6

RANK	CTRY	ATHLETES	TIME
1	HOL	VAN DER VELDE, Petrys / MOS, Jacob VELDHOVEN, Carolus / SUYTEN, Richard	7:29.05 WR
2	ITA	HERRNHOF, Hugo / PERETTI, Roberto FAGONE, Orazio / PERETTI, Enrico	7:30.39
3	CAN	GRENIER, Louis / VINCENT, Mario DOBREUIL, Robert / DAIGNAULT, Michel	7:35.47
4	USA	MOORE, Patrick / ARSENEAU, Brian BESTEMAN, David / GABEL, Andy	7:47.59

DISABLED SKIING
(EXHIBITION EVENT)

WOMEN'S MODIFIED GIANT SLALOM / February 21

No. of countries: 3   No. of entries: 5
No. of finishers: 5

RANK	CTRY	ATHLETE	1ST RUN	2ND RUN	TOTAL
1	USA	GOLDEN, Diana	47.68	38.73	1:26.41
2	USA	GENTILE, Catherine	51.42	41.44	1:32.86
3	USA	HILL, Martha	53.63	41.24	1:34.87

MEN'S MODIFIED GIANT SLALOM / February 21

No. of countries: 8   No. of entries: 13
No. of finishers: 13

RANK	CTRY	ATHLETE	1ST RUN	2ND RUN	TOTAL
1	FRG	SPITZ, Alexander	44.04	37.06	1:21.10
2	USA	MANNINO, Greg	44.94	37.93	1:22.87
3	SUI	BERGER, Fritz	45.98	39.62	1:25.60
5	USA	JAMISON, David	46.33	39:62	1:25.95
6	USA	EMERSON, Robert	46.99	40.23	1:27.22

WOMEN'S 5 KM / February 17

No. of countries: 3   No. of entries: 5
No. of finishers: 5

RANK	CTRY	ATHLETE / GUIDE	TIME
1	AUT	PREINING, Veronika / HABERL, Siegfried	22:56.3
2	FIN	PENNANEN, Kirsti / VILJAJARJU, Anja Vila	23:00.1
3	AUT	HEGER, Margaret / PUCHER, Manfred	26:59.3
(no USA entry)			

MEN'S 5 KM / February 17

No. of countries: 8   No. of entries: 10
No. of finishers: 10

RANK	CTRY	ATHLETE / GUIDE	TIME
1	NOR	AALIEN, Hans Anton / HOMB, Arne	18:51.2
2	SWE	PETTERSSON, Ake / STRIDH, Raland	19:29.7
3	NOR	VEIT, Asmund / ULVANG, Kjetil	19:48.6
6	USA	NOVOTNY, John / WARD, Craig	20:45.5

GAMES OF THE XXIVth OLYMPIAD

Seoul, Korea — September 17 - October 2, 1988

ARCHERY

WOMEN'S INDIVIDUAL / September 30

RANK	CTRY	ATHLETE	SCORE
1	KOR	KIM, Soo-nyung	344
2	KOR	WANG, Hee-kyung	332
3	KOR	YUN, Young-sook	327
4	URS	ARJANNIKOVA, Lyudmila	327
5	SWE	SJÖWALL, Jenny	325
6	FRG	KRIZ, Claudia	318
10	USA	SKILLMAN, Melanie	elim. semifinals
21	USA	PARKER, Denise	elim. eighthfinals
26	USA	OCHS, Debra	elim. open round

WOMEN'S TEAM / October 1

RANK	CTRY	ATHLETES	SCORE	SHOOT-OFF
1	KOR	KIM, Soo-nyung / WANG, Hee-kyung YUN, Young-sook	982	
2	INA	HANDAYANI, Lilies / SAIMAN, Nurfitriyana / WARDHANI, Kusuma	952	72
3	USA	OCHS, Debra / PARKER, Denise SKILLMAN, Melanie	952	67
4	URS		951	
5	GBR		933	
6	FRG		931	

MEN'S INDIVIDUAL / September 30

RANK	CTRY	ATHLETE	SCORE
1	USA	BARRS, Jay	338
2	KOR	PARK, Sung-soo	336
3	URS	ECHEEV, Vladimir	335
4	KOR	CHUNG, In-soo	331
5	HOL	RENIERS, Martinus	327
6	USA	McKINNEY, Rick	324
9	USA	PACE, Darrell	elim. semifinals

MEN'S TEAM / October 1

RANK	CTRY	ATHLETES	SCORE
1	KOR	CHUN, In-soo / LEE, Han-sup PARK, Sung-soo	986
2	USA	BARRS, Jay / McKINNEY, Rick PACE, Darrell	972
3	GBR	HALLARD, Steven / PRIESTMAN, Richard / WATSON, Leroy	968
4	FIN		956
5	URS		949
6	JPN		948

ATHLETICS

WOMEN'S 100 METERS / September 25

RANK	CTRY	ATHLETE	TIME
1	USA	GRIFFITH JOYNER, Florence	10.54 *
2	USA	ASHFORD, Evelyn	10.83
3	GDR	DRECHSLER, Heike	10.85
4	JAM	JACKSON, Grace	10.97
5	USA	TORRENCE, Gwen	10.97
6	URS	POMOCHTCHNIKOVA, Natalia	11.00

* wind-aided, +3.0 mps

WOMEN'S 200 METERS / September 29

RANK	CTRY	ATHLETE	TIME
1	USA	GRIFFITH JOYNER, Florence	21.34 WR
2	JAM	JACKSON, Grace	21.72
3	GDR	DRECHSLER, Heike	21.95
4	JAM	OTTEY, Merlene	21.99
5	GDR	MOELLER, Silke	22.09
6	USA	TORRENCE, Gwen	22.17
—	USA	MARSHALL, Pam	injured first round

WOMEN'S 400 METERS / September 26

RANK	CTRY	ATHLETE	TIME
1	URS	BRYZGUINA, Olga	48:65 OR
2	GDR	MUELLER, Petra	49:45
3	URS	NAZAROVA, Olga	49:90
4	USA	BRISCO, Valerie	50:16
5	USA	DIXON, Diane	50:72
6	USA	HOWARD-HILL, Denean	51.12

WOMEN'S 800 METERS / September 26

RANK	CTRY	ATHLETE	TIME
1	GDR	WODARS, Sigurn	1:56.10
2	GDR	WACHTEL, Christine	1:56.64
3	USA	GALLAGHER, Kim	1:56.91
4	YUG	COLOVIC, Slobodanka	1:57.50
5	USA	WALTON-FLOYD, Delisa	1:57.80
6	URS	EVSEEVA, Inna	1:59.37
—	USA	CLARK, Joetta	elim. semifinals

WOMEN'S 1,500 METERS / October 1

RANK	CTRY	ATHLETE	TIME
1	ROM	IVAN, Paula	3:53.96 OR
2	URS	BAIKAUSKAITE, Lailoute	4:00.24
3	URS	SAMOLENKO, Tatiana	4:00.30
4	GBR	CAHILL, Christina	4:00.64
5	CAN	WILLIAMS, Lynn	4:00.86
6	GDR	HAHMANN, Andrea	4:00.96
8	USA	SLANEY, Mary	4:02.49
11	USA	GALLAGHER, Kim	4:16.25
—	USA	JACOBS, Regina	elim. first round

WOMEN'S 3,000 METERS / September 25

RANK	CTRY	ATHLETE	TIME
1	URS	SAMOLENKO, Tatiana	8:26.53 OR
2	ROM	IVAN, Paula	8:27.15
3	GBR	MURRAY, Yvonne	8:29.02
4	URS	ROMANOVA, Elena	8:30.45
5	URS	ARTEMOVA, Matalia	8:31.67
6	USA	HUBER, Vicki	8:37.25
10	USA	SLANEY, Mary	8:47.13
13	USA	PLUMER, PattiSue	8:59.17

WOMEN'S 10,000 METERS / September 30

RANK	CTRY	ATHLETE	TIME
1	URS	BONDARENKO, Olga	31:05.21 OR
2	GBR	McCOLGAN, Elizabeth	31:08.44
3	URS	JOUPIFVA, Flena	31:19.82
4	GDR	ULLRICH, Kathrin	31:29.27
5	USA	LARRIEU-SMITH, Francie	31:35.52
6	USA	JENNINGS, Lynn	31:39.93
15	USA	NELSON, Lynn	32:32.24

WOMEN'S MARATHON / September 23

RANK	CTRY	ATHLETE	TIME
1	POR	MOTA, Rosa	2:25:40
2	AUS	MARTIN, Lisa	2:25:53
3	GDR	DOERRE, Kathrin	2:26:21
4	URS	POLOVINSKAIA, Tatiana	2:27:05
5	CHN	ZHAO, Youfeng	2:27:06
6	ITA	FOGLI, Laura	2:27:49
17	USA	DITZ, Nancy	2:33:42
39	USA	GROOS, Margaret	2:40:59
40	USA	O'BRIEN, Cathy	2:41:04

WOMEN'S 100-METER HURDLES / September 30

RANK	CTRY	ATHLETE	TIME
1	BUL	DONKOVA, Jordanka	12.38 OR
2	GDR	SIEBERT, Gloria	12.61
3	FRG	ZACKIEWICZ, Claudia	12.75
4	URS	GRIGORIEVA, Natalia	12.79
5	FRA	COLLE, Florence	12.98
6	CAN	ROCHELEAU, Julie	12.99
—	USA	MARTIN, LaVonna	elim. semifinals
—	USA	DEVERS-ROBERTS, Gail	elim. semifinals
—	USA	HUMPHREY, Jacqueline	elim. semifinals

WOMEN'S 400-METER HURDLES / September 28

RANK	CTRY	ATHLETE	TIME
1	AUS	FLINTOFF-KING, Debra	53.17 OR
2	URS	LEDOVSKAIA, Tatiana	53.18
3	GDR	FIEDLER, Ellen	53.63
4	GDR	BUSCH, Sabine	53.69
5	GBR	GUNNELL, Sally	54.03
6	FRG	ABT, Gudrun	54.04
8	USA	SHEFFIELD, LaTanya	55.32
—	USA	WILLIAMS, Schwonda	elim. semifinals
—	USA	MAXIE, Leslie	elim. first round

WOMEN'S 4x100-METER RELAY / October 1

RANK	CTRY	ATHLETES	TIME
1	USA	BROWN, Alice / ECHOLS, Shella GRIFFITH JOYNER, Florence ASHORD, Evelyn (*YOUNG, Danette)	41.98

Continued

WOMEN'S 4x100-METER RELAY — Continued

RANK	CTRY	ATHLETES	TIME
2	GDR	MOELLER, Silke / BEHRENDT, Kerstin LANGE, Ingrid / GÖHR, Marlies	42.09
3	URS	KONDRATIEVA, Lioudmila MALTCHOUGINA, Galina / JIROVA, Marina POMOCHTCHNIKOVA, Natalia	42.75
4	FRG		42.76
5	BUL		43.02
6	POL		43.93

* ran in preliminaries only.

WOMEN'S 4x400-METER RELAY / October 1

RANK	CTRY	ATHLETES	TIME
1	URS	LEDOVSKAIA, Tatiana / NAZAROVA, Olga PINIGUINA, Maria / BRYZGUINA, Olga	3:15.18 WR
2	USA	HOWARD-HILL, Denean / DIXON, Diane BRISCO, Valerie / GRIFFITH JOYNER, Florence (*HOWARD, Sherri / LEATHERWOOD, Lillie)	3:15.51
3	GDR	NEUBAUER, Dagmar / EMMELMANN, Kirsten BUSCH, Sabine / MUELLER, Petra	3:18.29
4	FRG		3:22.49
5	JAM		3:23.13
6	GBR		3:26.89

* ran in preliminaries only.

WOMEN'S HIGH JUMP / September 30

RANK	CTRY	ATHLETE	METERS	FT/IN	
1	USA	RITTER, Louise	2.03	6' 8"	OR
2	BUL	KOSTADINOVA, Stefka	2.01	6' 7"	
3	URS	BYKOVA, Tamara	1.99	6' 6-1/4"	
4	URS	TOURTCHAK, Olga	1.96	6' 5"	
5T	ROM	ASTAFEI, Galina	1.93	6' 4"	
5T	BUL	ANDONOVA, Lyudmila	1.93	6' 4"	
—	USA	KING, Patricia	elim. qualifying round		
—	USA	SOMMER, Coleen	elim. qualifying round		

WOMEN'S LONG JUMP / September 29

RANK	CTRY	ATHLETE	METERS	FT/IN	
1	USA	JOYNER-KERSEE, Jackie	7.40	24' 3-1/2"	OR
2	GDR	DRECHSLER, Heike	7.22	23' 8-1/4"	
3	URS	TCHISTIAKOVA, Galina	7.11	23' 4"	
4	URS	BELEVSKAIA, Elena	7.04	23' 1-1/4"	
5	AUS	BOEGMAN, Nicole	6.73	22' 1"	
6	GBR	MAY, Fiona	6.62	21' 8-3/4"	
—	USA	LEWIS, Carol	elim. qualifying round		
—	USA	ECHOLS, Susan	elim. qualifying round		

WOMEN'S SHOT PUT / October 1

RANK	CTRY	ATHLETE	METERS	FT/IN
1	URS	LISOVSKAYA, Natalia	22.24	72' 11-3/4"
2	GDR	NEIMKE, Kathrin	21.07	69' 01-1/2"
3	CHN	LI, MEISU	21.06	69' 01-1/4"
4	GDR	MUELLER, Ines	20.37	66' 10"
5	FRG	LOSCH, Claudia	20.27	66' 06"
6	GDR	HARTWIG, Heike	20.20	66' 03-1/4"
12	USA	DASSE, Bonnie	17.60	57' 09"
—	USA	PAGEL, Ramona	elim. qualifying round	
—	USA	PRICE, Connie	elim. qualifying round	

WOMEN'S DISCUS / September 29

RANK	CTRY	ATHLETE	METERS	FT/IN	
1	GDR	HELLMANN, Martina	72.30	237' 02"	OR
2	GDR	GANSKY, Diana	71.88	235' 10"	
3	BUL	HRISTOVA, Tzvetanka	69.74	228' 10"	
4	BUL	MITKOVA, Svetla	69.14	226' 10"	
5	URS	ZVEREVA, Ellina	68.94	226' 02"	
6	TCH	SILHAVA, Zdenka	67.84	222' 07"	
11	USA	CADY, Carol	63.42	208' 01"	
—	USA	PAGEL, Ramona	elim. qualifying round		
—	USA	PRICE, Connie	elim. qualifying round		

WOMEN'S JAVELIN / September 26

RANK	CTRY	ATHLETE	METERS	FT/IN	
1	GDR	FELKE, Petra	74.68	245' 00"	OR
2	GBR	WHITBREAD, Fatima	70.32	230' 08"	
3	GDR	KOCH, Beate	67.30	220' 09"	
4	URS	KOSTIOUTCHENKOVA, Irina	67.00	219' 10"	
5	GDR	RENK, Silke	66.38	217' 09"	
6	URS	ERMOLOVITCH, Natalia	64.84	212' 09"	
7	USA	MAYHEW, Donna	61.78	202' 08"	
—	USA	SUTFIN, Lynda	elim. qualifying round		
—	USA	SMITH, Karin	elim. qualifying round		

HEPTATHLON / September 23-24

RANK	CTRY	ATHLETE	POINTS
1	USA	JOYNER-KERSEE, Jackie	7,291 WR
2	GDR	JOHN, Sabine	6,897
3	GDR	BEHMER, Anke	6,858
4	URS	CHOUBENKOVA, Natalia	6,540
5	URS	SABLOVSKAITE, Remiguiia	6,456
6	GDR	SCHULZ, Ines	6,411
8	USA	GREINER, Cindy	6,297
18	USA	BROWN, Wendy	5,972

MEN'S 100 METERS / September 24

RANK	CTRY	ATHLETE	TIME
1 *	USA	LEWIS, Carl	9.92 OR
2	GBR	CHRISTIE, Linford	9.97
3	USA	SMITH, Calvin	9.99
4	USA	MITCHELL, Dennis	10.04
5	BRA	SILVA, Robson	10.11
6	CAN	WILLIAMS, Desai	10.11

*Ben Johnson (CAN), original gold medalist, tested positive for use of a banned substance.

MEN'S 200 METERS / September 28

RANK	CTRY	ATHLETE	TIME
1	USA	DELOACH, Joe	19.75 OR
2	USA	LEWIS, Carl	19.79
3	BRA	SILVA, Robson	20.04
4	GBR	CHRISTIE, Linford	20.09
5	CAN	MAHORN, Atlee Anthony	20.39
6	FRA	QUENEHERVE, Gilles	20.40
—	USA	MARTIN, Roy	elim. semifinals

MEN'S 400 METERS / September 28

RANK	CTRY	ATHLETE	TIME
1	USA	LEWIS, Steven	43.87
2	USA	REYNOLDS, Harry "Butch"	43.93
3	USA	EVERETT, Danny	44.09
4	AUS	CLARK, Darren	44.55
5	NGR	EGBUNIKE, Innocent	44.72
6	JAM	CAMERON, Bertland	44.94

MEN'S 800 METERS / September 26

RANK	CTRY	ATHLETE	TIME
1	KEN	ERENG, Paul	1:43.45
2	BRA	CRUZ, Joaquim	1:43.90
3	MAR	AOUITA, Said	1:44.06
4	GBR	ELLIOTT, Peter	1:44.12
5	USA	GRAY, Johnny	1:44.80
6	BRA	BARBOSA, Jose	1:46.39
—	USA	EVERETT, Mark	elim. first round
—	USA	BASKIN, Tracy	elim. first round

MEN'S 1,500 METERS / October 1

RANK	CTRY	ATHLETE	TIME
1	KEN	RONO, Peter	3:35.96
2	GBR	ELLIOTT, Peter	3:36.15
3	GDR	HEROLD, Jens-Peter	3:36.21
4	GBR	CRAM, Steve	3:36.24
5	USA	SCOTT, Steve	3:36.99
6	HOL	KULKER, Han	3:37.08
10	USA	ATKINSON, Jeff	3:40.80
—	USA	DEADY, Mark	elim. semifinals

MEN'S 5,000 METERS / October 1

RANK	CTRY	ATHLETE	TIME
1	KEN	NGUGI, John	13:11.70
2	FRG	BAUMANN, Dieter	13:15.72
3	GDR	KUNZE, Hansjoerg	13:15.73
4	POR	CASTRO, Domingos	13:16.09
5	USA	MAREE, Sydney	13:23.69
6	GBR	BUCKNER, Jack	13:23.85
—	USA	PADILLA, Doug	elim. semifinals
—	USA	BRAHM, Terry	elim. sminfinals

MEN'S 10,000 METERS / September 26

RANK	CTRY	ATHLETE	TIME
1	MAR	BOUTAIB, Mly. Brahim	27:21.46 OR
2	ITA	ANTIBO, Salvatore	27:23.55
3	KEN	KIMELI, Kipkemboi	27:25.16
4	FRA	PRIANON, Jean-Louis	27:36.43
5	MEX	BARRIOS, Arturo	27:39.32
6	GDR	KUNZE, Hansjoerg	27:39.35
18	USA	BICKFORD, Bruce	29:09.74
—	USA	PORTER, Pat	elim. first round
—	USA	PLASENCIA, Steve	elim. first round

MEN'S MARATHON / October 2

RANK	CTRY	ATHLETE	TIME
1	ITA	BORDIN, Gelindo	2:10:32
2	KEN	WAKIIHURI, Douglas	2:10:47
3	DJI	AHMED SALEH, Houssein	2:10:59
4	JPN	NAKAYAMA, Takeyuki	2:11.05
5	AUS	MONEGHETTI, Stephen	2:11:49
6	GBR	SPEDDING, Charles	2:12:19
14	USA	PFITZINGER, Peter	2:14:44
29	USA	EYESTONE, Ed	2:19:09
DNF	USA	CONOVER, Mark	

MEN'S 110-METER HURDLES / September 26

RANK	CTRY	ATHLETE	TIME
1	USA	KINGDOM, Roger	12.98 OR
2	GBR	JACKSON, Colin	13.28
3	USA	CAMPBELL, Anthony	13.38
4	URS	CHICHKINE, Vladimir	13.51
5	GBR	RIDGEON, Jonathan	13.52
6	GBR	JARRETT, Tony	13.54
8	USA	BLAKE, Arthur	13.96

MEN'S 400-METER HURDLES / September 25

RANK	CTRY	ATHLETE	TIME
1	USA	PHILLIPS, Andre	47.19 OR
2	SEN	BA, El Hadj Dia	47.23
3	USA	MOSES, Edwin	47.56
4	USA	YOUNG, Kevin	47.94
5	JAM	GRAHAM, Winthrop	48.04
6	GBR	AKABUSI, Kriss	48.69

3,000-METER STEEPLECHASE / September 30

RANK	CTRY	ATHLETE	TIME
1	KEN	KARIUKI, Julius	8:05.51 OR
2	KEN	KOECH, Peter	8:06.79
3	GBR	ROWLAND, Mark	8:07.96
4	ITA	LAMBRUSCHINI, Alessandro	8:12.17
5	BEL	VAN DIJCK, William	8:13.99
6	USA	MARSH, Henry	8:14.39
—	USA	DIEMER, Brian	elim. semifinals
—	USA	ABSHIRE, Brian	elim. semifinals

MEN'S 4x100-METER RELAY / October 1

RANK	CTRY	ATHLETES	TIME
1	URS	BRYZGINE, Victor / KRYLOV, Vladimir MOURAVIEV, Vladimir / SAVINE, Vitali	38.19
2	GBR	BUNNEY, Elliot / REGIS, John McFARLANE, Michael / CHRISTIE, Linford	38.28
3	FRA	MARIE-ROSE, Bruno / SANGOUMA, Daniel QUENEHERVE, Gilles / MORINIERE, Max	38.40
4	JAM		38.47
5	ITA		38.54
6	FRG		38.55
DQ*	USA	MITCHELL, Dennis / ROBINSON, Albert SMITH, Calvin / McNEILL, Lee	—

* disqualified in round 1, heat 1.

MEN'S 4x400-METER RELAY / October 1

RANK	CTRY	ATHLETES	TIME
1	USA	EVERETT, Danny / LEWIS, Steven ROBINZINE, Kevin / REYNOLDS, Harry "Butch" (*VALMON, Andrew / McKAY, Antonio)	2:56.16 EWR
2	JAM	DAVIS, Howard / MORRIS, Devon GRAHAM, Winthrop / CAMERON, Bertland	3:00.30
3	FRG	DOBELEIT, Norbert / ITT, Edgar VAIHINGER, Jorg / LUBKE, Raif	3:00.56
4	GDR		3:01.13
5	GBR		3:02.00
6	AUS		3:02.49

* ran in preliminaries only.

MEN'S 20 KM WALK / September 23

RANK	CTRY	ATHLETE	TIME
1	TCH	PRIBILINEC, Jozef	1:19:57 OR
2	GDR	WEIGEL, Ronald	1:20:00
3	ITA	DAMILANO, Maurizio	1:20:14
4	ESP	MARIN, Jose	1:20:34
5	TCH	MRAZEK, Roman	1:20:43
6	URS	CHTCHENNIKOV, Mikhail	1:20:47
37	USA	MORGAN, Gary	1:27:26
38	USA	HEIRING, Jim	1:27:30
44	USA	LEWIS, Timothy	1:31:00

MEN'S 50 KM WALK / September 30

RANK	CTRY	ATHLETE	TIME
1	URS	IVANENKO, Viacheslav	3:38:29 OR
2	GDR	WEIGEL, Ronald	3:38:56
3	GDR	GAUDER, Hartwig	3:39:45
4	URS	POTACHEV, Alexandre	3:41:00
5	ESP	MARIN, Jose	3:43:03
6	AUS	BAKER, Simon	3:44:07
			Continued

MEN'S 50 KM WALK — Continued

RANK	CTRY	ATHLETE	TIME
22	USA	EVONIUK, Marco	3:56:55
23	USA	SCHUELER, Carl	3:57:44
34	USA	KAESTNER, Andrew	4:12:49

MEN'S HIGH JUMP / September 25

RANK	CTRY	ATHLETE	METERS	FT/IN	
1	URS	AVDEENKO, Guennadi	2.38	7' 9-3/4"	OR
2	USA	CONWAY, Hollis	2.36	7' 8-3/4"	
3T	URS	POVARNITSYNE, Roudolf	2.36	7' 8-3/4"	
3T	SWE	SJÖBERG, Patrik	2.36	7' 8-3/4"	
5	BER	SAUNDERS, Clarence	2.34	7' 8"	
6	FRG	MÖGENBURG, Dietmar	2.34	7' 8"	
10	USA	HOWARD, Jim	2.31	7' 7"	
11	USA	STANTON, Brian	2.31	7' 7"	

MEN'S POLE VAULT / September 29

RANK	CTRY	ATHLETE	METERS	FT/IN	
1	URS	BUBKA, Sergei	5.90	19' 4-1/4"	OR
2	URS	GATAOULLINE, Radion	5.85	19' 2-1/4"	
3	URS	EGOROV, Grigori	5.80	19' 0-1/4"	
4	USA	BELL, Earl	5.70	18' 8-1/4"	
5T	FRA	VIGNERON, Thierry	5.70	18' 8-1/4"	
5T	FRA	COLLET, Philippe	5.70	18' 8-1/4"	
10	USA	TARPENNING, Kory	5.50	18' 0-1/2"	
12	USA	OLSON, BILLY	5.50	18' 0-1/2"	

MEN'S LONG JUMP / September 26

RANK	CTRY	ATHLETE	METERS	FT/IN
1	USA	LEWIS, Carl	8.72	28' 07-1/2"
2	USA	POWELL, MIKE	8.49	27' 10-1/4"
3	USA	MYRICKS, Larry	8.27	27' 01-3/4"
4	ITA	EVANGELISTI, Giovanni	8.08	26' 06-1/4"
5	ESP	CORGOS, Antonio	8.03	26' 04-1/4"
6	HUN	SZALMA, Laszlo	8.00	26' 03"

MEN'S TRIPLE JUMP / September 24

RANK	CTRY	ATHLETE	METERS	FT/IN	
1	BUL	MARKOV, Hristo	17.61	57' 09-1/2"	OR
2	URS	LAPCHINE, Igor	17.52	57' 05-3/4"	
3	URS	KOVALENKO, Alexandre	17.42	57' 02"	
4	URS	PROTSENKO, Oleg	17.38	57' 00-1/4"	
5	USA	SIMPKINS, Charlie	17.29	56' 08-3/4"	
6	USA	BANKS, Willie	17.03	55' 10-1/2"	
—	USA	CANNON, Robert	elim. qualifying round		

MEN'S SHOT PUT / September 23

RANK	CTRY	ATHLETE	METERS	FT/IN	
1	GDR	TIMMERMANN, Ulf	22.47	73' 08-3/4"	OR
2	USA	BARNES, Randy	22.39	73' 05-1/2"	
3	SUI	GUENTHOER, Werner	21.99	72' 01-3/4"	
4	GDR	BEYER, Udo	21.40	70' 02-1/2"	
5	TCH	MACHURA, Remigius	20.57	67' 06"	
6	CHI	WEIL, Gert	20.38	66' 10-1/2"	
9	USA	TAFRALIS, Gregg	20.16	66' 1-3/4"	
11	USA	DOEHRING, Jim	19.89	65'3-1/4''	

MEN'S DISCUS / October 1

RANK	CTRY	ATHLETE	METERS	FT/IN	
1	GDR	SCHULT, Jurgen	68.82	225' 09"	OR
2	URS	OUBARTAS, Romas	67.48	221' 05"	
3	FRG	DANNEBERG, Rolf	67.38	221' 01"	
4	URS	DOUMTCHEV, Iouri	66.42	217' 11"	
5	USA	WILKINS, Mac	65.90	216' 02"	
6	TCH	VALENT, Gejza	65.80	215' 10"	
10	USA	BUNCIC, Mike	62.46	204' 11"	
—	USA	HEISLER, Randy	elim. qualifying round		

HAMMER THROW / September 26

RANK	CTRY	ATHLETE	METERS	FT/IN	
1	URS	LITVINOV, Serguei	84.80	278' 02"	OR
2	URS	SEDYKH, Yuriy	83.76	274' 10"	
3	URS	TAMM, Iouri	81.16	266' 03"	
4	GDR	HABER, Ralf	80.44	263' 11"	
5	FRG	WEIS, Heinz	79.16	259' 08"	
6	HUN	GECSEK, Tibor	78.36	275' 01"	
—	USA	DEAL, Lance	elim. qualifying round		
—	USA	FLAX, Ken	elim. qualifying round		

MEN'S JAVELIN / September 25

RANK	CTRY	ATHLETE	METERS	FT/IN
1	FIN	KORJUS, Tapio	84.28	276' 06"
2	TCH	ZELEZNY, Jan	84.12	276' 00"
3	FIN	RATY, Seppo	83.26	273' 02"
4	FRG	TAFELMEIER, Klaus	82.72	271' 05"
5	URS	EVCIOUKOV, Viktor	82.32	270' 01"
6	GDR	WEISS, Gerald	81.30	266' 09"
—	USA	STEPHENS, David	elim. qualifying round	
—	USA	PETRANOFF, Tom	elim. qualifying round	
—	USA	CROUSER, Brian	elim. qualifying round	

DECATHLON / September 28-29

RANK	CTRY	ATHLETE	POINTS
1	GDR	SCHENK, Christian	8,488
2	GDR	VOSS, Torsten	8,399
3	CAN	STEEN, Dave	8,328
4	GBR	THOMPSON, Daley	8,306
5	FRA	PLAZIAT, Christian	8,272
6	FRA	BLONDEL, Alain	8,268
7	USA	BRIGHT, Tim	8,216
9	USA	JOHNSON, David	8,180
36	USA	KINDER, Gary	3,900

BASKETBALL

WOMEN / September 29

OVERALL		MEDAL ROUND				
RANK	CTRY	WON	LOST	SCORES		USA GAME SCORES
1	USA	5	0	77-70	(Final)	USA vs. TCH 87-81
2	YUG	3	2			USA vs. YUG 101-74
3	URS	3	2	68-53	(3rd-4th)	USA vs. CHN 94-79
4	AUS	2	3			USA vs. URS 102-88
5	BUL	3	2	102-74	(5th-6th)	USA vs. YUG 77-70
6	CHN	2	3			

MEN / September 30

OVERALL		MEDAL ROUND				
RANK	CTRY	WON	LOST	SCORES		USA GAMES SCORES
1	URS	7	1	76-63	(Final)	USA vs. ESP 97-53
2	YUG	6	2			USA vs. CAN 76-70
3	USA	7	1	78-49	(3rd-4th)	USA vs. BRA 78-49
4	AUS	4	4			USA vs. CHN 108-57
5	BRA	5	3	106-90	(5th-6th)	USA vs. EGY 102-35
6	CAN	3	5			USA vs. PUR 94-57
						USA vs. URS 76-82
						USA vs. AUS 78-49

BOXING

RSC - Referee stopped contest
KO - Knockout

LIGHT FLYWEIGHT - 48 KG / October 1

RANK	CTRY	ATHLETE		DECISION
1	BUL	HRISTOV, Ivailo		5-0
2	USA	CARBAJAL, Michael		
3T	PHI	SERANTES, Leopoldo		
3T	HUN	ISASZEGI, Robert		

FLYWEIGHT - 51 KG / October 2

RANK	CTRY	ATHLETE		DECISION
1	KOR	KIM, Kwang sun		4-1
2	GDR	TEWS, Andreas		
31	MEX	GONZALEZ, Mario		
3T	URS	SKRIABIN, Timofei		
—	USA	JOHNSON, Arthur		elim. eighthfinals

BANTAMWEIGHT - 54 KG / October 1

RANK	CTRY	ATHLETE		DECISION
1	USA	McKINNEY, Kennedy		5-0
2	BUL	HRISTOV, Alexandar		
3T	THA	MOOLSAN, Phajol		
3T	COL	JULIO ROCHA, Jorge		

FEATHERWEIGHT - 57 KG / October 2

RANK	CTRY	ATHLETE		DECISION
1	ITA	PARISI, Giovanni	RSC-1	1:41
2	ROM	DUMITRESCU, Daniel		
3T	KOR	LEE, Jae-hyuk		
3T	MAR	ACHIK, Abdelhak		
—	USA	BANKS, Kelcie		elim. first round

LIGHTWEIGHT - 60 KG / October 1

RANK	CTRY	ATHLETE		DECISION
1	GDR	ZUELOW, Andreas		5-0
2	SWE	CRAMNE, George		
3T	USA	ELLIS, Romallis		
3T	MGL	ENKHBAT, Nerguy		

LIGHT WELTERWEIGHT - 63.5 KG / October 2

RANK	CTRY	ATHLETE		DECISION
1	URS	JANOVSKI, Viatcheslav		5-0
2	AUS	CHENEY, Grahame		
3T	FRG	GIES, Reiner		
3T	SWE	MYRBERG, Lars		
—	USA	FOSTER, Todd		elim. quarterfinals

WELTERWEIGHT - 67 KG / October 1

RANK	CTRY	ATHLETE		DECISION
1	KEN	WANGILA, Robert	RSC-2	0:44
2	FRA	BOUDOUANI, Laurent		
3T	USA	GOULD, Kenneth		
3T	POL	DYDAK, Jan		

LIGHT MIDDLEWEIGHT - 71 KG / October 2

RANK	CTRY	ATHLETE		DECISION
1	KOR	PARK, Si-hun		3-2
2	USA	JONES, Roy		
3T	CAN	DOWNEY, Raymond		
3T	GBR	WOODHALL, Richard		

MIDDLEWEIGHT - 75 KG / October 1

RANK	CTRY	ATHLETE		DECISION
1	GDR	MASKE, Henry		5-0
2	CAN	MARCUS, Egerton		
3T	KEN	SANDE, Chris		
3T	PAK	SYED, Hussain Shah		
—*	USA	HEMBRICK, Anthony		elim. first round

* walkover

LIGHT HEAVYWEIGHT - 81 KG / October 2

RANK	CTRY	ATHLETE		DECISION
1	USA	MAYNARD, Andrew		5-0
2	URS	CHANAVAZOV, Nourmagomed		
3T	YUG	SKARO, Damir		
3T	POL	PETRICH, Henryk		

HEAVYWEIGHT - 91 KG / October 1

RANK	CTRY	ATHLETE		DECISION
1	USA	MERCER, Ray	KO-1	2:16
2	KOR	BAIK, Hyun-man		
3T	HOL	VANDERLIJDE, Arnold		
3T	POL	GOLOTA, Andrzej		

SUPER HEAVYWEIGHT - 91 KG / October 2

RANK	CTRY	ATHLETE		DECISION
1	CAN	LEWIS, Lennox	RSC-2	0:43
2	USA	BOWE, Riddick		
3T	POL	ZARENKIEWICZ, Janusz		
3T	URS	MIROCHNITCHENKO, Alexandre		

CANOE AND KAYAK

MEN'S C-1, 500 METERS / September 30

RANK	CTRY	ATHLETE	TIME
1	GDR	HEUKRODT, Olaf	1:56.42
2	URS	SLIVINSKII, Mikhail	1:57.26
3	BUL	MARINOV, Martin	1:57.27
4	HUN	SZABO, Attila	1:59.87
5	POL	PINCZURA, Jan	1:59.90
6	ROM	MACARENCU, Aurel	2:00.98
—	USA	TERRELL, James	elim. semifinals

MEN'S C-2, 500 METERS / September 30

RANK	CTRY	ATHLETES	TIME
1	URS	RENEISKI, Victor / JOURAVSKI, Nikolai	1:41.77
2	POL	DOPIERALA, Marek / LBIK, Marek	1:43.61
3	FRA	RENAUD, Philippe / BETTIN, Joel	1:43.81
4	BUL	BONEV, Deyan / BOJILOV, Petar	1:44.32
5	GDR	SCHUCK, Alexander / ZERESKE, Thomas	1:44.36
6	HUN	SARUSI KIS, Janos / VASKUTI, Istvan	1:44.85
—	USA	McLAIN, Rodney / MERRITT, Bruce	elim. semifinals

MEN'S C-1, 1,000 METERS / October 1

RANK	CTRY	ATHLETE	TIME
1	URS	KLEMENTIEV, Ivan	4:12.78
2	GDR	SCHMIDT, Joerg	4:15.83
3	BUL	BOUKHALOV, Nikolai	4:18.94
4	CAN	CAIN, Larry	4:20.70
5	ROM	MACARENCU, Aurel	4:21.72
6	HUN	PULAI, Imre	4:21.86
—	USA	MERRITT, Bruce	elim. semifinals

MEN'S C-2, 1,000 METERS / October 1

RANK	CTRY	ATHLETES	TIME
1	URS	RENEISKI, Victor / JOURAVSKI, Nikolai	3:48.36
2	GDR	HEUKRODT, Olaf / SPELLY, Ingo	3:51.44
3	POL	DOPIERALA, Marek / LBIK, Marek	3:54.33
4	DEN	FREDERIKSEN, Christian / NIELSSON, Arne	3:54.94
5	FRG	FAUST, Hartmut / FAUST, Wolfram	3:55.62
6	ROM	OBREJA, Grigore / ANDRIEV, Gheorghe	3:56.56
—	USA	STEWARD, Gregory / URICK, Ronald	elim. repechage

WOMEN'S K-1, 500 METERS / September 30

RANK	CTRY	ATHLETE	TIME
1	BUL	GUECHEVA, Vania	1:55.19
2	GDR	SCHMIDT, Birgit	1:55.31
3	POL	DYLEWSKA, Izabela	1:57.38
4	HUN	KOBAN, Rita	1:57.58
5	DEN	KNUDSEN, Yvonne B.	1:58.80
6	USA	PHILLIPS, Traci	2:00.81

WOMEN'S K-2, 500 METERS / September 30

RANK	CTRY	ATHLETES	TIME
1	GDR	SCHMIDT, Birgit / NOTHNAGEL, Anke	1:43.46
2	BUL	GUECHEVA, Vania / PALIISKA, Diana	1:44.06
3	HOL	DERCKX, Annemiek / COX, Annemarie	1:46.00
4	HUN	MESZAROS, Erika / RAKUSZ, Eva	1:46.58
5	URS	SALOMYKOVA, Irina / KHMELEVSKAIA, Irina	1:47.68
6	SWE	OLSSON, Anne / ANDERSSON, Agneta	1:48.39
7	USA	CONOVER, Sheila / MARINO GEERS, Cathy	1:50.33

WOMEN'S K-4, 500 METERS / October 1

RANK	CTRY	ATHLETES	TIME
1	GDR	SCHMIDT, Birgit / NOTHNAGEL, Anke PORTWICH, Ramona / SINGER, Heike	1:40.78
2	HUN	GECZI, Erika / MESZAROS, Erika RAKUSZ, Eva / KOBAN, Rita	1:41.88
3	BUL	GUECHEVA, Vania / PALIISKA, Diana PETKOVA, Ogniana / IVANOVA, Borislava	1:42.63
4	URS		1:44.26
5	FRG		1:45.62
6	SWE		1:45.67
9	USA	PHILLIPS, Traci / CONOVER, Sheila MARINO GEERS, Cathy / DERY-BATLIK, Shirley	1:47.94

MEN'S K-1, 500 METERS / September 30

RANK	CTRY	ATHLETE	TIME
1	HUN	GYULAY, Zsolt	1:44.82
2	GDR	STAEHLE, Andreas	1:46.38
3	NZL	MacDONALD, Paul	1:46.46
4	USA	HERBERT, Michael	1:46.73
5	SWE	SUNDKVIST, Karl	1:46.76
6	TCH	SZABO, Attila	1:47.38

MEN'S K-2, 500 METERS / September 30

RANK	CTRY	ATHLETES	TIME
1	NZL	FERGUSON, Ian / MacDONALD, Paul	1:33.98
2	URS	NAGAEV, Igor / DENISSOV, Victor	1:34.15
3	HUN	ABRAHAM, Attila / CSIPES, Ferenc	1:34.32
4	FRG	SCHOLL, Reiner / PFRANG, Thomas	1:34.40
5	ROM	STOIAN, Daniel / VELEA, Angelin	1:35.96
6	POL	FREIMUT, Maciej / KURPIEWSKI, Wojciech	1:36.22
8	USA	KENT, Olney "Terry" / WHITE, Carl "Terry"	1:36.62

MEN'S K-1, 1,000 METERS / October 1

RANK	CTRY	ATHLETE	TIME
1	USA	BARTON, Greg	3:55.27
2	AUS	DAVIES, Grant	3:55.28
3	GDR	WOHLLEBE, Andre	3:55.55
4	URS	BANKOVSKI, Dmitri	3:56.49
5	SWE	OLSSON, Gunnar	3:56.84
6	NZL	THOMPSON, Alan	3:56.91

MEN'S K-2, 1,000 METERS / October 1

RANK	CTRY	ATHLETES	TIME
1	USA	BARTON, Greg / BELLINGHAM, Norman	3:32.42
2	NZL	FERGUSON, Ian / MacDONALD, Paul	3:32.71
3	AUS	FOSTER, Peter / GRAHAM, Kelvin	3:33.76
4	FRG	ELLWANGER, Niels / LOEMKER, Carsten	3:34.63
5	GDR	BEHLING, Guido / KRENTZ, Torsten	3:35.44
6	ROM	STOIAN, Daniel / VELEA, Angelin	3:35.75

MEN'S K-4, 1,000 METERS / October 1

RANK	CTRY	ATHLETES	TIME
1	HUN	GYULAY, Zsolt / CSIPES, Ferenc HODOSI, Sandor / ABRAHAM, Attila	3:00.20
2	URS	MOTOUZENKO, Alexandre / KIRSANOV, Sergei NAGAEV, Igor / DENISSOV, Victor	3:01.40
3	GDR	BLUHM, Kay / WOHLLEBE, Andre STAEHLE, Andreas / BLIESENER, Hans-Joerg	3:02.37
4	AUS		3:03.70
5	POL		3:04.73
6	FRG		3:05.43
—	USA	HARBOLD, Michael / WHITE, Carl "Terry" BADER, Curt / KENT, Olney "Terry"	elim. semifinals

CYCLING

WOMEN'S MATCH SPRINT / September 24

RANK	CTRY	ATHLETE	1 RD	2 RD	3 RD
1	URS	SALOUMIAE, Erika		12.00	12.58
2	GDR	ROTHENBURGER-LUDING, Christa	11.68		
3	USA	PARASKEVIN YOUNG, Connie	14.07	12.41	
4	FRA	GAUTHERON, Isabelle			
5	AUS	SPEIGHT, Julie		12.56	
6	CHN	ZHOU, Suying			

WOMEN'S 82 KM IND. ROAD RACE / September 26

RANK	CTRY	ATHLETE	TIME
1	HOL	KNOL, Monique	2:00.52
2	FRG	NIEHAUS, Jutta	same time
3	URS	ZILPORITEE, Laima	same time
4	CAN	BRUNET, Genevieve	same time
5	URS	EVPAK, Valentina	same time
6	GBR	BLOWER, Maria	same time
8	USA	THOMPSON-BENEDICT, Inga	same time
14	USA	BANKAITIS-DAVIS, Bunki	same time
16	USA	ZACK, Sally	same time

MEN'S MATCH SPRINT / September 24

RANK	CTRY	ATHLETE	1 RD	2 RD	3 RD
1	GDR	HESSLICH, Lutz	13.98	11.82	
2	URS	KOVCHE, Nikolai			
3	AUS	NEIWAND, Gary	10.97	10.88	
4	GBR	ALEXANDER, Edward			
5	TCH	SUSTR, Vratislav	11.34		
6	BEL	SCHOEFS, Erik			
—	USA	CARPENTER, Ken	elim. first round repechage		

MEN'S 4,000 M INDIVIDUAL PURSUIT / September 22

RANK	CTRY	ATHLETE	TIME
1	URS	UMARAS, Gintaoutas	4:32.00
2	AUS	WOODS, Dean	4:35.00
3	GDR	DITTERT, Bernd	4:34.17
4	GBR	STURGESS, Colin	4:34.90
5	POL	DAWIDOWICZ, Ryszard	4:39.44
6	DEN	CLAUSEN, Peter	4:42.62
—	USA	BRINTON, David	elim. eighthfinals

MEN'S 4,000 M TEAM PURSUIT / September 24

RANK	CTRY	ATHLETES	TIME
1	URS	EKIMOV, Viatcheslav / KASPOUTIS, Artouras NELUBINE, Dmitri / UMARAS, Gintaoutas	4:13.31
2	GDR	BLOCHWITZ, Steffen / HENNIG, Roland MEIER, Dirk / WOLF, Carsten	4:14.09
3	AUS	DUTTON, Brett / McCARNEY, Wayne McGLEDE, Stephen / WOODS, Dean	4:16.02
4	FRA		4:22.23
5	TCH		4:19.05
6	ITA		4:20.90
—	USA	LETTIERI, Dave / McCARTHY, Michael NITZ, Leonard Harvey / SUNDQUIST, Carl	elim. qual. round

MEN'S 50 KM POINT RACE / September 24

RANK	CTRY	ATHLETE	LAPS DOWN	PTS.
1	DEN	FROST, Dan	00	038
2	HOL	PEELEN, Leo	00	026
3	URS	GANEEV, Marat	01	046
4	AUS	BURNS, Robert	01	020
5	ARG	CURUCHET, Juan Esteban	01	018
6	FRG	MESSERSCHMIDT, Uwe	02	028
8	USA	ANDREU, Frankie	02	021

MEN'S 100 KM TEAM TIME TRIAL / September 18

RANK	CTRY	ATHLETES	TIME
1	GDR	AMPLER, Uwe / KUMMER, Mario LANDSMANN, Maik / SCHUR, Jan	1:57:47.7
2	POL	HALUPCZOK, Joachim / JASKULA, Zenon LESNIEWSKI, Marek / SYPYTKOWSKI, Andrzej	1:57:54.2
3	SWE	JOHANSSON, Björn / KARLSSON, Jan LAFIS, Michel / JARL, Anders	1:59:47.3
4	FRA		1:59:49.8
5	ITA		1:59:58.3
6	FRG		2:00:06.3
10	USA	ALVIS, Norm / COPELAND, James PALMER, Tony / PAULIN, Andy	2:02:35.7

MEN'S ONE KM TIME TRIAL / September 20

RANK	CTRY	ATHLETE	TIME
1	URS	KIRITCHENKO, Alexandre	1:04.499
2	AUS	VINNICOMBE, Martin	1:04.784
3	FRG	LECHNER, Robert	1:05.114
4	DEN	ROPKE, Kurt Kenneth	1:05.168
5	ESP	GONZALEZ, Bernardo	1:05.281
6	GDR	MALCHOW, Maic	1:05.393
14	USA	LIVINGSTON, Bobby	1:06.926

MEN'S 196.8 KM ROAD RACE / September 27

RANK	CTRY	ATHLETE	TIME
1	GDR	LUDWIG, Olaf	4:32.22
2	FRG	GROENE, Bernd	4:32.25
3	FRG	HENN, Christian	4:32.46
4	USA	MIONSKE, Robert	same time
5	URS	ABDOUJAPAROV, Djamolidin	same time
6	AUS	SALAS, Edward	same time
65	USA	McKINLEY, Scott	4:32.56
69	USA	SCHOMMER, Craig	4:32.56

EQUESTRIAN

INDIVIDUAL DRESSAGE / September 27

RANK	CTRY	ATHLETE / HORSE	TOTAL
1	FRG	UPHOFF, Nicole / Rembrandt 24	1,521
2	FRA	OTTO-CREPIN, Margitt / Corlandus	1,462
3	SUI	STUECKELBERGER, Chris / Gauguin de Lully Ch.	1,417
4	CAN	ISHOY, Cynthia / Dynasty	1,401
5	FIN	KYRKLUND, Kyra / Matador	1,393
6	FRG	THEORDORESCU, Monica / Ganimedes	1,385
13	USA	DOVER, Robert / Federleicht	1,320
17	USA	RANSEHOUSEN, Jessica / Orpheus	1,282

TEAM DRESSAGE / September 25

RANK	CTRY	ATHLETE / HORSE	TOTAL
1	FRG	KLIMKE, Dr. Reiner / Ahlerich 2 LINSENHOFF, Annkathri / Courage 10 THEODORESCU, Monica / Ganimedes UPHOFF, Nicole / Rembrandt 24	4,302
2	SUI	HOFER, Otto / Andiamo STUECKELBERGER, Chris / Gaugin de Lully Ch. RAMSEIER, Daniel / Random SCHATZMANN, Samuel / Rochus	4,164
3	CAN	ISHOY, Cynthia / Dynasty PRACHT, Eva Maria / Emirage SMITH, Gina / Malte NICOLL, Ashley / Reipo	3,969
4	URS		3,926
5	HOL		3,903
6	USA	BAUDIN, Belinda / Christopher DOVER, Robert / Federleicht GRAY, Lendon / Later On RANSEHOUSEN, Jessica / Orpheus	3,883

INDIVIDUAL THREE-DAY EVENT / October 2

RANK	CTRY	ATHLETE / HORSE	TOTAL
1	NZL	TODD, Mark / Charisma	42.60
2	GBR	STARK, Ian / Sir Wattie	52.80
3	GBR	LENG, Virginia / Master Craftsman	62.00
4	FRG	ERHORN, Claus / Justyn Thyme	62.35
5	NZL	POTTINGER, Tinks / Volunteer	65.80
6	FRG	BAUMANN, Matthias / Shamrock 11	68.80
10	USA	DAWSON, Phyllis / Albany II	99.60
18	USA	DAVIDSON, Bruce / Dr. Peaches	141.80
—	USA	SUTTON, Ann / Tarzan	withdrew
—	USA	LENDE, Karen / The Optimist	eliminated

TEAM THREE-DAY EVENT / September 22

RANK	CTRY	ATHLETE / HORSE	TOTAL
1	FRG	ERHORN, Claus / Justyn Thyme BAUMANN, Matthias / Shamrock 11 KASPAREIT, Thies / Sherry 42 EHRENBRINK, Ralf / Uncle Todd	225.95
2	GBR	PHILLIPS, Mark / Cartier STRAKER, Karen / Get Smart LENG, Virginia / Master Craftsman STARK, Ian / Sir Wattie	271.20
3	NZL	TODD, Mark / Charisma KNIGHTON, Marges / Enterprise BENNIE, Andrew / Grayshott POTTINGER, Tinks / Volunteer	256.80
4	POL		389.60
5	AUS		457.60
6	FRA		498.80
—	USA	DAWSON, Phyllis / Albany II DAVIDSON, Bruce / Dr. Peaches SUTTON, Ann / Tarzan LENDE, Karen / The Optimist	eliminated

INDIVIDUAL JUMPING / October 2

RANK	CTRY	ATHLETE / HORSE	TOTAL
1	FRA	DURAND, Pierre / Jappeloup	1.25
2*	USA	BEST, Greg / Gem Twist	4.00
3	FRG	HUCK, Karsten / Nepomuk 8	4.00
4T	USA	KURSINSKI, Anne / Starman	8.00
4T	GBR	BROOME, David / Countryman	8.00
6	MEX	AZCARRAGA, Jaime / Chin Chin	8.25
7T	USA	FARGIS, Joe / Mill Pearl	12.00

* won silver medal based on lower total time.

TEAM JUMPING / September 28

RANK	CTRY	ATHLETE / HORSE	TOTAL
1	FRG	BEERBAUM, Ludger / The Freak BRINKMANN, Wolfgang / Pedro HAFEMEISTER, Dirk / Orchidee 76 SLOOTHAAK, Franke / Walzerkonig 19	17.25
2	USA	BEST, Greg / Gem Twist JACQUIN, Lisa / For The Moment KURSINSKI, Anne / Starman FARGIS, Joe / Mill Pearl	20.50

Continued

TEAM JUMPING — Continued

RANK	CTRY	ATHLETE / HORSE	TOTAL
3	FRA	BOURDY, Hubert / Morgat COTTIER, Frederic / Flambeauc ROBERT, Michel / La Fayette DURAND, Pierre / Jappeloup	27.50
4	CAN		28.75
5	HOL		32.25
6	GBR		40.00

FENCING

WOMEN'S INDIVIDUAL FOIL / September 22

RANK	CTRY	ATHLETE
1	FRG	FICHTEL, Anja
2	FRG	BAU, Sabine
3	FRG	FUNKENHAUSER, Zita
4	HUN	JANOSI, Zsuzsanna
5	URS	SADOVSKAIA, Tatiana
6	HUN	STEFANEK, Gertrud
11	USA	BILODEAU, Caitlin
35	USA	MONPLAISIR, Sharon
36	USA	O'NEILL, Mary Jane

WOMEN'S TEAM FOIL / September 28

RANK	CTRY	ATHLETES
1	FRG	BAU, Sabine / FICHTEL, Anja FUNKENHAUSER, Zita / KLUG, Annette WEBER, Christiane
2	ITA	BORTOLOZZI, Francesca / GANDOLFI, Annapia / TRAVERSA, Lucia / VACCARONI, Dorina / ZALAFFI, Margherita
3	HUN	JANOSI, Zsuzsanna / KOVACS, Edit STEFANEK, Gertrud / SZOCS, Zsusanna TUSCHAK, Katalin
4	URS	
5	CHN	
6	USA	BILODEAU, Caitlin / CHERIS, Elaine MONPLAISIR, Sharon / O'NEILL, Mary Jane / SULLIVAN, Molly

MEN'S INDIVIDUAL EPÉE / September 24

RANK	CTRY	ATHLETE
1	FRG	SCHMITT, Arnd
2	FRA	RIBOUD, Philippe
3	URS	CHOUVALOV, Andrei
4	ITA	CUOMO, Sandro
5	GDR	KUEHNEMUND, Torsten
6	SWE	BERGSTROM, Jerri
38	USA	TREVOR, Stephen
47	USA	STULL, Robert
71	USA	MARX, Robert

MEN'S TEAM EPÉE / September 30

RANK	CTRY	ATHLETES
1	FRA	DELPLA, Frederic / HENRY, Jean Michel LENGLET, Olivier / RIBOUD, Philippe / SRECKI, Eric
2	FRG	BORRMANN, Elmar / FISCHER, Volker / GERULL, Thomas / PUSCH, Alexander / SCHMITT, Arnd
3	URS	CHOUVALOV, Andrei / KOLOBKOV, Pavel REZNITCHENKO, Vladimir / TICHKO, Mikhail TIKHOMIROV, Igor
4	ITA	
5	SUI	
6	HUN	
11	USA	MARX, Robert / MOREAU, John / SHELLEY, Lee / STULL, Robert / TREVOR, Stephen

MEN'S INDIVIDUAL FOIL / September 22

RANK	CTRY	ATHLETE
1	ITA	CERIONI, Stefano
2	GDR	WAGNER, Udo
3	URS	ROMANKOV, Alexandre
4	FRG	SCHRECK, Ulrich
5	HUN	ERSEK, Zsolt
6	ITA	NUMA, Mauro
12	USA	LEWISON, Peter
36	USA	MARX, Michael
43	USA	LITTELL, David

MEN'S TEAM FOIL / September 27

RANK	CTRY	ATHLETES
1	URS	ROMANKOV, Alexandre / MAMEDOV, Ilgar / APTSIAOURI, Vladimir / IBRAGUIMOV, Anvar / KORESTSKII, Boris
2	FRG	GEY, Mathias / WEIDNER, Thorsten / BEHR, Matthias / SCHRECK, Ulrich / ENDRES, Thomas
3	HUN	ERSEK, Zsolt / SZEKERES, Pal / SZELEI, Istvan / BUSA, Istvan / GATAI, Robert
4	GDR	
5	POL	
6	FRA	
14	USA	LEWISON, Peter / LITTELL, David / MARX, Michael MASSIALAS, Gregory / NOMOMURA, George

MEN'S INDIVIDUAL SABRE / September 23

RANK	CTRY	ATHLETE
1	FRA	LAMOUR, Jean François
2	POL	OLECH, Janusz
3	ITA	SCALZO, Giovanni
4	FRA	DELRIEU, Philippe
5	HUN	NEBALD, Gyorgy
6	URS	POGOSSOV, Gueorgui
16	USA	MORMANDO, George
20	USA	WESTBROOK, Peter
32	USA	LOFTON, Michael

MEN'S TEAM SABRE / September 29

RANK	CTRY	ATHLETES
1	HUN	BUJDOSO, Imre / CSONGRADI, Laszlo GEDOEVARI, Imre / NEBALD, Gyorgy / SZABO, Bence
2	URS	ALCHAN, Andrei / BOURTSEV, Mikhail KORIAJKINE, Serguei / MINDIRGASSOV, Serguei POGOSSOV, Gueorgui
3	ITA	CAVALIERE, Massimo / MARIN, Marco / DALLA BARBA, Gianfranco / MEGLIO, Ferdinando / SCALZO, Giovanni
4	FRA	
5	POL	
6	FRG	
7	USA	COTTINGHAM, Robert / FRIEDBERG, Paul / LOFTON, Michael / MORMANDO, Steve / WESTBROOK, Peter

FIELD HOCKEY

WOMEN / September 30

RANK	CTRY	WON	LOST	TIED	SCORE	USA GAME SCORES
1	AUS	3	0	2	2-0 (Final)	USA vs. HOL 1-3
2	KOR	3	1	1		USA vs. ARG 1-2
3	HOL	4	1	0	3-1 (3rd-4th)	USA vs. GBR 2-2
4	GBR	1	3	1		USA vs. FRG 1-2
5	FRG	3	2	0	4-2 (5th-6th)	USA vs. ARG 1-3
6	CAN	1	3	1		
7	ARG	2	3	0	3-1 (7th-8th)	
8	USA	0	4	1		

MEN / October 1

RANK	CTRY	WON	LOST	TIED	SCORE
1	GBR	5	1	1	3-1 (Final)
2	FRG	5	1	1	
3	HOL	4	2	1	2-1 (3rd-4th)
4	AUS	5	2	0	
5	PAK	5	2	0	2-1 (5th-6th)
6	IND	2	3	2	

(no USA entry)

GYMNASTICS

WOMEN'S TEAM COMPETITION / September 21

RANK	CTRY	ATHLETES	TOTAL
1	URS	BAITOVA, Svetlana / CHEVTCHENKO, Elena STRAJEVA, Olga / BOGUINSKAIA, Svetlana LACHTCHENOVA, Natalia SHOUSHOUNOVA, Elena	395.475
2	ROM	VOINEA, Camelia / GOLEA, Eugenia POPA, Celestina / POTORAC, Gabriela SILIVAS, Daniela / DOBRE, Aurelia	394.125
3	GDR	JENTSCH, Martina / FAEHNRICH, Gabriele KLOTZ, Ulrike / SCHIEFERDECKER, Bettina THUEMMLER, Doerte / KERSTEN, Dagmar	390.875
4	USA	MARLOWE, Melissa / STACK, Chelle GARRISON-STEVES, Kelly / SPIVEY, Theresa "Hope" / JOHNSON, Brandy / MILLS, Phoebe	390.575
5	BUL		390.550
6	CHN		388.400

WOMEN'S INDIVIDUAL ALL-AROUND / September 23

RANK	CTRY	ATHLETE	PRELIM.	VAULT BEAM	U BARS FLOOR	TOTAL
1	URS	SHOUSHOUNOVA, Elena	39.837	10.000 9.925	9.900 10.000	79.662
2	ROM	SILIVAS, Daniela	39.787	9.950 9.900	10.000 10.000	79.637
3	URS	BOGUINSKAIA, Svetlana	39.700	9.950 9.900	9.950 9.900	79.400
4	ROM	POTORAC, Gabriela	39.462	9.800 9.950	9.900 9.925	79.037
5	URS	LACHTCHENOVA, Natalia	39.450	9.825 9.875	9.825 9.900	78.875
6	ROM	DOBRE, Aurelia	39.337	9.825 9.900	9.900 9.850	78.812
10	USA	JOHNSON, Brandy	39.275	9.825 9.825	9.875 9.725	78.525
15	USA	MILLS, Phoebe	39.337	9.800 9.275	9.850 9.775	78.037
16	USA	GARRISON-STEVES, Kelly	38.912	9.825 9.675	9.750 9.775	77.937

WOMEN'S BALANCE BEAM / September 25

RANK	CTRY	ATHLETE	TOTAL
1	ROM	SILIVAS, Daniela	19.924
2	URS	SHOUSHOUNOVA, Elena	19.875
3T	USA	MILLS, Phoebe	19.837
3T	ROM	POTORAC, Gabriela	19.837
5	URS	BOGUINSKAIA, Svetlana	19.787
6	BUL	DOUDEVA, Diana	19.724
7	USA	GARRISON-STEVES, Kelly	19.649

WOMEN'S FLOOR EXERCISE / September 25

RANK	CTRY	ATHLETE	TOTAL
1	ROM	SILIVAS, Daniela	19.937
2	URS	BOGUINSKAIA, Svetlana	19.887
3	BUL	DOUDEVA, Diana	19.850
4	BUL	VODENITCHAROVA, Deliana	19.837
5	HUN	STORCZER, Beata	19.675
6	USA	MILLS, Phoebe	19.662

WOMEN'S UNEVEN BARS / September 25

RANK	CTRY	ATHLETE	TOTAL
1	ROM	SILIVAS, Daniela	20.000
2	GDR	KERSTEN, Dagmar	19.987
3	URS	SHOUSHOUNOVA, Elena	19.962
4	GDR	THUEMMLER, Doerte	19.900
5	URS	BOGUINSKAIA, Svetlana	19.899
6	TCH	POLOKOVA, Iveta	19.837
8	USA	MILLS, Phoebe	19.787

WOMEN'S HORSE VAULT / September 25

RANK	CTRY	ATHLETE	TOTAL
1	URS	BOGUINSKAIA, Svetlana	19.905
2	ROM	POTORAC, Gabriela	19.830
3	ROM	SILIVAS, Daniela	19.818
4	BUL	STOYANOVA, Boriana	19.780
5	USA	JOHNSON, Brandy	19.774
6	GDR	KERSTEN, Dagmar	19.756

MEN'S TEAM COMPETITION / September 20

RANK	CTRY	ATHLETES	TOTAL
1	URS	GOGOLADZE, Vladimir / NOUVIKOV, Vladimir KHARIKOV, Serguei / BILOZERTCHEV, Dmitri ARTEMOV, Vladimir / LIOUKINE, Valeri	593.350
2	GDR	HOFFMANN, Ulf / WECKER, Andreas / TIPPELT, Sven / BUECHNER, Ralf / BEHRENDT, Holger KROLL, Sylvio	588.450
3	JPN	KONISHI, Hiroyuki / YAMADA, Takahiro SATO, Toshiharu / NISHIKAWA, Daisuke MIZUSHIMA, Koichi / IKETANI, Yukio	585.600
4	CHN		585.250
5	BUL		585.100
6	HUN		582.300
11	USA	LAKES, Charles / JOHNSON, Scott MINICUCCI, Dominick / SUTER, Kenneth "Wes" DAVIS, Kevin / RINGNALD, Lance	576.850

MEN'S INDIVIDUAL ALL-AROUND / September 22

RANK	CTRY	ATHLETE	PRELIM.	FLOOR VAULT	P. HORSE P. BARS	RINGS H. BAR	TOTAL
1	URS	ARTEMOV, Vladimir	59.475	9.900 9.900	9.900 10.000	9.900 10.000	119.125
2	URS	LIOUKINE, Valeri	59.425	9.900 9.900	9.950 9.900	9.950 10.000	119.025
3	URS	BILOZERTCHEV, Dmitri	59.225	9.900 10.000	10.000 9.950	10.000 9.900	118.975
4	GDR	TIPPELT, Sven	58.800	9.800 9.900	9.950 9.800	9.950 9.800	118.000
5	ROM	GHERMAN, Marius	58.775	9.800 9.800	9.900 9.800	9.850 9.900	117.825
6T	BUL	HRISTOZOV, Kalofer	58.850	9.800 9.650	9.900 9.850	9.900 9.800	117.750
6T	CHN	WANG, Chongsheng	58.600	9.750 9.900	9.900 9.850	9.850 9.900	117.750
19	USA	LAKES, Charles	58.225	9.900 9.850	9.750 9.700	9.800 9.950	117.175
34	USA	DAVIS, Kevin	57.375	9.650 9.500	9.800 9.650	9.650 9.700	115.325
35	USA	RINGNALD, Lance	57.625	9.500 9.550	9.800 9.850	9.650 9.100	115.075

MEN'S FLOOR EXERCISE / September 24

RANK	CTRY	ATHLETE	TOTAL
1	URS	KHARIKOV, Serguei	19.925
2	URS	ARTEMOV, Vladimir	19.900
3T	CHN	LOU, Yun	19.850
3T	JPN	IKETANI, Yukio	19.850
5	CHN	LI, Ning	19.800
6	ITA	PRETI, Boris	19.775

MEN'S HORIZONTAL BAR / September 24

RANK	CTRY	ATHLETE	TOTAL
1T	URS	ARTEMOV, Vladimir	19.900
1T	URS	LIOUKINE, Valeri	19.900
3T	GDR	BEHRENDT, Holger	19.800
3T	ROM	GHERMAN, Marius	19.800
5	CHN	WANG, Chongsheng	19.775
6	CHN	XU, Zhiqiang	19.700

MEN'S HORSE VAULT / September 24

RANK	CTRY	ATHLETE	TOTAL
1	CHN	LOU, Yun	19.875
2	GDR	KROLL, Sylvio	19.862
3	KOR	PARK, Jong-hoon	19.775
4	BUL	KOLEV, Dian	19.737
5	GDR	BEHRENDT, Holger	19.650
6	URS	KHARIKOV, Serguei	19.600

MEN'S PARALLEL BARS / September 24

RANK	CTRY	ATHLETE	TOTAL
1	URS	ARTEMOV, Vladimir	19.925
2	URS	LIOUKINE, Valeri	19.900
3	GDR	TIPPELT, Sven	19.750
4	BUL	HRISTOZOV, Kalofer	19.725
5	ROM	GHERMAN, Marius	19.700
6	CAN	HIBBERT, Curtis	19.675

MEN'S RINGS / September 24

RANK	CTRY	ATHLETE	TOTAL
1T	GDR	BEHRENDT, Holger	19.925
1T	URS	BILOZERTCHEV, Dmitri	19.925
3	GDR	TIPPELT, Sven	19.875
4T	BUL	HRISTOZOV, Kalofer	19.825
4T	URS	LIOUKINE, Valeri	19.825
6T	CHN	LOU, Yun	19.800
6T	ITA	CHECHI, Juri	19.800

MEN'S POMMEL HORSE / September 24

RANK	CTRY	ATHLETE	TOTAL
1T	BUL	GUERASKOV, Lyubomir	19.950
1T	HUN	BORKAI, Zsolt	19.950
1T	URS	BILOZERTCHEV, Dmitri	19.950
4	JPN	MIZUSHIMA, Koichi	19.900
5	URS	LIOUKINE, Valeri	19.875
6	JPN	NISHIKAWA, Daisuke	19.850

WOMEN'S RHYTHMIC ALL-AROUND / September 30

RANK	CTRY	ATHLETE	ROPES	HOOP	CLUBS	RIBB.	PRELIM	TOTAL
1	URS	LOBATCH, Marina	10.000	10.000	10.000	10.000	20.000	60.000
2	BUL	DOUNAVSKA, Adriana	10.000	10.000	10.000	9.950	19.950	59.950
3	URS	TIMOCHENKO, Alexandra	10.000	10.000	10.000	10.000	19.875	59.875
4	BUL	PANOVA, Bianka	10.000	10.000	10.000	10.000	19.725	59.725
5	ESP	LLORET, Maria Isabel	9.850	9.850	9.850	9.850	19.500	58.900
6	HUN	SINKO, Andrea	9.850	9.800	9.800	9.800	19.525	58.775
—	USA	BERUBE, Michelle			elim. preliminary round			
—	USA	SIMPSON, Diane			elim. preliminary round			

JUDO

EXTRA-LIGHTWEIGHT (Up to 60 KG) / September 25

RANK	CTRY	ATHLETE
1	KOR	KIM, Jae-yup
2	USA	ASANO, Kevin
3T	JPN	HOSOKAWA, Shinji
3T	URS	TOTIKACHVILI, Amiran

HALF-LIGHTWEIGHT (Up to 65 KG) / September 26

RANK	CTRY	ATHLETE
1	KOR	LEE, Kyung-keun
2	POL	PAWLOWSKI, Janusz
3T	FRA	CARABETTA, Bruno
3T	JPN	YAMAMOTO, Yosuke
—	USA	MARCHAL, Joe — elim. third round

LIGHTWEIGHT (Up to 71 KG) / September 27

RANK	CTRY	ATHLETE
1	FRA	ALEXANDRE, Marc
2	GDR	LOLL, Sven
3T*	USA	SWAIN, Michael
3T	URS	TENADZE, Gueorgui

*Kerrith Brown (GBR), original bronze medalist, tested positive for use of a banned substance.

HALF-MIDDLEWEIGHT (Up to 78 KG) / September 28

RANK	CTRY	ATHLETE
1	POL	LEGIEN, Waldemar
2	FRG	WIENEKE, Frank
3T	FRG	BRECHOT, Torsten
3T	URS	VARAEV, Bachir
—	USA	MORRIS, Jason — elim. second round

MIDDLEWEIGHT (Up to 86 KG) / September 29

RANK	CTRY	ATHLETE	
1	AUT	SEISENBACHER, Peter	
2	URS	CHESTAKOV, Vladmir	
3T	HOL	SPIJKERS, Ben	
3T	JPN	OSAKO, Akinobu	
—	USA	CAPO, Rene	elim. first round

HALF-HEAVYWEIGHT (Up to 95 KG) / September 30

RANK	CTRY	ATHLETE	
1	BRA	MIGUEL, Aurelio	
2	FRG	MEILING, Marc	
3T	BEL	VAN DE WALLE, Robert	
3T	GBR	STEWART, Dennis	
—	USA	BERLAND, Bob	elim. first round

HEAVYWEIGHT (Over 95 KG) / October 1

RANK	CTRY	ATHLETE	
1	JPN	SAITO, Hitoshi	
2	GDR	STOEHR, Henry	
3T	KOR	CHO, Yong-Chul	
3T	URS	VERITCHEV, Grigori	
—	USA	COHEN, Steve	elim. second round

MODERN PENTATHLON

INDIVIDUAL / September 22

RANK	CTRY	ATHLETE	EQU.	FEN.	SWIM.	SHO.	XC	TOTAL
					POINTS			
1	HUN	MARTINEK, Janos	1,066	990	1,264	868	1,216	5,404
2	ITA	MASSULLO, Carlo	1,010	881	1,204	1,044	1,240	5,379
3	URS	IAGORACHVILI, Vakhtang	980	915	1,344	978	1,150	5,367
4	HUN	MIZSER, Attila	1,010	847	1,196	934	1,294	5,281
5	FRA	RUER, Christophe	968	779	1,348	934	1,213	5,242
6	GBR	PHELPS, Richard	964	898	1,304	868	1,195	5,229
18	USA	NIEMAN, Robert	944	932	1,248	1,000	910	5,034
49	USA	STULL, Robert	470	983	1,240	868	1,027	4,588
60	USA	GOSTIGIAN, Michael	0	820	1,264	1,044	895	4,023

TEAM / September 22

RANK	CTRY	ATHLETE	TOTAL
1	HUN	MARTINEK, Janos / MIZSER, Attila FABIAN, Laszlo	15,886
2	ITA	MASSULLO, Carlo / MASALA, Daniele TIBERTI, Gianluca	15,571
3	GBR	PHELPS, Richard / MAHONY, Dominic BROOKHOUSE, Graham	15,276
4	FRA		15,268
5	URS		15,214
6	TCH		15,043
16	USA	NIEMAN, Robert / STULL, Robert GOSTIGIAN, Michael	13,645

ROWING

WOMEN'S SINGLE SCULLS / September 25

RANK	CTRY	ATHLETE	TIME
1	GDR	BEHRENDT, Jutta	7:47.19
2	USA	MARDEN, Anne	7:50.28
3	BUL	GUEORGUIEVA, Magdalena	7:53.65
4	HOL	VAN ETTEKOVEN, Harriet	7:57.29
5	ROM	POPESOU, Marioara	7:59.44
6	DEN	PORS, Inger	7:59.77

WOMEN'S DOUBLE SCULLS / September 24

RANK	CTRY	ATHLETES	TIME
1	GDR	PETER, Birgit / SCHROETER, Martina	7:00.48
2	ROM	COGEANU, Veronica / LIPA, Elisabeta	7:04.36
3	BUL	NINOVA, Violeta / MADINA, Stefka	7:06.03
4	URS	JOUKOVA, Marina / OMELIANOVITCH, Maria	7:12.67
5	CHN	GUO, Mei / CAO, Mianying	7:18.69
6	USA	HAVELKA, Monica / TIPPETT, Cathy	7:21.28

WOMEN'S PAIR W/O COXSWAIN / September 24

RANK	CTRY	ATHLETES	TIME
1	ROM	ARBA, Rodica / HOMEGHI, Olga	7:28.13
2	BUL	STOYANOVA, Radka / BERBEROVA, Lalka	7:31.95
3	NZL	PAYNE, Nicola / HANNEN, Lynley	7:35.68
4	GDR	SPITTLER, Kerstin / SCHROEDER, Katrin	7:40.47
5	URS	STONE, Sarmite / SMORODINA, Marina	7:53.19
6	USA	KIRCH, Barbara / KEGGI, Mara	7:56.27

WOMEN'S QUADRUPLE SCULLS / September 25

RANK	CTRY	ATHLETES	TIME
1	GDR	FOERSTER, Kerstin / MUNDT, Kristina SCHRAMM, Beate / SORGERS, Jana	6:21.06
2	URS	KALIMBET, Irina / MAZYI, Svetlana FROLOVA, Inna / DOUMTCHEVA, Antonina	6:23.47

Continued

WOMEN'S QUADRUPLE SCULLS — Continued

RANK	CTRY	ATHLETES	TIME
3	ROM	BALAN, Anisoara / MINEA, Anisoara COGEANU, Veronica / LIPA, Elisabeta	6:23.81
4	BUL		6:24.10
5	TCH		6:41.86
6	BEL		6:43.79
—	USA	CASSUTO, Sherry / HERRON, Angie MARSHALL, Jennie / MARTIN, Ann	elim. repechage

WOMEN'S FOUR OARS W/COXSWAIN / September 24

RANK	CTRY	ATHLETES	TIME
1	GDR	WALTHER, Martina / DOBERSCHEUTZ, Gerlinde / HORNIG, Carola SIECH, Birte / ROSE, Sylvia	6:56.00
2	CHN	ZHANG, Xianghua / HU, Yadong YANG, Xiao / ZHOU, Shouying / LI, Ronghua	6:58.78
3	ROM	TRASCA, Marioara / NECULA, Veronica ANITAS, Herta / BALAN, Doina Lilian OANCIA, Ecaterina	7:01.13
4	BUL		7:02.27
5	USA	CORBET, Jennifer / GENGLER, Sarah BRADLEY, Elizabeth / ECKERT, Cynthia SANTIAGO, Kimberly	7:09.12
6	GBR	JOHNSTON, Fiona / GROSE, Katherine GOUGH, Joanne / SMITH, Susan NORRISH, Alison	7:10.80

WOMEN'S EIGHT OARS W/COXSWAIN / September 25

RANK	CTRY	ATHLETES	TIME
1	GDR		6:15.17
2	ROM		6:17.44
3	CHN		6:21.83
4	URS		6:22.35
5	BUL		6:25.02
6	USA	THOMPSON, Juliet / CAMPBELL, Christine PECK, Abigail / MALLERY, Margaret BROOME, Susan / MAXWELL, Stephanie SEATON, Anna / TOWNLEY, Alison BEARD, Elizabeth "Betsy"	6:26.66

MEN'S SINGLE SCULLS / September 24

RANK	CTRY	ATHLETE	TIME
1	GDR	LANGE, Thomas	6:49.86
2	FRG	KOLBE, Peter Michael	6:54.77
3	NZL	VERDONK, Eric	6:58.66
4	AUS	McGLASHAN, Hamish	7:01.43
5	POL	BRONIEWSKI, Kajetan	7:03.67
6	USA	SUDDUTH, Andrew	7:11.45

MEN'S DOUBLE SCULLS / September 24

RANK	CTRY	ATHLETES	TIME
1	HOL	FLORIJN, Ronald / RIENKS, Nicolas	6:21.13
2	SUI	SCHWERZMANN, Beat / BODENMANN, Ueli	6:22.59
3	URS	MARTCHENKO, Alexandre / IAKOUCHA, Vassily	6:22.87
4	FRG	HAENDLE, Christian / THIENEL, Ralf	6:24.97
5	GDR	MUND, Uwe / HEPPNER, Uwe	6:26.20
6	DEN	RASMUSSEN, Per H.S. / ELTANG, Bjarne	6:26.98
—	USA	FLORIO, Glen / STILL, Kevin	elim. repechage

MEN'S PAIR W/O COXSWAIN / September 24

RANK	CTRY	ATHLETES	TIME
1	GBR	HOLMES, Andrew / REDGRAVE, Steven	6:36.84
2	ROM	NEAGU, Dragos / DOBRE, Danut	6:38.06
3	YUG	PRESERN, Bojan / MUJKIC, Sadik	6:41.01
4	BEL	LEWUILLON, Alain / VAN BELLEGHEM, Wim	6:45.47
5	GDR	ERTEL, Carl / GASCH, Uwe	6:48.86
6	URS	ZUBORENKO, Igor / VYRVITCH, Yaleri	6:51.11
—	USA	BAUSBACK, Kurt / IVES, Edward	elim. semifinals

MEN'S PAIRS W/COXSWAIN / September 25

RANK	CTRY	ATHLETES	TIME
1	ITA	ABBAGNALE, Carmine / ABBAGNALE, Guiseppe DI CAPUA, Guiseppe	6:58.79
2	GDR	STREIT, Mario / KIRCHHOFF, Detlef RENSCH, Rene	7:00.63
3	GBR	HOLMES, Andrew / REDGRAVE, Steven SWEENEY, Patrick	7:01.95
4	ROM		7:02.60
5	BUL		7:03.04
6	URS		7:06.07
—	USA	ESPESETH, Robert / FISH, Jonathan LYONS, Daniel	elim. semifinals

MEN'S QUADRUPLE SCULLS / September 25

RANK	CTRY	ATHLETE	TIME
1	ITA	POLI, Piero / FARINA, Gianluca TIZZANO, Davide / ABBAGNALE, Agostino	5:53.37
2	NOR	BJONNESS, Lars / VINJE, Vetle THORSEN, Rolf Bernt / HANSEN, Alf John	5:55.08

Continued

MEN'S QUADRUPLE SCULLS — Continued

RANK	CTRY	ATHLETE	TIME
3	GDR	BOGS, Steffen / ZUEHLKE, Steffen HABERMANN, Heiko / KOEPPEN, Jens	5:56.13
4	URS		5:57.18
5	AUS		5:59.15
6	FRG		5:59.59
—	USA	ALTEKRUESE, Charles / FRACKELTON, John MONTESI, Greg / STROTBECK, John	elim. repechage

MEN'S FOUR OARS W/O COXSWAIN / September 25

RANK	CTRY	ATHLETES	TIME
1	GDR	SCHROEDER, Roland / GREINER, Thomas BRUDEL, Ralf / FOERSTER, Olaf	6:03.11
2	USA	RODRIGUEZ, Raoul / BOHRER, Thomas KRMPOTICH, David / KENNELLY, Richard	6:05.53
3	FRG	KESSLAU, Norbert / GRABOW, Volker PUTTLITZ, Jorg / GRABOW, Guido	6:06.22
4	GBR		6:06.74
5	ITA		6:09.55
6	URS		11:03.77

MEN'S FOUR OARS W/COXSWAIN / September 24

RANK	CTRY	ATHLETES	TIME
1	GDR	KLAWONN, Frank / EICHWURZEL, Bernd NIESECKE, Frank / SCHMELING, Karsten REIHER, Hendrik	6:10.74
2	ROM	POPESCU, Dimitrie / SNEP, Ioan ROBU, Valentin / TOMOIAGA, Vasile LOVRENSKI, Ladislau	6:13.58
3	NZL	KEYS, George / WRIGHT, Ian JOHNSTON, Gregory / WHITE, Christopher BIRD, Andrew	6:15.78
4	GBR		6:18.08
5	USA	TERWILLIGER, John / HUNTINGTON, Christopher / DARLING, Tom / WALTERS, John / ZEMBSCH, Mark	6:18.47
6	YUG		6:23.28

MEN'S EIGHT OARS W/COXSWAIN / September 25

RANK	CTRY	ATHLETE	TIME
1	FRG		5:46.05
2	URS		5:48.01
3	USA	TETI, Mike / SMITH, John / PATTON, Ted RUSHER, John / NORDELL, Peter McLAUGHLIN, Jeff / BURDEN, Doug PESCATORE, John / BAUER, Seth	5:48.26
4	GBR		5:51.59
5	AUS		5:53.73
6	CAN		5:54.26

SHOOTING

WOMEN'S AIR PISTOL / September 21

RANK	CTRY	ATHLETE	SCORE	GRAND TOTAL
1	YUG	SEKARIC, Jasna	389	489.5 FWR
2	URS	SALOUKVADZE, Nino	390 WR	487.9
3	URS	DOBRANTCHEVA, Marina	385	485.2
4	BEL	GOFFIN, Anne	381	480.2
5	GDR	VOELKER, Anke	383	479.3
6	CHN	LIU, Haiying	380	476.9
16T	USA	DYER, Kimberly	377	—
22T	USA	FOX, Ruby	375	

WOMEN'S SPORT PISTOL / September 19

RANK	CTRY	ATHLETE	SCORE	GRAND TOTAL
1	URS	SALOUKVADZE, Nino	591 OR	690.0
2	JPN	HASEGAWA, Tomoko	587	686.0
3	YUG	SEKARIC, Jasna	591	686.0
4	FRG	BREKER, Lieselotte	585	685.0
5	HUN	FERENCZ, Agnes	585	685.0
6	SWE	FRIES, Kristina	586	685.0
24T	USA	DYER, Kim	578	
26	USA	FOX, Ruby	577	

WOMEN'S AIR RIFLE / September 18

RANK	CTRY	ATHLETE	SCORE	GRAND TOTAL
1	URS	CHILOVA, Irina	395 OR	498.5
2	FRG	SPERBER, Silvia	393	497.5
3	URS	MALOUKHINA, Anna	394	495.8
4	CHN	ZHANG, Qiuping	395 OR	494.7
5	FIN	PELTOLA, Pirjo	393	493.6
6	USA	MEILI, Launi	395 OR	493.3
10	USA	WIGGER, Deena	392	—

WOMEN'S SMALLBORE STANDARD RIFLE, THREE-POSITIONS / September 21

RANK	CTRY	ATHLETE	SCORE	GRAND TOTAL
1	FRG	SPERBER, Silvia	590 OR	685.6
2	BUL	LETCHEVA, Vessela	583	683.2
3	URS	TCHERKASSOVA, Valentina	586	681.4
4	GDR	KLEPP, Katja	584	680.5
5	CAN	BOWES, Sharon	584	680.5
6	URS	MALOUKHINA, Anna	585	678.4
7	USA	MEILI, Launi	582	676.5
13T	USA	JEWELL, Wanda	579	

MEN'S AIR PISTOL / September 24

RANK	CTRY	ATHLETE	SCORE	GRAND TOTAL
1	BUL	KIRIAKOV, Taniou	585	687.9
2	USA	BULJUNG, Erich	590 EWR	687.9
3	CHN	XU, Haifeng	584	684.5
4	ROM	BABII, Sorin	588	683.3
5	URS	BASSINSKI, Igor	583	683.2
6	TCH	RUZICKA, Miroslav	582	681.4
28	USA	NYGORD, Donald	574	

MEN'S FREE PISTOL / September 18

RANK	CTRY	ATHLETE	SCORE	GRAND TOTAL
1	ROM	BABII, Sorin	566	660.0
2	SWE	SKANAKER, Ragnar	564	657.0
3	URS	BASSINSKI, Igor	570	657.0
4	BUL	KIRIAKOV, Taniou	566	656.0
5	GDR	EDER, Gernot	561	654.0
6	HUN	KARACSONY, Gyula	564	654.0
11	USA	NYGORD, Donald	559	—
16T	USA	YOUNG, Darius	556	—

MEN'S RAPID-FIRE PISTOL / September 23

RANK	CTRY	ATHLETE	SCORE	GRAND TOTAL
1	URS	KOUZMINE, Afanasi	598 OR	698.0 FWR
2	GDR	SCHUMANN, Ralf	597	696.0
3	HUN	KOVACS, Zoltan	594	693.0
4	ITA	SEVIERI, Alberto	596	693.0
5	POL	KACZMAREK, Adam	595	691.0
6	COL	TOVAR, Bernardo	593	690.0
7	USA	McNALLY, John	597	690.0
13T	USA	ARREDONDO, Rojelio	590	

MEN'S RUNNING GAME TARGET / September 23

RANK	CTRY	ATHLETE	SCORE	GRAND TOTAL
1	NOR	HELESTAD, Tor	591 OR	689.0
2	CHN	HUANG, Shiping	589	687.0
3	URS	AVRAMENKO, Guennadi	591 OR	686.0
4	TCH	KERMIET, Jan	588	679.0
5	HUN	DOLESCHALL, Andras	588	—
6	HUN	SOLTI, Attila	588	—
17	USA	BENSLEY, Todd	581	—
18	USA	SWINNEY, Scott	580	—

MEN'S AIR RIFLE / September 20

RANK	CTRY	ATHLETE	SCORE	GRAND TOTAL
1	YUG	MAKSIMOVIC, Goran	594 OR	695.6
2	FRA	BERTHELOT, Nicolas	593	694.2
3	FRG	RIEDERER, Johann	592	694.0
4	USA	FOTH, Robert	591	692.5
5	NOR	STENVAAG, Harald	591	692.0
6	HUN	ZAHONYI, Attila	591	691.4
17T	USA	FITZ-RANDOLPH, Roderick	587	

MEN'S SMALLBORE RIFLE, ENGLISH MATCH / September 19

RANK	CTRY	ATHLETE	SCORE	GRAND TOTAL
1	TCH	VARGA, Miroslav	600 EWR	703.9
2	KOR	CHA, Young-Chul	598	702.8
3	HUN	ZAHONYI, Attila	597	701.9
4	TCH	SOUKENIK, Pavel	598	701.2
5	GBR	ALLAN, Alister	598	700.9
6	CHN	XU, Xiaoguang	597	700.6
15T	USA	DUBIS, Glenn	595	
24T	USA	WRIGHT III, Webster	594	

MEN'S SMALLBORE RIFLE, THREE-POSITIONS / September 22

RANK	CTRY	ATHLETE	SCORE	GRAND TOTAL
1	GBR	COOPER, Malcolm	1180	1,279.3
2	GBR	ALLAN, Alister	1181 OR	1,275.6
3	URS	IVANOV, Kirill	1173	1,275.0
4	DEN	CHRISTENSEN, Klavs Jorn	1177	1,273.6
5	USA	DUBIS, Glenn	1174	1,273.5
6	URS	PETIKIANE, Gratchia	1173	1,272.2
13T	USA	DURBEN, Daniel	1169	—

OLYMPIC SKEET / September 24

RANK	CTRY	ATHLETE	SCORE	GRAND TOTAL
1	GDR	WEGNER, Axel	198 EOR	222
2	CHI	DE IRUARRIZAGA, Alfonso	198 EOR	221
3	ESP	GUARDIOLA, Jorge	196	220
4	USA	CARLISLE, Daniel	197	220
5	CHN	ZHANG, Weigang	196	219
6	GDR	RAABE, Juergen	196	219
24	USA	DRYKE, Matthew	193	—
25T	USA	SMITH, Richard	145	—
52	USA	CARLISLE, Terry	67	—

OLYMPIC TRAP / September 20

RANK	CTRY	ATHLETE	SCORE	GRAND TOTAL	SHOOT-OFF
1	URS	MONAKOV, Dmitri	197	222	8
2	TCH	BEDNARIK, Miloslav	197	222	7
3	BEL	PEETERS, Frans	195	219	16
4	PER	BOZA, Francisco	195	219	15
5	HOL	VAN LIMBEEK, Bean	195	219	7
6	JPN	WATANABE, Kazumi	195	216	
9	USA	CARLISLE, Daniel	194	—	
12T	USA	BALLARD, Brian	192	—	
12T	USA	HAAS III, George	192	—	
47	USA	KOCH, Carolyn	130	—	

SOCCER (FOOTBALL)

FINAL STANDING / October

RANK	CTRY	GAMES WON	LOST	TIE	SCORE	USA GAME SCORES
1	URS	5	0	1	3-2 (final)	USA vs. ARG 1-1
2	BRA	4	0	2		USA vs. KOR 0-0
3	FRG	4	1	1	3-0 (3rd-4th)	USA vs. URS 2-4
4	ITA	3	3	0		
—	USA	0	1	2		

SWIMMING

COMPETITIVE SWIMMING

WOMEN'S 50-METER FREESTYLE / September 25

RANK	CTRY	ATHLETE	TIME
1	GDR	OTTO, Kristin	25.49 OR
2	CHN	YANG, Wenyi	25.64
3T	GDR	MEISSNER, Katrin	25.71
3T	USA	STERKEL, Jill	25.71
5	USA	FETTER, Leigh	25.78
6	ROM	COSTACHE, Tamara	25.80

WOMEN'S 100-METER FREESTYLE / September 19

RANK	CTRY	ATHLETE	TIME
1	GDR	OTTO, Kristin	54.93
2	CHN	ZHUANG, Yong	55.47
3	FRA	PLEWINSKI, Catherine	55.49
4	GDR	STELLMACH, Manuela	55.52
5	CRC	POLL, Silvia	55.90
6	HOL	BRIENESSE, Karin	56.15
7	USA	TORRES, Dara	56.25
12	USA	KREMER, Mitzi	56.83 #

- Final B

WOMEN'S 200-METER FREESTYLE / September 21

RANK	CTRY	ATHLETE	TIME
1	GDR	FRIEDRICH, Heike	1:57.65 OR
2	CRC	POLL, Silvia	1:58.67
3	GDR	STELLMACH, Manuela	1:59.01
4	USA	WAYTE, Mary	1:59.04
5	URS	TREFILOVA, Natalia	1:59.24
6	USA	KREMER, Mitzi	2:00.23

WOMEN'S 400-METER FREESTYLE / September 22

RANK	CTRY	ATHLETE	TIME
1	USA	EVANS, Janet	4:03.85 WR
2	GDR	FRIEDRICH, Heike	4:05.94
3	GDR	MOEHRING, Anke	4:06.62
4	USA	BRUCE, Tami	4:08.16
5	AUS	ELFORD, Janelle	4:10.64
6	BEL	ARNOULD, Isabelle	4:11.73

WOMEN'S 800-METER FREESTYLE / September 24

RANK	CTRY	ATHLETE	TIME
1	USA	EVANS, Janet	8:20.20 OR
2	GDR	STRAUSS, Astrid	8:22.09
3	AUS	McDONALD, Julie	8:22.93
4	GDR	MOEHRING, Anke	8:23.09
5	USA	BRUCE, Tami	8:30.86
6	AUS	ELFORD, Janelle	8:30.94

WOMEN'S 100-METER BACKSTROKE / September 22

RANK	CTRY	ATHLETE	TIME
1	GDR	OTTO, Kristin	1:00.89
2	HUN	EGERSZEGI, Krisztina	1:01.56
3	GDR	SIRCH, Cornelia	1:01.57
4	USA	MITCHELL, Betsy	1:02.71
5	USA	BARR, Beth	1:02.78
6	CRC	POLL, Silvia	1:03.34

WOMEN'S 200-METER BACKSTROKE / September 25

RANK	CTRY	ATHLETE	TIME
1	HUN	EGERSZEGI, Krisztina	2:09.29 OR
2	GDR	ZIMMERMANN, Kathrin	2:10.61
3	GDR	SIRCH, Cornelia	2:11.45
4	USA	BARR, Beth	2:12.39
5	AUS	LIVINGSTONE, Nicole	2:13.43
6	USA	HAYES, Andrea	2:15.02

WOMEN'S 100-METER BREASTSTROKE / September 23

RANK	CTRY	ATHLETE	TIME
1	BUL	DANGALAKOVA, Tania	1:07.95 OR
2	BUL	FRENKEVA, Antoaneta	1:08.74
3	GDR	HOERNER, Silke	1:08.83
4	CAN	HIGSON, Allison	1:08.86
5	URS	VOLKOVA, Elena	1:09.24
6	USA	McFARLANE, Tracey	1:09.60
13	USA	JOHNSON, Susan	1:11.08 #

- Final B

WOMEN'S 200-METER BREASTSTROKE / September 21

RANK	CTRY	ATHLETE	TIME
1	GDR	HOERNER, Silke	2:26.71 WR
2	CHN	HUANG, Xiaomin	2:27.49
3	BUL	FRENKEVA, Antoaneta	2:28.34
4	BUL	DANGALAKOVA, Tania	2:28.43
5	URS	BOGATCHEVA, Ioulia	2:28.54
6	BEL	LEMPEREUR, Ingrid	2:29.42
13	USA	RAPP, Susan	2:32.90 #
14	USA	McFARLANE, Tracy	2:33.46 #

- Final B

WOMEN'S 100-METER BUTTERFLY / September 23

RANK	CTRY	ATHLETE	TIME
1	GDR	OTTO, Kristin	59.00 OR
2	GDR	WEIGANG, Birte	59.45
3	CHN	QIAN, Hong	59.52
4	FRA	PLEWINSKI, Catherine	59.58
5	USA	JORGENSEN, Janel	1:00.48
6	HOL	VAN BENTUM, Cornelia	1:00.62
7	USA	MEAGHER, Mary T.	1:00.97

WOMEN'S 200-METER BUTTERFLY / September 25

RANK	CTRY	ATHLETE	TIME
1	GDR	NORD, Kathleen	2:09.51
2	GDR	WEIGANG, Birte	2:09.91
3	USA	MEAGHER, Mary T.	2:10.80
4	ROM	PURA, Stela Marian	2:11.28
5	USA	RADKE, Trina	2:11.55
6	JPN	TAKAHASHI, Kiyomi	2:11.62

WOMEN'S 200-METER INDIVIDUAL MEDLEY / September 24

RANK	CTRY	ATHLETE	TIME
1	GDR	HUNGER, Daniela	2:12.59 OR
2	URS	DENDEBEROVA, Elena	2:13.31
3	ROM	LUNG, Noemi Ildiko	2:14.85
4	AUS	CLATWORTHY, Jodie	2:16.31
5	HOL	MUIS, Marianne	2:16.40
6	ROM	PATRASCOIU, Aneta	2:16.70
8	USA	HEDGEPETH, Whitney	2:17.99
—	USA	WAYTE, Mary	DQ heats

WOMEN'S 400-METER INDIVIDUAL MEDLEY / September 19

RANK	CTRY	ATHLETE	TIME
1	USA	EVANS, Janet	4:37.76
2	ROM	LUNG, Noemi Ildiko	4:39.46
3	GDR	HUNGER, Daniela	4:39.76
4	URS	DENDEBEROVA, Elena	4:40.44
5	GDR	NORD, Kathleen	4:41.64
6	AUS	CLATWORTHY, Jodie	4:45.86
11	USA	HANSEN, Erika	4:51.93 #

- B final

WOMEN'S 4x100-METER FREESTYLE RELAY / September 22

RANK	CTRY	ATHLETES	TIME
1	GDR	OTTO, Kristin / MEISSNER, Katrin HUNGER, Daniela / STELLMACH, Manuela	3:40.63 OR
2	HOL	MUIS, Marianne / MUIS, Mildred VAN BENTUM, Cornelia / BRIENESSE, Karin	3:43.39
3	USA	WAYTE, Mary / KREMER, Mitzi WALKER, Laura / TORRES, Dara (*ZEMINA, Paige / STERKEL, Jill)	3:44.25
4	CHN		3:44.69
5	URS		3:44.99
6	CAN		3:46.75

* swam in preliminaries only.

WOMEN'S 4x100-METER MEDLEY RELAY / September 24

RANK	CTRY	ATHLETES	TIME
1	GDR	OTTO, Kristin / HOERNER, Silke WEIGANG, Birte / MEISSNER, Katrin	4:03.74 OR
2	USA	BARR, Beth / McFARLANE, Tracy JORGENSEN, Janel / WAYTE, Mary (*MITCHELL, Betsy / MEAGHER, Mary T. TORRES, Dara)	4:07.90
3	CAN	MELIEN, Lori / HIGSON, Allison KERR, Jane / NUGENT, Andrea	4:10.49
4	AUS		4:11.57
5	HOL		4:12.19
6	BUL		4:12.36

* swam in preliminaries only.

MEN'S 50-METER FREESTYLE / September 24

RANK	CTRY	ATHLETE	TIME
1	USA	BIONDI, Matthew	22.14 WR
2	USA	JAGER, Thomas	22.36
3	URS	PRIGODA, Gennadi	22.71
4	SUI	HALSALL, Dano	22.83
5	SUI	VOLERY, Stefan	22.84
6	URS	TKASHENKO, Vladimir	22.88

MEN'S 100-METER FREESTYLE / September 22

RANK	CTRY	ATHLETE	TIME
1	USA	BIONDI, Matthew	48.63 OR
2	USA	JACOBS, Christopher	49.08
3	FRA	CARON, Stephan	49.62
4	URS	PRIGODA, Gennadi	49.75
5	URS	BACHKATOV, Iouri	50.08
6	AUS	BAILDON, Andrew	50.23

MEN'S 200-METER FREESTYLE / September 19

RANK	CTRY	ATHLETE	TIME
1	AUS	ARMSTRONG, Duncan	1:47.25 WR
2	SWE	HOLMERTZ, Anders	1:47.89
3	USA	BIONDI, Matthew	1:47.99
4	POL	WOJDAT, Artur	1:48.40
5	FRG	GROSS, Michael	1:48.59
6	GDR	ZESSNER, Steffen	1:48.77
7	USA	DALBEY, Troy	1:48.86

MEN'S 400-METER FREESTYLE / September 23

RANK	CTRY	ATHLETE	TIME
1	GDR	DASSLER, Uwe	3:46.95 WR
2	AUS	ARMSTRONG, Duncan	3:47.15
3	POL	WOJDAT, Artur	3:47.34
4	USA	CETLINSKI, Matthew	3:48.09
5	POL	PODKOSCIELNY, Mariusz	3:48.59
6	FRG	PFEIFFER, Stefan	3:49.96
14	USA	JORGENSEN, Daniel	3:55.34 #

- Final B

MEN'S 1,500-METER FREESTYLE / September 25

RANK	CTRY	ATHLETE	TIME
1	URS	SALNIKOV, Vladimir	15:00.40
2	FRG	PFEIFFER, Stefan	15:02.69
3	GDR	DASSLER, Uwe	15:06.15
4	USA	CETLINSKI, Matthew	15:06.42
5	POL	PODKOSCIELNY, Mariusz	15:14.76
6	FRG	HENKEL, Rainer	15:18.19
—	USA	JORGENSEN, Lars	elim. in heats

MEN'S 100-METER BACKSTROKE / September 24

RANK	CTRY	ATHLETE	TIME
1	JPN	SUZUKI, Daichi	55.05
2	USA	BERKOFF, David	55.18
3	URS	POLIANSKI, Igor	55.20
4	URS	ZABOLOTNOV, Serguei	55.37
5	CAN	TEWKSBURY, Mark	56.09
6	GDR	BALTRUSCH, Frank	56.10
11	USA	MORTENSON, Jay	57.06 #

- Final B

MEN'S 200-METER BACKSTROKE / September 22

RANK	CTRY	ATHLETE	TIME
1	URS	POLIANSKI, Igor	1:59.37
2	GDR	BALTRUSCH, Frank	1:59.60
3	NZL	KINGSMAN, Paul	2:00.48
4	URS	ZABOLOTNOV, Serguei	2:00.52
5	GDR	RICHTER, Dirk	2:01.67
6	FRG	BERNDT, Jens-Peter	2:01.84
7	USA	VEATCH, Daniel	2:02.26
10	USA	BIGELOW, Steve	2:02.95 #

- Final B

MEN'S 100-METER BREASTSTROKE / September 19

RANK	CTRY	ATHLETE	TIME
1	GBR	MOORHOUSE, Adrian	1:02.04
2	HUN	GUTTLER, Karoly	1:02.05
3	URS	VOLKOV, Dmitri	1:02.20
4	CAN	DAVIS, Victor	1:02.38
5	HUN	DEBNAR, Tamas	1:02.50
6	USA	SCHROEDER, Richard	1:02.55
15	USA	WATTERS, Daniel	1:04.72 #

- Final B

MEN'S 200-METER BREASTSTROKE / September 23

RANK	CTRY	ATHLETE	TIME
1	HUN	SZABO, Jozsef	2:13.52
2	GBR	GILLINGHAM, Nick	2:14.12
3	ESP	LOPEZ, Sergio	2:15.21
4	USA	BARROWMAN, Mike	2:15.45
5	URS	LOZIK, Valeri	2:16.16
6	URS	ALEXEEV, Vadim	2:16.70
—	USA	STACKLE, Kirk	elim. heats

MEN'S 100-METER BUTTERFLY / September 21

RANK	CTRY	ATHLETE	TIME
1	SUR	NESTY, Anthony	53.00 OR
2	USA	BIONDI, Matthew	53.01
3	GBR	JAMESON, Andy	53.30
4	AUS	SIEBEN, Jonathan	53.33
5	FRG	GROSS, Michael	53.44
6	USA	MORTENSON, Jay	54.07

MEN'S 200-METER BUTTERFLY / September 24

RANK	CTRY	ATHLETE	TIME
1	FRG	GROSS, Michael	1:56.94 OR
2	DEN	NIELSEN, Benny	1:58.24
3	NZL	MOSSE, Anthony	1:58.28
4	CAN	PONTING, Thomas	1:58.91
5	USA	STEWART, Melvin	1:59.19
6	AUS	WILSON, David	1:59.20
9	USA	DEAN, Mark	2:00.26 #

- Final B

MEN'S 200-METER INDIVIDUAL MEDLEY / September 25

RANK	CTRY	ATHLETE	TIME
1	HUN	DARNYI, Tamas	2:00.17 WR
2	GDR	KUEHL, Patrick	2:01.61
3	URS	IAROCHTCHOUK, Vadim	2:02.40
4	URS	ZOUBKOV, Mikhail	2:02.92
5	FRG	BERMEL, Peter	2:03.81
6	AUS	BRUCE, Robert	2:04.34
9	USA	WHARTON, David	2:03.05 #
16	USA	STAPLETON, Bill	2:06.32 #

- Final B

MEN'S 400-METER INDIVIDUAL MEDLEY / September 21

RANK	CTRY	ATHLETE	TIME
1	HUN	DARNYI, Tamas	4:14.75 WR
2	USA	WHARTON, David	4:17.36
3	ITA	BATTISTELLI, Stefano	4:18.01
4	HUN	SZABO, Jozsef	4:18.15
5	GDR	KUEHL, Patrick	4:18.44
6	FRG	BERNDT, Jens-Peter	4:21.71
9	USA	KOSTOFF, Jeff	4:22.95 #

- Final B, 1st

MEN'S 4x100-METER FREESTYLE RELAY / September 23

RANK	CTRY	ATHLETES	TIME
1	USA	JACOBS, Christopher / DALBEY, Troy JAGER, Thomas / BIONDI, Matthew (*LANG, Brent / GJERTSEN, Doug JORDAN, Shawn)	3:16.53 WR
2	URS	PRIGODA, Gennadi / BACHKATOV, Iouri EVSEEV, Nikolai / TKASHENKO, Vladimir	3:18.33
3	GDR	RICHTER, Dirk / FLEMMING, Thomas HINNEBURG, Lars / ZESNER, Steffen	3:19.82
4	FRA		3:20.02
5	SWE		3:21.07
6	FRG		3:21.65

* swam in preliminaries only.

MEN'S 4x200-METER FREESTYLE RELAY / September 21

RANK	CTRY	ATHLETES	TIME
1	USA	DALBEY, Troy / CETLINSKI, Matthew GJERTSEN, Douglas / BIONDI, Matthew (* OPPEL, Craig / JORGENSEN, Daniel)	7:12.51 WR
2	GDR	DASSLER, Uwe / LODZIEWSKI, Sven FLEMMING, Thomas / ZESNER, Steffen	7:13.68
3	FRG	HOCHSTEIN, Erik / FAHRNER, Thomas HENKEL, Rainer / GROSS, Michael	7:14.35
4	AUS		7:15.23
5	ITA		7:16.00
6	SWE		7:19.10

* swam in preliminaries only.

MENS 4x100-METER MEDLEY RELAY / September 25

RANK	CTRY	ATHLETES	TIME
1	USA	BERKOFF, David / SCHROEDER, Richard BIONDI, Matthew / JACOBS, Christopher (*MORTENSON, Jay / JAGER, Thomas)	3:36.93 WR
2	CAN	TEWKSBURY, Mark / DAVIS, Victor PONTING, Thomas / GOSS, Donald	3:39.28
3	URS	POLIANSKI, Igor / VOLKOV, Dmitri IAROCHTCHOUK, Vadim / PRIGODA, Gennadi	3:39.96
4	FRG		3:42.98
5	JPN		3:44.36
6	AUS		3:45.85

* swam in preliminaries only.

DIVING

WOMEN'S PLATFORM / September 18

RANK	CTRY	ATHLETE	TOTAL
1	CHN	XU, Yanmei	445.20
2	USA	MITCHELL, Michele	436.95
3	USA	WILLIAMS, Wendy	400.44
4	URS	STASSIOULEVITCH, Anjela	386.22
5	CHN	CHEN, Xiaodan	384.15
6	URS	MIROCHINA, Elena	381.93

WOMEN'S SPRINGBOARD / September 25

RANK	CTRY	ATHLETE	TOTAL
1	CHN	GAO, Min	580.23
2	CHN	LI, Qing	534.33
3	USA	McCORMICK, Kelly	533.19
4	URS	LACHKO, Irina	526.65
5	URS	BABKOVA, Marina	506.43
6	USA	LUCERO, Wendy	498.81

MEN'S PLATFORM / September 27

RANK	CTRY	ATHLETE	TOTAL
1	USA	LOUGANIS, Gregory	638.61
2	CHN	XIONG, Ni	637.47
3	MEX	MENA, Jesus	594.39
4	URS	TCHOGOVADZE, Gueorgui	585.96
5	GDR	HEMPEL, Jan	583.77
6	CHN	LI, Kongzheng	543.81
12	USA	JEFFREY, Patrick	483.54

MEN'S SPRINGBOARD / September 20

RANK	CTRY	ATHLETE	TOTAL
1	USA	LOUGANIS, Gregory	730.80
2	CHN	TAN, Liangde	704.88
3	CHN	LI, Deliang	665.28
4	FRG	KILLAT, Albin	661.47
5	USA	BRADSHAW, Mark	642.99
6	MEX	MONDRAGON, Jorge	616.02

SYNCHRONIZED SWIMMING

SOLO / September 30

RANK	CTRY	ATHLETE	POINTS
1	CAN	WALDO, Carolyn	200.150
2	USA	RUIZ-CONFORTO, Tracie	197.633
3	JPN	KOTANI, Mikako	191.850
4	FRA	HERMINE, Muriel	190.100
5	SUI	SINGER, Karin	185.600
6	GBR	SHEARN, Nicola	181.933

DUET / October 1

RANK	CTRY	ATHLETES	POINTS
1	CAN	WALDO, Carolyn / CAMERON, Michelle	197.717
2	USA	JOSEPHSON, Sarah / JOSEPHSON, Karen	197.284
3	JPN	TANAKA, Miyako / KOTANI, Mikako	190.159
4	FRA	SCHULER, Karine / CAPRON, Anne	184.792
5	SUI	BOSS, Edith / SINGER, Karin	183.950
6	URS	TSCHERNIAEVA, Mariia / TITOVA, Tatiana	182.667

WATER POLO / October 1

RANK	CTRY	WON	LOST	TIED	SCORE	USA GAME SCORES
1	YUG	6	1	0	9-7 (Final)	USA vs. YUG 7-6
2	USA	5	2	0		USA vs. ESP 7-9
3	URS	4	2	1	14-13 (3rd-4th)	USA vs. CHN 14-7
4	FRG	5	2	0		USA vs. GRE 18-9
5	HUN	3	2	3		USA vs. HUN 10-9
6	ESP	4	2	2		USA vs. URS 8-7
						USA vs. YUG 7-9

TABLE TENNIS

WOMEN'S SINGLES / October 1

RANK	CTRY	ATHLETE	MATCH SCORE
1	CHN	CHEN, Jing	3-2 (Final)
2	CHN	LI, Huifen	2-0 (3rd-4th)
3	CHN	JIAO, Zhimin	
4	TCH	HRACHOVA, Marie	3-0 (5th-6th)
5	URS	BOULATOVA, Flyura	
6	URS	POPOVA, Valentina	
—	USA	BHUSHAN, Insook	elim. first round
—	USA	GEE, Diana	elim. first round

WOMEN'S DOUBLES / September 30

RANK	CTRY	ATHLETE	MATCH SCORE
1	KOR	HYUN, Jung-hwa / YANG, Young-ja	2-1 (Final)
2	CHN	CHEN, Jing / JIANO, Zhimin	
3	YUG	FAZLIC, Jasna / PERKUCIN, Gordana	2-1 (3rd-4th)
4	JPN	HOSHINO, Mika / ISHIDA, Kiyomi	
5	TCH	HRACHOVA, Marie / KASALOVA, Renata	2-1 (5th-6th)
6	URS	BOULATOVA, Flyura / KOVTOUN, Elena	
—	USA	BHUSHAN, Insook / GEE, Diana	elim. first round

MEN'S SINGLES / October 1

RANK	CTRY	ATHLETE	MATCH SCORE
1	KOR	YOO, Nam-kyu	3-1 (Final)
2	KOR	KIM, Ki-taik	
3	SWE	LINDH, Erik	3-1 (3rd-4th)
4	HUN	KLAMPAR, Tiber	
5	CHN	JIANG, Jialiang	3-0 (5th-6th)
6	CHN	CHEN, Longcan	
—	USA	O'NEILL, Sean	elim. first round

MEN'S DOUBLES / September 30

RANK	CTRY	ATHLETE	MATCH SCORE
1	CHN	CHEN, Longcan / WEI, Qingguang	2-1 (Final)
2	YUG	LUPULESKU, Ilija / PRIMORAC, Zoran	
3	KOR	AHN, Jae-hyung / YOO, Nam-kyu	2-0 (3rd-4th)
4	KOR	KIM, Ki-taik / KIM, Wan	
5	CHN	JIANG, Jialiang / XU, Zengcai	2-0 (5th-6th)
6	POL	GRUBBA, Andrezej / KUCHARSKI, Leszek	

(No USA entry)

TEAM HANDBALL

WOMEN / September 29

RANK	CTRY	WON	LOST	TIED	USA GAME SCORES
1	KOR	4	2	0	USA vs. YUG 18-19
2	NOR	3	1	2	USA vs. TCH 19-33
3	URS	3	1	2	USA vs. KOR 18-24
4	YUG	3	3	0	USA vs. CHN 22-31
5	TCH	5	1	0	USA vs. CIV 27-16
6	CHN	3	3	0	
7	USA	1	5	0	

MEN / October 1

RANK	CTRY	WON	LOST	TIED	USA GAME SCORES
1	URS	6	0	0	USA vs. ISL 15-22
2	KOR	4	2	0	USA vs. YUG 23-31
3	YUG	4	1	1	USA vs. URS 14-26
4	HUN	3	3	0	USA vs. SWE 12-26
5	SWE	4	2	0	USA vs. ALG 17-20
6	TCH	3	3	0	USA vs. JPN 20-24
12	USA	0	6	0	

TENNIS

WOMEN'S SINGLES / October 1

RANK	CTRY	ATHLETE	
1	FRG	GRAF, Steffi	
2	ARG	SABATINI, Gabriela	
3T	USA	GARRISON, Zina	
3T	BUL	MALEEVA, Manuela	
—	USA	SHRIVER, Pam	elim. quarterfinals
—	USA	EVERT, Chris	elim. third round

WOMEN'S DOUBLES / September 30

RANK	CTRY	ATHLETES	
1	USA	SHRIVER, Pam / GARRISON, Zina	
2	TCH	NOVOTNA, Jana / SUKOVA, Helena	
3T	AUS	SMYLIE, Elizabeth / TURNBULL, Wendy	
3T	FRG	GRAF, Steffi / KOHDE-KILSCH, Claudia	

MEN'S SINGLES / September 30

RANK	CTRY	ATHLETE	
1	TCH	MECIR, Miloslav	
2	USA	MAYOTTE, Tim	
3T	USA	GILBERT, Brad	
3T	SWE	EDBERG, Stefan	

MEN'S DOUBLES / September 30

RANK	CTRY	ATHLETE	
1	USA	FLACH, Ken / SEGUSO, Robert	
2	ESP	SANCHEZ, Emilio / CASAL, Sergio	
3T	TCH	MECIR, Miloslav / SREJBER, Milan	
3T	SWE	EDBERG, Stefan / JARRYD, Anders	

VOLLEYBALL

WOMEN / September 29

RANK	CTRY	WON	LOST	MATCH	GAME SCORES
1	URS	4	1	3-2	10-15,12-15,15-13,15-7,17-15 (Final)
2	PER	4	1		
3	CHN	3	2	3-0	15-13,15-6,15-6 (3rd-4th)
4	JPN	2	3		
5	GDR	3	2	3-1	15-9,15-4,11-15,15-11 (5th-6th)
6	BRA	1	4		
7	USA	2	3	3-2	15-4,12-15,13-15,15-9,15-8 (7th-8th)
8	KOR	1	4		

USA MATCH (GAME) SCORES

CHN 3,	USA 0	(15-9,15-5,15-7)
USA 3,	BRA 2	(14-16,15-5,15-13,12-15,15-7)
PER 3,	USA 2	(12-15,9-15,15-4,15-5,15-9)
GDR 3,	USA 1	(15-13,15-11,10-15,15-8 — semifinals)
USA 3,	KOR 2	(15-4,12-15,13-15,15-9,15-8 — 7th-8th)

MEN / October 2

RANK	CTRY	WON	LOST	MATCH	GAME SCORES
1	USA	7	0	3-1	13-15,15-10,15-4,15-8 (Final)
2	URS	5	2		
3	ARG	4	3	3-2	15-10,15-17,15-8,12-15,15-9 (3rd-4th)
4	BRA	4	3		
5	HOL	5	2	3-0	15-6,15-8,15-10 (5th-6th)
6	BUL	3	4		

USA MATCH SCORES

USA 3,	JPN 0	(15-13,15-2,15-2)
USA 3,	HOL 1	(15-7,12-15,15-1,15-11)
USA 3,	ARG 2	(11-15,11-15,15-4,17-15,15-7)
USA 3,	FRA 0	(17-15,15-6,15-13)
USA 3,	TUN 0	(15-4,15-6,15-4)
USA 3,	BRA 0	(15-3,15-5,15-11 — semifinals)
USA 3,	URS 1	(13-15,15-10,15-4,15-8 — final)

WEIGHTLIFTING

52 KG / September 18

RANK	CTRY	ATHLETE	SNATCH	CLEAN & JERK	TOTAL KG
1	BUL	MARINOV, Sevdalin	120.0 WR	150.0	270.0 WR
2	KOR	CHUN, Byung-kwan	112.5	147.5	260.0
3#	CHN	HE, Zhuoqiang	112.5	145.0	257.5
4	CHN	ZHANG, Shoulie	115.0	142.5	257.5
5	POL	GUTOWSKI, Jacek	112.5	135.0	247.5
6	ROM	CIHAREAN, Traian Ioach	110.0	130.0	240.0

(no USA entry)
awarded bronze based on lower body weight.

56 KG / September 19

RANK	CTRY	ATHLETE	SNATCH	CLEAN & JERK	TOTAL KG
1*	URS	MIRZOIAN, Oxen	127.5 OR	165.0 OR	292.5 OR
2	CHN	HE, Yingqiang	125.0	162.5	287.5
3	CHN	LIU, Shoubin	127.5	140.0	267.5
4	INA	WIHARDJA, Dirdja	112.5	142.5	255.0
5#	JPN	ICHIBA, Takashi	107.5	145.0	252.5
6	KOR	KIM, Kwi-shik	110.0	142.5	252.5

(no USA entry)
* Mitko Grablev (BUL), original gold medalist, tested positive for use of a banned substance.
# awarded fifth place based on lower body weight.

60 KG / September 20

RANK	CTRY	ATHLETE	SNATCH	CLEAN & JERK	TOTAL KG
1	TUR	SULEYMANOGLU, Naim	152.5 WR	190.0 WR	342.5 WR
2	BUL	TOPOUROV, Stefan	137.5	175.0	312.5
3	CHN	YE, Huanming	127.5	160.0	287.5
4	KOR	MIN, Joon-ki	125.0	155.0	280.0
5	JPN	MURAKI, Yosuke	127.5	150.0	277.5
6	GRE	SIDIROPOULOS, Gianni	120.0	145.0	265.0

(no USA entry)

67.5 KG / September 21

RANK	CTRY	ATHLETE	SNATCH	CLEAN & JERK	TOTAL KG
1*	GDR	KUNZ, Joachim	150.0	190.0	340.0
2	URS	MILITOSSIAN, Israel	155.0 OR	182.5	337.5
3	CHN	LI, Jinhe	147.5	177.5	325.0
4#	POL	SEWERYN, Marek	145.0	172.5	317.5
5	TUR	BATMAZ, Ergun	145.0	172.5	317.5
6	CHN	XIAO, Minglin	132.5	172.5	305.0
13	USA	JACQUES, Michael	125.0	157.5	282.5

* Angel Guenchev (BUL), original gold medalist, tested positive for use of a banned substance.
# awarded fourth place based on lower body weight.

75 KG / September 22

RANK	CTRY	ATHLETE	SNATCH	CLEAN & JERK	TOTAL KG
1	BUL	GUIDIKOV, Borislav	167.5 OR	207.5 OR	375.0 OR
2	GDR	STEINHOEFEL, Ingo	165.0	195.0	360.0
3	BUL	VARBANOV, Alexander	157.5	200.0	357.5
4*#	CHN	CAI, Yanshu	157.5	190.0	347.5
5	ROM	SOCACI, Andrei	152.5	195.0	347.5
6#	POL	KOSINSKI, Waldemar	152.5	180.0	332.5
8	USA	URRUTIA, Roberto	150.0	177.5	327.5

* Kalman Csengeri (HUN), original fourth-place finisher, tested positive for use of a banned substance.
# awarded placement(s) based on lower body weight.

82.5 KG / September 24

RANK	CTRY	ATHLETE	SNATCH	CLEAN & JERK	TOTAL KG
1	URS	ARSAMAKOV, Israil	167.5	210.0	377.5
2	HUN	MESSZI, Istvan	170.0	200.0	370.0
3	KOR	LEE, Hyung-kun	160.0	207.5	367.5
4	GBR	MORGAN, David	165.0	200.0	365.0
5	POL	SIEMION, Krzysztof	162.5	195.0	357.5
6	JPN	ISAOKA, Ryoji	155.0	195.0	350.0
11	USA	CRASS, Derrick	140.0	175.0	315.0
14	USA	WHITE, Curt	140.0	165.0	305.0

90 KG / September 25

RANK	CTRY	ATHLETE	SNATCH	CLEAN & JERK	TOTAL KG
1	URS	KHRAPATYI, Anatoli	187.5 OR	225.0 OR	412.5 OR
2#	URS	MOUKHAMEDIAROV, Nail	177.5	222.5	400.0
3	POL	ZAWADA, Slawomir	180.0	220.0	400.0
4	POL	PIOTROWSKI, Andrzej	165.0	200.0	365.0
5	HUN	BUDA, Attila	175.0	185.0	360.0
6	GBR	MERCER, David	157.5	200.0	357.5
11	USA	KRITSKY, Arn	147.5	185.0	332.5
14	USA	BRIAN, Bret	140.0	180.0	320.0

awarded silver based on lower body weight.

100 KG / September 26

RANK	CTRY	ATHLETE	SNATCH	CLEAN & JERK	TOTAL KG
1*	URS	KOUZNETSOV, Pavel	190.0 OR	235.0 OR	425.0 OR
2	ROM	VLAD, Nicu	185.0	217.5	402.5
3	FRG	IMMESBERGER, Peter	175.0	220.0	395.0
4	HUN	BOKFI, Janos	180.0	212.5	392.5
5	FRA	TOURNEFIER, Francis	170.0	215.0	385.0
6	CAN	GARON, Denis	160.0	222.5	382.5

(no USA entry)
* Andor Szanyi (HUN), original gold medalist, tested positive for use of a banned substance.

110 KG / September 27

RANK	CTRY	ATHLETE	SNATCH	CLEAN & JERK	TOTAL KG
1	URS	ZAKHAREVITCH, Yuri	210.0 WR	245.0 OR	455.0 WR
2	HUN	JACSO, Jozsef	190.0	237.5	427.5
3#	GDR	WELLER, Ronny	190.0	235.0	425.0
4	GDR	SCHUBERT, Michael	190.0	235.0	425.0
5	URS	POPOV, Alexandre	187.5	232.5	420.0
6	ITA	OBERBURGER, Norberto	187.5	227.5	415.0
11#*	USA	SCHUTZ, Rich	160.0	200.0	360.0
13	USA	MICHELS, Jeff	167.5	192.5	360.0

awarded placement(s) based on lower body weight.
* did not make weight at 100 KG and moved up one weight class.

OVER 110 KG / September 29

RANK	CTRY	ATHLETE	SNATCH	CLEAN & JERK	TOTAL KG
1	URS	KOURLOVITCH, Alexandre	212.5 OR	250.0	462.5 OR
2	FRG	NERLINGER, Manfred	190.0	240.0	430.0
3	FRG	ZAWILJA, Martin	182.5	232.5	415.0
4	USA	MARTINEZ, Mario	175.0	232.5	407.5
5	TCH	HUDECEK, Petr	175.0	225.0	400.0
6	EGY	ELBATOTY, Reda	175.0	217.5	392.5
10	USA	BERGMAN, John	167.5	185.0	352.5

WRESTLING

FREESTYLE

48 KG / September 29

RANK	CTRY	ATHLETE
1	JPN	KOBAYASHI, Takashi
2	BUL	TZONOV, Ivan
3	URS	KARAMTCHAKOV, Serguei
4	USA	VANNI, Tim
5	FRG	HEUGABEL, Reiner
6	TUR	SUKRUOGLU, Ilyas

52 KG / September 30

RANK	CTRY	ATHLETE	
1	JPN	SATO, Mitsuru	
2	YUG	TRSTENA, Saban	
3	URS	TOGOUZOV, Vladimir	
4	HUN	BIRO, Laszlo	
5	TUR	SEYHANLI, Aslan	
6	KOR	KIM, Jong-oh	
—	USA	CHERTOW, Ken	elim. third round

57 KG / October 1

RANK	CTRY	ATHLETE	
1	URS	BELOGLAZOV, Serguei	
2	IRN	MOHAMMADIAN, Askari	
3	KOR	NOH, Kyung-sun	
4	TUR	AK, Ahmet	
5	BUL	IVANOV, Valentin	
6	HUN	NAGY, Bela	
—	USA	DAVIS, Barry	elim. third round

62 KG / September 29

RANK	CTRY	ATHLETE
1	USA	SMITH, John
2	URS	SARKISSIAN, Stepan
3	BUL	CHTEREV, Simeon
4	IRN	FALLAH, Akbar
5	FRG	HELMDACH, Joerg
6	MGL	ENHE, Avirmed

68 KG / October 1

RANK	CTRY	ATHLETE
1	URS	FADZAEV, Arsen
2	KOR	PARK, Jang-soon
3	USA	CARR, Nate
4	JPN	AKAISHI, Kosei
5	CAN	McKAY, David
6	FIN	RAUHALA, Jukka

74 KG / September 30

RANK	CTRY	ATHLETE
1	USA	MONDAY, Kenneth
2	URS	VARAEV, Adlan
3	BUL	SOFIADI, Rakhmad
4	MGL	ENHBAYAR, Lodoy
5	FIN	RAUHALA, Pekka
6	IRN	VAGOZARI, Ayatollah

82 KG / October 1

RANK	CTRY	ATHLETE
1	KOR	HAN, Myung-woo
2	TUR	GENCALP, Necmi
3	TCH	LOHYNA, Josef
4	URS	TAMBOUVTSEV, Alexandre
5	MGL	SUHBAT, Puntsag
6	USA	SCHULTZ, Mark

90 KG / September 29

RANK	CTRY	ATHLETE
1	URS	KHADARTSEV, Makharbek
2	JPN	OTA, Akira
3	KOR	KIM, Tae-woo
4	HUN	TOTH, Gabor
5	USA	SCHERR, Jim
6	BUL	ALABAKOV, Roumen

100 KG / September 30

RANK	CTRY	ATHLETE
1	ROM	PUSCASU, Vasile
2	URS	KHABELOV, Leri
3	USA	SCHERR, William
4	GDR	NEUPERT, Uwe
5	BUL	KARADOUCHEV, Gueorgui
6	MGL	JAVHLANTUGS, Bold

130 KG / October 1

RANK	CTRY	ATHLETE
1	URS	GOBEDJICHVILI, David
2	USA	BAUMGARTNER, Bruce
3	GDR	SCHROEDER, Andreas
4	HUN	KLAUZ, Laszlo
5	BUL	ATANASSOV, Atanas
6	CAN	PAYNE, Daniel

GRECO-ROMAN

48 KG / September 20

RANK	CTRY	ATHLETE	
1	ITA	MAENZA, Vincenzo	
2	POL	GLAB, Andrzej	
3	BUL	TZENOV, Bratan	
4	URS	ALLAKHVERDIEV, Maguiatdine	
5	SYR	ALFARAJ, Khaled	
6	FRG	SCHERER, Markus	
—	USA	FULLER, Mark	elim. third round

52 KG / September 21

RANK	CTRY	ATHLETE	
1	NOR	RONNINGEN, Jon	
2	JPN	MIYAHARA, Atsuji	
3	KOR	LEE, Jae-suk	
4	URS	IGNATENKO, Alexandre	
5	POL	KIERPACZ, Roman	
6	TCH	JANKOVICS, Tobor	
—	USA	SHELDON, Shawn	elim. second round

57 KG / September 22

RANK	CTRY	ATHLETE	
1	HUN	SIKE, Andras	
2	BUL	BALOV, Stoyan	
3	GRE	HOLIDIS, Charalambos	
4	CHN	YANG, Changling	
5	KOR	HUH, Byung-ho	
6	IRQ	SALAH, Ghazi	
—	USA	AMADO, Anthony	elim. fourth round

62 KG / September 20

RANK	CTRY	ATHLETE
1	URS	MADJIDOV, Kamandar
2	BUL	VANGUELOV, Jivko
3	KOR	AN, Dae-hyun
4	HUN	BODI, Jeno
5	FRG	BEHL, Peter
6	USA	ANDERSON, Isaac

68 KG / September 22

RANK	CTRY	ATHLETE	
1	URS	DJOULFALAKIAN, Levon	
2	KOR	KIM, Sung-moon	
3	FIN	SIPILA, Tapio	
4	ROM	CARARE, Petrica	
5	POL	KOPANSKI, Jerzy	
6	JPN	OKUBO, Yasuhiro	
—	USA	SERAS, Andrew	elim. fourth round

74 KG / September 21

RANK	CTRY	ATHLETE	
1	KOR	KIM, Young-nam	
2	URS	TOURLYKHANOV, Daoulet	
3	POL	TRACZ, Jozef	
4	HUN	TAKACS, Janos	
5	FRA	MISCHLER, Martial	
6	BUL	VELITCHKOV, Borislav	
—	USA	BUTLER, David	elim. fourth round

82 KG / September 22

RANK	CTRY	ATHLETE
1	URS	MAMIACHVILI, Mikhail
2	HUN	KOMAROMI, Tibor
3	KOR	KIM, Sang-kyu
4	NOR	KLEVEN, Stig Arild
5	YUG	KASUM, Goran
6	SWE	FREDRIKSSON, Magnus
7	USA	MORGAN, John

90 KG / September 20

RANK	CTRY	ATHLETE	
1	BUL	KOMCHEV, Atanas	
2	FIN	KOSKELA, Harri	
3	URS	POPOV, Vladimir	
4	SWE	GULLDEN, Christer	
5	FRG	STEINBACH, Andreas	
6	AUT	PITSCHMANN, Franz	
—	USA	FOY, Michial	elim. third round

100 KG / September 21

RANK	CTRY	ATHLETE
1	POL	WRONSKI, Andrzej
2	FRG	HIMMEL, Gerhard
3	USA	KOSLOWSKI, Dennis
4	BUL	GUEORGUIEV, Ilia
5	YUG	TERTEI, Jozef
6	KOR	YOO, Young-tai

130 KG / September 22

RANK	CTRY	ATHLETE
1	URS	KARELINE, Alexandre
2	BUL	GUEROVSKI, Ranguel
3	SWE	JOHANSSON, Tomas
4	EGY	ELHADAD, Hassan
5	HUN	KLAUZ, Laszlo
6	JPN	DEGUCHI, Kazuya
8	USA	KOSLOWSKI, Duane

YACHTING

WOMEN'S 470 / September 27

RANK	CTRY	ATHLETES	NET POINTS
1	USA	JOLLY, Allison / JEWELL, Lynne	26.70
2	SWE	SODERSTROM, Marit / BENGTSSON, Birgitta	40.00
3	URS	MOSKALENKO, Larissa / TCHOUNIKHOVSKAI, Irina	45.40
4	FIN	LEMSTROM, Bettina / LEMSTROM, Annika	47.00
5	FRG	MEYER, Susanne / ADLKOFER, Katrin	56.40
6	AUS	GREEN, Nicola / DAVIS, Karyn	57.00

MEN'S 470 / September 27

RANK	CTRY	ATHLETES	NET POINTS
1	FRA	PEPONNET, Thierry / PILLOT, Luc	34.70
2	URS	TYNISTE, Tynou / TYNISTE, Toomas	46.00
3	USA	SHADDEN, John / McKEE, Charlie	51.00
4	ESP	LEON, Feranado / SANCHEZ, Luna F.	55.00
5	FRG	HUNGER, Wolfgang / HUNGER, Joachim	58.70
6	NZL	EVANS, Peter / MANDER, Simon	62.70

DIVISION II SAILBOARD / September 27

RANK	CTRY	ATHLETE	NET POINTS
1	NZL	KENDALL, Bruce	35.40
2	AHO	BOERSMA, Jan	42.70
3	USA	GEBHARDT, Michael	48.00
4	HOL	VERSCHOOR, Bart	53.40
5	FRA	NAGY, Robert	61.70
6	ITA	WIRZ, Francesco	63.00

FINN / September 27

RANK	CTRY	ATHLETE	NET POINTS
1	ESP	DORESTE, Jose Luis	38.10
2	ISV	HOLMBERG, Peter	40.40
3	NZL	CUTLER, John	45.00
4	GBR	CHILDERLEY, Stuart	50.70
5	DEN	HJORTNES, Lasse	51.00
6	FRG	SCHMID, Thomas	72.10
10	USA	LEDBETTER, Brian	91.00

FLYING DUTCHMAN / September 27

RANK	CTRY	ATHLETES	NET POINTS
1	DEN	BOJSEN-MOLLER, Jorgen / GRONBORG, Christian	31.40
2	NOR	POLLEN, Olepetter / BJORKUM, Erik	37.40
3	CAN	McLAUGHLIN, Frank / MILLEN, John	48.40
4	ISR	SELA, Yoel / AMIR, Eldad	59.70
5	NZL	JONES, Murray / KNOWLES, Gregory	60.00
6	GBR	YEOMAN, Roger / McDONALD, Neal	72.70
11	USA	FOERSTER, Paul / GOLDMAN, Andrew	85.70

TORNADO / September 27

RANK	CTRY	ATHLETES	POINTS
1	FRA	LE DEROFF, Jean-Yves / HENARD, Nicolas	16.00
2	NZL	TIMMS, Christopher / SELLERS, Rex	35.40
3	BRA	GRAEL, Lars / FREITAS, Clinio	40.10
4	AUT	PETSCHEL, Norbert / CLAUS, Christian	46.00
5	ITA	ZUCCOLI, Giorgio / SANTELLA, Luca	60.10
6	NOR	NILSEN, Per Arne / JOHANNESSEN, Carl	67.70
14	USA	MELVIN, James / MUGLIA, Patrick	110.70

STAR / September 27

RANK	CTRY	ATHLETES	POINTS
1	GBR	McINTYRE, Michael / VAILE, Philip Bryn	45.70
2	USA	REYNOLDS, Mark / HAENEL, Hal	48.00
3	BRA	GRAEL, Torben / FALCAO, Nelson	50.00
4	SWE	JOHANSSON, Mats / HANSSON, Mats	56.70
5	ITA	GORLA, Giorgio / PERABONI, Alfio	63.10
6	CAN	MacDONALD, David / MacDONALD, Donald	63.70

SOLING / September 27

RANK	CTRY	ATHLETES	POINTS
1	GDR	SCHUEMANN, Jochen / FLACH, Thomas JAEKEL, Bernd	11.70
2	USA	KOSTECKI, John / BAYLIS, William BILLINGHAM, Robert	14.00
3	DEN	BANK, Jesper / MATHIASEN, Jan Dupont SECHER, Steen	52.70
4	GBR		67.10
5	BRA		67.40
6	FRA		68.40

BASEBALL
(DEMONSTRATION SPORT) / September 28

RANK	CTRY	RECORD	SCORE	USA GAME SCORES
1	USA	4-1	5-3 (Final)	USA vs. KOR 5-3
2	JPN	4-1		USA vs. AUS 12-2 6-2/3 Inn.
3	PUR	3-2	7-0 (3rd-4th)	USA vs. CAN 7-8
4	KOR	2-3		USA vs. PUR 7-2
				USA vs. JPN 5-3

WOMEN'S JUDO
(DEMONSTRATION EVENT)

EXTRA-LIGHTWEIGHT (Up to 48 KG) / September 25

RANK	CTRY	ATHLETE
1	CHN	LI, Zhongyun
2	JPN	ESAKI, Fumiko
3T	AUS	REARDON, Julie
3T	KOR	CHO, Min-sun

(no USA entry)

HALF-LIGHTWEIGHT (Up to 52 KG) / September 26

RANK	CTRY	ATHLETE
1	GBR	RENDLE, Sharon
2	FRA	BRUN, Dominique
3T	ITA	GUINGI, Alessandra
3T	JPN	YAMAGUCHI, Kaori

(no USA entry)

LIGHTWEIGHT (Up to 56 KG) / September 27

RANK	CTRY	ATHLETE	
1	AUS	WILLIAMS, Suzanne	
2	CHN	LIU, Guizhu	
3T	FRA	ARNAUD, Catherine	
3T	FRG	PHILIPS, Regina	
—	USA	TRIVELLA, Eve	elim. first round

HALF-MIDDLEWEIGHT (Up to 61 KG) / September 28

RANK	CTRY	ATHLETE
1	GBR	BELL, Diane
2	USA	ROETHKE, Lynn
3T	JPN	MOCHIDA, Noriko
3T	POL	OLECHNOWICZ, Boguslawa

MIDDLEWEIGHT (Up to 66 KG) / September 29

RANK	CTRY	ATHLETE
1	JPN	SASAKI, Hikari
2	FRA	DEYDIER, Brigitte
3T	AUT	HARTL, Roswitha
3T	KOR	PARK, Ji-young

(no USA entry)

HALF-HEAVYWEIGHT (Up to 72 KG) / September 30

RANK	CTRY	ATHLETE
1	BEL	BERGHMANS, Ingrid
2	KOR	BAE, Mi-jung
3T	FRG	CLASSEN, Barbara
3T	JPN	TANABE, Yoko

(no USA entry)

HEAVYWEIGHT (Over 72 KG) / October 1

RANK	CTRY	ATHLETE
1	HOL	SERIESE, Angelique
2	CHN	GAO, Fenglian
3T	USA	CASTRO-GOMEZ, Margaret
3T	FRG	SIGMUND, Regina

TAEKWONDO
(DEMONSTRATION SPORT)

WOMEN'S FINWEIGHT (Up to 43 KG) / September 19

RANK	CTRY	ATHLETE	
1	TPE	CHIN, Yu-fang	
2	KOR	LEE, Hwa-jin	
3T	MAL	MARATHAMUTHU, Vasugi	
3T	MEX	TORRES, Moni	
—	USA	KALANOC, Cheryl	elim. first round

WOMEN'S FLYWEIGHT (43-47 KG) / September 17

RANK	CTRY	ATHLETE
1	KOR	CHOO, Nan-yool
2	ESP	NARANJO, Maria Angela
3T	USA	PEJO, Mayumi
3T	TPE	PAI, Yun-yao

WOMEN'S BANTAMWEIGHT (47-51 KG) / September 18

RANK	CTRY	ATHLETE
1	TPE	CHEN, Yi-an
2	USA	HOLLOWAY, Debra
3T	ESP	LOPEZ, Josefina
3T	KOR	PARK, Sun-young

WOMEN'S FEATHERWEIGHT (51-55 KG) / September 20

RANK	CTRY	ATHLETE	
1	DEN	CHRISTENSEN, Annemette	
2	TUR	TAN, Zuleyha	
3T	ESP	DOLLS, Amparo	
3T	KOR	KIM, So-young	
—	USA	DOTSON, Kim	elim. first round

WOMEN'S LIGHTWEIGHT (55-60 KG) / September 19

RANK	CTRY	ATHLETE
1	USA	HEE, Dana
2	DEN	SCHWARTZ, Karin
3T	HOL	VAN DUREN, Jolanda
3T	TPE	CHEN, Jiun-feng

WOMEN'S WELTERWEIGHT (60-65 KG) / September 17

RANK	CTRY	ATHLETE
1	USA	LIMAS, Arlene
2	KOR	KIM, Ji-sook
3T	ESP	BISTUER, Coral
3T	FRG	SEIDEL, Sonny

WOMEN'S MIDDLEWEIGHT (65-70 KG) / September 18

RANK	CTRY	ATHLETE
1	KOR	KIM, Hyun-hee
2	HOL	DE JONGH, Margaretha
3T	USA	JEWELL, Sharon
3T	ESP	NAVAZ, Elena

WOMEN'S HEAVYWEIGHT (Over 70 KG) / September 20

RANK	CTRY	ATHLETE
1	USA	LOVE, Lynnette
2	KOR	JANG, Yoon-jung
3T	CAN	FRANSSEN, Yvonne
3T	FRG	GUESTER, Ute

MEN'S FINWEIGHT (Up to 50 KG) / September 19

RANK	CTRY	ATHLETE	
1	KOR	KWON, Tae-ho	
2	USA	MORENO, Juan	
3T	MEX	TORRUELLA, Enrique	
3T	NEP	LAMA, Bidhan	

MEN'S FLYWEIGHT (50-54 KG) / September 17

RANK	CTRY	ATHLETE	
1	KOR	HA, Tae-kyung	
2	ESP	GARCIA, Gabriel	
3T	BRN	DARRAJ, Adel	
3T	JOR	ABUSHEKHA, Ihsan	
—	USA	PHAM, Loung	elim. second round

MEN'S BANTAMWEIGHT (54-58 KG) / September 18

RANK	CTRY	ATHLETE
1	KOR	JI, Yong-suk
2	ESP	SANABRIA, Jose
3T	USA	LEE, Han-Won
3T	IRN	DANESH, Feisal

MEN'S FEATHERWEIGHT (58-64 KG) / September 20

RANK	CTRY	ATHLETE
1	KOR	CHANG, Myung-sam
2	TUR	YAGIZ, Cengiz
3T	JOR	KAMAL, Samer
3T	KSA	AL GAFAR, Ibrahim

(no USA entry)

MEN'S LIGHTWEIGHT (64-70 KG) / September 19

RANK	CTRY	ATHLETE
1	KOR	PARK, Bong-kwon
2	ESP	SANCHEZ, Jose Maria
3T	USA	BAKER, Greg
3T	MEX	JURADO, Manuel

MEN'S WELTERWEIGHT (70-76 KG) / September 17

RANK	CTRY	ATHLETE
1	KOR	CHUNG, Kook-hyun
2	ITA	D'ORIANO, Luigi
3T	USA	WARWICK, Jay
3T	TPE	WU, Tsung-che

MEN'S MIDDLEWEIGHT (76-83 KG) / September 18

RANK	CTRY	ATHLETE	
1	KOR	LEE, Kye-haeng	
2	EGY	HUSSEIN, Amr	
3T	FRG	WOZNICKI, Markus	
3T	TUR	SAHIN, Metin	
—	USA	HASAN, Na'im	elim. second round

MEN'S HEAVYWEIGHT (Over 83 KG) / September 20

RANK	CTRY	ATHLETE
1	USA	KIM, Jimmy
2	KOR	KIM, Jong-suk
3T	ESP	ALVAREZ, Jose Luis
3T	FRG	ARNDT, Michael

BADMINTON
(EXHIBITION SPORT)
(no USA entry)

WOMEN'S SINGLES / September 19

RANK	CTRY	ATHLETE
1	KOR	HWANG, Hye-young
2	CHN	HAN, Aiping
3	JPN	SUMIKO, Kitada

WOMEN'S DOUBLES / September 19

RANK	CTRY	ATHLETES
1	KOR	CHUNG, Young / KIM, Yun-ja
2	CHN	LING, Ying / GUAN, Weizhen
3	DEN	DORTE, Kjaer / NETTIE, Nielsen

MEN'S SINGLES / September 19

RANK	CTRY	ATHLETE
1	CHN	YANG, Yang
2	INA	SUGIARTO, Ichuk
3	KOR	PARK, Sung bac

MEN'S DOUBLES / September 19

RANK	CTRY	ATHLETES
1	CHN	LI, Yohgho / TIAN, Bingyi
2	KOR	LEE, Sang-bok / LEE, Kwang-jin
3	JPN	SHUUJI, Matsumo / SHINJU, Matsuura

BOWLING
(EXHIBITION SPORT)

WOMEN / September 18

RANK	CTRY	ATHLETE	TOTAL
1	PHI	CERDENA, Arianne	2,354
2	FIN	MAATTOLA, Annikki	2,315
3	JPN	ASAI, Atsuko	2,281
7	USA	McMULLEN, Debbie	2,137

MEN / September 18

RANK	CTRY	ATHLETE	TOTAL
1	KOR	YUL, Keon-jong	2,435
2	SIN	CHIN, Jack Loke	2,333
3	FIN	PELTOLA, Tapani	2,274
6	USA	LEWIS, Mark	2,237

WHEELCHAIR
(EXHIBITION EVENT)

WOMEN'S 800 METERS / September 30

RANK	CTRY	ATHLETE	TIME
1	USA	HEDRICK, Sharon	2:11.49
2	DEN	ANNE-HANSEN, Connie	—
3	USA	CABLE-BROOKS, Candace	2:18.68
6	USA	CODY-MORRIS, Ann	2:28.78

MEN'S 1,500 METERS / September 30

RANK	CTRY	ATHLETE	TIME
1	FRA	BADID, Mustapha	—
2	BEL	VAN WINKEL, Paul	—
3	USA	BLANCHETTE, Craig	3:34.37

(no other USA entry)

A LOOK BACK AT STATS

CALGARY 1988
PARTICIPATING NATIONS

TOTAL NUMBER OF COUNTRIES: 57
TOTAL NUMBER OF ATHLETES: 1,576 (ENTERED)

AHO	NETHERLANDS ANTILLES
AND	ANDORRA
ARG	ARGENTINA
AUS	AUSTRALIA
AUT	AUSTRIA
BEL	BELGIUM
BOL	BOLIVIA
BUL	BULGARIA
CAN	CANADA
CHI	CHILE
CHN	PEOPLE'S REPUBLIC OF CHINA
CRC	COSTA RICA
CYP	CYPRUS
DEN	DENMARK
ESP	SPAIN
FIJ	FIJI ISLANDS
FIN	FINLAND
FRA	FRANCE
FRG	FEDERAL REPUBLIC OF GERMANY
GBR	GREAT BRITAIN
GDR	GERMAN DEMOCRATIC REPUBLIC
GRE	GREECE
GUA	GUATEMALA
GUM	GUAM
HOL	NETHERLANDS
HUN	HUNGARY
IND	INDIA
ISL	ICELAND
ISV	VIRGIN ISLANDS
ITA	ITALY
JAM	JAMAICA
JPN	JAPAN
KOR	KOREA
LIB	LEBANON
LIE	LIECHTENSTEIN
LUX	LUXEMBURG
MAR	MOROCCO
MEX	MEXICO
MGL	MONGOLIA
MON	MONACO
NOR	NORWAY
NZL	NEW ZEALAND
PRK	NORTH KOREA
PHI	PHILIPPINES
POL	POLAND
POR	PORTUGAL
PUR	PUERTO RICO
ROM	ROMANIA
SMR	SAN MARINO
SUI	SWITZERLAND
SWE	SWEDEN
TCH	CZECHOSLOVAKIA
TPE	CHINESE TAIPEI
TUR	TURKEY
USA	UNITED STATES
URS	USSR
YUG	YUGOSLAVIA

SEOUL 1988
PARTICIPATING NATIONS

TOTAL NUMBER OF COUNTRIES: 160
TOTAL NUMBER OF ATHLETES: 9,593 (ENTERED)

AFG	AFGHANISTAN
AHO	NETHERLANDS ANTILLES
ALG	ALGERIA
AND	ANDORRA
ANG	ANGOLA
ANT	ANTIGUA
ARG	ARGENTINA
ARU	ARUBA
ASA	AMERICAN SAMOA
AUS	AUSTRALIA
AUT	AUSTRIA
BAH	BAHAMAS
BAN	BANGLADESH
BAR	BARBADOS
BEL	BELGIUM
BEN	BENIN
BER	BERMUDAS
BHU	BHUTAN
BIR	BURMA
BIZ	BELIZE
BOL	BOLIVIA
BOT	BOTSWANA
BRA	BRAZIL
BRN	BAHRAIN
BRU	BRUNEI
BUL	BULGARIA
BUR	BURKINA FASO
CAF	CENTRAL AFRICA
CAN	CANADA
CAY	CAYMAN ISLANDS
CHA	CHAD
CHI	CHILE
CHN	PEOPLE'S REPUBLIC OF CHINA
CIV	IVORY COAST
CMR	CAMEROON
COK	COOK ISLANDS
COL	COLOMBIA
CRC	COSTA RICA
CYP	CYPRUS
DEN	DENMARK
DJI	DJIBOUTI
DOM	DOMINICAN REPUBLIC
ECU	ECUADOR
EGY	EGYPT
ESA	EL SALVADOR
ESP	SPAIN
FIJ	FIJI ISLANDS
FIN	FINLAND
FRA	FRANCE
FRG	FEDERAL REPUBLIC OF GERMANY
GAB	GABON
GAM	GAMBIA
GBR	GREAT BRITAIN
GDR	GERMAN DEMOCRATIC REPUBLIC
GEQ	EQUATORIAL GUINEA
GHA	GHANA
GRE	GREECE
GRN	GRENADA

GUA	GUATEMALA
GUI	GUINEA
GUM	GUAM
GUY	GUYANA
HAI	HAITI
HKG	HONG KONG
HOL	NETHERLANDS
HON	HONDURAS
HUN	HUNGARY
INA	INDONESIA
IND	INDIA
IRL	IRELAND
IRN	IRAN
IRQ	IRAQ
ISL	ICELAND
ISR	ISRAEL
ISV	VIRGIN ISLANDS
ITA	ITALY
IVB	BRITISH VIRGIN ISLANDS
JAM	JAMAICA
JOR	JORDAN
JPN	JAPAN
KEN	KENYA
KOR	KOREA
KSA	SAUDI ARABIA
KUW	KUWAIT
LAO	LAOS
LBA	LIBYA
LBR	LIBERIA
LES	LESOTHO
LIB	LEBANON
LIE	LIECHTENSTEIN
LUX	LUXEMBURG
MAL	MALAYSIA
MAR	MOROCCO
MAW	MALAWI
MDV	MALDIVES
MEX	MEXICO
MGL	MONGOLIA
MLI	MALI
MLT	MALTA
MON	MONACO
MOZ	MOZAMBIQUE
MRI	MAURITIUS
MTN	MAURITANIA
NEP	NEPAL
NGR	NIGERIA
NGU	PAPUA-NEW GUINEA
NIG	NIGER
NOR	NORWAY
NZL	NEW ZEALAND
OMA	OMAN
PAK	PAKISTAN
PAN	PANAMA
PAR	PARAGUAY
PER	PERU
PHI	PHILIPPINES
POL	POLAND
POR	PORTUGAL
PUR	PUERTO RICO
QAT	QATAR
ROM	ROMANIA
RWA	RWANDA
SAM	WESTERN SAMOA

SEN	SENEGAL
SIN	SINGAPORE
SLE	SIERRA LEONE
SMR	SAN MARINO
SOL	SOLOMON ISLANDS
SOM	SOMALIA
SRI	SRI LANKA
SUD	SUDAN
SUI	SWITZERLAND
SUR	SURINAM
SWE	SWEDEN
SWZ	SWAZILAND
SYR	SYRIA
TAN	TANZANIA
TCH	CZECHOSLOVAKIA
TGA	TONGA
THA	THAILAND
TOG	TOGO
TPE	CHINESE TAIPEI
TRI	TRINIDAD AND TOBAGO
TUN	TUNISIA
TUR	TURKEY
UAE	UNITED ARAB EMIRATES
UGA	UGANDA
URS	USSR
URU	URUGUAY
USA	UNITED STATES
VAN	VANUATU
VEN	VENEZUELA
VIE	VIETNAM
VIN	ST. VINCENT & GRENADINES
YAR	YEMEN ARAB REPUBLIC
YMD	DEMOCRATIC REPUBLIC OF YEMEN
YUG	YUGOSLAVIA
ZAI	ZAIRE
ZAM	ZAMBIA
ZIM	ZIMBABWE

CALGARY 1988
MEDAL COUNT

CTRY	GOLD	SILVER	BRONZE	TOTAL
URS	11	9	9	29
GDR	9	10	6	25
SUI	5	5	5	15
AUT	3	6	2	11
FRG	3	4	2	9
FIN	4	1	2	7
HOL	3	2	2	7
SWE	4	0	2	6
USA	**2**	**1**	**3**	**6**
NOR	0	3	3	6
ITA	2	1	2	5
CAN	0	2	3	5
YUG	0	2	1	3
TCH	0	1	2	3
FRA	1	0	1	2
JPN	0	0	1	1
LIE	0	0	1	1

ABOVE / *American Carl Lewis, as usual, came up with the longest jump —*
28' 7-1/2". He also won the 100 meters and placed second in the 200. (Lori Adamski-Peek)

SEOUL 1988 MEDAL COUNT

CTRY	GOLD	SILVER	BRONZE	TOTAL
URS	55	31	46	132
GDR	37	35	30	102
USA	**36**	**31**	**27**	**94**
FRG	11	14	15	40
BUL	10	12	13	35
KOR	12	10	11	33
CHN	5	11	12	28
ROM	7	11	6	24
GBR	5	10	9	24
HUN	11	6	6	23
FRA	6	4	6	16
POL	2	5	9	16
ITA	6	4	4	14
JPN	4	3	7	14
AUS	3	6	5	14
NZL	3	2	8	13
YUG	3	4	5	12
SWE	0	4	7	11
CAN	3	2	5	10
KEN	5	2	2	9
HOL	2	2	5	9
TCH	3	3	2	8
BRA	1	2	3	6
NOR	2	3	0	5
DEN	2	1	1	4
FIN	1	1	2	4
ESP	1	1	2	4
SUI	0	2	2	4
MOR	1	0	2	3
TUR	1	1	0	2
JAM	0	2	0	2
ARG	0	1	1	2
BEL	0	0	2	2
MEX	0	0	2	2
AUT	1	0	0	1
POR	1	0	0	1
SUR	1	0	0	1
CHI	0	1	0	1
CRC	0	1	0	1
INA	0	1	0	1
IRN	0	1	0	1
AHO	0	1	0	1
PER	0	1	0	1
SEN	0	1	0	1
ISV	0	1	0	1
COL	0	0	1	1
DJI	0	0	1	1
GRE	0	0	1	1
MGL	0	0	1	1
PAK	0	0	1	1
PHI	0	0	1	1
THA	0	0	1	1

OLYMPIC HOSTS OF THE PAST: 1896–1988

YEAR	#	WINTER HOST
1924	I	Chamonix (FRA)
1928	II	St. Moritz (SUI)
1932	III	Lake Placid (USA)
1936	IV	Garmisch-Partenkirchen (GER)
1948	V	St. Moritz (SUI)
1952	VI	Oslo (NOR)
1956	VII	Cortina D'Ampezzo (ITA)
1960	VIII	Squaw Valley (USA)
1964	IX	Innsbruck (AUT)
1968	X	Grenoble (FRA)
1972	XI	Sapporo (JPN)
1976	XII	Innsbruck (AUT)
1980	XIII	Lake Placid (USA)
1984	XIV	Sarajevo (YUG)
1988	XV	Calgary (CAN)

NOTE: The 10-year anniversary celebration of the Modern Olympics (1906) is not numbered. The 1916 Summer Olympics were not held due to World War I. The 1940 and 1944 Summer and Winter Olympics were not held due to World War II.

YEAR	#	SUMMER HOST
1896	I	Athens (GRE)
1900	II	Paris (FRA)
1904	III	St. Louis (USA)
1906	—	Athens (GRE)
1908	IV	London (GBR)
1912	V	Stockholm (SWE)
1920	VII	Antwerp (BEL)
1924	VIII	Paris (FRA)
1928	IX	Amsterdam (HOL)
1932	X	Los Angeles (USA)
1936	XI	Berlin (GER)
1948	XIV	London (GBR)
1952	XV	Helsinki (FIN)
1956	XVI	Melbourne (AUS)
1960	XVII	Rome (ITA)
1964	XVIII	Tokyo (JPN)
1968	XIX	Mexico City (MEX)
1972	XX	Munich (FRG)
1976	XXI	Montreal (CAN)
1980	XXII	Moscow (URS)
1984	XXIII	Los Angeles (USA)
1988	XXIV	Seoul (KOR)

BEST U.S. FINAL FINISHES IN OLYMPIC EVENTS

WR = world record
OR = Olympic record
DNS = did not start

EWR = equals world record
EOR = equals Olympic record
T = tie

WINTER EVENTS

BIATHLON
1924-1976 not held

10 KILOMETERS

YEAR	RANK	ATHLETE	TIME
1980	19	Lyle Nelson	35:40.56
1984	20	Willie Carow	33:05.8
1988	27	Josh Thompson	27:27.7

20 KILOMETERS
1924-1956 not held

YEAR	RANK	ATHLETE	TIME
1960	14	John Burritt	1:46:36.8
1964	16	Charles Akers	1:32:24.9
1968	27	Ralph Wakeley	1:27:32.9
1972	14	Peter Karns	1:20:59.67
1976	35	Lyle Nelson	1:25:27.50
1980	36	Martin Hagen	1:21:02.95
1984	26	Lyle Nelson	1:21:05.4
1988	25	Josh Thompson	1:01:29.4

4x7.5-KM RELAY
1924-1964 not held

YEAR	RANK	TEAM	TIME
1968	8	Ralph Wakely / Edward Williams / William Spencer / John Ehrensbeck	2:28:35.5
1972	6	Peter Karns / Dexter Morse / Dennis Donahue / William Bowerman	1:57:24.32

Continued

4x7.5-KM RELAY—Continued

YEAR	RANK	TEAM	TIME
1976	11	Lyle Nelson / Dennis Donahue / John Morton / Peter Dascoulias	2:10:17.72
1980	8	Martin Hagen / Lyle Nelson / Donald Nielsen / Peter Hoag	1:39:24.29
1984	11	Willie Carow / Donald Nielsen / Lyle Nelson / Josh Thompson	1:44:31.9
1988	9	Lyle Nelson / Curtis Schreiner / Darin Binning / Josh Thompson	1:29.33.0

BOBSLED

TWO-MAN
1924-1928/1960 not held

YEAR	RANK	TEAM	TIME
1932	1	J. Hubert Stevens / Curtis Stevens	8:14.74
1936	1	Ivan Brown / Alan Washbond	5:29.29
1948	3	Frederick Fortune / Schuyler Carron	5:35.30
1952	2	Stanley Benham / Patrick Martin	5:26.89
1956	5	Waightman Washbond / Pat Biesiadecki	5:38.16
1964	5	Lawrence McKillip / James Ernest Lamy	4:24.60
1968	6	Paul Lamey / Robert Huscher	4:46.03
1972	16	Paul Lamey / Howard Siler	5:06.62
1976	14	James Morgan / Tom Becker	3:50.76
1980	5	Howard Siler / Dick Nalley	4:11.73
1984	15	Brent Rushlaw / Jim Tyler	3:30.75
1988	16	Matt Roy / Jim Herberich	3:59.34

FOUR-MAN
1924 no U.S. entry
1960 not held

YEAR	RANK	TEAM	TIME
1928	1	William Fiske / Nion Tucker / Geoffrey Mason / Clifford Gray / Richard Parke	3:20.5
1932	1	William Fiske / Edward Eagan / Clifford Gray /Jay O'Brien	7:53.68

Continued

FOUR-MAN—Continued

YEAR	RANK	TEAM	TIME
1936	4	J. Hubert Stevens / Crawford Merkel Robert Martin / John Shene	5:24.13
1948	1	Francis Tyler / Patrick Martin Edward Rimkus / William D'Amico	5:20.1
1952	2	Stanley Benham / Patrick Martin Howard Crossett / James Atkinson	5:10.48
1956	3	Arthur Tyler / William Dodge Charles Butler / James Lamy	5:12.39
1964	6	William Hickey / Charles Randolph Reginald Benham / William Dundon	4:17.23
1968	10	Boris Said / David Dunn Robert Crowley / Philip Duprey	2:19.56
1972	14	Boris Said / Philip Duprey John Copley / Kenneth Morris	4:48.43
1976	15	Thomas Becker / Peter Brennan James Morgan / John Proctor	3:46.72
1980	12	Bob Hickey / Jeff Jordan Willie Davenport / Jeff Gadley	4:06.11
1984	5	Jeff Jost / Joe Briski Thomas Barnes / Hal Hoye	3:23.33
1988	4	Brent Rushlaw / Hal Hoye Mike Wasko / Bill White	3:48.28

FIGURE SKATING

FP = factor placement

WOMEN'S SINGLES
1908 no U.S. entry

YEAR	RANK	ATHLETE	POINTS	FP
1920	3	Theresa Weld	898.00	
1924	2	Beatrix Loughran	279.85	
1928	3	Beatrix Loughran	2254.50	
1932	3	Maribel Vinson	2158.5	
1936	5	Maribel Vinson	388.7	
1948	6	Yvonne Sherman	149.833	
1952	2	Tenley Albright	1432.2	
1956	1	Tenley Albright	169.67	
1960	1	Carol Heiss	1490.1	
1964	6	Peggy Fleming	1819.6	
1968	1	Peggy Fleming	1970.5	
1972	3	Janet Lynn	2663.1	
1976	1	Dorothy Hamill	193.80	
1980	2	Linda Fratianne	188.30	
1984	2	Rosalyn Sumners		4.6
1988	3	Debi Thomas		6.0

MEN'S SINGLES

YEAR	RANK	ATHLETE	POINTS	FP
1908	6	Irving Brokaw	1201.0	
1920	6	Nathaniel Niles	1976.25	
1924	6	Nathaniel Niles	274.47	
1928	10	Roger Turner	2245.5	
1932	6	Roger Turner	2297.6	
1936	12	Roger Lee	2541.0	
1948	4	John Lettengarver	176.400	
1952	3	James Grogan	1627.4	
1956	1	Hayes Alan Jenkins	166.43	
1960	1	David Jenkins	1440.2	
1964	3	Scott Allen	1873.6	
1968	2	Timothy Wood	1891.6	
1972	4	Kenneth Shelley	2596.0	
1976	6	David Santee	184.28	
1980	3	Charles Tickner	187.06	
1984	1	Scott Hamilton		3.4
1988	1	Brian Boitano		3.0

PAIRS
1908 no U.S. entry

YEAR	RANK	ATHLETES	POINTS	FP
1920	4	Theresa Weld / Nathaniel Niles	62.50	
1924	6	Theresa Blanchard-Weld / Nathaniel Niles	9.07	
1928	4	Beatrix Loughran / Sherwin Badger	87.50	
1932	2	Beatrix Loughran / Sherwin Badger	77.5	
1936	5	Maribel Vinson / George Hill	10.4	
1948	4	Yvonne Sherman / Robert Swenning	10.581	
1952	2	Karol Kennedy / Michael Kennedy	100.6	
1956	5	Carol Ormaca / Robin Greiner	10.71	
1960	3	Nancy Ludington / Ronald Ludington	76.2	
1964	3	Vivian Joseph / Ronald Joseph	98.2	
1968	6	Cynthia Kauffman / Ronald Kauffman	297.0	
1972	4	Alicia "Jojo" Starbuck / Kenneth Shelley	406.8	
1976	5	Tai Babilonia / Randy Gardner	134.24	
1980	5	Caitlin Carruthers / Peter Carruthers	137.38	
1984	2	Caitlin Carruthers / Peter Carruthers		2.8
1988	3	Jill Watson / Peter Oppegard		4.2

ICE DANCING
1924-1972 not held

YEAR	RANK	ATHLETES	POINTS	FP
1976	3	Colleen O'Conner / James Millns	204.88	
1980	7	Judy Blumberg / Michael Seibert	190.30	
1984	4	Judy Blumberg / Michael Seibert		7.0
1988	6	Suzanne Semanick / Scott Gregory		12.0

ICE HOCKEY
1928 no U.S. entry

YEAR	RANK	WIN	LOSS	TIE	PF	PA
1920	2	3	1	0	52	2
1924	2	4	1	0	73	6
1932	2	4	1	1	27	5
1936	3	5	2	1	10	4
1948	—	5	3	0	86	33
1952	2	6	1	1	43	21
1956	2	5	2	0	33	16
1960	1	7	0	0	48	17
1964	5	2	5	0	29	33
1968	6	2	4	1	23	28
1972	2	4	2	0	23	18
1976	5	2	3	0	15	21
1980	1	6	0	1	33	15
1984	7	2	2	2	23	21
1988	7	3	3	0	35	31

LUGE

WOMEN'S SINGLES
1896-1960 not held

YEAR	RANK	ATHLETE	TIME
1964	DNS	Dorothy Ann Hirschland	
1968	14	Kathleen Roberts	2:33.60
1972	15	Kathleen Roberts Homstad	3:05.98
1976	21	Kathleen Roberts Homstad	3:01.351
1980	15	Deborah Genovese	2:42.926
1984	15	Bonny Warner	2:51.910
1988	6	Bonny Warner	3:06.056

MEN'S SINGLES
1924-1960 not held

YEAR	RANK	ATHLETE	TIME
1964	13	Francis Lloyd Feltman	3:35.05
1968	26	Kim Layton	2:58.64
1972	28	James Murray	3:37.93
1976	25	Richard Cavanaugh	3:41.357
1980	12	Jeff Tucker	3:01.296
1984	14	Frank Masley	3:07.750
1988	12	Frank Masley	3:07.943

MEN'S DOUBLES
1924-1960 not held

YEAR	RANK	TEAM	TIME
1964	13	Raymond Fales / Nicholas Mastromatteo	2:11.93
1968	DNS	Michael Hessel / James Moriarty	
1972	15	Jack Elder / F. Jones	1:32.59
1976	23	Robert Berkley / Richard Cavanaugh	1:32.009
1980	11	Richard Healey / Walter Danco	1:21.341
1984	9	Ron Rossi / Doug Bateman	1:24.651
1988	11	Miroslav Zajonc / Tim Nardiello	1:33.320

SKIING

ALPINE

WOMEN'S DOWNHILL
1924-1936 not held

YEAR	RANK	ATHLETE	TIME
1948	12	Brynhild Grasmoen	2:36.0
1952	17	Andrea Mead Lawrence	1:55.3
1956	10	Gladys "Skeeter" Werner	1:49.6
1960	2	Penelope "Penny" Pitou	1:38.6
1964	14	Starr Walton	2:01.45
1968	17	Kiki Cutter	1:44.94
1972	3	Susan Corrock	1:37.68
1976	3	Cynthia Nelson	1:47.50
1980	4	Heidi Preuss	1:39.51
1984	16	Holly Flanders	1:15.11
1988	18	Edith Thys	1:28.53

WOMEN'S SLALOM
1924-1936 not held
1968/1984 no U.S. finishers

YEAR	RANK	ATHLETE	TIME
1948	1	Gretchen Fraser	1:57.2
1952	1	Andrea Mead Lawrence	2:10.6
1956	20	Dorothy Surgenor	1:37.3
1960	2	Betsy Snite	1:52.9
1964	3	Jean Saubert	1:31.36
1972	1	Barbara Ann Cochran	1:31.24
1976	6	Lindy Cochran	1:33.24
1980	8	Christin Cooper	1:29.28
1988	11	Beth Madsen	1:41.18

WOMEN'S GIANT SLALOM
1924-1948 not held

YEAR	RANK	ATHLETE	TIME
1952	1	Andrea Mead Lawrence	2:06.8
1956	4T	Andrea Mead Lawrence	1:58.3
1960	2	Penelope "Penny" Pitou	1:40.0
1964	2	Jean Saubert	1:53.11
1968	12	Judy Nagel	1:57.39
1972	11	Barbara Ann Cochran	1:33.16
1976	12	Lindy Cochran	1:31.33
1980	7	Christin Cooper	2:44.71
1984	1	Debbie Armstrong	2:20.98
1988	12	Diann Roffe	2:10.72

WOMEN'S SUPER GS
1924-1984 not held

YEAR	RANK	ATHLETE	TIME
1988	9	Edith Thys	1:20.93

WOMEN'S COMBINED
1924-1932/1952-1984 not held

YEAR	RANK	ATHLETE	POINTS
1936	19	Elizabeth Woolsey	69.24
1948	2	Gretchen Fraser	6.95
1988	15	Beth Madsen	108.64

ABOVE / *Soviet gymnast — and local heartthrob — Vladimir Artemov won the men's individual all-around title with a score of 119.125. Overall he won four gold medals and one silver.* (Dave Black)

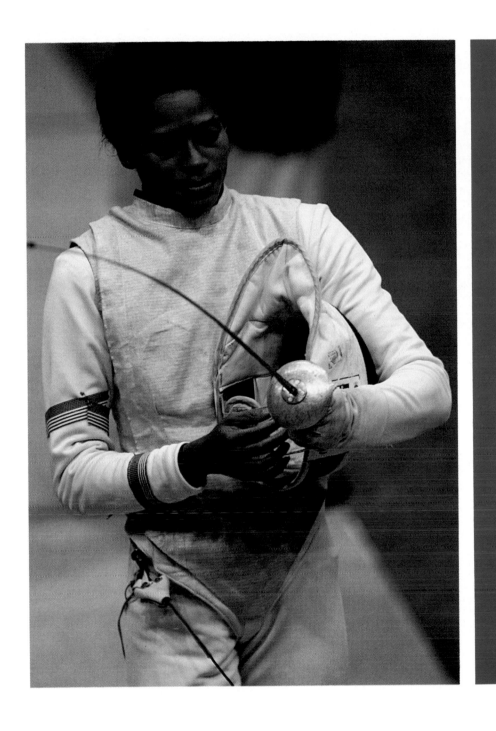

LEFT / *Sharon Monplaisir was a member of the U.S. team foil squad that placed sixth.* (R.L. Hagedohm/LPI)

MEN'S DOWNHILL
1924-1936 not held

YEAR	RANK	ATHLETE	TIME
1948	42	Dick Movitz	3:25.2
1952	5	William Beck	2:33.3
1956	11	Wallace "Bud" Werner	3:05.8
1960	14	Dave Gorsuch	2:11.0
1964	14	Annibale John Orsi, Jr.	2:21.59
1968	18	William Kidd	2:03.4
1972	8	Robert Cochran	1:53.39
1976	6	Andy Mill	1:47.06
1980	5	Pete Patterson	1:47.04
1984	1	William Johnson	1:45.59
1988	26	A.J. Kitt	2:04.94

MEN'S SLALOM
1924-1936 not held
1988 no U.S. finishers

YEAR	RANK	ATHLETE	TIME
1948	7	Jack Reddish	2:15.5
1952	9	Joseph Brooks Dodge	2:04.7
1956	4	Joseph Brooks Dodge	3:21.8
1960	9	Thomas Corcoran	2:14.7
1964	2	William Kidd	2:11.27
1968	5	Vladimir "Spider" Sabich	1:40.49
1972	9	Tyler Palmer	1:52.05
1976	13	Cary Adgate	2:09.53
1980	2	Phil Mahre	1:44.76
1984	1	Phil Mahre	1:39.41

MEN'S GIANT SLALOM
1924-1948 not held

YEAR	RANK	ATHLETE	TIME
1952	6	Joseph Brooks Dodge	2:32.6
1956	13	Ralph Miller	3:15.8
1960	4	Thomas Corcoran	1:49.7
1964	7	William Kidd	1:49.97
1968	5	William Kidd	3:32.37
1972	17	Robert Cochran	3:15.54
1976	5	Phil Mahre	3:28.20
1980	10	Phil Mahre	2:44.33
1984	8	Phil Mahre	2:43.25
1988	12	Tiger Shaw	2:10.23

MEN'S SUPER GS
1924-1984 not held

YEAR	RANK	ATHLETE	TIME
1988	18	Tiger Shaw	1:44.46

MEN'S COMBINED
1924-1932 not held
1952-1984 not held
1988 no U.S. finishers

YEAR	RANK	ATHLETE	POINTS
1936	10	Richard Durrance	87.74
1948	12	Jack Reddish	13.24

NORDIC

WOMEN'S 5 KILOMETERS
1924-1960 not held
1964-1968 no U.S. entry

YEAR	RANK	ATHLETE	TIME
1972	18	Martha Rockwell	17:50.34
1976	28	Martha Rockwell	17:33.07
1980	22	Alison Owen-Spencer	16:05.04
1984	27	Lynn Spencer-Galanes	18:30.8
1988	31	Leslie Krichko	16:31.1

WOMEN'S 10 KILOMETERS
1924-1948 not held
1952-1968 no U.S. entry

YEAR	RANK	ATHLETE	TIME
1972	16	Martha Rockwell	36:34.22
1976	36	Martha Rockwell	34:21.34
1980	22	Alison Owen-Spencer	32:41.33
1984	26	Judy Rabinowitz	34:35.1
1988	36	Leslie Krichko	33:25.1

WOMEN'S 20 KILOMETERS
1924-1980 not held

YEAR	RANK	ATHLETE	TIME
1984	27	Judy Rabinowitz	1:07:11.4
1988	23	Dorcas Denhartog	1:00:48.6

WOMEN'S 4x5-KM RELAY
1924-1952 not held
1956-1972 3x5-km relay
1956-1968 no U.S. entry

YEAR	RANK	TEAM	TIME
1972	11	Barbara Britch / Alison Owen Martha Rockwell	53:38.60
1976	9	Martha Rockwell / Jana Hlavaty Terry Porter / Twila Hinkle	1:17:58.18
1980	7	Alison Owen-Spencer / Beth Paxson Leslie Bancroft / Margaret Spencer	1:06:55.41
1984	7	Susan Long / Judy Rabinowitz Lynn Spencer-Galanes / Patricia Ross	1:10:48.4
1988	8	Dorcas Denhartog / Leslie Thompson Nancy Fiddler / Leslie Krichko	1:04:08.8

MEN'S 15 KILOMETERS
1924-1952 18 km course

YEAR	RANK	ATHLETE	TIME
1924	19	Sigurd Overby	1:34:56.0
1928	42	Anders Haugen	2:30:30.0
1932	23	Olle Zetterstrom	1:38:26
1936	34	Karl Magnus Satre	1:25:56
1948	65	Wendell Broomhall	1:31:40
1952	43	Ted Farwell	1:11:54
1956	41	Andrew M. Miller	56:08.0
1960	22	Andrew M. Miller	54:49.0
1964	38	Michael Gallagher	56:19.4
1968	34	Michael Gallagher	52:02.4
1972	44	Everett Dunklee	49:52.20
1976	37	Timothy Caldwell	47:33.59
1980	16	William Koch	43:38.56
1984	18	Dan Simoneau	43:03.4
1988	29	Dan Simoneau	44:53.8

MEN'S 30 KILOMETERS
1924-1952 not held

YEAR	RANK	ATHLETE	TIME
1956	38	Andrew M. Miller	2:00:38
1960	27	Andrew M. Miller	2:03.05.4
1964	30	Michael Elliott	1:40:11.7
1968	27	Michael Gallagher	1:41:58.2
1972	26	Michael Elliott	1:43:15.03
1976	2	William Koch	1:30:57.84
1980	30	Stanley Dunklee	1:33:48.02
1984	21T	William Koch	1:33:44.4
1988	49	Dan Simoneau	1:35:21.4

MEN'S 50 KILOMETERS
1924-1956/1964 no U.S. entry

YEAR	RANK	ATHLETE	TIME
1960	17	Andrew M. Miller	—
1968	22	Michael Gallagher	2:36:26.1
1972	24	Gene Morgan	2:54:01.52
1976	13	William Koch	2:44:34.69
1980	13	William Koch	2:34:31.62
1984	17	William Koch	2:24:02.3
1988	47	Kevin Brochman	2:19:45.5

MEN'S 4x10-KM RELAY
1924-1932 not held
1948 no U.S. entry

YEAR	RANK	TEAM	TIME
1936	11	Birger Torrissen / Warren Chivers Richard Parsons / Karl Magnus Satre	3:06:26
1952	12	George Hoveland / John Burton Ted Farwell / Wendell Broomhall	2:53:28
1956	12	Ted Farwell / Andrew M. Miller Lawrence Damon / Marvin Crawford	2:32:04
1960	11	Andrew M. Miller / Karl Bohlin John Dendahl / Peter Lahdenpera	2:38:01.8
1964	13	Michael Gallagher / Michael Elliot James Shea / John Bower	2:42:55.8
1968	12	Michael Gallagher / Michael Elliot Robert Gray / John Bower	2:21:30.4
1972	12	Timothy Caldwell / Michael Gallagher Larry Martin / Michael Elliot	2:14:37.28
1976	6	Douglas Peterson / Timothy Caldwell William Koch / Ronny Yaeger	2:11:41.35
1980	8	William Koch / Timothy Caldwell James Galanes / Stanley Dunklee	2:04:12.17
1984	8	Dan Simoneau / Timothy Caldwell James Galanes / William Koch	1:59:52.30
1988	13	Todd Boonstra / Dan Simoneau Bill Spencer / Joseph Galanes	1:50:27.6

INDIVIDUAL NORDIC COMBINED

YEAR	RANK	ATHLETE	70-METER JUMP POINTS	15 KM SKI TIME	TOTAL POINTS
1924	11	Sigurd Overby	—	—	12.219
1928	25	Anders Haugen	—	—	7.447
1932	9	Rolf Monsen	201.9	1:42.36	369.3
1936	27	Karl Magnus Satre	91.5	1:25.56	355.8
1948	26	Corey Engen	—	—	346.8
1952	11	Ted Farwell	196	—	401.4
1956	23	Marvin Crawford	196.5	—	419.2
1960	26	Alfred Vincelette	190.5*	—	395.274
1964	15	John Bower	—	—	403.76
1968	13	John Bower	—	—	411.16
1972	21	Mike Devecka	—	—	362.835
1976	17	James Galanes	184.1	—	381.13
1980	12	Walter Malmquist	—	—	395.300
1984	13	Kerry Lynch	181.8	48:02.9	388.165
1988	19	Joseph Holland	210.4	41:01.8	—

*60-meter

TEAM NORDIC COMBINED
1924-1984 not held

YEAR	RANK	ATHLETE	JUMP POINTS	3x10-KM SKI TIME
1988	10	Joseph Holland / Todd Wilson Hans Johnstone	516.9	1:23:42.9

INDIVIDUAL 70-METER SKI JUMPING
1924-1960 not held

YEAR	RANK	ATHLETE	POINTS
1964	10	John Balfanz	206.50
1968	33	John Balfanz	189.7
1972	34	Jerry Martin	197.2
1976	21	Jim Denney	218.9
1980	17	Jeffrey Davis	225.30
1984	9	Jeffrey Hastings	203.5
1988	18	Mark Konopacke	188.2

INDIVIDUAL 90-METER SKI JUMPING
1924-1956 various lengths
1960-1964 80 meters

YEAR	RANK	ATHLETE	POINTS
1924	3	Anders Haugen	17.916
1928	6	Rolf Monsen	16.687
1932	5	Caspar Oimen	216.7
1936	11	Sverre Fredheim	214.1

Continued

INDIVIDUAL 90-METER SKI JUMPING—Cont.

YEAR	RANK	ATHLETE	POINTS
1948	5	Gordon Wren	222.8
1952	12	Keith Wegeman	204.5
1956	21	Art Devlin	194.5
1960	7	Ansten Samuelstuen	211.5
1964	24	Gene Kotlarek	197.50
1968	34	Bill Bakke	175.5
1972	25	Ron Steele	177.7
1976	18	Jim Denney	191.1
1980	8	Jim Denney	239.1
1984	4	Jeffrey Hastings	201.2
1988	32	Michael Holland	170.6

TEAM 90-METER SKI JUMPING
1924-1984 not held

YEAR	RANK	TEAM	POINTS
1988	10	Tad Langlois / Mark Konopacke Dennis McGrane / Michael Holland	496.8

SPEEDSKATING

WOMEN'S 500 METERS
1924-1956 not held

YEAR	RANK	ATHLETE	TIME
1960	3	Jeanne Ashworth	46.1
1964	4	Jeanne Ashworth	46.2
1968	2	Jennifer Fish	46.3
1972	1	Anne Henning	43.33 OR
1976	1	Sheila Young	42.76 OR
1980	2	Leah Mueller	42.26
1984	8	Bonnie Blair	42.53
1988	1	Bonnie Blair	39.10 WR

WOMEN'S 1,000 METERS
1924-1956 not held

YEAR	RANK	ATHLETE	TIME
1960	8	Jeanne Ashworth	1:36.5
1964	7	Janice Smith	1:36.7
1968	3	Dianne Holum	1:33.4
1972	3	Anne Henning	1:31.62
1976	2	Leah Mueller Poulos	1:28.57
1980	2	Leah Mueller Poulos	1:25.41
1984	13	Lydia Stephans	1:26.73
1988	3	Bonnie Blair	1:18.31

WOMEN'S 1,500 METERS
1924-1956 not held

YEAR	RANK	ATHLETE	TIME
1960	11	Jeanne Ashworth	2:33.7
1964	15	Judith Morstein	2:33.3
1968	13	Dianne Holum	2:28.5
1972	1	Dianne Holum	2:20.85 OR
1976	2	Sheila Young	2:17.06
1980	7	Beth Heiden	2:13.10
1984	14	Mary Docter	2:12.14
1988	4	Bonnie Blair	2:04.02

WOMEN'S 3,000 METERS
1924-1956 not held

YEAR	RANK	ATHLETE	TIME
1960	8	Jeanne Ashworth	5:28.5
1964	11	Jeanne Ashworth	5:30.3
1968	10	Jeanne Ashworth	5:14.0
1972	2	Dianne Holum	4:58.67
1976	7	Nancy Swider	4:48.46
1980	3	Beth Heiden	4:33.77
1984	6	Mary Docter	4:36.25
1988	11	Janet Goldman	4:25.26

WOMEN'S 5,000 METERS
1924-1984 not held

YEAR	RANK	ATHLETE	TIME
1988	10	Janet Goldman	7:36.98

MEN'S 500 METERS

YEAR	RANK	ATHLETE	TIME	
1924	1	Charles Jewtraw	44.0	
1928	3	John O'Neil Farrell	43.6	
1932	1	John Shea	43.4	EOR
1936	3	Leo Freisinger	44.0	
1948	2	Kenneth Bartholomew	43.2	
1952	1	Kenneth Henry	43.2	
1956	6	William Carow	41.8	
1960	2	William Disney	40.3	
1964	1	Richard "Terry" McDermott	40.1	OR
1968	2	Richard "Terry" McDermott	40.5	
1972	11	Peter Eberling	40.58	
1976	3	Daniel Immerfall	39.54	
1980	1	Eric Heiden	38.03	OR
1984	4	Dan Jansen	38.55	
1988	8	Nick Thometz	37.19	

MEN'S 1,000 METERS
1924-1972 not held

YEAR	RANK	ATHLETE	TIME
1976	1	Peter Mueller	1:19.32
1980	1	Eric Heiden	1:15.18 OR
1984	4	Nick Thometz	1:16.85
1988	17	Tom Cushman	1:14.68

MEN'S 1,500 METERS

YEAR	RANK	ATHLETE	TIME
1924	7	Harry Kaskey	2:29.8
1928	5	Edward Murphy	2:25.9
1932	1	John Shea	2:57.5
1936	4	Leo Freisinger	2:21.3
1948	6	John Werket	2:20.2
1952	12	John Werket	2:43.3
1956	20	Matthew McNamara	2:15.2
1960	17	Richard Hunt	2:17.7
1964	15	Richard Hunt	2:13.4
1968	19	Richard Wurster	2:08.4
1972	7	Daniel Carroll	2:07.24
1976	5	Daniel Carroll	2:02.26
1980	1	Eric Heiden	1:55.44 OR
1984	14	Nick Thometz	2:00.77
1988	2	Eric Flaim	1:52.12

MEN'S 5,000 METERS

YEAR	RANK	ATHLETE	TIME
1924	8	Richard Donovan	9:05.3
1928	4	Irving Jaffee	9:01.3
1932	1	Irving Jaffee	9:40.8
1936	11	Robert Petersen	8:46.5
1948	17	Raymond Blum	8:54.4
1952	24	Matthew McNamara	8:53.4
1956	17	Matthew McNamara	8:10.6
1960	14	Arnold Uhrlass	8:18.0
1964	20	Richard Hunt	8:09.7
1968	24	William Lanigan	7:57.7
1972	10	Daniel Carroll	7:44.72
1976	6	Daniel Carroll	7:36.46
1980	1	Eric Heiden	7:02.29 OR
1984	12	Michael Woods	7:24.81
1988	4	Eric Flaim	6:47.09

MEN'S 10,000 METERS

YEAR	RANK	ATHLETE	TIME
1924	8	Valentine Bialas	18:34.0
1928	1	Irving Jaffee	18:36.5
			Continued

MEN'S 10,000 METERS—Continued

YEAR	RANK	ATHLETE	TIME
1932	1	Irving Jaffee	19:13.6
1936	8	Edward Schroeder	17:52.0
1948	11	John Werket	19:44.0
1952	16	Matthew McNamara	18:08.7
1956	27	Matthew McNamara	17:45.6
1960	10	Ross Zucco	16:37.6
1964	30	Arthur Le Bombard	17:30.6
1968	21	William Lanigan	16:50.1
1972	9	Daniel Carroll	15:44.41
1976	7	Daniel Carroll	15:19.29
1980	1	Eric Heiden	14:28.13 WR
1984	7	Michael Woods	14:57.30
1988	4	Eric Flaim	14:05.57

A SAMPLING OF SUMMER EVENTS

NOTE: United States boycotted the 1980 Moscow Olympic Games

ARCHERY
1896-1968 not held

WOMEN'S INDIVIDUAL

YEAR	RANK	ATHLETE	POINTS
1972	1	Doreen Wilber	2424 WR
1976	1	Luann Ryon	2499 WR
1984	6T	Katrina King	2508
1988	10	Melanie Skillman	elim. semifinals

MEN'S INDIVIDUAL
1896-1968 not held

YEAR	RANK	ATHLETE	POINTS
1972	1	John Williams	2528 WR
1976	1	Darrell Pace	2571 WR
1984	1	Darrell Pace	2616 OR
1988	1	Jay Barrs	338

ATHLETICS (TRACK & FIELD)
w = wind-aided

WOMEN'S 100 METERS
1896-1924 not held

YEAR	RANK	ATHLETE	TIME	
1928	1	Elizabeth Robinson	12.2	EWR
1932	3	Wilhelmina Von Bremen	12.0	
1936	1	Helen Stephens	11.5	w
1948	—	Audrey Patterson	12.8	(3rd; heat 3)
	—	Mabel E. Walker	12.8	(3rd; heat 4)
1952	6	Mae Faggs	12.1	
1956	4	Isabelle Daniels	11.8	
1960	1	Wilma Rudolph	11.0	w
1964	1	Wyomia Tyus	11.4	
1968	1	Wyomia Tyus	11.0	WR
1972	4	Iris Davis	11.32	
1976	5	Evelyn Ashford	11.24	
1984	1	Evelyn Ashford	10.97 OR	
1988	1	Florence Griffith Joyner	10.54 w	

WOMEN'S MARATHON
1896-1980 not held

YEAR	RANK	ATHLETE	TIME
1984	1	Joan Benoit	2:24:52
1988	17	Nancy Ditz	2:33.42

LEFT / *Asko Peltoniemi cleared 5.60 meters before being eliminated. He placed ninth, the best Finnish finish in an Olympic pole vault competition.* (Bob Long/LPI)

ABOVE / *Seventeen-year-old Hope Spivey was a member of the U.S. women's gymnastics team that finished fourth with a score of 390.575, just .3 of a point from the bronze medal.* (Dave Black)

WOMEN'S LONG JUMP
1896-1936 not held

YEAR	RANK	ATHLETE	METERS	FT-IN	
1948	12	Emma Reed	4.845	15' 10-1/4"	
1952	7	Mabel Landry	5.75	18' 10-1/2"	
1956	2	Willye White	6.09	19' 11-3/4"	
1960	16	Willye White	—	18' 11-1/4"	
1964	12	Willye White	6.07	19' 11"	
1968	10	Martha Watson	—	20' 04"	
1972	11	Willye White	—	20' 07"	
1976	2	Kathy McMillan	6.66	21' 10-1/4"	
1984	4	Angela Thacker	6.78	22' 03"	
1988	1	Jackie Joyner-Kersee	7.40	24' 03-1/2"	OR

MEN'S 100 METERS

YEAR	RANK	ATHLETE	TIME	
1896	1	Thomas Burke	12.0	
1900	1	Frank Jarvis	11.0	
1904	1	Archibald Hahn	11.0	
1906	1	Archibald Hahn	11.2	
1908	2	James Rector	10.9	
1912	1	Ralph Craig	10.8	
1920	1	Charles Paddock	10.8	
1924	2	Jackson Scholz	10.7	
1928	4	Frank Wykoff	11.0	
1932	1	Thomas "Eddie" Tolan	10.3	OR
1936	1	Jesse Owens	10.3	EOR
1948	1	Harrison Dillard	10.3	EOR
1952	1	Lindy Remigino	10.4	
1956	1	Bobby Joe Morrow	10.5	
1960	2	David Sime	10.2	
1964	1	Robert Hayes	10.0	EWR
1968	1	James Hines	9.95	WR
1972	2	Robert Taylor	10.24	
1976	4	Harvey Glance	10.19	
1984	1	Carl Lewis	9.99	
1988	1	Carl Lewis	9.92	OR

MEN'S MARATHON
42,195 m = 26.2 miles
1896 no U.S. entry

YEAR	RANK	ATHLETE	TIME	
1900	5	Arthur Newton	4:04:12	(40,260 m)
1904	1	Thomas Hicks	3:28:63	(40,000 m)
1906	3	William Frank	3:00:46.8	(41,860 m)
1908	1	John Hayes	2:55:18.4	
1912	3	Gaston Strobino	2:38:42.4	(40,200 m)
1920	7	Joseph Organ	2:41:30.8	(42,750 m)
1924	3	Clarence DeMar	2:48:14.0	
1928	5	Joie Ray	2:36:04.0	
1932	7	Albert Michelsen	2:39:38.0	
1936	18	John A. Kelley	2:49:32.4	
1948	14	Theodore J. Vogel	2:45:27.0	
1952	13	Victor Dyrgall	2:32:52.4	
1956	20	Nick Costes	2:42:20.0	
1960	19	John Kelley	2:24:58.0	
1964	6	Leonard "Buddy" Edelen	2:18:12.4	
1968	14	Kenneth Moore	2:29:49.4	
1972	1	Frank Shorter	2:12:19.8	
1976	2	Frank Shorter	2:10:45.8	
1984	11	Peter Pfitzinger	2:13:53.0	
1988	14	Peter Pfitzinger	2:14:44.0	

MEN'S LONG JUMP

YEAR	RANK	ATHLETE	METERS	FT-IN	
1896	1	Ellery Clark	6.35	20' 10"	
1900	1	Alvin Kraenzlein	7.18	23' 06-3/4"	OR
1904	1	Meyer Prinstein	7.34	24' 01"	OR
1906	1	Meyer Prinstein	7.20	23' 07-1/2"	
1908	1	Frank Irons	7.48	24' 06-1/2"	OR

Continued

MEN'S LONG JUMP—Continued

YEAR	RANK	ATHLETE	METERS	FT-IN	
1912	1	Albert Gutterson	7.60	24' 11-1/4"	OR
1920	2	Carl Johnson	7.09	23' 03-1/4"	
1924	1	William De Hart Hubbard	7.44	24' 05"	
1928	1	Edward Hamm	7.73	25' 04-1/2"	OR
1932	1	Edward Gordon	7.64	25' 00-3/4"	
1936	1	Jesse Owens	8.06	26' 05-1/2"	OR
1948	1	Willie Steele	7.82	25' 08"	
1952	1	Jerome Biffle	7.57	24' 10"	
1956	1	Gregory Bell	7.83	25' 08-1/4"	
1960	1	Ralph Boston	8.12	26' 07-3/4"	OR
1964	2	Ralph Boston	8.03	26' 04-1/4"	
1968	1	Bob Beamon	8.90	29' 02-1/2"	WR
1972	1	Randy Williams	8.24	27' 00-1/2"	
1976	1	Arnie Robinson	8.35	27' 04-3/4"	
1984	1	Carl Lewis	8.54	28' 00-1/4"	
1988	1	Carl Lewis	8.72	28' 07-1/2"	

BASKETBALL
PF - points for
PA - points against

WOMEN
1896-1972 not held

YEAR	RANK	WON	LOST	PF	PA
1976	2	3	2	415	417
1984	1	6	0	516	320
1988	1	5	0	461	392

MEN
1896-1932 not held

YEAR	RANK	WON	LOST	PF	PA
1936	1	4	0	152	69
1948	1	8	0	524	256
1952	1	8	0	562	406
1956	1	8	0	793	365
1960	1	8	0	815	476
1964	1	9	0	704	434
1968	1	9	0	739	505
1972	2	8	1	660	401
1976	1	7	0	584	500
1984	1	8	0	763	506
1988	3	7	1	733	490

BOXING

DEC - decision   RET - retired
KO - knock out   DQ - disqualified
RSC - referee stopped contest

SUPER HEAVYWEIGHT (+90 kg - 198 lbs)

1904–1908 (+71.67 kg - 158 lbs)
1920–1936 (+79.38 kg - 175 lbs)
1948   (+80 kg - 176.5 lbs)
1952–1980 (+81 kg - 179 lbs)

1896-1900/1906/1912 not held
1908 no U.S. entry

YEAR	RANK	ATHLETE	DECISION
1904	1	Samuel Berger	DEC
1920	4	William Spengler	
1924	5T	H.G. Greathouse	
1928	5T	Alexander Kaletchetz	
1932	3	Frederick Feary	
1936	—	Arthur Oliver	BYE / defeated in 2nd
1948	5T	Jay Lambert	
1952	1	H. Edward Sanders	DQ-2nd
1956	1	T. Peter Rademacher	RSC-1st 2:27

Continued

SUPER HEAVYWEIGHT—Continued

YEAR	RANK	ATHLETE	DECISION
1960	5T	Percy Price	
1964	1	Joseph Frazier	DEC 3-2
1968	1	George Foreman	RSC-2nd
1972	5T	Duane Bobick	
1976	3	Johnny Tate	
1984	1	Tyrell Biggs	DEC 4-1
1988	2	Riddick Bowe	RSC-2nd 0:43

CANOE AND KAYAK

WOMEN'S K-2, 500 METERS
1896-1956 not held

YEAR	RANK	ATHLETE	TIME
1960	—	Mary Ann Duchai / Dianne Jerome	2:21.13*
1964	2	Francine Fox / Gloriane Perrier	1:59.16
1968	7	Sperry Rademaker / Marcia Smoke	2:02.97
1972	—	Nancy Pervis / Linda Murray	2:11.50**
1976	—	Linda Dragan / Ann Turner	1:57.10***
1984	5	Shirley Dery / Leslie Klein	1:49.51
1988	7	Sheila Conover / Cathy Marino Geers	1:50.33

* 5th; semifinal repechage
** 5th; heat 2
***4th; semifinals

MEN'S K-2, 500 METERS
1896-1972 not held

YEAR	RANK	ATHLETE	TIME
1976	—	Michael Johnson / William Leach	1:49.95*
1984	—	David Helpern / Olney "Terry" Kent	**
1988	8	Olney "Terry" Kent / Carl "Terry" White	1:36.22

* 4th; repechage
** did not qualify for final

CYCLING

WOMEN'S ROAD RACE
1896-1980 not held

YEAR	RANK	ATHLETE	TIME	COURSE-KM
1984	1	Connie Carpenter-Phinney	2:11:14.0	79.2
1988	8	Inga Thompson-Benedict	2:00:52.0	82

MEN'S ROAD RACE
1896/1906 no U.S. entry
1900-1904/1908 not held
1948 no U.S. finishers

YEAR	RANK	ATHLETE	TIME	COURSE-KM
1912	3	Carl Schutte	10:52:38.8	320
1920	13	Ernest P. Kockler	—	175
1924	33	John Bonlicault	7:15:51.6	188
1928	51	Chester Nelson	5:42:57.0	165
1932	11	Henry O'Brien, Jr.	2:33:36.0	100
1936	44	Albert Byrd	—	100
1952	32	Donald T. Sheldon	5:22:33.3	190.4
1956	44	Joseph H. Becker	5:47:02.0	187.73
1960	23	Michael Hiltner	4:20:57.0	175.38
1964	75	John Allis	4:39:51.83	194.83
1968	44	John Howard	4:52:45.8	196.2
1972	61	John Howard	4:17:13.0	182.4
1976	6	George Mount	4:47:23.0	175
1984	1	Alexi Grewal	4:59:57.0	190.2
1988	4	Robert Mionske	4:32:46.0	196.8

EQUESTRIAN

INDIVIDUAL THREE-DAY EVENT
1896-1908 not held
1956 no U.S. finishers

YEAR	RANK	ATHLETE/MOUNT	POINTS
1912	8	John Montgomery / Deceive	45.88
1920	6	Harry Chamberlin / Nigra	1568.75
1924	3	Sloan Doak / Pathfinder	1845.5
1928	17	Major Sloan Doak / Misty Morn	1841.68
1932	2	Earl Thomson / Jenny Camp	1811.00
1936	2	Earl Thomson / Jenny Camp	-99.9
1948	2	Frank Henry / Swing Low	-21
1952	9	Charles Hough, Jr. / Cassavellanus	70.66
1960	15	Michael Plumb / Markham	153.46
1964	4	Michael Page / Grasshopper	47.40
1968	3	Michael Page / Foster	-52.31
1972	5	Kevin Freeman / Good Mixture	-29.87
1976	1	Edmund Coffin / Bally-Cor	-114.99
1984	2	Karen Stives / Ben Arthur	-54.2
1988	10	Phyllis Dawson / Albany II	99.60

FENCING

B - barrage

WOMEN'S TEAM FOIL
1896-1956 not held

YEAR	RANK	ATHLETE	
1960	10	Jancie Lee Romary / Maxine Mitchell / Judy Goodrich / Evelyn Terhune / Harrriet King	
1964	—	Janice Lee Romary / Denise O'Connor / Ann Drungis / Tommy Angell / Harriet King	3rd; Pool B
1968	—	Janice Lee Romary / Maxine Mitchell / Sally Pechinsky / Harriet King / Veronica Smith	lost in last round pool
1972	7	Ruth White / Natalia Clovis / Tanya Adamovich / Harriet King / Ann O'Donnell	
1976	—	Denise O'Connor / Nikke Franke / Gay D'Asaro / Ann O'Donnell / Dorothy Armstrong	lost in pre-rounds
1984	6	Vincent Bradford / Sharon Monplaisir / Susan Badders ʄ Debra Waples / Jana Angelakis	
1988	6	Caitlin Bilodeau / Elaine Cheris / Sharon Monplaisir / Mary Jane O'Neill / Molly Sullivan	

MEN'S TEAM FOIL
1896-1900/1906-1912 not held
1904 two teams competed:
CUBA-USA Team and USA

YEAR	RANK	ATHLETE	MATCHES WON	LOST
1904	2	Charles Tatham / Fitzhugh Townsend / Arthur Fox	2	
1920	3	Henry Breckenridge / Francis Honeycutt / Arthur Lyon / Harold Rayner / Robert Sears	22	42
1924	—	Lt. P.W. Allison / Burke Boyce / Harold Bloomer / Lt. T.P. Jeter / A.P. Walker, Jr.	elim. quarterfinals	
1928	5	George Calnan / Rene Peroy / Joseph Levis / Harold Rayner / Henry Breckenridge / Dernell Every		
1932	3	George Calnan / Joseph Levis / Hugh Alessandroni / Dernell Every / Richard Steere / Frank Righeimer	22 6	26 20 B
1936	5	Joseph Levis / Hugh Alessandroni / John Potter / John Hurd / Warren Dow / William Pecora		

Continued

MEN'S TEAM FOIL—Continued

YEAR	RANK	ATHLETE	MATCHES WON	LOST
1948	4	Daniel Bukantz / Dean Cetrulo / Dernell Every / Silvio Giolito / Nathaniel Lubell / Austin Prokop	14	29
1952	8	Daniel Bukantz / Nathaniel Lubell / Albert Axelrod / Silvio Giolito / Bryon Krieger / Harold D. Goldsmith		
1956	4	Albert Axelrod / Daniel Bukantz / Harold Goldsmith / Bryon Kreiger / Nathaniel Lubell / Sewall Shurtz	18	28
1960	5	Gene Glazer / Harold Goldsmith / Joseph Paletta / Albert Alexrod / Daniel Bukantz		
1964	—	Lawrence Anastasi / Albert Axelrod / Herbert Cohen / Eugene Glazer / Edwin Richards	3rd; Pool A	
1968	—	Albert Alexrod / Lawrence Anastasi / Herbert Cohen / Uriah Jones	lost in last round pool	
1972	—	Martin Davis / Tyrone Simmonds / Lt. Joseph Freeman / Carl Borack / Seaman John Nonna	lost in last round pool	
1976	7T	Martin Lang / Edward Ballinger / Edward Wright / Edward Donofrio / Brooke Mackler		
1984	5	Michael Marx / Gregory Massialas / Peter Lewison / Mark Smith / Michael McCahey		
1988	14	Peter Lewison / David Littell / Michael Marx / Gregory Massialas / George Nomomura		

FIELD HOCKEY

WOMEN
1896-1976 not held

YEAR	RANK	WON	LOST	TIE	PF	PA
1984	3	2	2	1	9	7
1988	8	0	4	1	6	12

MEN
1896-1906/1912/1924 not held
1908/1920/1928/1952 no U.S. entry
1960-1976/1988 did not qualify

YEAR	RANK	WON	LOST	TIE	PF	PA	
1932	3	0	2	0	3	33	(3 teams competed - India, 1st; Japan, 2nd)
1936	—	0	3	0			(4th place; group A)
1948	—	0	3	0	1	16	(4th place; group B)
1956	11	0	3	1			
1984	12	0	5	0	4	14	*

* (USA tied Malaysia, 3-3, but was relegated to 12th place on basis of penalty strokes, 9-8, for Malaysia)

GYMNASTICS

WOMEN'S TEAM COMPETITION
1896-1924/1932 not held
1928 no U.S. entry

YEAR	RANK	ATHLETE	POINTS
1936	5	Consetta Caruccio / Jennie Caputo / Irma Haubold / Margaret Duff / Ada Lunardoni / Adelaide Meyer / Mary Wright / Marie Kibler (injured)	471.60
1948	3	Helen Schifano / Clara Schroth / Meta Elste / Marian Barone / Ladislava Bakanic / Consetta (Caruccio) Lenz / Anita Simonis / Dorothy Dalton	422.63
1952	15	Clara S. Lomady / Meta Elste / Marian T. Barone / Ruth Grulkowski / Dorothy Dalton / Ruth Topalian / Doris Kirkman / Marie Hoesly	471.41

Continued

WOMEN'S TEAM COMPETITION—Cont.

YEAR	RANK	ATHLETE	POINTS
1956	9	Muriel Davis / Jacquelyn Klein / Judith Howe / Sandra Ruddick / Joyce Racek / Doris Fuchs	413.20
1960	9	Doris Fuchs / Muriel Grossfeld / Betty Maycock / Theresa Montefusco / Sharon Richardson / Gail Sontgerath	363.053
1964	9	Kathleen Corrigan / Muriel Grossfeld / Dale McClements / Linda Metheny / Janie Speaks / Marie Walther	367.321
1968	6	Cathy Rigby / Linda Metheny / Joyce Tanac / Kathy Gleason / Colleen Mulvihill / Wendy Cluff	369.75
1972	4	Cathy Rigby / Kimberly Chace / Roxanne Pierce / Linda Metheny / Joan Moore / Nancy Thies	365.90
1976	6	Kimberly Chace / Debra Willcox / Leslie Wolfsberger / Colleen Casey / Carrie Englert / Doris Howard	448.20
1984	2	Mary Lou Retton / Julianne McNamara / Kathy Johnson / Michelle Dusserre / Tracee Talavera / Pamela Bileck	391.20
1988	4	Melissa Marlowe / Chelle Stack / Kelly Garrison-Steves / Theresa "Hope" Spivey / Brandy Johnson / Phoebe Mills	390.575

MEN'S TEAM COMPETITION
1896-1900 not held
1906-1920 no U.S. entry
1904 only U.S. teams competed

YEAR	RANK	ATHLETE	POINTS
1904	1	Turngemeinde Philadelphia	374.43
1924	5	Frank Kriz / Alfred Jochim / John Pearson / Frank Safanda / Curtis Rottman / Rudolph Novak / Max Wandrer / John Mais	715.117
1928	7	Alfred Jochim / Glenn Berry / Frank Kriz / Frank Haubold / Harold Newhart / John Pearson / Herman Witzig / Paul Krempel	1519.125
1932	2	Frank Haubold / Frederick Meyer / Alfred Joquim / Frank Cumiskey	522.275
1936	10	Frank Cumiskey / Frederick H. Meyer / George F. Wheeler / Chester W. Phillips / Arthur Pitt / Frank O. Haubold / Alfred A. Jochim / Kenneth Griffin	551.301
1948	7	Edward Scrobe / Vincent D'Autorio / William Roetzheim / Joseph Kotys / Frank Cumiskey / Raymond Sorensen	1252.50
1952	8	Edward Scrobe / Robert Stout / William Roetzheim / Donald Holder / John Beckner / Charles Simms / Walter Blattmann / Vincent D'Autorio	543.15
1956	6	John Beckner / Jose Armando Vega / Charles Simms / Richard Beckner / Abraham Grossfeld / William Torn	547.50
1960	5	Larry Banner / John Beckner / Donald Tonry / Abraham Grossfeld / Fred Orlofsky / Garland O'Quinn	555.20
1964	7	Makoto Sakamoto / Russell Mitchell / Ronald Barak / Larry Banner / Gregor Weiss / Arthur Shurlock	556.95
1968	7	David Thor / Fred Roethlisberger / Stephen Hug / Stephen Cohen / Sidney Freudenstein / Kanati Allen	548.90
1972	10	Marshall Averner / John Crosby, Jr. / James Culhane, Jr. / George Grennfield / Steven Hug / Makato Sakomoto	533.85
1976	7	Wayne Young / Kurt Thomas / Peter Kormann / Thomas Beach / Marshall Avener / Bart Conner	556.10
1984	1	Peter Vidmar / Bart Conner / Mitchell Gaylord / Timothy Daggett / Jim Hartung / Scott Johnson	591.40
1988	11	Charles Lakes / Scott Johnson / Dominick Minicucci / Kenneth "Wes" Suter / Kevin Davis / Lance Ringnald	576.850

ABOVE / *Yun Young-sook is the picture of composure and tranquility as her arrow speeds accurately toward its tiny target. Yun won the bronze for her score of 327 points in the individual competition and the gold for being a member of the Korean team that scored 982 points.* (Lori Adamski-Peek)

JUDO

HEAVYWEIGHT (+ 95 kg - + 209 lbs)
1896-1960/1968 not held

YEAR	RANK	ATHLETE	
1964	*	George L. Harris	(+80 kg - +176 lbs)
1972	5	Doug Nelson	(+93 kg - +205 lbs)
1976	3	Allen Coage	(+93 kg - +205 lbs)
1984	5T	Doug Nelson	
1988	—	Steve Cohen	elim. 2nd round

* Lost in qualifying rounds / won 1 match

MODERN PENTATHLON

TEAM
1896-1948 not held

YEAR	RANK	ATHLETE	POINTS
1952	4	Frederick Denman / W. Thad McArthur / Guy Troy	215
1956	2	George Lambert / William Andre / Jack Daniels	13482
1960	3	Robert Beck / Jack Daniels / George Lambert	14192
1964	2	James Moore / David Kirkwood / Paul Pesthy	14189
1968	2	James Moore / Robert Beck / M. Thomas Lough	13280
1972	4	Charles Richard / John Fitzgerald / Scott Taylor	14802
1976	5	John Fitzgerald / Michael Burley / Robert Nieman	15285
1984	2	Michael Storm / Robert Losey / Dean Glenesk	15568
1988	16	Robert Nieman / Robert Stull / Michael Gostigian	13645

ROWING

WOMEN'S SINGLE SCULLS
1896-1972 not held

YEAR	RANK	ATHLETE	TIME
1976	2	Joan Lind	4:06.21
1984	2	Charlotte Geer	3:43.89
1988	2	Anne Marden	7:50.28

MEN'S SINGLE SCULLS
1896/1906 not held
1900/1908/1912 no U.S. entry
1904 only U.S. competed

YEAR	RANK	ATHLETE	TIME
1904	1	Frank Greer	10:08.5
1920	1	John Kelly, Sr.	7:35.0
1924	2	William Gilmore	7:54.0
1928	2	Kenneth Myers	7:20.8
1932	2	William Miller	7:45.2
1936	3	Daniel Barrow	8:28.0
1948	4	John Kelly, Jr.	—
1952	—	John Kelly, Jr.	7:42.0 *
1956	3	John Kelly, Jr.	8:11.8
1960	5	Harry Parker	7:29.26
1964	6	Donald Spero	8:37.53
1968	4	John Van Blom	8:00.51
1972	5	James Dietz	7:24.81
1976	7	James Dietz	—
1984	2	John Biglow	7:12.00
1988	6	Andrew Sudduth	7:11.45

* elim. semifinals

SHOOTING

WOMEN'S SMALLBORE RIFLE, 3 POSITIONS
1896-1980 not held

YEAR	RANK	ATHLETE	SCORE
1984	3	Wanda Jewell	578
1988	7	Launi Meili	582

MEN'S SMALLBORE RIFLE, 3 POSITIONS
1896-1948 not held

YEAR	RANK	ATHLETE	SCORE
1952	12	Arthur Jackson	1155
1956	12	Arthur Jackson	1153
1960	7	Daniel Puckel	1137
1964	1	Lones Wigger	1164 WR
1968	2	John Writer	1156
1972	1	John Writer	1166 WR
1976	1	Lanny Bassham	1162
1984	6	Glenn Dubis	1151
1988	5	Glenn Dubis	1174

SWIMMING

COMPETITIVE SWIMMING

WOMEN'S 50-METER FREESTYLE
1896-1984 not held

YEAR	RANK	ATHLETE	TIME
1988	3T	Jill Sterkel	25:11

WOMEN'S 100-METER FREESTYLE
1896-1908 not held
1912 no U.S. entry

YEAR	RANK	ATHLETE	TIME	
1920	1	Ethelda Bleibtrey	1:13.6	WR
1924	1	Ethel Lackie	1:12.4	
1928	1	Albina Osipowich	1:11.0	OR
1932	1	Helene Madison	1:06.8	OR
1936	6	Olive McKean	1:08.4	
1948	2	Ann Curtis	1:06.5	
1952	5	Joan Alderson	1:07.1	
1956	4	Joan Rosazza	1:05.2	
1960	2	S. Christine Von Saltza	1:02.8	
1964	2	Sharon Stouder	59.9	
1968	1	Jan Henne	1:00.0	
1972	1	Sandra Neilson	58.59	OR
1976	4	Kim Peyton	56.81	
1984	1	Nancy Hogshead	55.92	
1988	7	Dara Torres	56.25	

WOMEN'S 100-METER BUTTERFLY
1896-1952 not held

YEAR	RANK	ATHLETE	TIME	
1956	1	Shelly Mann	1:11.0	OR
1960	1	Carolyn Schuler	1:09.5	OR
1964	1	Sharon Stouder	1:04.7	WR
1968	2	Ellie Daniel	1:05.8	
1972	4	Deena Deardurff	1:03.95	
1976	3	Wendy Boglioli	1:01.17	
1984	1	Mary T. Meagher	59.26	
1988	5	Janel Jorgensen	1:00.48	

WOMEN'S 4x100-METER MEDLEY RELAY
1896-1956 not held

YEAR	RANK	ATHLETE	TIME	
1960	1	Lynn Burke / Patty Kempner / Carolyn Schuler / S. Christine Von Saltza	4:41.1	WR
1964	1	Cathy Ferguson / Cynthia Goyette Sharon Stouder / Kathleen Ellis	4:33.9	WR
1968	1	Kaye Hall / Catie Ball Ellie Daniel / Susan Pedersen	4:28.3	OR
1972	1	Melissa Belote / Catherine Carr Deena Deardurff / Sandra Neilson	4:20.75	WR
1976	2	Linda Jezek / Lauri Siering Camille Wright / Shirley Babashoff	4:14.55	
1984	1	Theresa Andrews / Tracy Caulkins Mary T. Meagher / Nancy Hogshead	4:08.34	
1988	2	Beth Barr / Tracy McFarlane Janel Jorgensen / Mary Wayte	4:07.90	

MEN'S 50-METER FREESTYLE
1896-1900/1906-1984 not held
1904 47.52 m (50 yards)

YEAR	RANK	ATHLETE	TIME	
1904	2	J. Scott Leary	28.2	
1988	1	Matthew Biondi	22.14	WR

MEN'S 100-METER FREESTYLE
1900 not held

YEAR	RANK	ATHLETE	TIME	
1896	5	Gardner Williams	—	
1904	2	Charles Daniels	—	
1906	1	Charles Daniels	1:13.4	
1908	1	Charles Daniels	1:05.6	WR
1912	1	Duke Paoa Kahanamoku	1:03.4	
1920	1	Duke Paoa Kahanamoku	1:00.4	WR
1924	1	Johnny Weissmuller	59.0	OR
1928	1	Johnny Weissmuller	58.6	OR
1932	3	Albert Schwartz	58.8	
1936	6	Peter Fick	59.7	
1948	1	Walter Ris	57.3	OR
1952	1	Clarke Scholes	57.4	
1956	4	Logan Reid Patterson	57.2	
1960	2	Lance Larson	55.2	OR
1964	1	Donald Schollander	53.4	OR
1968	2	Kenneth Walsh	52.8	
1972	1	Mark Spitz	51.22	WR
1976	1	Jim Montgomery	49.99	WR
1984	1	Ambrose "Rowdy" Gaines	49.80	OR
1988	1	Matthew Biondi	48.63	OR

MEN'S 100-METER BUTTERFLY
1896-1964 not held

YEAR	RANK	ATHLETE	TIME	
1968	1	Douglas Russell	55.9	OR
1972	1	Mark Spitz	54.27	WR
1976	1	Matt Vogel	54.35	
1984	2	Pablo Morales	53.23	
1988	2	Matthew Biondi	53.01	

MEN'S 4x100-METER MEDLEY RELAY
1896-1956 not held

YEAR	RANK	ATHLETE	TIME	
1960	1	Frank McKinney / Paul Hait Lance Larson / F. Jeffrey Farrell	4:05.4	WR
1964	1	Harold Thompson Mann / William Craig / Fred Schmidt / Stephen Clark	3:58.4	WR
1968	1	Charles Hickcox / Donald McKenzie Douglas Russell / Kenneth Walsch	3:54.9	WR
1972	1	Michael Stamm / Thomas Bruce Mark Spitz / Jerry Heidenreich	3:48.16	WR
1976	1	John Naber / John Hencken Matt Vogel / Jim Montgomery	3:42.22	WR
1984	1	Richard Carey / Steve Lundquist / Pablo Morales / Ambrose "Rowdy" Gaines	3:39.30	WR
1988	1	David Berkoff / Richard Schroeder Matthew Biondi / Christopher Jacobs	3:36.93	WR

DIVING

WOMEN'S SPRINGBOARD
1896 1912 not held
1920 only U.S. competed

YEAR	RANK	ATHLETE	POINTS
1920	1	Aileen Riggen	539.9
1924	1	Elizabeth Becker	474.5
1928	1	Helen Meany	78.62
1932	1	Georgia Coleman	87.52
1936	1	Marjorie Gestring	89.27
1948	1	Victoria Draves	108.74
1952	1	Patricia McCormick	147.30
1956	1	Patricia McCormick	142.36
1960	2	Paula Jean Pope	141.24

WOMEN'S SPRINGBOARD—Cont.

YEAR	RANK	ATHLETE	POINTS
1964	2	Jeanne Collier	138.36
1968	1	Sue Gossick	150.77
1972	1	Maxine "Micki" King	450.03
1976	1	Jennifer Chandler	506.19
1984	2	Kelly McCormick	527.46
1988	3	Kelly McCormick	533.19

MEN'S SPRINGBOARD
1896-1906 not held

YEAR	RANK	ATHLETE	POINTS
1908	3	George Gaidzik	85.3
1912	8	George Gaidzik	68.01
1920	1	Louis Kuehn	675.4
1924	1	Albert White	696.4
1928	1	Ulise "Pete" DesJardins	185.04
1932	1	Michael Galitzen	161.38
1936	1	Richard Degener	163.57
1948	1	Bruce Harlan	163.64
1952	1	David Browning	205.29
1956	1	Robert Clotworthy	159.56
1960	1	Gary Tobian	170.00
1964	1	Kenneth Sitzberger	159.90
1968	1	Bernard Wrightson	170.15
1972	3	Craig Lincoln	577.29
1976	1	Philip Boggs	619.05
1984	1	Gregory Louganis	754.41
1988	1	Gregory Louganis	730.80

SYNCHRONIZED SWIMMING

DUET
1896-1980 not held

YEAR	RANK	ATHLETE	POINTS
1984	1	Candy Costie / Tracie Ruiz	195.584
1988	2	Sarah Josephson / Karen Josephson	197.284

WATER POLO
1896/1906 not held
1900/1908/1912 no U.S. entry
1904 only U.S. competed
1976 did not qualify

YEAR	RANK	WON	LOST	TIE	PF	PA
1904	1	2	0		11	0
1920	4	2	3		16	19
1924	3	3	3		14	13
1928	6	0	1		0	5
1932	3	2	1	1	20	12
1936	9	1	2		7	8
1948	10	1	1	1	11	11
1952	4	5	6	0	43	41
1956	5	2	5	1	18	25
1960	7	4	5	0	42	48
1964	9	1	2	0	12	9
1968	5	5	2	1	49	43
1972	3	7	1	2	55	41
1984	2	6	0	1	65	43
1988	2	5	2	0	71	56

TEAM HANDBALL

WOMEN
1896-1972 not held
1976 no U.S. entry

YEAR	RANK	WON	LOST	TIE	PF	PA
1984	4	2	3	0	114	123
1988	7	1	5	0	104	121

MEN
1896-1932/1948-1968 not held

YEAR	RANK	WON	LOST	TIE	PF	PA
1936	6	0	3		6	46
1972	15	1	4		86	111
1976	10	0	5		100	149
1984	9	1	4	1	115	116
1988	12	0	6	0	102	149

TENNIS

WOMEN'S SINGLES
1896/1904/1928-1984 not held
1906-1920 no U.S. entry

YEAR	RANK	ATHLETE	FINAL
1900	3	Marion Jones	
1924	1	Helen Wills	6-2 6-2
1988	3T	Zina Garrison	

MEN'S SINGLES
1928-1984 not held
1896/1900/1906/1920 no U.S. entry
1904 only U.S. competed

YEAR	RANK	ATHLETE	FINAL
1904	1	Beals Wright	6-4 6-4
1908	1	Jay Gould	
1912	—	Theodore R. Pell	elim. 4th round
1920	—	Theodore R. Pell	elim. 2nd round
1924	1	Vincent Richards	6-4 6-4 5-7 4-6 6-2
1988	2	Tim Mayotte	

VOLLEYBALL

WOMEN
1896-1960 not held
1972-1976 U.S. did not qualify

YEAR	RANK	MATCHES WON	MATCHES LOST	SETS WON	SETS LOST	PF	PA
1964	5	1	4	3	12	98	213
1968	8	0	7	4	21	196	353
1984	2	4	1	12	6	239	218
1988	7	2	3	9	15	238	307

MEN
1896-1960 not held
1972-1976 did not qualify

YEAR	RANK	MATCHES WON	MATCHES LOST	SETS WON	SETS LOST	PF	PA
1964	9	2	7	10	23	360	450
1968	7	4	5	15	18	382	414
1984	1	5	1	15	4	258	159
1988	1	7	0	21	4	366	211

WEIGHTLIFTING

SUPER HEAVYWEIGHT (+ 110 kg - 242.5 lbs)
1900/1908-1912 not held
1896/1906/1920-1928 no U.S. entry
1896-1968 Heavyweight
* two-hand lift
+ OR / # WR / = EOR

YEAR	RANK	ATHLETE	PRESS	SNATCH	CLEAN & JERK	TOTAL KG
1904	2	Oscar Osthoff				84.37*
1932	5	Albert Manger	100.0	92.5	122.5	315.0
1936	9	John C. Grimek	115.0	105.0	137.5	357.5
1948	1	John Davis	137.5+	137.5	177.5#	452.5+
1952	1	John Davis	150.0+	145.0	165.0	460.0+
1956	1	Paul Anderson	167.5	145.0=	187.5+	500.0+
1960	2	James Bradford	180.0+	150.0	182.5	512.5
1964	3	Norbert Schemansky	180.0	165.0	192.5	537.5
						Continued

SUPER HEAVYWEIGHT —Continued

YEAR	RANK	ATHLETE	PRESS	SNATCH	CLEAN & JERK	TOTAL KG
1968	3	Joseph Dube	200.0+	145.0	210.0	555.0
1972	DQ	Ken Patera	212.5	(failed 2 lifts)		
1976	5	Bruce Wilhelm		172.5	215.0	387.5
1984	2	Mario Martinez		185.0	225.0	410.0
1988	4	Mario Matrinez		175.0	232.5	407.5

WRESTLING

FREESTYLE

LIGHT HEAVYWEIGHT (90 kg - 198 lbs)
1896-1912 not held

YEAR	RANK	ATHLETE	ROUND ELIM.	BAD PTS.	FINAL ROUND	FINAL MATCH
1920	3	Walter Maurer				
1924	1	John Spellman				
1928	4	Heywood Edwards				
1932	1	Peter Mehringer				
1936	5	Ray Clemons	4	7		
1948	1	Henry Wittenberg	—	1	2	
1952	2	Henry Wittenberg	—	4	3	
1956	3	Peter Blair	—	4	6	
1960	5	Daniel Brand	5	7		
1964	6	Gerald Conine	4	6		
1968	6	Jess Lewis	4	7		
1972	1	Benjamin Peterson	—	4	2	
1976	2	Benjamin Peterson	—	3.5	4	
1984	1	Ed Banach			15-3	4:02
1988	5	Jim Scherr				

GRECO-ROMAN

LIGHT HEAVYWEIGHT (90 kg - 198 lbs)
1896-1906 not held
1908-1952 no U.S. entry

YEAR	RANK	ATHLETE	ROUND ELIM.	BAD PTS.	FINAL MATCH
1956	6	Dale Thomas	3	6	
1960	14	Howard George	2	(won 2 decisions)	
1964	—	William Lovell	2	(lost on foul)	
1968	—	Henk Schenk	2	(disqualification and draw)	
1972	—	Capt. Wayne Baughman	2		
1976	7T	James Johnson	3	8	
1984	1	Steven Fraser		1-1	6:00
1988	—	Michail Foy	3		

YACHTING

STAR
1896-1928/1976 not held

YEAR	RANK	ATHLETE	POINTS
1932	1	Gilbert Gray / Andrew Libano	46
1936	5	William Waterhouse / Woodbridge Metcalf	51
1948	1	Hilary Smart / Paul Smart	5828
1952	2	John Reid / John Price	7126
1956	1	Herbert Williams / Laurence Low	5876
1960	3	William Parks / Robert Halperin	6269
1964	2	Richard Stearns / Lynn Williams	5585
1968	1	Lowell North / Peter Barrett	14.4
1972	10	Alan Holt / Richard Gates	89.0
1984	1	William E. Buchan / Stephen Erickson	29.7
1988	2	Mark Reynolds / Hal Haenal	48.00

LEFT / *Twenty-four-year-old Charles Lakes finished 19th -- the best U.S. men's result -- in the 36-man all-around field. Encouraged by his performance in Seoul, Lakes is looking toward Barcelona in 1992 and a possible medal.* (Dave Black)   ·